HORI-san and
MIYAMURA-KUN

HORIMIYA

HERO × DAISUKE HAGIWARA

13

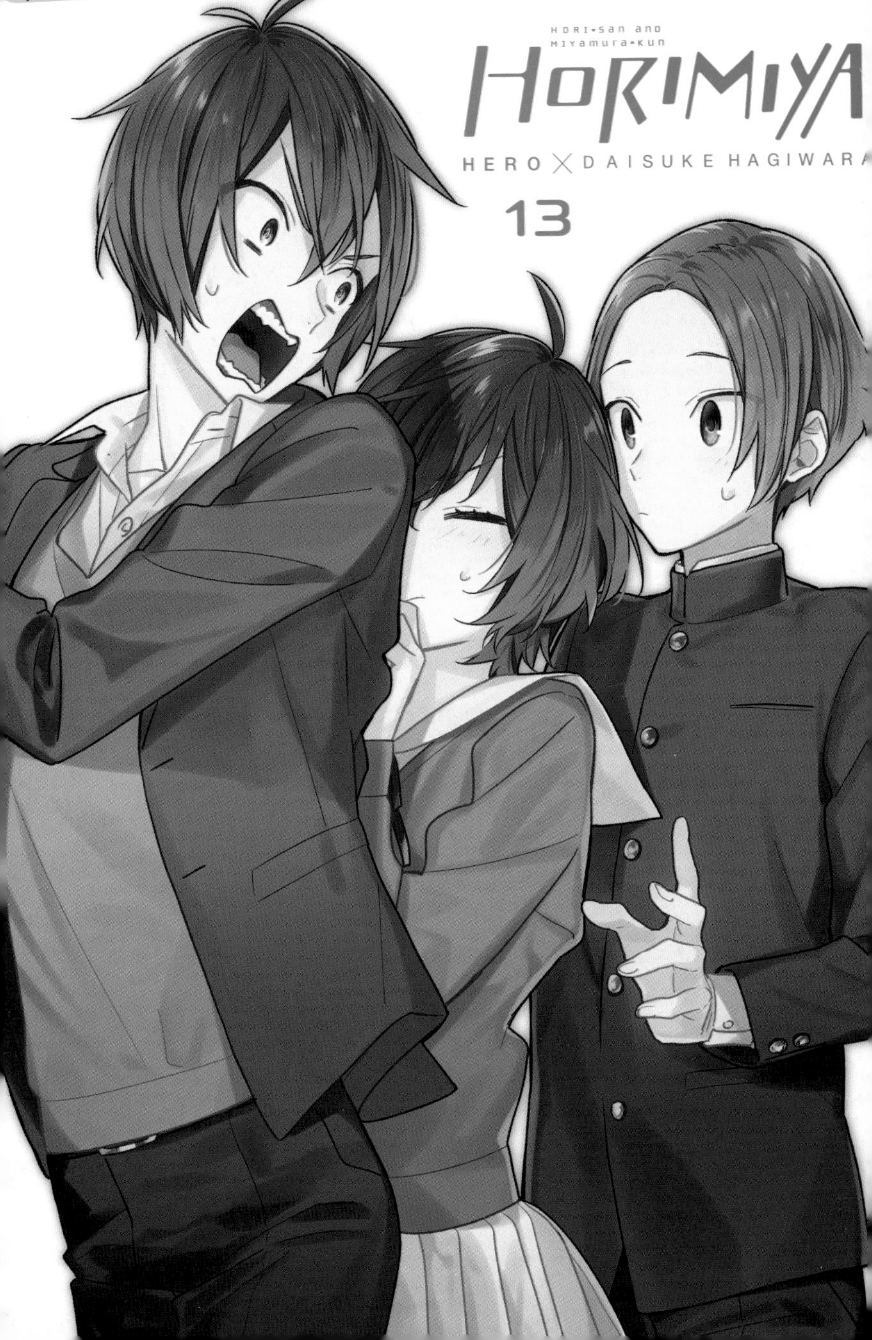

HORI-san and
MIYamura-kun

HORIMIYA

13

C O N T E N T S ✶

page·**91**	3
page·**92**	29
page·**93**	47
page·**94**	65
page·**95**	87
page·**96**	107
page·**97**	121
page·**98**	135
page·**99**	151
page·**100**	183

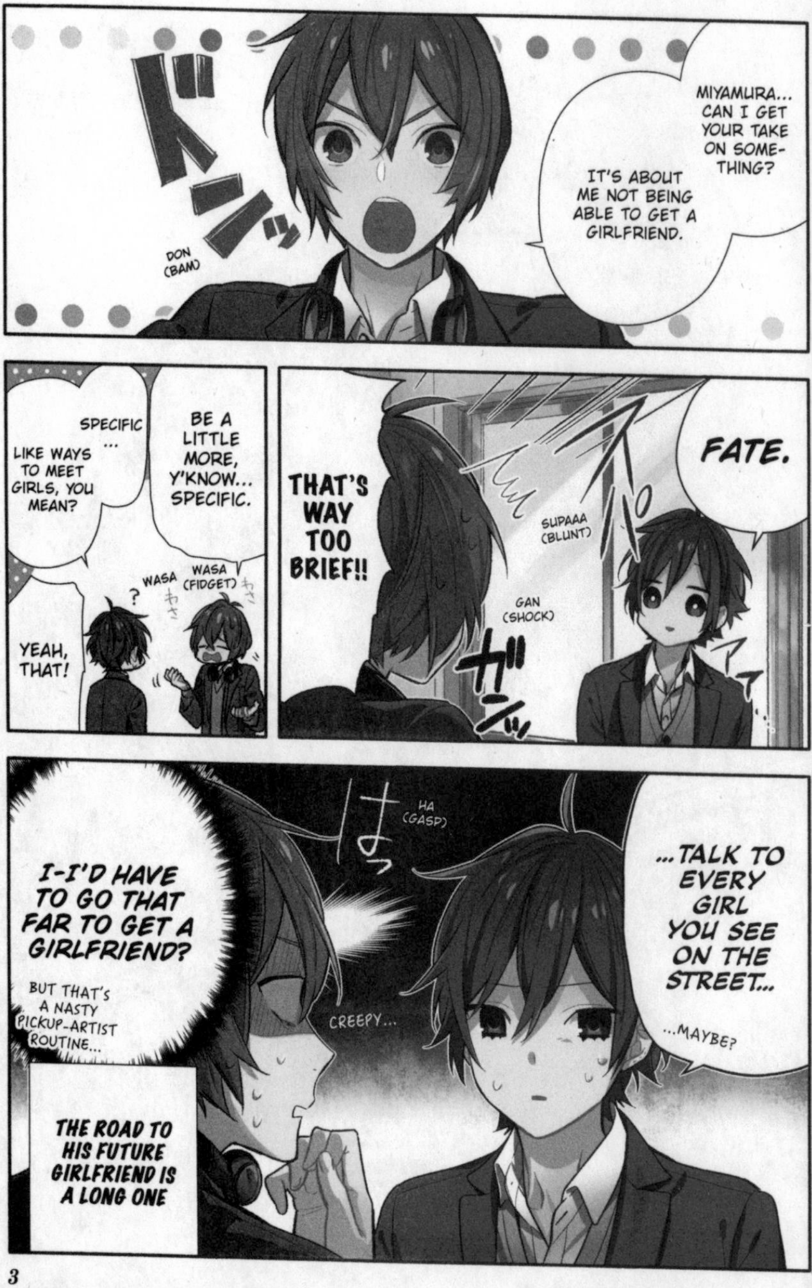
MIYAMURA... CAN I GET YOUR TAKE ON SOME-THING?
IT'S ABOUT ME NOT BEING ABLE TO GET A GIRLFRIEND.
DON (BAM)
FATE.
SUPAAA (BLUNT)
THAT'S WAY TOO BRIEF!!
GAN (SHOCK)
BE A LITTLE MORE, Y'KNOW... SPECIFIC.
WASA WASA (FIDGET)
SPECIFIC ... LIKE WAYS TO MEET GIRLS, YOU MEAN?
?
YEAH, THAT!
...TALK TO EVERY GIRL YOU SEE ON THE STREET...
...MAYBE?
HA (GASP)
CREEPY...
I-I'D HAVE TO GO THAT FAR TO GET A GIRLFRIEND?
BUT THAT'S A NASTY PICKUP-ARTIST ROUTINE...
THE ROAD TO HIS FUTURE GIRLFRIEND IS A LONG ONE

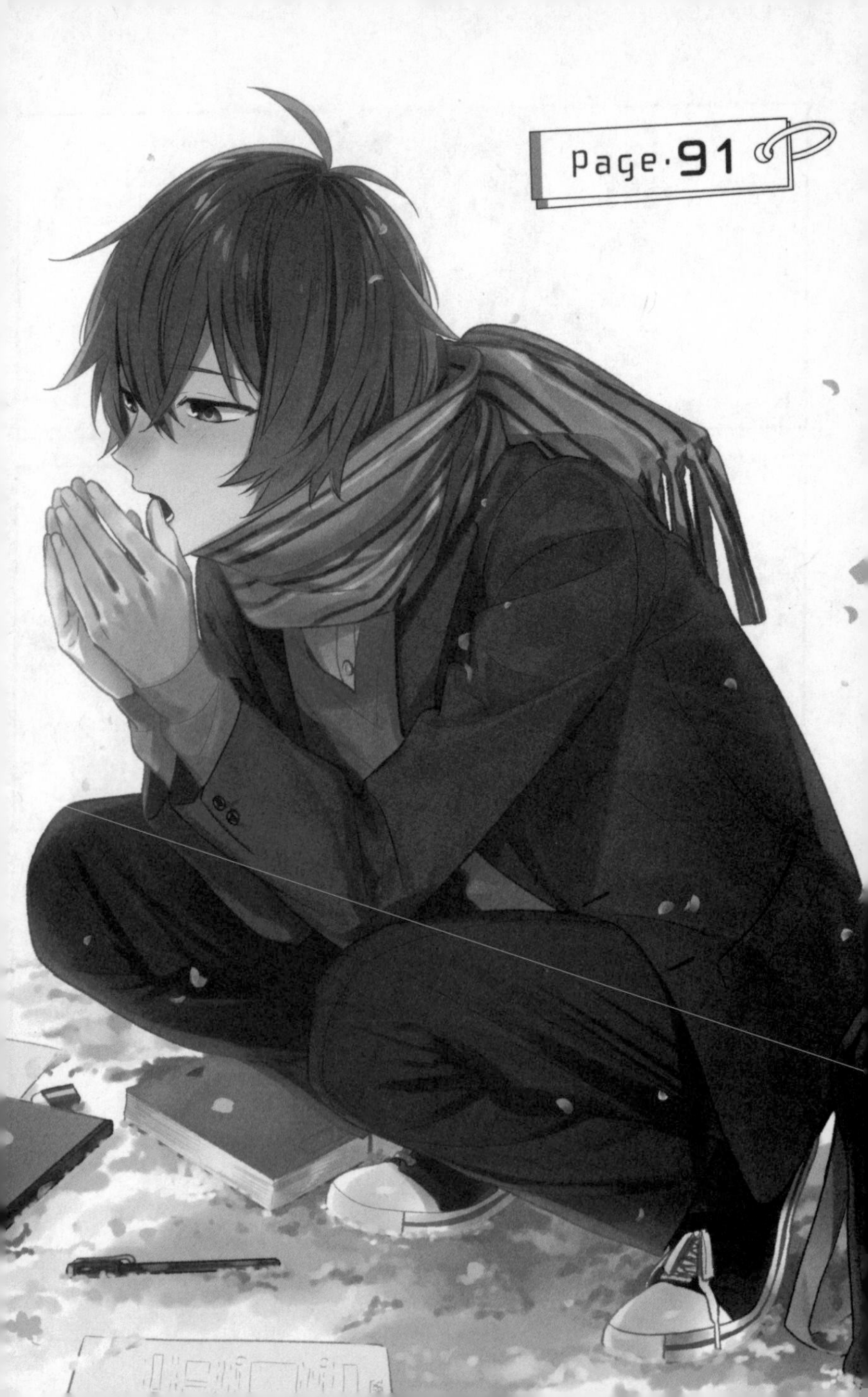
page·91

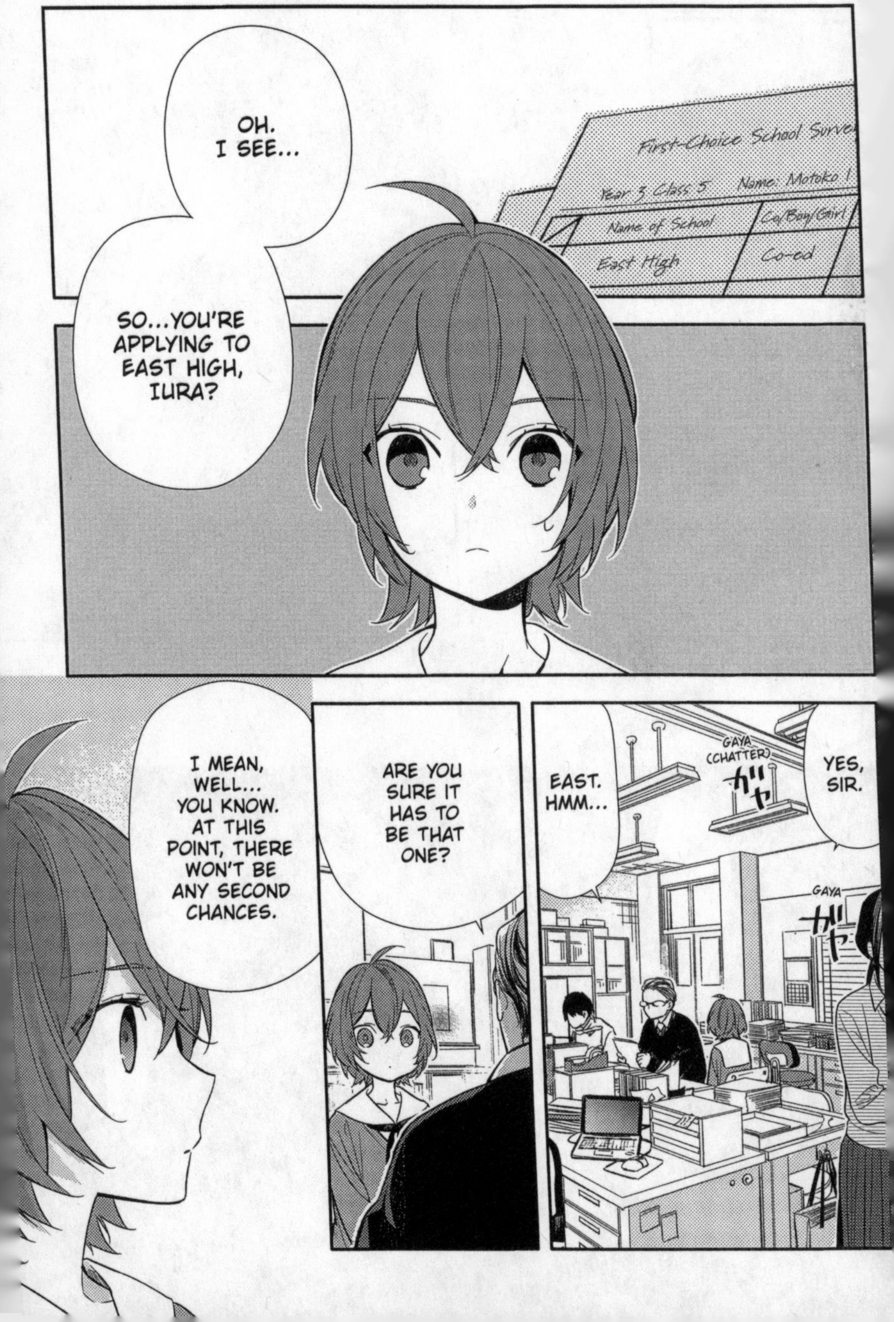
OH. I SEE...
First-Choice School Surve
Year 3 Class 5
Name: Motoko I
Name of School
Co/Boy/Girl
East High
Co-ed
SO...YOU'RE APPLYING TO EAST HIGH, IURA?
YES, SIR.
GAYA (CHATTER)
EAST. HMM...
GAYA
ARE YOU SURE IT HAS TO BE THAT ONE?
I MEAN, WELL... YOU KNOW. AT THIS POINT, THERE WON'T BE ANY SECOND CHANCES.

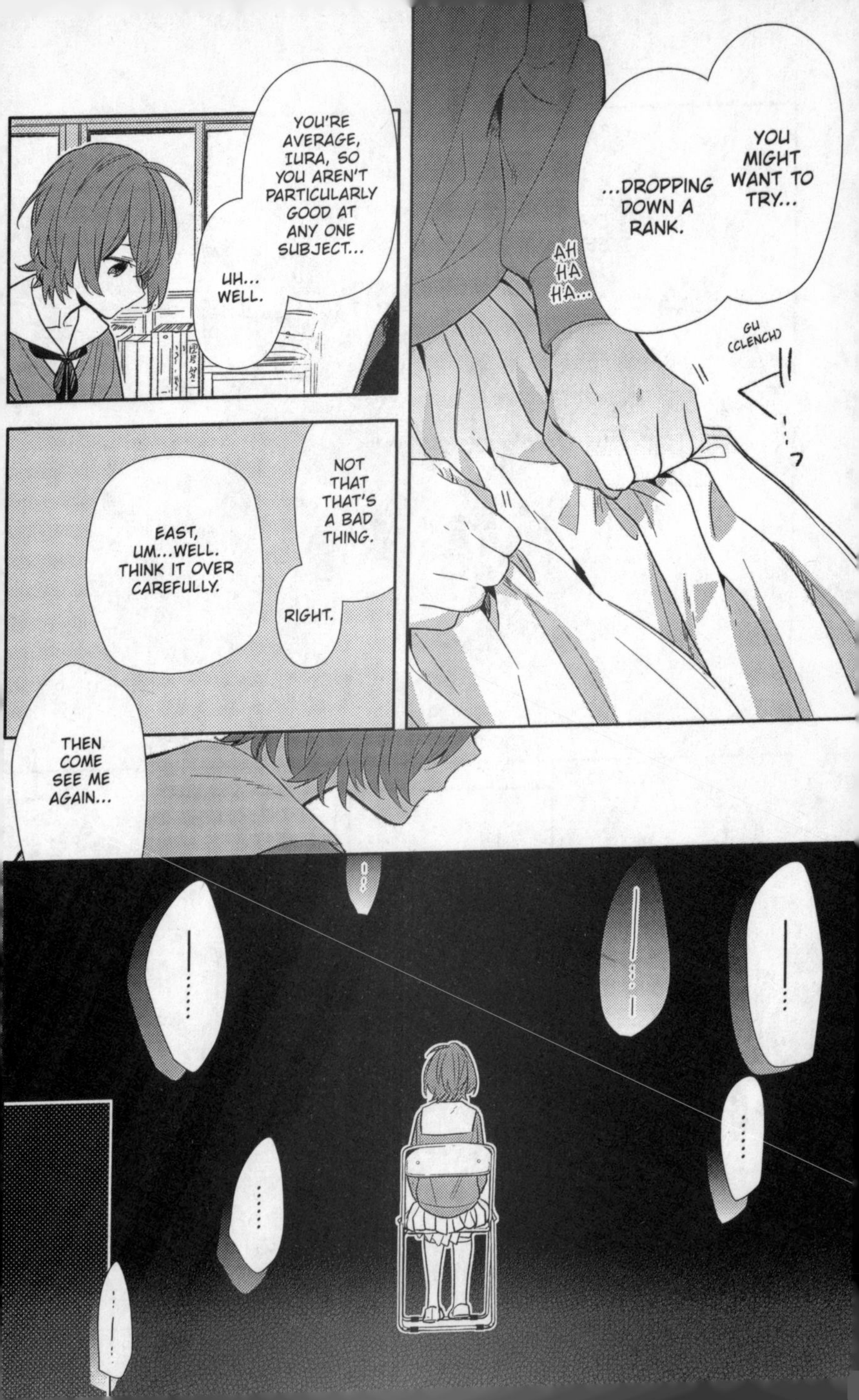
YOU MIGHT WANT TO TRY...
...DROPPING DOWN A RANK.
AH HA HA...
GU (CLENCH)
YOU'RE AVERAGE, IURA, SO YOU AREN'T PARTICULARLY GOOD AT ANY ONE SUBJECT...
UH... WELL.
NOT THAT THAT'S A BAD THING.
EAST, UM...WELL. THINK IT OVER CAREFULLY.
RIGHT.
THEN COME SEE ME AGAIN...

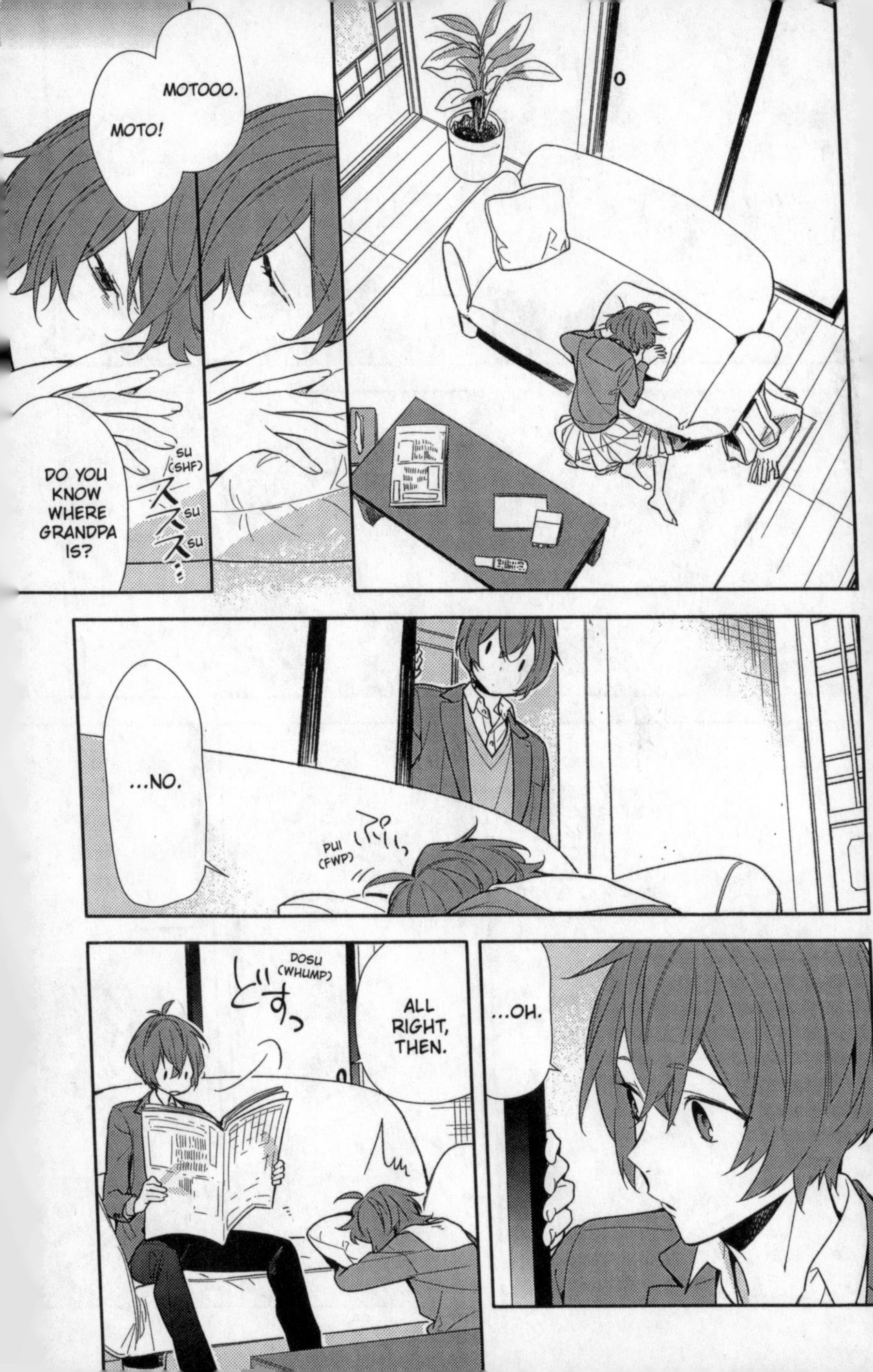
MOTOOO.
MOTO!
SU (SHF) スススス... SU SU
DO YOU KNOW WHERE GRANDPA IS?
...NO.
PUI (FWP) ぷい
...OH.
ALL RIGHT, THEN.
DOSU (WHUMP) どすっ

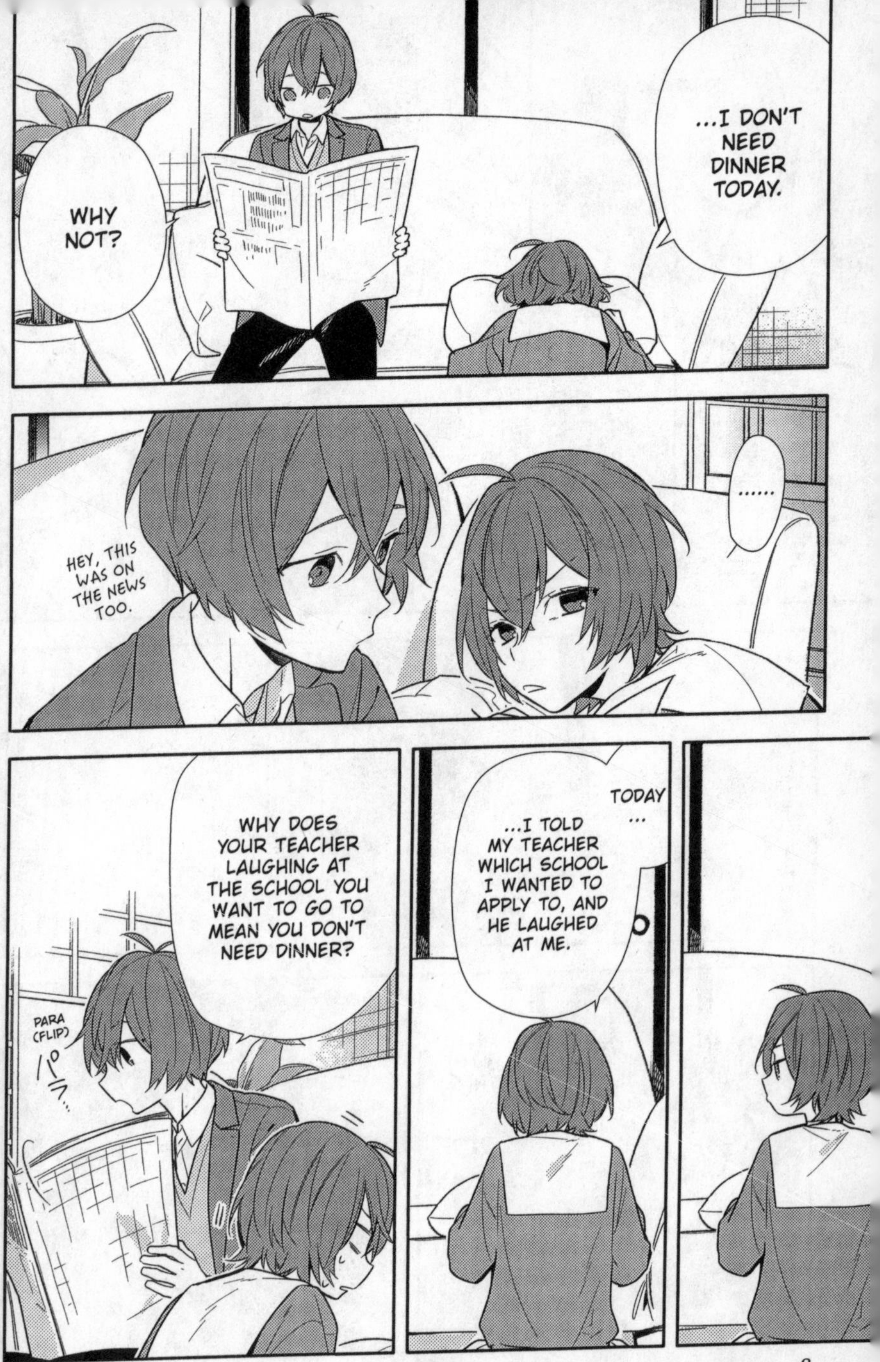
...I DON'T NEED DINNER TODAY.
WHY NOT?
......
HEY, THIS WAS ON THE NEWS TOO.
TODAY...
...I TOLD MY TEACHER WHICH SCHOOL I WANTED TO APPLY TO, AND HE LAUGHED AT ME.
WHY DOES YOUR TEACHER LAUGHING AT THE SCHOOL YOU WANT TO GO TO MEAN YOU DON'T NEED DINNER?
PARA (FLIP)

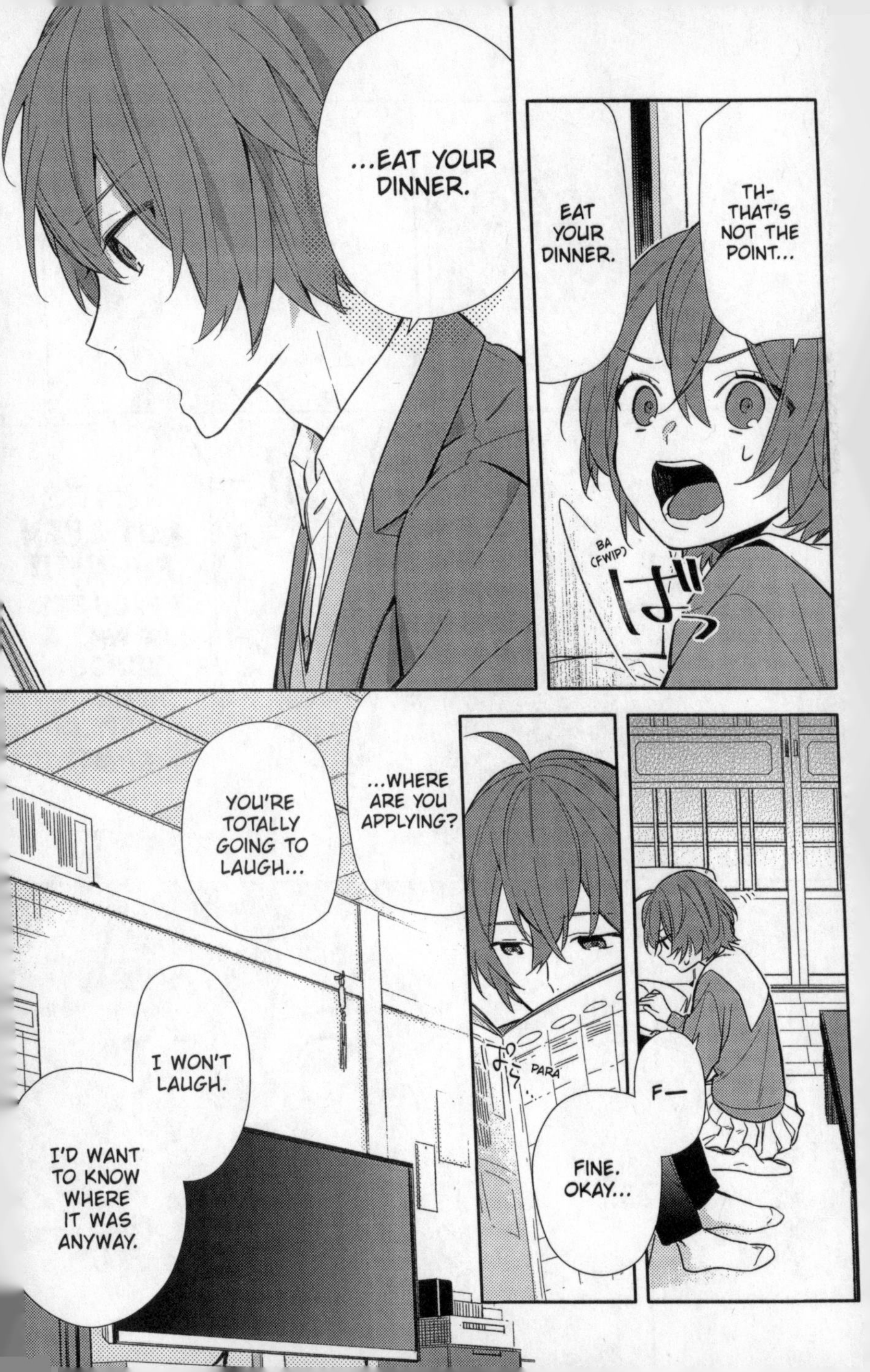
TH- THAT'S NOT THE POINT...
EAT YOUR DINNER.
BA (FWIP)
...EAT YOUR DINNER.
PARA
F—
FINE. OKAY...
...WHERE ARE YOU APPLYING?
YOU'RE TOTALLY GOING TO LAUGH...
I WON'T LAUGH.
I'D WANT TO KNOW WHERE IT WAS ANYWAY.

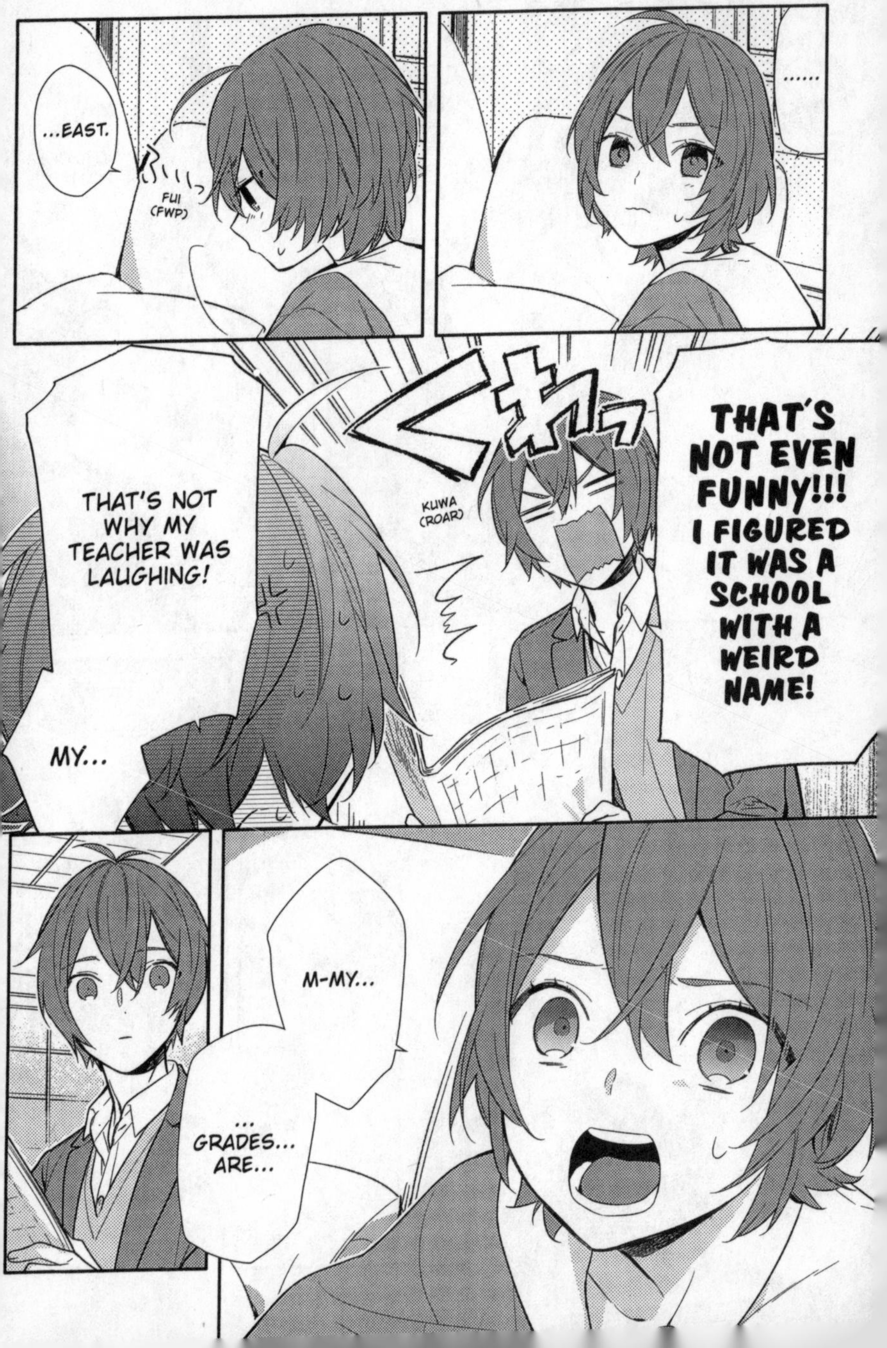
......
...EAST.
FUI (FWP)
THAT'S NOT EVEN FUNNY!!! I FIGURED IT WAS A SCHOOL WITH A WEIRD NAME!
KUWA (ROAR)
THAT'S NOT WHY MY TEACHER WAS LAUGHING!
MY...
M-MY...
... GRADES... ARE...

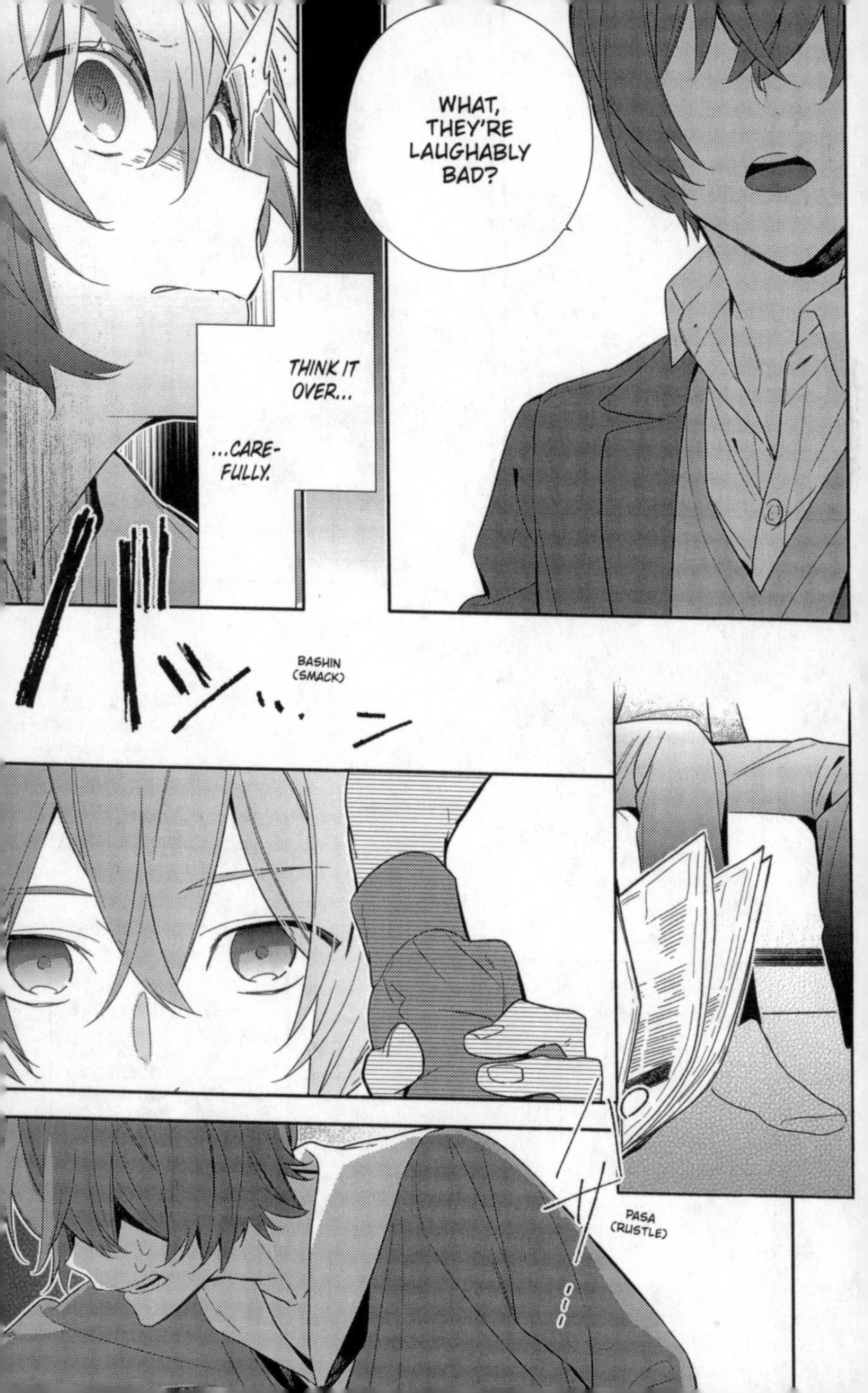
WHAT, THEY'RE LAUGHABLY BAD?
THINK IT OVER...
...CARE-FULLY.
BASHIN (SMACK)
PASA (RUSTLE)

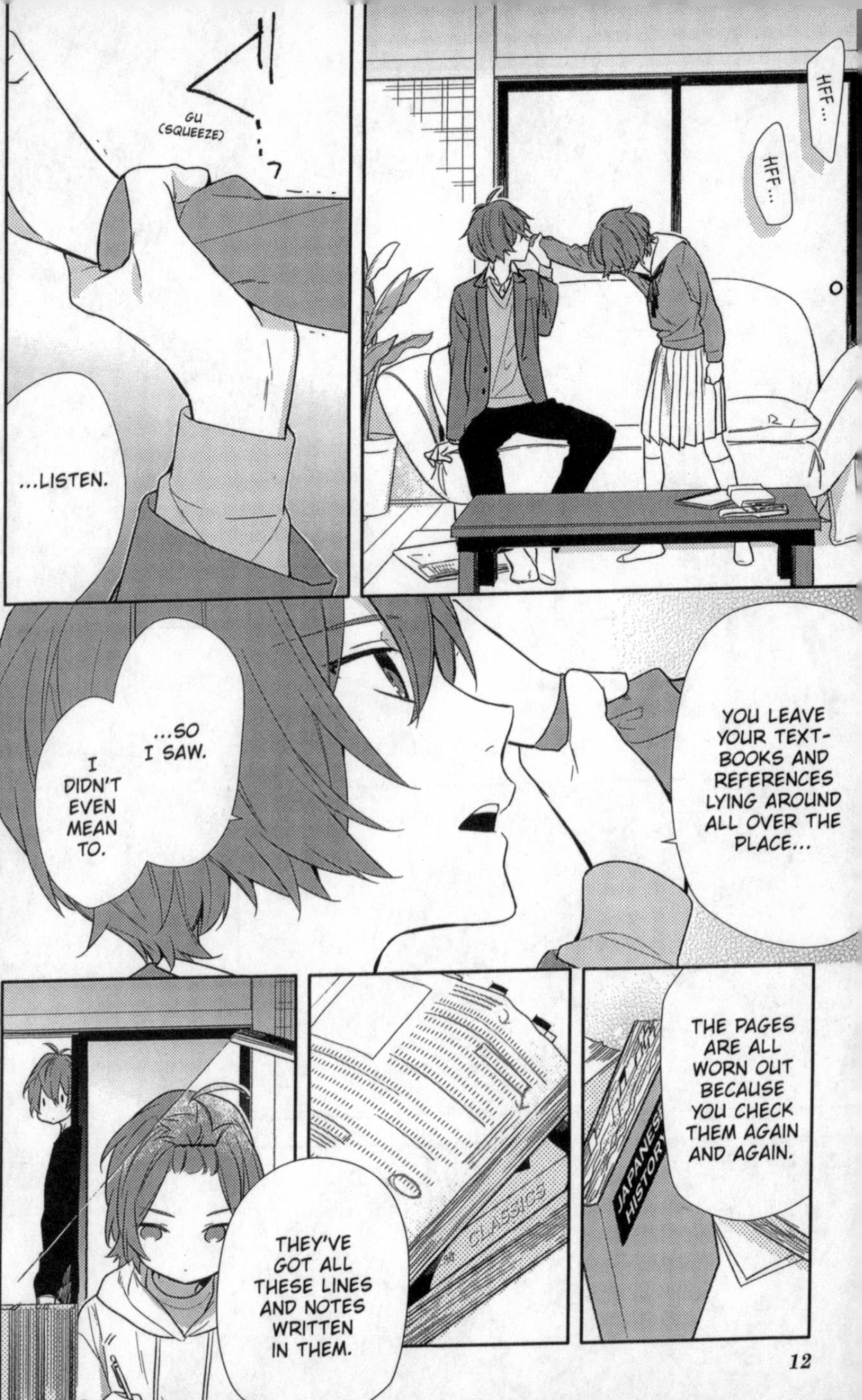
HFF...
HFF...
GU (SQUEEZE)
...LISTEN.
YOU LEAVE YOUR TEXT-BOOKS AND REFERENCES LYING AROUND ALL OVER THE PLACE...
...SO I SAW.
I DIDN'T EVEN MEAN TO.
THE PAGES ARE ALL WORN OUT BECAUSE YOU CHECK THEM AGAIN AND AGAIN.
JAPANESE HISTORY
CLASSICS
THEY'VE GOT ALL THESE LINES AND NOTES WRITTEN IN THEM.

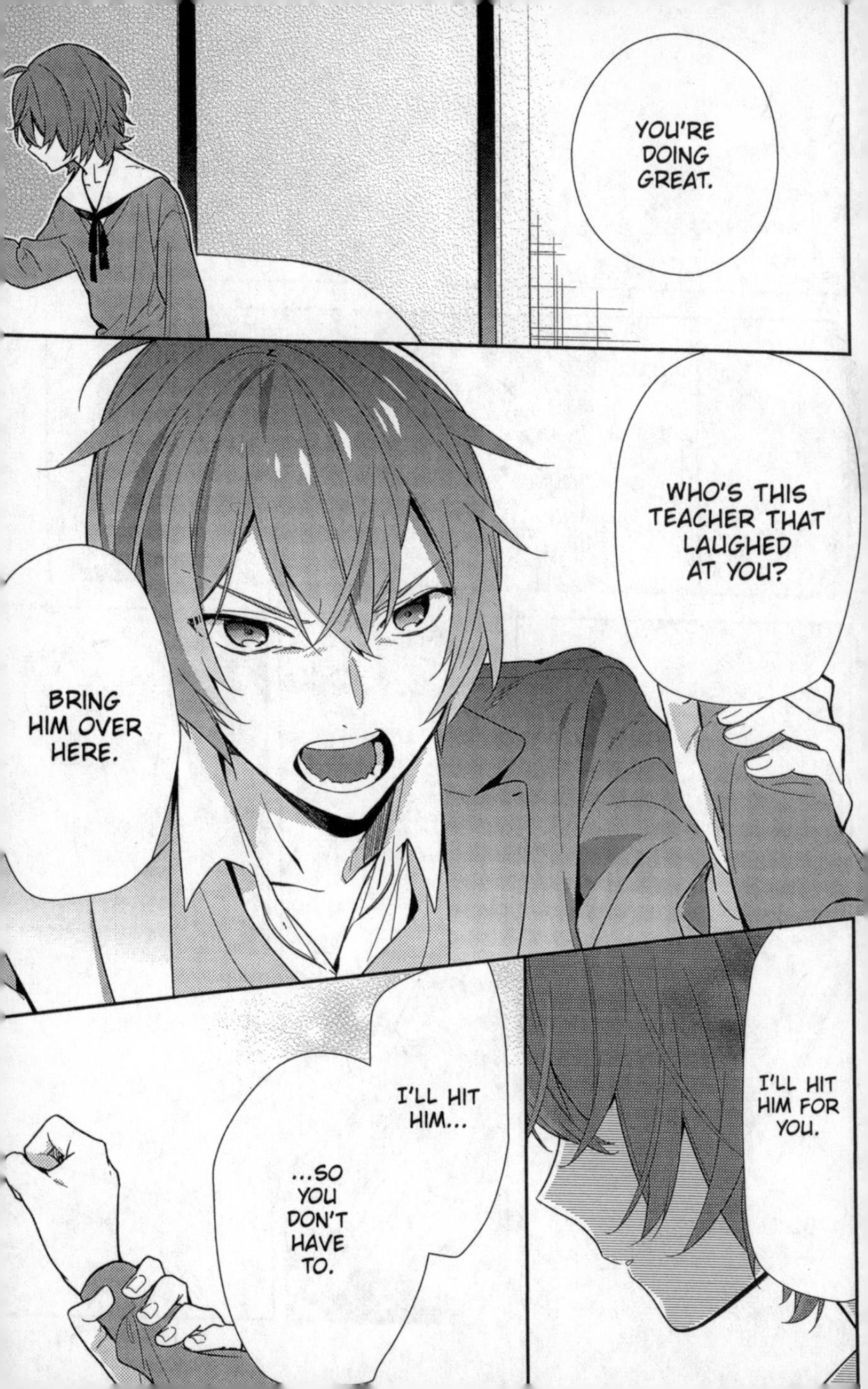
YOU'RE DOING GREAT.
WHO'S THIS TEACHER THAT LAUGHED AT YOU?
BRING HIM OVER HERE.
I'LL HIT HIM FOR YOU.
I'LL HIT HIM...
...SO YOU DON'T HAVE TO.

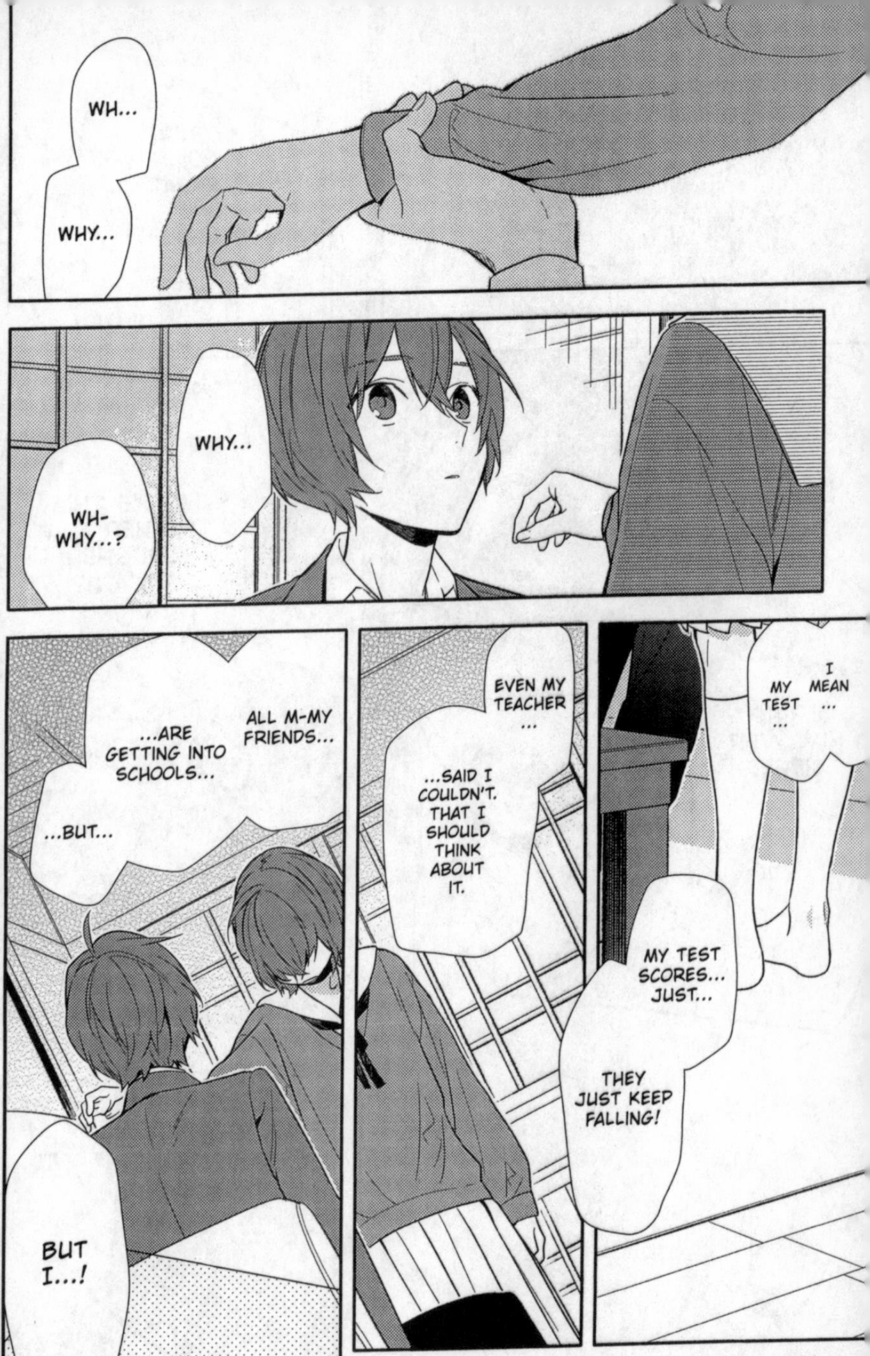
WH...
WHY...
WHY...
WH- WHY...?
I MEAN...
MY TEST...
MY TEST SCORES... JUST...
THEY JUST KEEP FALLING!
EVEN MY TEACHER...
...SAID I COULDN'T. THAT I SHOULD THINK ABOUT IT.
ALL M-MY FRIENDS...
...ARE GETTING INTO SCHOOLS...
...BUT...
BUT I...!

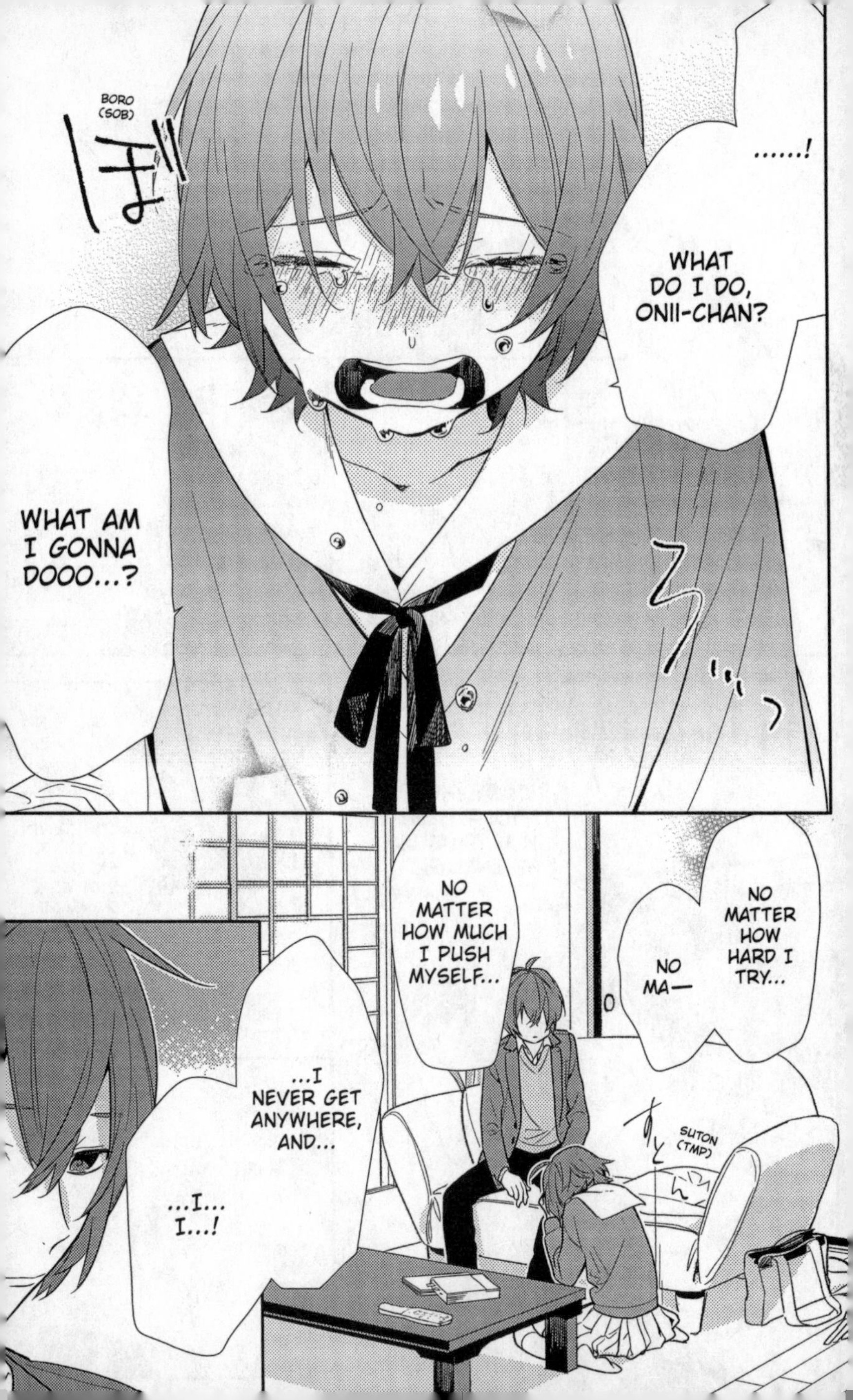
......!
WHAT DO I DO, ONII-CHAN?
BORO (SOB)
WHAT AM I GONNA DOOO...?
NO MATTER HOW HARD I TRY...
NO MA—
NO MATTER HOW MUCH I PUSH MYSELF...
SUTON (TMP)
...I NEVER GET ANYWHERE, AND...
...I... I...!

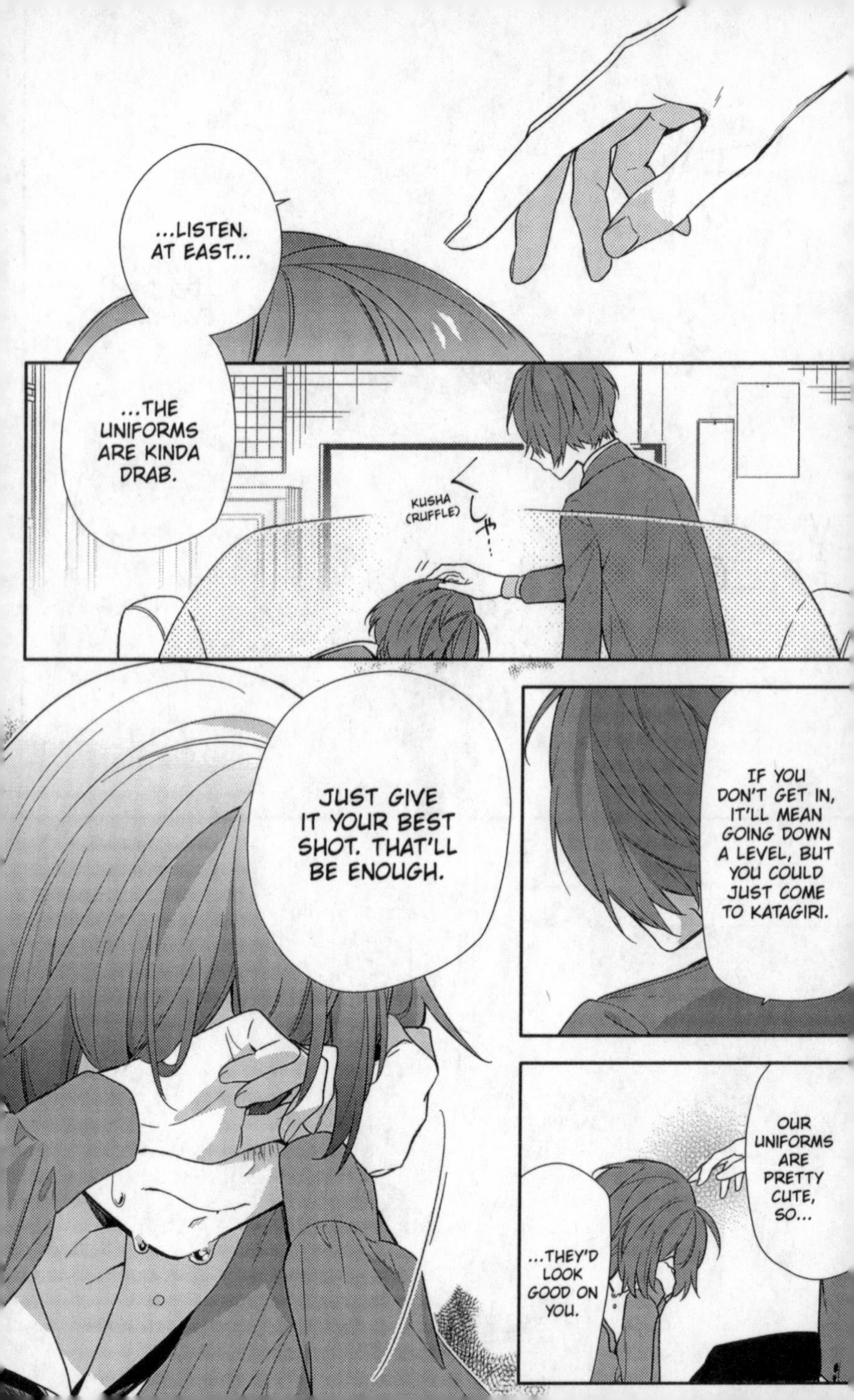
...LISTEN. AT EAST...
...THE UNIFORMS ARE KINDA DRAB.
KUSHA (RUFFLE)
IF YOU DON'T GET IN, IT'LL MEAN GOING DOWN A LEVEL, BUT YOU COULD JUST COME TO KATAGIRI.
OUR UNIFORMS ARE PRETTY CUTE, SO...
...THEY'D LOOK GOOD ON YOU.
JUST GIVE IT YOUR BEST SHOT. THAT'LL BE ENOUGH.

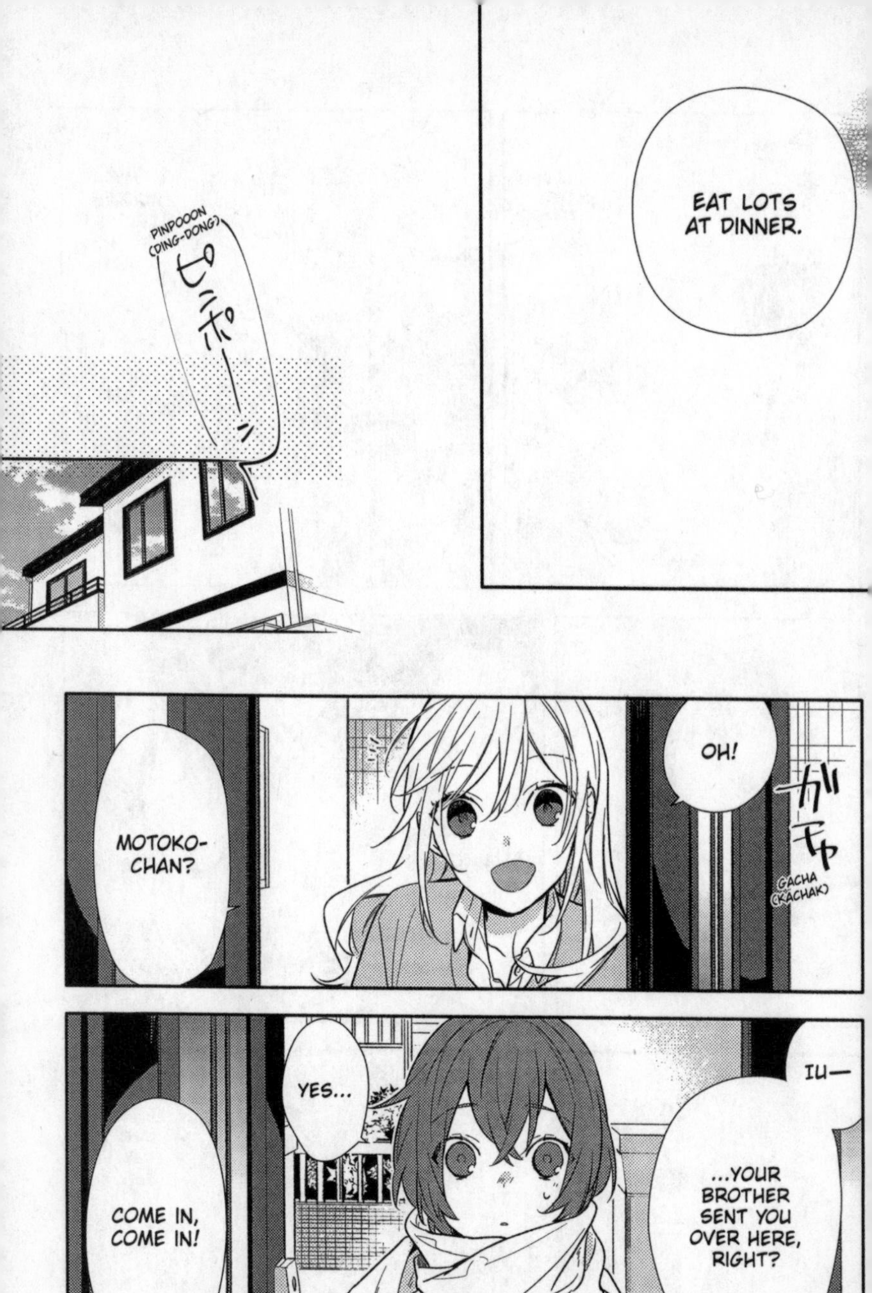
EAT LOTS AT DINNER.
PINPOOON (DING-DONG)
ピンポーン
OH!
ガチャ
GACHA (KACHAK)
MOTOKO-CHAN?
IU—
...YOUR BROTHER SENT YOU OVER HERE, RIGHT?
YES...
COME IN, COME IN!

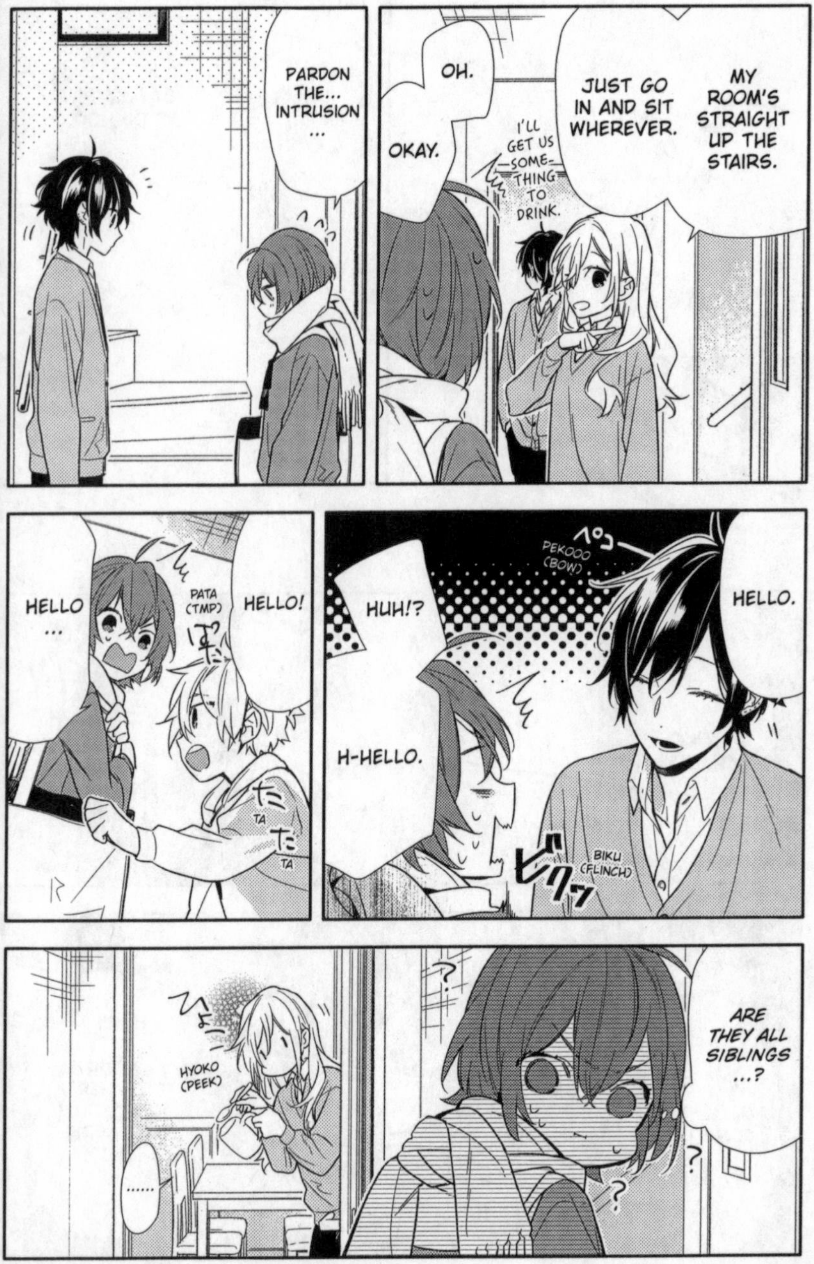
MY ROOM'S STRAIGHT UP THE STAIRS.
JUST GO IN AND SIT WHEREVER.
I'LL GET US SOMETHING TO DRINK.
OH.
OKAY.
PARDON THE... INTRUSION ...
HELLO.
PEKOOO (BOW)
HUH!?
H-HELLO.
BIKU (FLINCH)
HELLO!
PATA (TMP)
HELLO ...
TA
TA
ARE THEY ALL SIBLINGS ...?
HYOKO (PEEK)
......

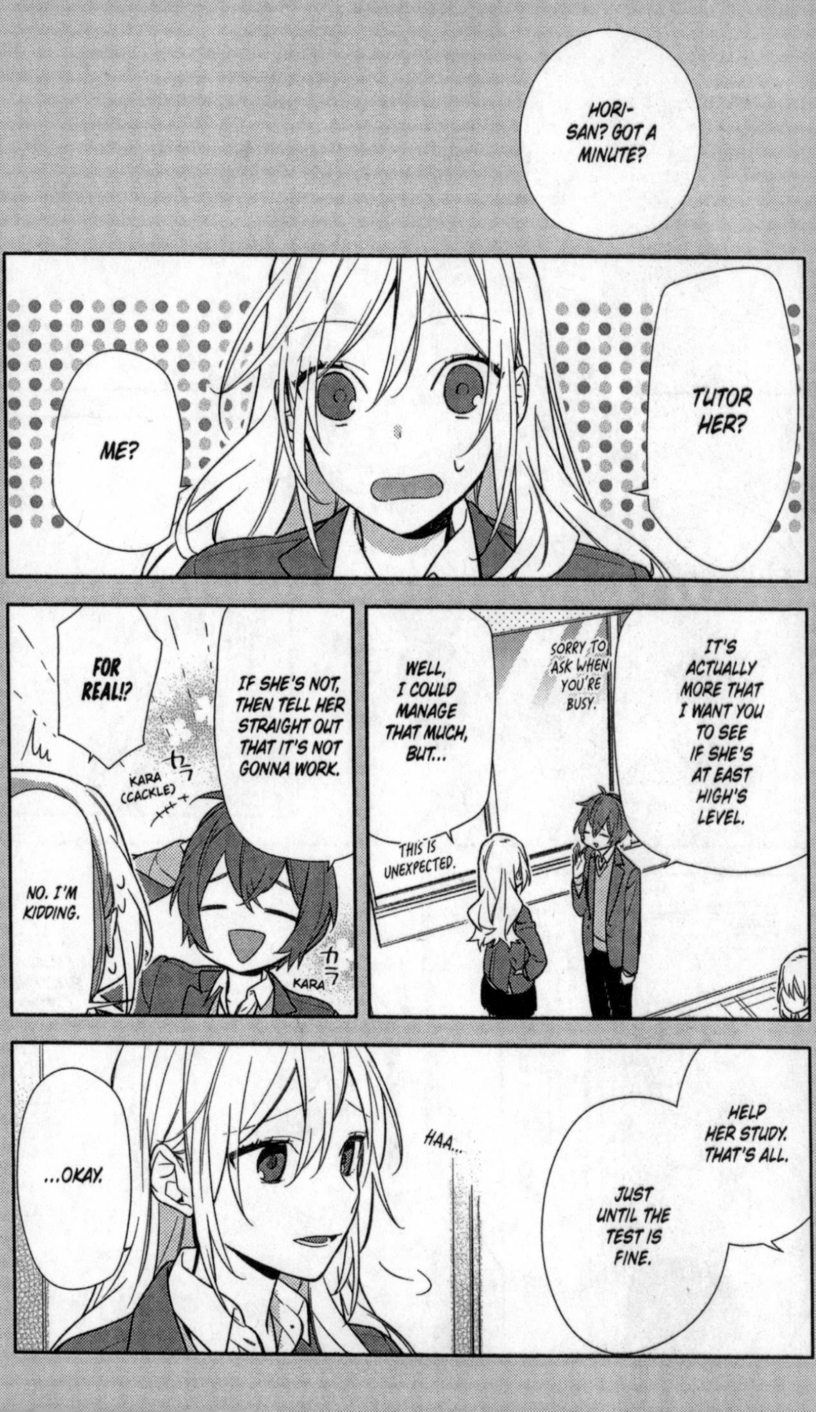
HORI-SAN? GOT A MINUTE?
TUTOR HER?
ME?
IT'S ACTUALLY MORE THAT I WANT YOU TO SEE IF SHE'S AT EAST HIGH'S LEVEL.
SORRY TO ASK WHEN YOU'RE BUSY.
WELL, I COULD MANAGE THAT MUCH, BUT...
THIS IS UNEXPECTED.
IF SHE'S NOT, THEN TELL HER STRAIGHT OUT THAT IT'S NOT GONNA WORK.
FOR REAL!?
カラ
KARA (CACKLE)
NO. I'M KIDDING.
カラ
KARA
HELP HER STUDY. THAT'S ALL.
JUST UNTIL THE TEST IS FINE.
HAA...
...OKAY.

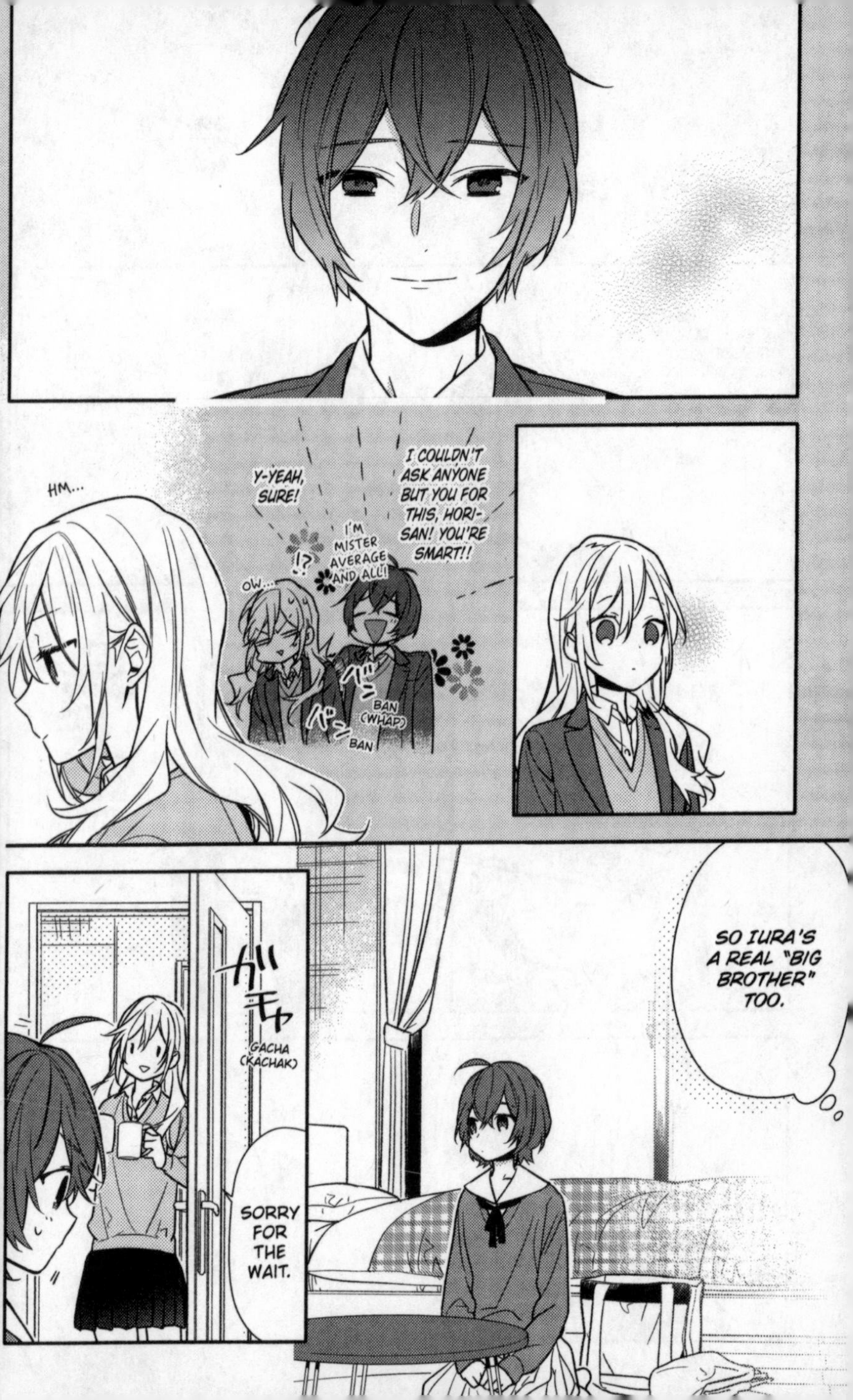
I COULDN'T ASK ANYONE BUT YOU FOR THIS, HORI-SAN! YOU'RE SMART!!
I'M MISTER AVERAGE AND ALL!
Y-YEAH, SURE!
!?
OW...
BAN (WHAP)
BAN
HM...
SO IURA'S A REAL "BIG BROTHER" TOO.
GACHA (KACHAK)
SORRY FOR THE WAIT.

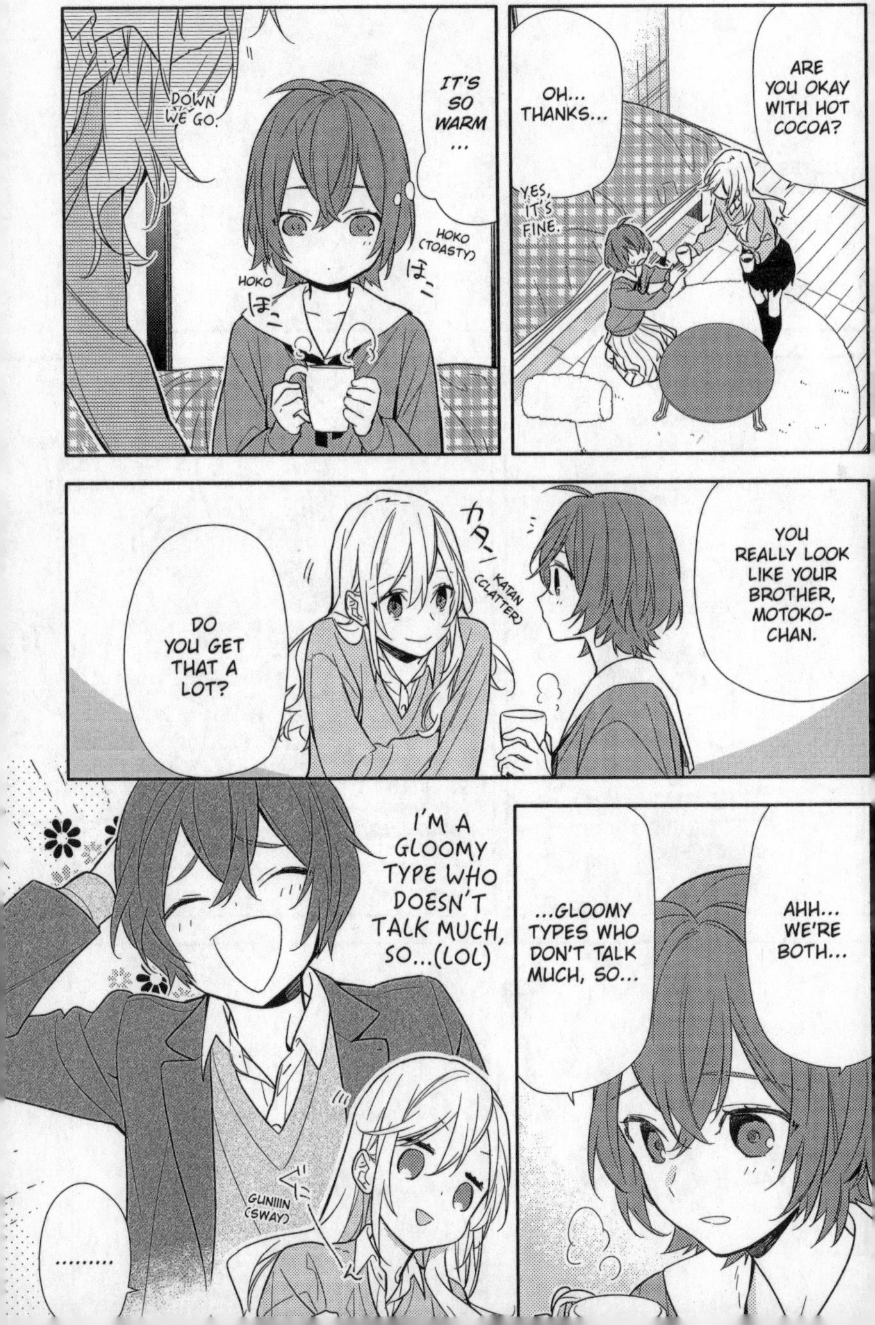
ARE YOU OKAY WITH HOT COCOA?
OH... THANKS...
YES, IT'S FINE.
IT'S SO WARM...
HOKO (TOASTY)
ほこ
HOKO
ほこ
DOWN WE GO.
YOU REALLY LOOK LIKE YOUR BROTHER, MOTOKO-CHAN.
カタ
KATAN (CLATTER)
DO YOU GET THAT A LOT?
AHH... WE'RE BOTH...
...GLOOMY TYPES WHO DON'T TALK MUCH, SO...
I'M A GLOOMY TYPE WHO DOESN'T TALK MUCH, SO...(LOL)
GUNIIIN (SWAY)
....

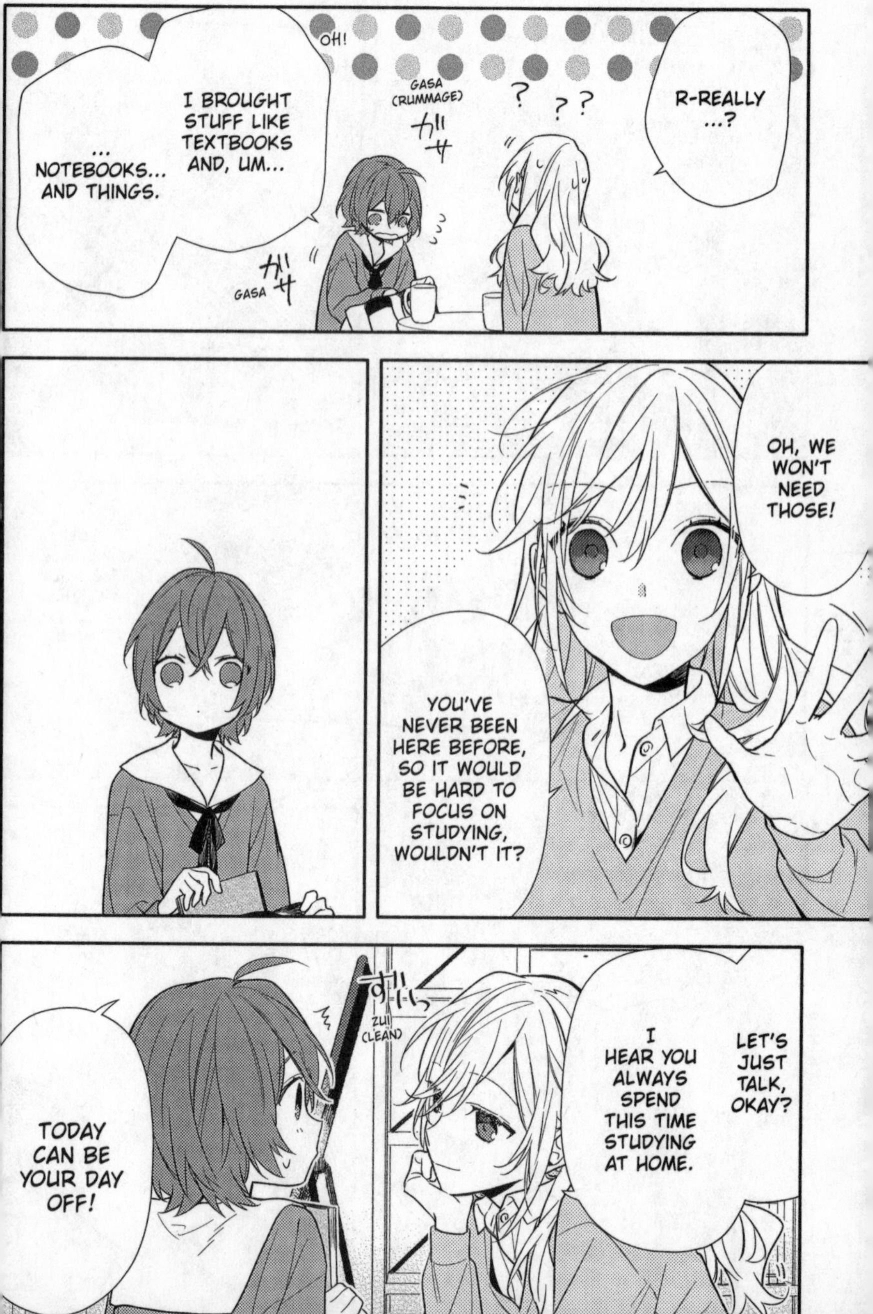
R-REALLY ...?
? ? ?
GASA (RUMMAGE)
OH!
I BROUGHT STUFF LIKE TEXTBOOKS AND, UM...
... NOTEBOOKS... AND THINGS.
GASA
OH, WE WON'T NEED THOSE!
YOU'VE NEVER BEEN HERE BEFORE, SO IT WOULD BE HARD TO FOCUS ON STUDYING, WOULDN'T IT?
LET'S JUST TALK, OKAY?
I HEAR YOU ALWAYS SPEND THIS TIME STUDYING AT HOME.
ZUI (CLEAN)
TODAY CAN BE YOUR DAY OFF!

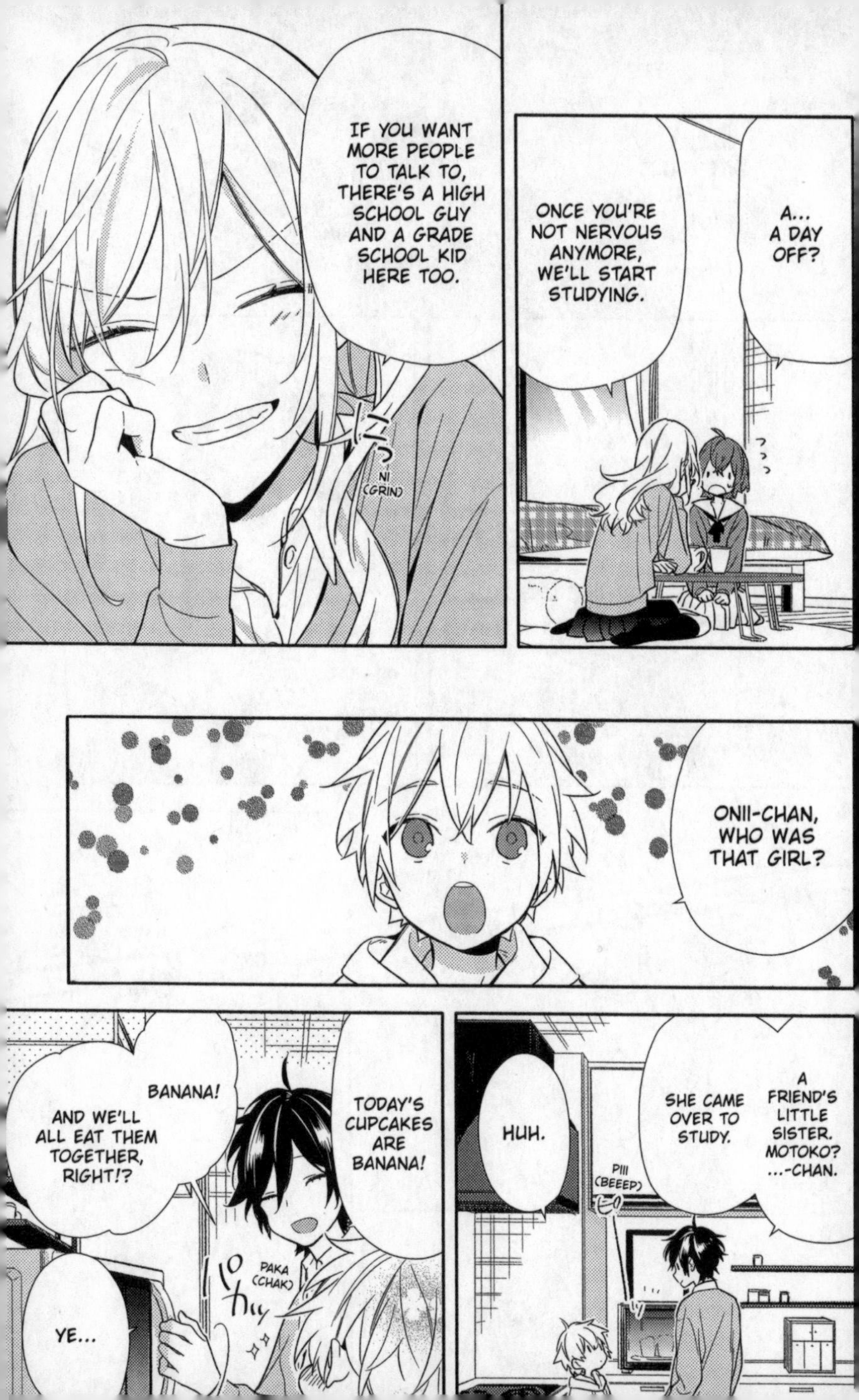
A... A DAY OFF?
ONCE YOU'RE NOT NERVOUS ANYMORE, WE'LL START STUDYING.
IF YOU WANT MORE PEOPLE TO TALK TO, THERE'S A HIGH SCHOOL GUY AND A GRADE SCHOOL KID HERE TOO.
NI (GRIN)
ONII-CHAN, WHO WAS THAT GIRL?
A FRIEND'S LITTLE SISTER. MOTOKO? ...-CHAN.
SHE CAME OVER TO STUDY.
PIII (BEEEP)
HUH.
TODAY'S CUPCAKES ARE BANANA!
BANANA!
AND WE'LL ALL EAT THEM TOGETHER, RIGHT!?
PAKA (CHAK)
YE...

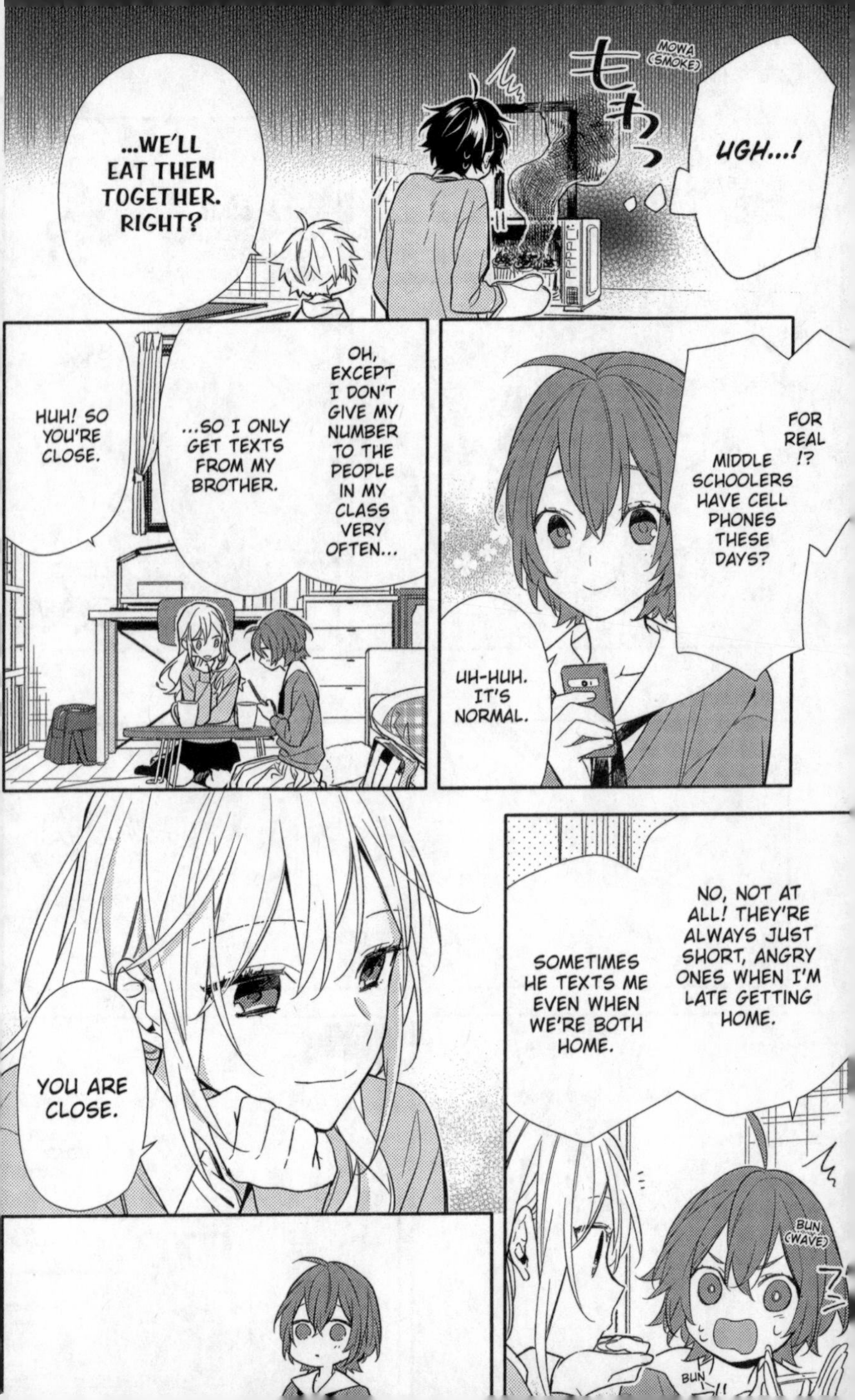
MOWA (SMOKE)
UGH...!
...WE'LL EAT THEM TOGETHER. RIGHT?
FOR REAL!?
MIDDLE SCHOOLERS HAVE CELL PHONES THESE DAYS?
UH-HUH. IT'S NORMAL.
OH, EXCEPT I DON'T GIVE MY NUMBER TO THE PEOPLE IN MY CLASS VERY OFTEN...
...SO I ONLY GET TEXTS FROM MY BROTHER.
HUH! SO YOU'RE CLOSE.
NO, NOT AT ALL! THEY'RE ALWAYS JUST SHORT, ANGRY ONES WHEN I'M LATE GETTING HOME.
SOMETIMES HE TEXTS ME EVEN WHEN WE'RE BOTH HOME.
BUN (WAVE)
BUN
YOU ARE CLOSE.

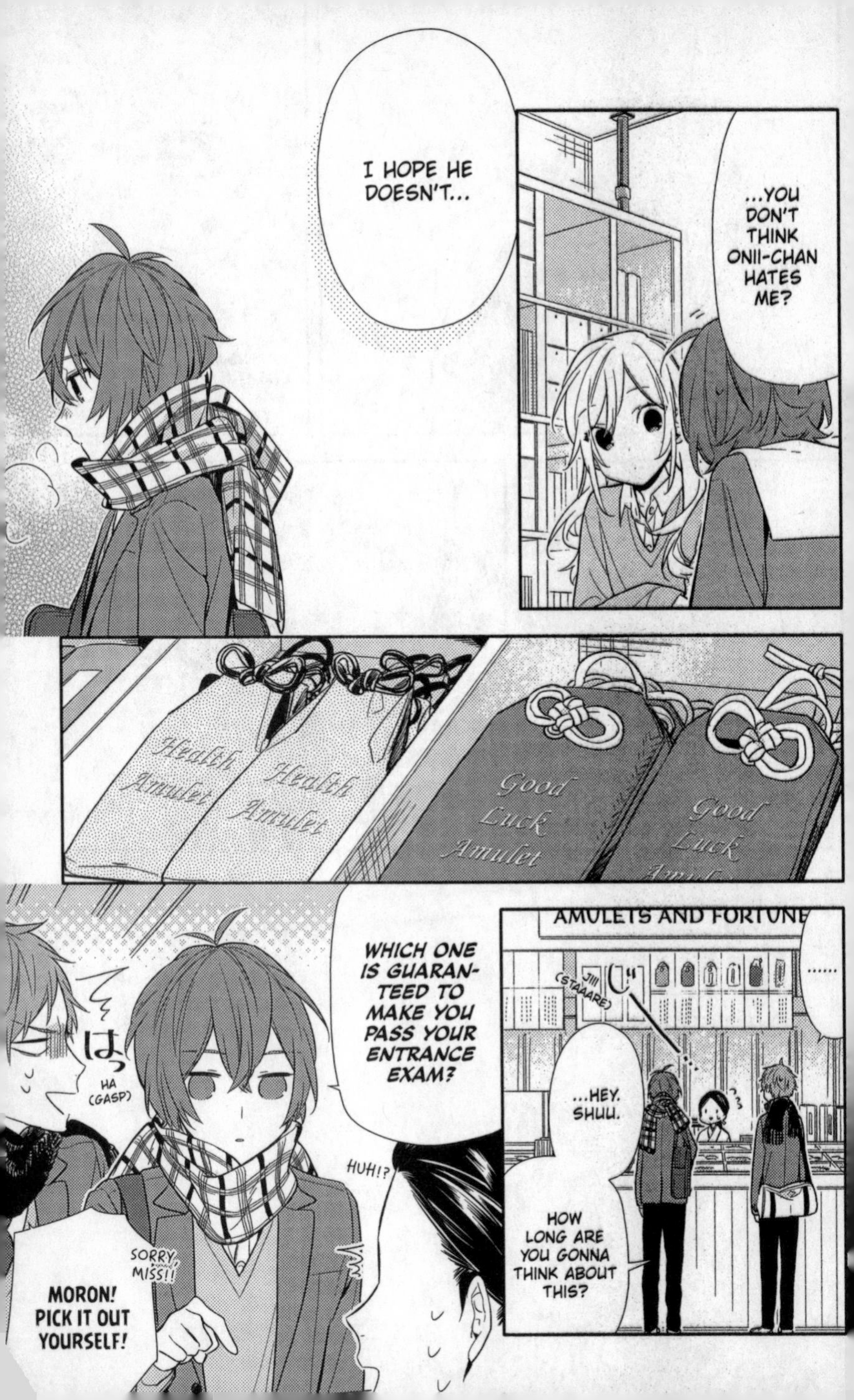
...YOU DON'T THINK ONII-CHAN HATES ME?
I HOPE HE DOESN'T...
Health Amulet
Health Amulet
Good Luck Amulet
Good Luck
AMULETS AND FORTUNE
......
JIII (STAAARE)
...HEY. SHUU.
HOW LONG ARE YOU GONNA THINK ABOUT THIS?
WHICH ONE IS GUARAN-TEED TO MAKE YOU PASS YOUR ENTRANCE EXAM?
HUH!?
はっ
HA (GASP)
SORRY, MISS!!
MORON! PICK IT OUT YOURSELF!

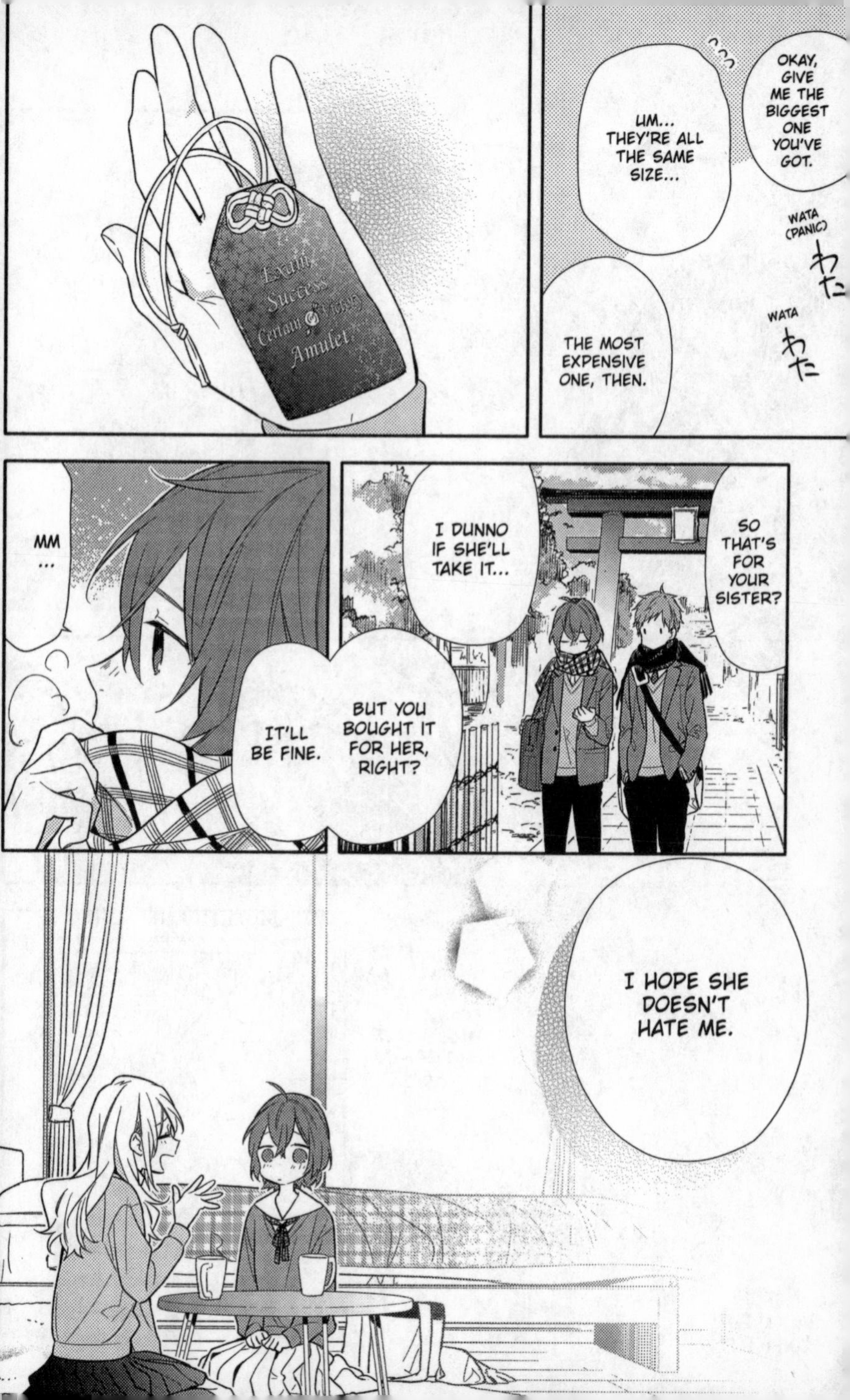

OKAY, GIVE ME THE BIGGEST ONE YOU'VE GOT.
UM... THEY'RE ALL THE SAME SIZE...
WATA (PANIC) わた
WATA わた
THE MOST EXPENSIVE ONE, THEN.
Exam Success Certain Victory Amulet
SO THAT'S FOR YOUR SISTER?
I DUNNO IF SHE'LL TAKE IT...
BUT YOU BOUGHT IT FOR HER, RIGHT?
IT'LL BE FINE.
MM...
I HOPE SHE DOESN'T HATE ME.

HORIMIYA

HORIMIYA

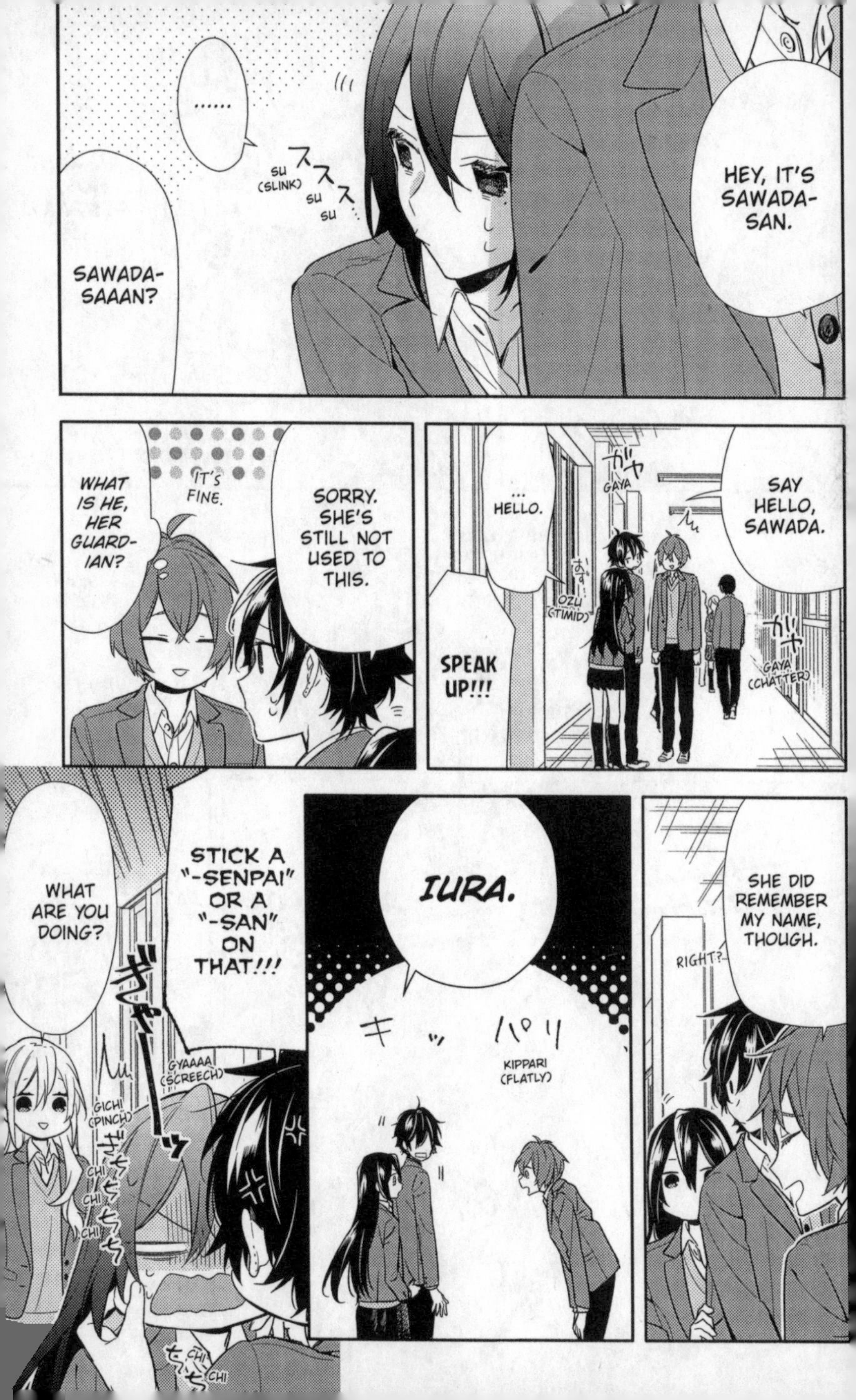
HEY, IT'S SAWADA-SAN.
......
SU (SLINK) SU SU
SAWADA-SAAAN?
SAY HELLO, SAWADA.
GAYA
... HELLO.
OZU (TIMID)
GAYA (CHATTER)
SPEAK UP!!!
SORRY. SHE'S STILL NOT USED TO THIS.
IT'S FINE.
WHAT IS HE, HER GUARDIAN?
SHE DID REMEMBER MY NAME, THOUGH.
RIGHT?
IURA.
KIPPARI (FLATLY)
STICK A "-SENPAI" OR A "-SAN" ON THAT!!!
WHAT ARE YOU DOING?
GYAAAA (SCREECH)
GICHI (PINCH)
CHI CHI CHI
CHI CHI

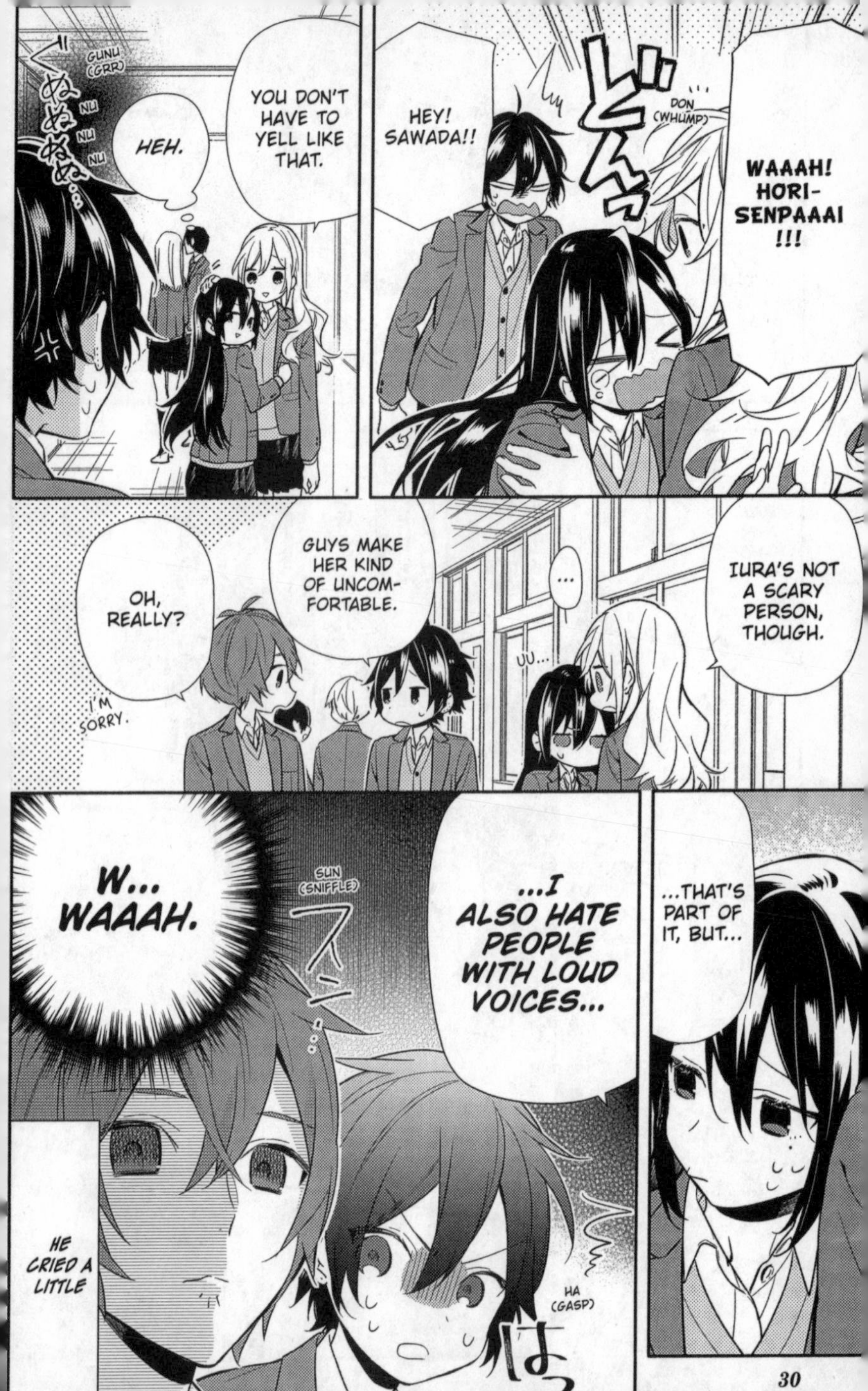
WAAAH! HORI-SENPAAAI!!!
DON (WHUMP)
HEY! SAWADA!!
YOU DON'T HAVE TO YELL LIKE THAT.
HEH.
GUNU (GRR)
NU NU NU
IURA'S NOT A SCARY PERSON, THOUGH.
...
UU...
GUYS MAKE HER KIND OF UNCOM-FORTABLE.
OH, REALLY?
I'M SORRY.
...THAT'S PART OF IT, BUT...
...I ALSO HATE PEOPLE WITH LOUD VOICES...
HA (GASP)
SUN (SNIFFLE)
W... WAAAH.
HE CRIED A LITTLE

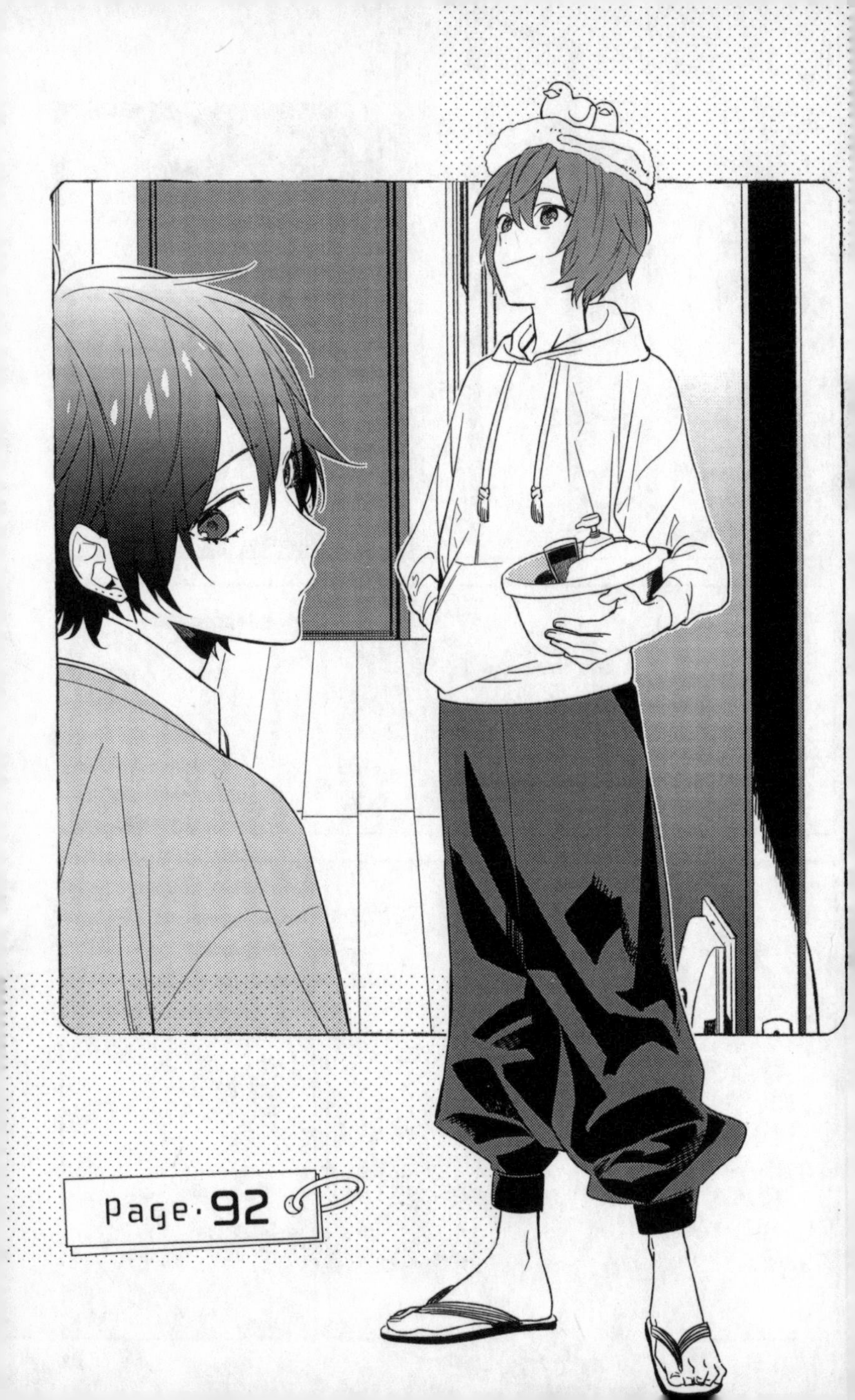
Page·92

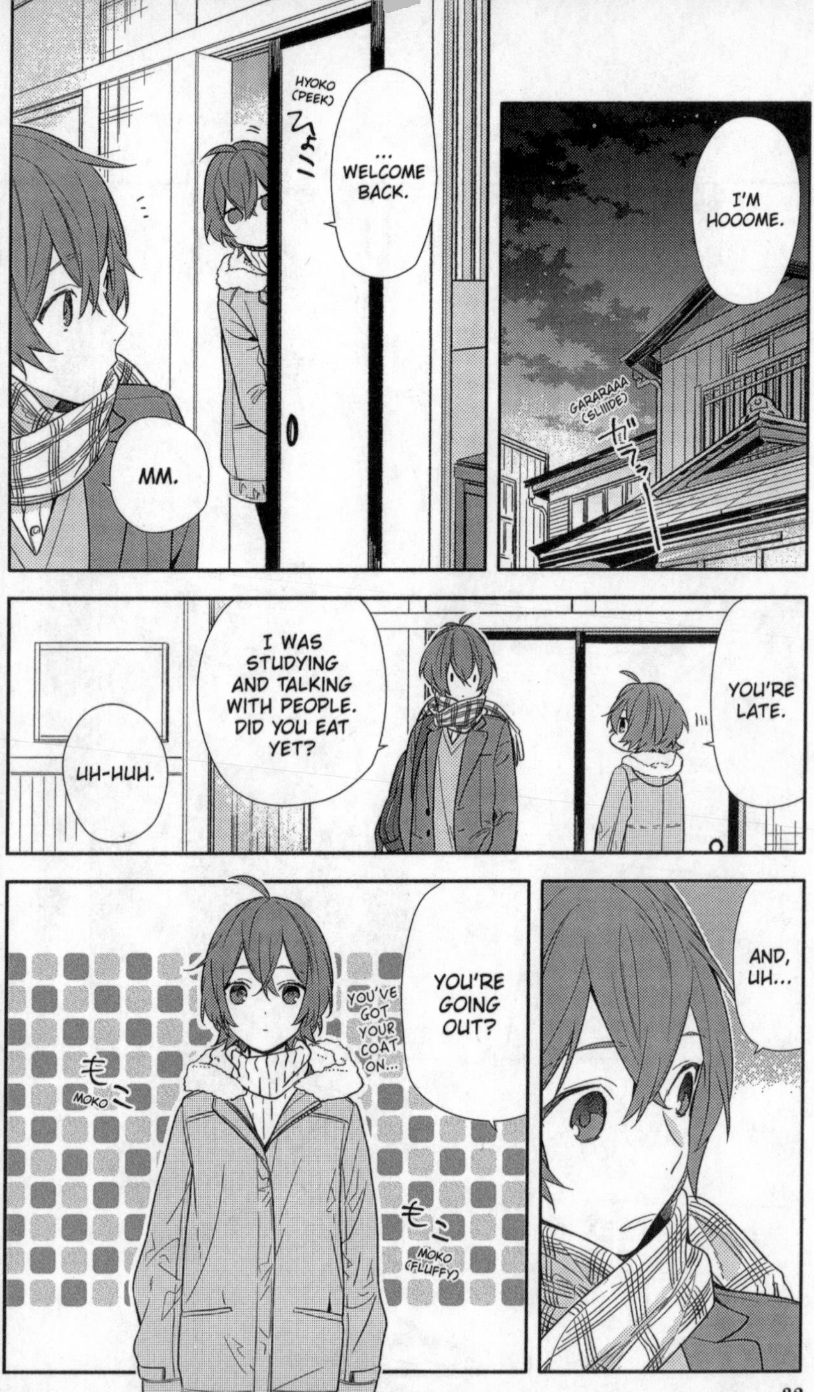
I'M HOOOME.
GARARAAA (SLIIIDE)
HYOKO (PEEK)
ひょこ
...WELCOME BACK.
MM.
YOU'RE LATE.
I WAS STUDYING AND TALKING WITH PEOPLE. DID YOU EAT YET?
UH-HUH.
AND, UH...
YOU'RE GOING OUT?
YOU'VE GOT YOUR COAT ON...
もこ
MOKO
もこ
MOKO (FLUFFY)

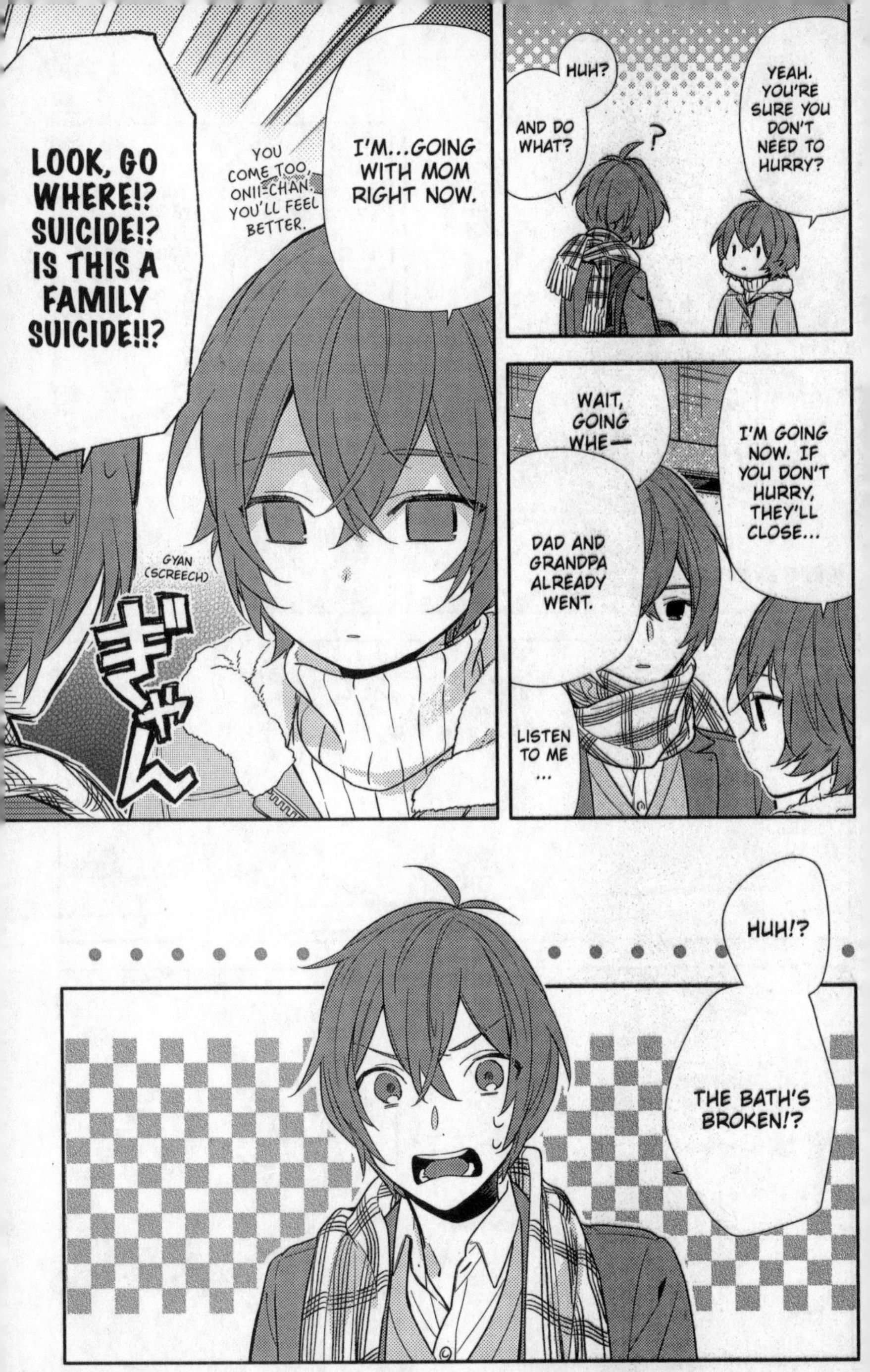
YEAH. YOU'RE SURE YOU DON'T NEED TO HURRY?
HUH?
AND DO WHAT?
?
I'M GOING NOW. IF YOU DON'T HURRY, THEY'LL CLOSE...
WAIT, GOING WHE—
DAD AND GRANDPA ALREADY WENT.
LISTEN TO ME ...
I'M...GOING WITH MOM RIGHT NOW.
YOU COME TOO, ONII-CHAN. YOU'LL FEEL BETTER.
LOOK, GO WHERE!? SUICIDE!? IS THIS A FAMILY SUICIDE!!?
ぎゃん
GYAN (SCREECH)
HUH!?
THE BATH'S BROKEN!?

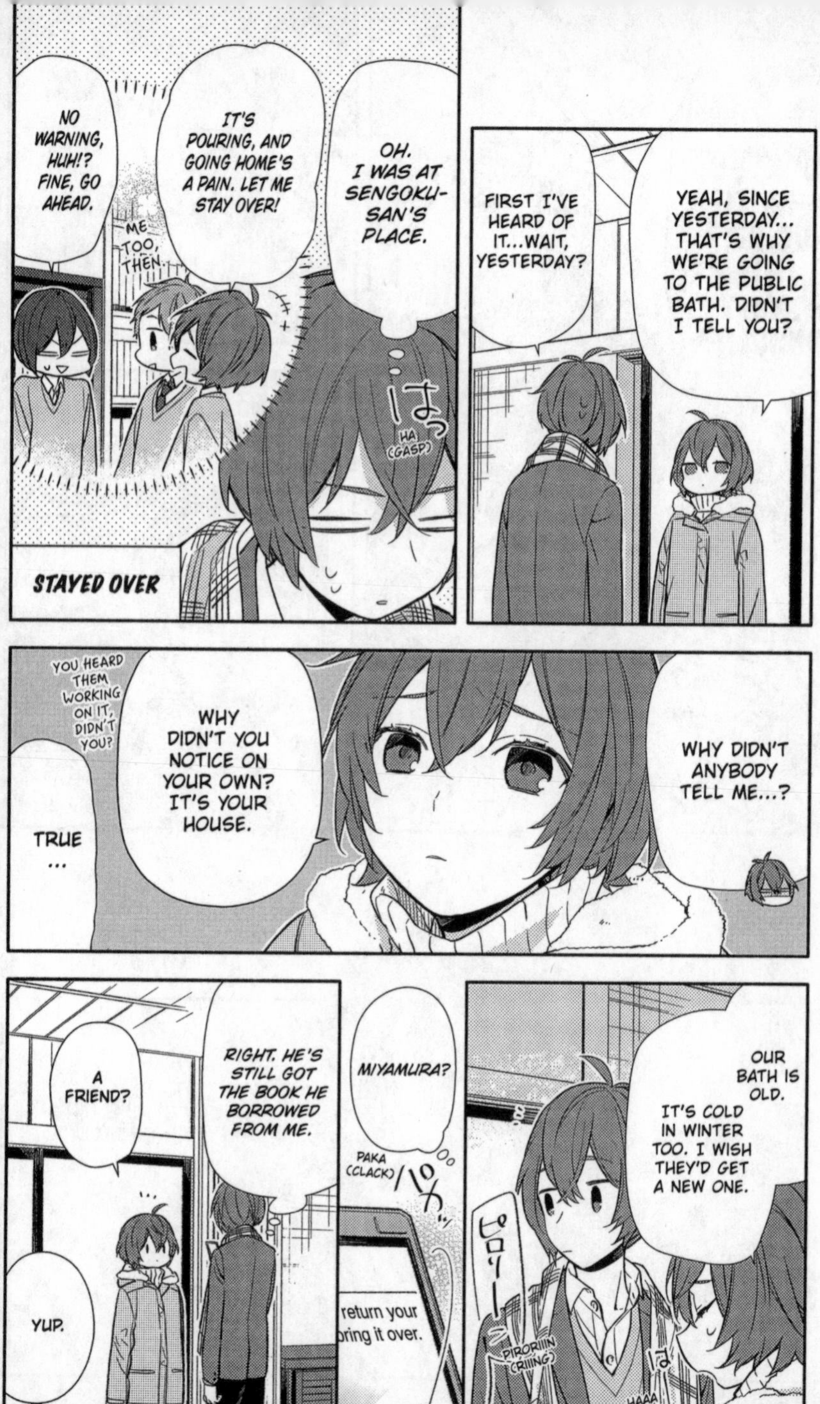
YEAH, SINCE YESTERDAY... THAT'S WHY WE'RE GOING TO THE PUBLIC BATH. DIDN'T I TELL YOU?
FIRST I'VE HEARD OF IT...WAIT, YESTERDAY?
OH. I WAS AT SENGOKU-SAN'S PLACE.
HA (GASP)
IT'S POURING, AND GOING HOME'S A PAIN. LET ME STAY OVER!
ME TOO, THEN.
NO WARNING, HUH!? FINE, GO AHEAD.
STAYED OVER
WHY DIDN'T ANYBODY TELL ME...?
WHY DIDN'T YOU NOTICE ON YOUR OWN? IT'S YOUR HOUSE.
YOU HEARD THEM WORKING ON IT, DIDN'T YOU?
TRUE...
OUR BATH IS OLD.
IT'S COLD IN WINTER TOO. I WISH THEY'D GET A NEW ONE.
PIRORIIIN (RIIING)
HAAA (SIGH)
MIYAMURA?
PAKA (CLACK)
RIGHT. HE'S STILL GOT THE BOOK HE BORROWED FROM ME.
return your
ring it over.
A FRIEND?
...
YUP.

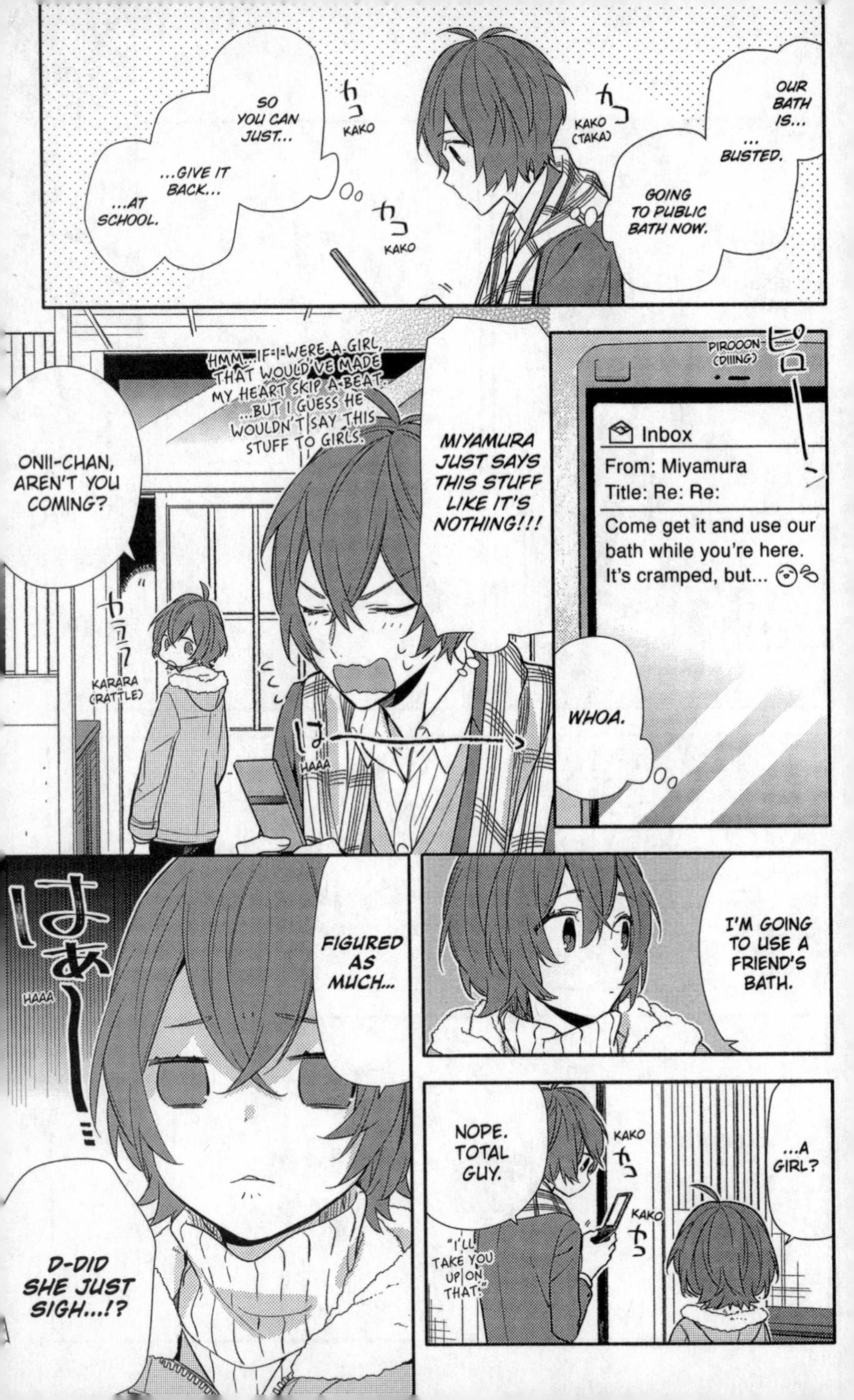
OUR BATH IS... ...BUSTED.
GOING TO PUBLIC BATH NOW.
カコ
KAKO (TAKA)
SO YOU CAN JUST...
...GIVE IT BACK...
...AT SCHOOL.
カコ
KAKO
カコ
KAKO
ピロ
PIROOON (DIIING)
Inbox
From: Miyamura
Title: Re: Re:
Come get it and use our bath while you're here. It's cramped, but...
WHOA.
MIYAMURA JUST SAYS THIS STUFF LIKE IT'S NOTHING!!!
HMM... IF I WERE A GIRL, THAT WOULD'VE MADE MY HEART SKIP A BEAT ...BUT I GUESS HE WOULDN'T SAY THIS STUFF TO GIRLS.
は
HAAA
ONII-CHAN, AREN'T YOU COMING?
カララ
KARARA (RATTLE)
I'M GOING TO USE A FRIEND'S BATH.
...A GIRL?
NOPE. TOTAL GUY.
KAKO
カコ
KAKO
カコ
"I'LL TAKE YOU UP ON THAT."
はあ
HAAA
FIGURED AS MUCH...
D-DID SHE JUST SIGH...!?

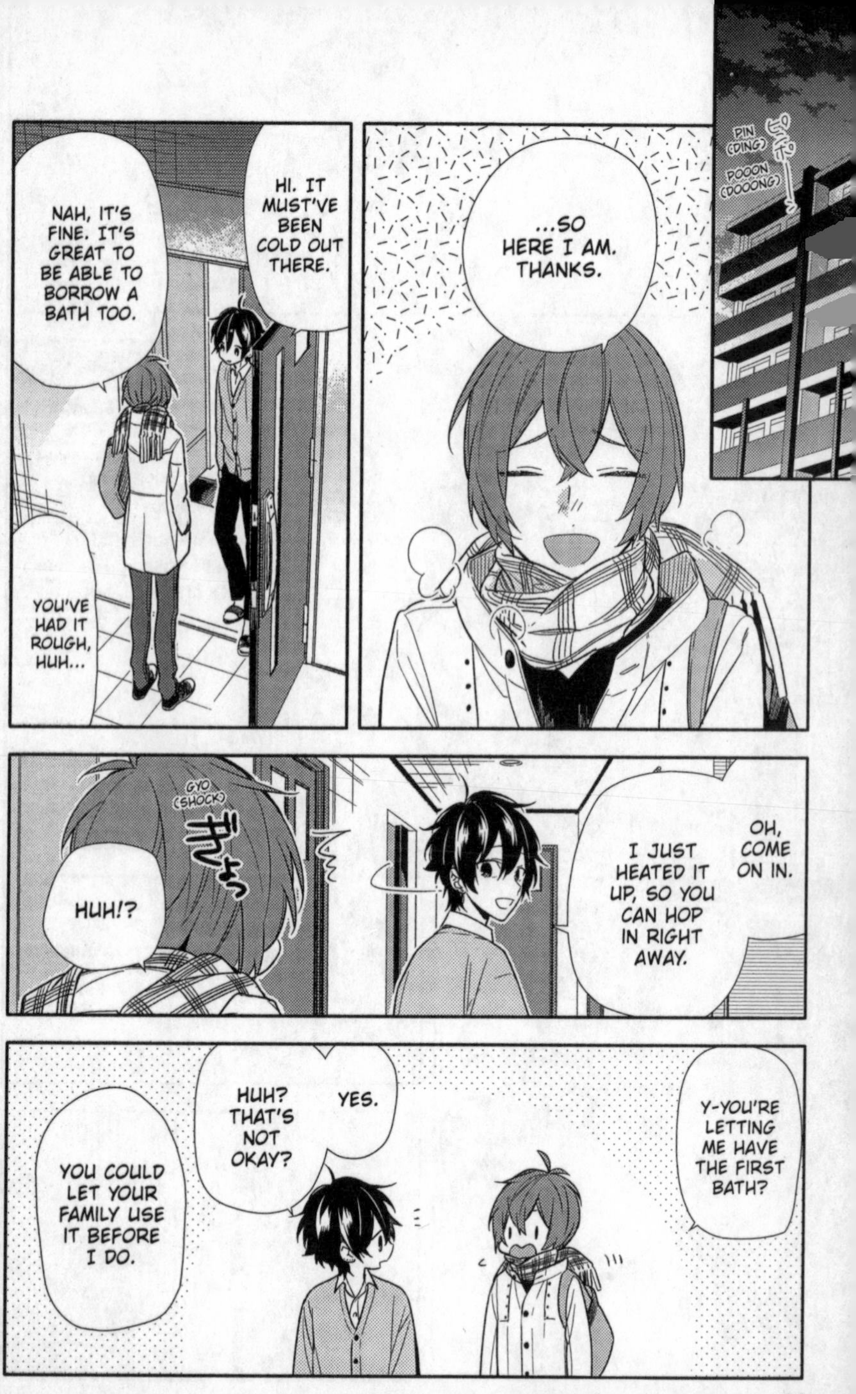
PIN (DING)
POOON (DOOONG)
...SO HERE I AM. THANKS.
HI. IT MUST'VE BEEN COLD OUT THERE.
NAH, IT'S FINE. IT'S GREAT TO BE ABLE TO BORROW A BATH TOO.
YOU'VE HAD IT ROUGH, HUH...
OH, COME ON IN.
I JUST HEATED IT UP, SO YOU CAN HOP IN RIGHT AWAY.
GYO (SHOCK)
ぎょっ
HUH!?
Y-YOU'RE LETTING ME HAVE THE FIRST BATH?
YES.
HUH? THAT'S NOT OKAY?
YOU COULD LET YOUR FAMILY USE IT BEFORE I DO.

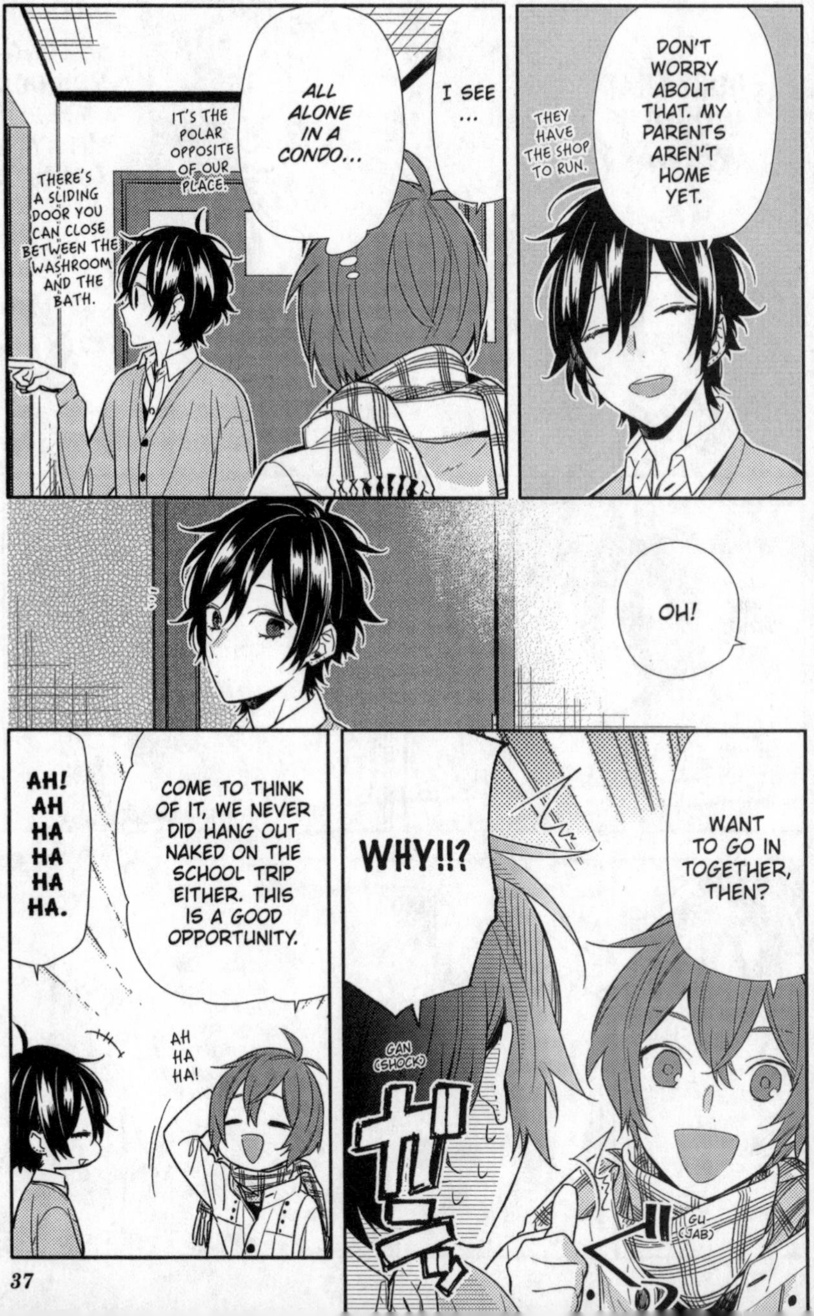
DON'T WORRY ABOUT THAT. MY PARENTS AREN'T HOME YET.
THEY HAVE THE SHOP TO RUN.
I SEE...
ALL ALONE IN A CONDO...
IT'S THE POLAR OPPOSITE OF OUR PLACE.
THERE'S A SLIDING DOOR YOU CAN CLOSE BETWEEN THE WASHROOM AND THE BATH.
OH!
WANT TO GO IN TOGETHER, THEN?
WHY!!?
GAN (SHOCK)
GU (JAB)
COME TO THINK OF IT, WE NEVER DID HANG OUT NAKED ON THE SCHOOL TRIP EITHER. THIS IS A GOOD OPPORTUNITY.
AH! AH HA HA HA HA.
AH HA HA!

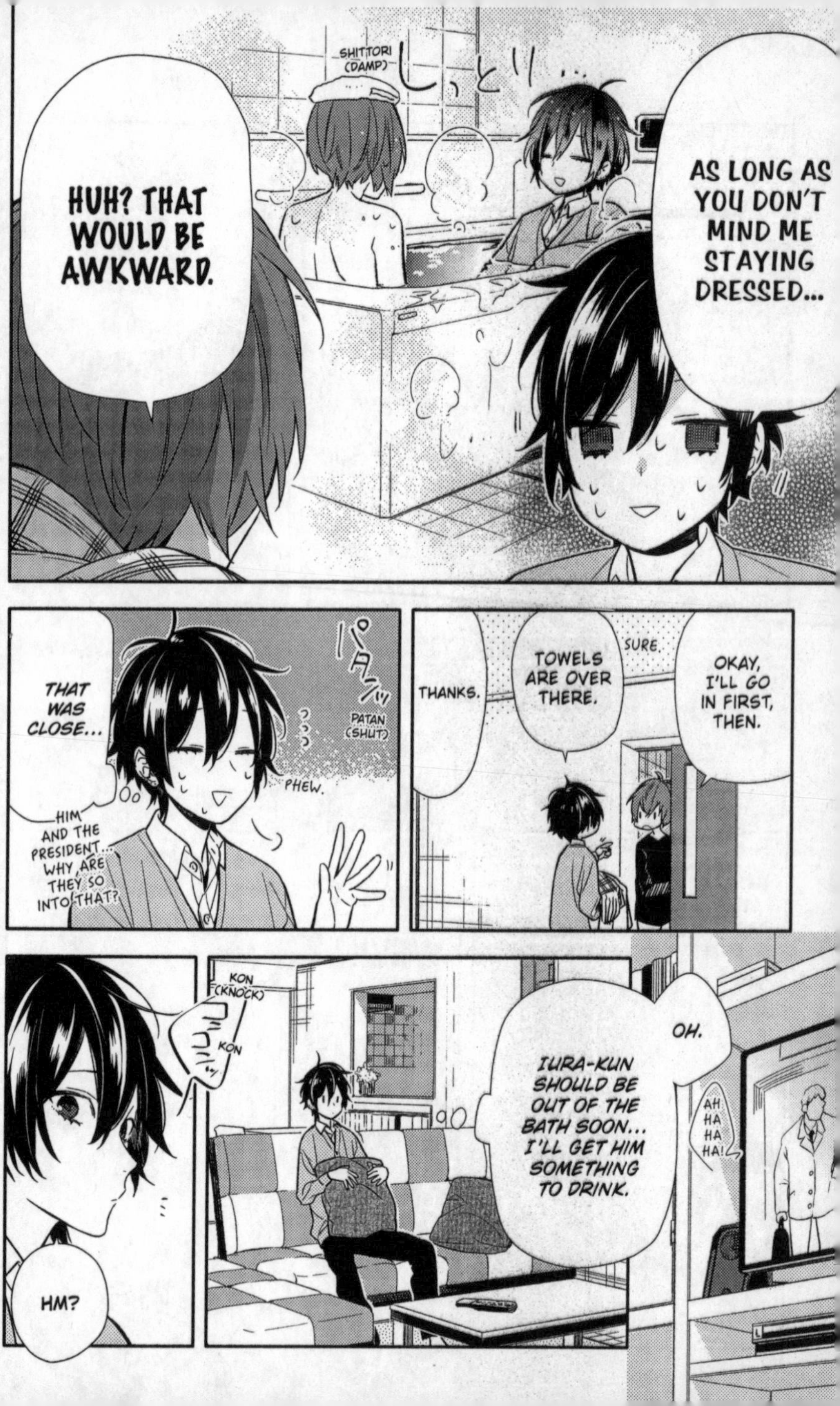
AS LONG AS YOU DON'T MIND ME STAYING DRESSED...
SHITTORI (DAMP)
HUH? THAT WOULD BE AWKWARD.
OKAY, I'LL GO IN FIRST, THEN.
SURE.
TOWELS ARE OVER THERE.
THANKS.
PATAN (SHUT)
THAT WAS CLOSE...
PHEW.
HIM AND THE PRESIDENT... WHY ARE THEY SO INTO THAT?
OH.
IURA-KUN SHOULD BE OUT OF THE BATH SOON... I'LL GET HIM SOMETHING TO DRINK.
AH HA HA HA!
KON (KNOCK)
KON
HM?

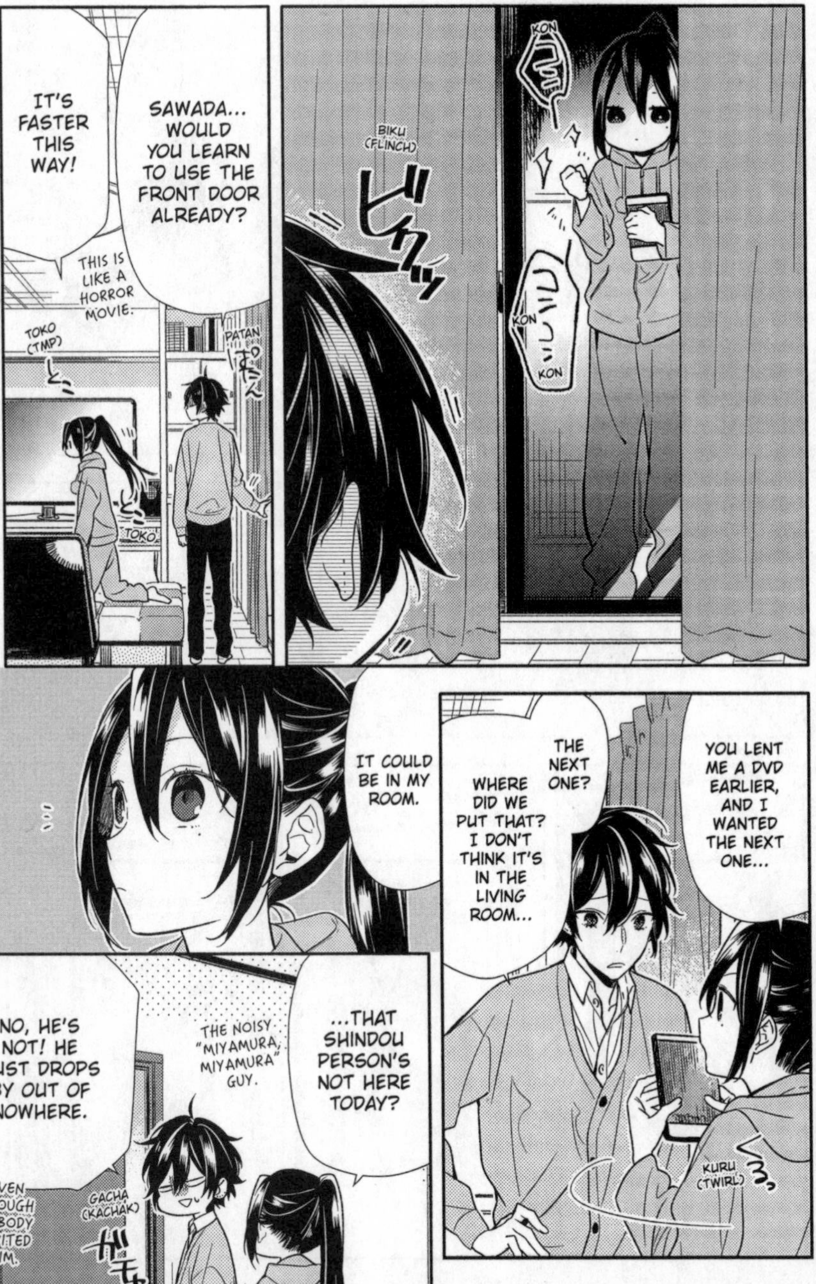
KON
KON
KON
BIKU (FLINCH)
SAWADA... WOULD YOU LEARN TO USE THE FRONT DOOR ALREADY?
IT'S FASTER THIS WAY!
THIS IS LIKE A HORROR MOVIE.
PATAN
TOKO (TMP)
TOKO
YOU LENT ME A DVD EARLIER, AND I WANTED THE NEXT ONE...
THE NEXT ONE?
WHERE DID WE PUT THAT? I DON'T THINK IT'S IN THE LIVING ROOM...
KURU (TWIRL)
IT COULD BE IN MY ROOM.
...THAT SHINDOU PERSON'S NOT HERE TODAY?
THE NOISY "MIYAMURA, MIYAMURA" GUY.
NO, HE'S NOT! HE JUST DROPS BY OUT OF NOWHERE.
GACHA (KACHAK)
EVEN THOUGH NOBODY INVITED HIM.

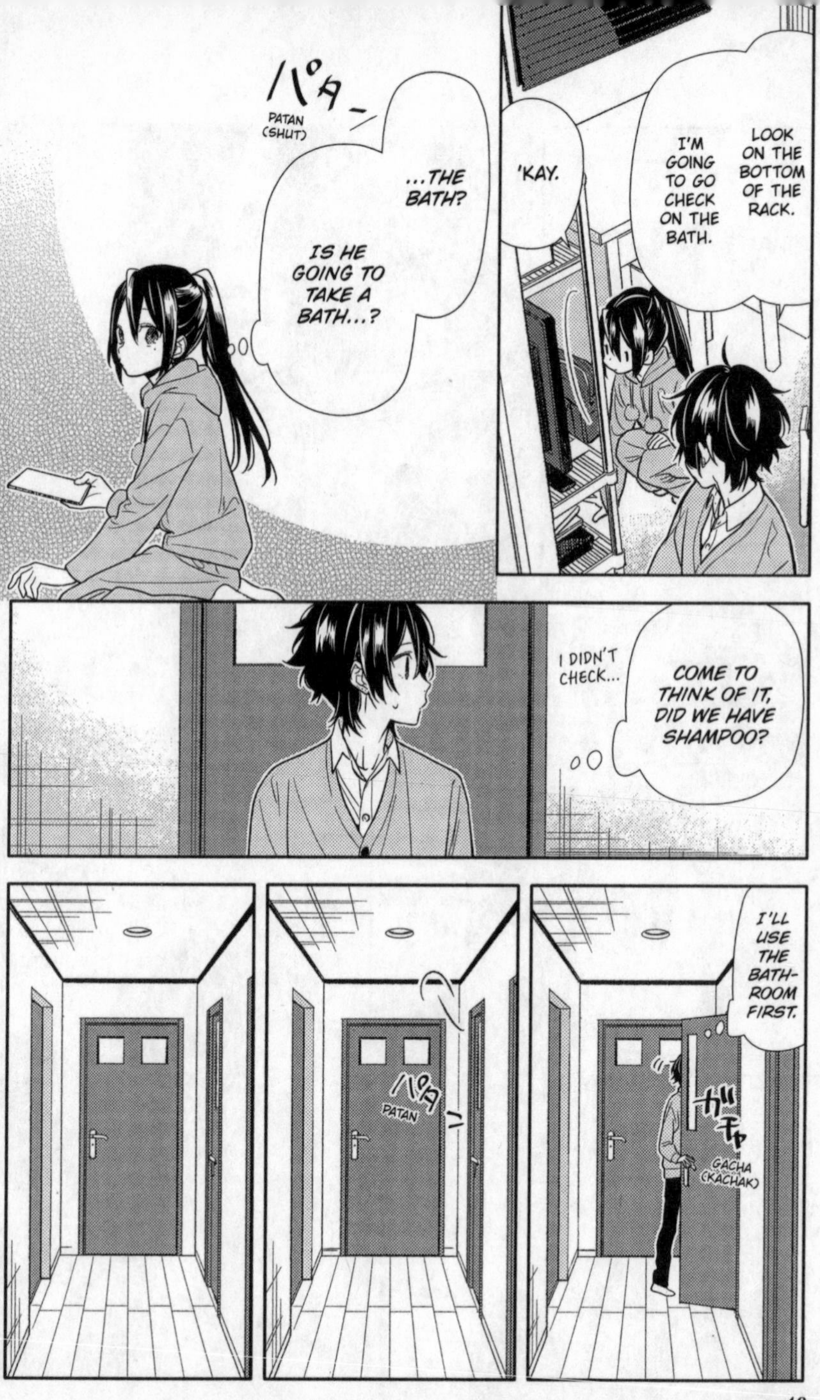
LOOK ON THE BOTTOM OF THE RACK.
I'M GOING TO GO CHECK ON THE BATH.
'KAY.
パタン
PATAN (SHUT)
...THE BATH?
IS HE GOING TO TAKE A BATH...?
COME TO THINK OF IT, DID WE HAVE SHAMPOO?
I DIDN'T CHECK...
I'LL USE THE BATHROOM FIRST.
ガチャ
GACHA (KACHAK)
パタン
PATAN

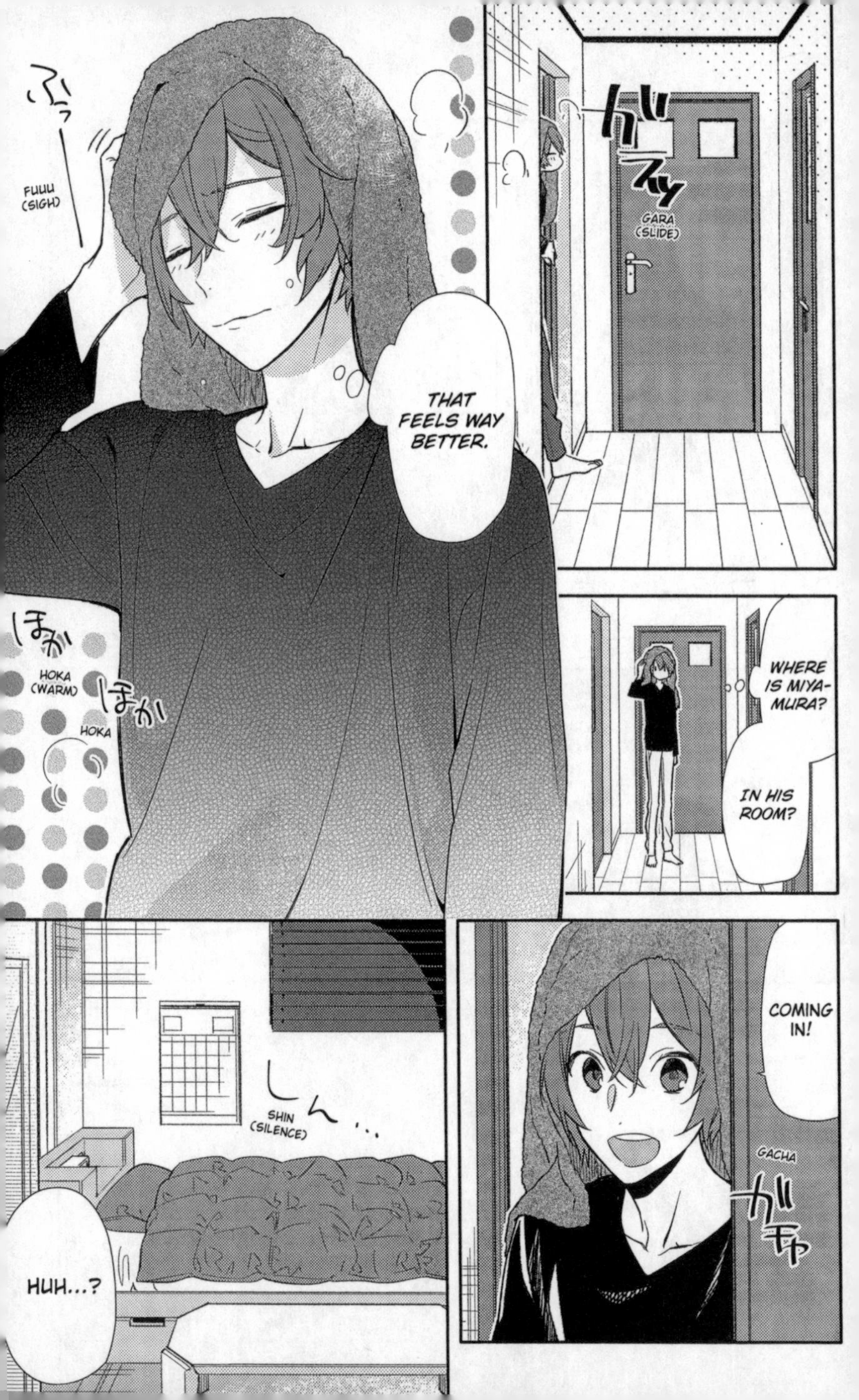
GARA (SLIDE)
WHERE IS MIYA-MURA?
IN HIS ROOM?
FUUU (SIGH)
THAT FEELS WAY BETTER.
HOKA (WARM)
HOKA
COMING IN!
GACHA
SHIN (SILENCE)
HUH...?

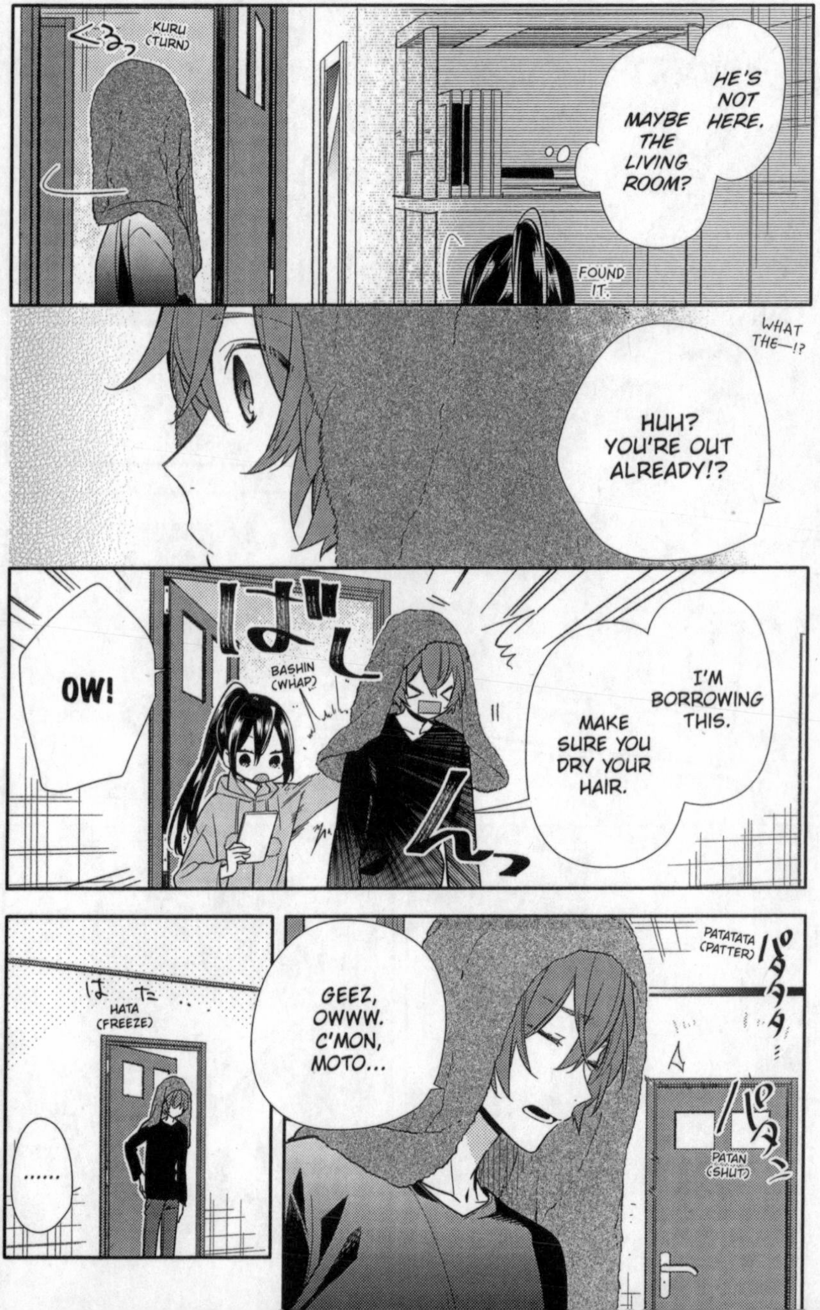
HE'S NOT HERE.
MAYBE THE LIVING ROOM?
FOUND IT.
KURU (TURN)
WHAT THE—!?
HUH? YOU'RE OUT ALREADY!?
I'M BORROWING THIS.
MAKE SURE YOU DRY YOUR HAIR.
BASHIN (WHAP)
OW!
PATATATA (PATTER)
GEEZ, OWWW. C'MON, MOTO...
PATAN (SHUT)
HATA (FREEZE)
......

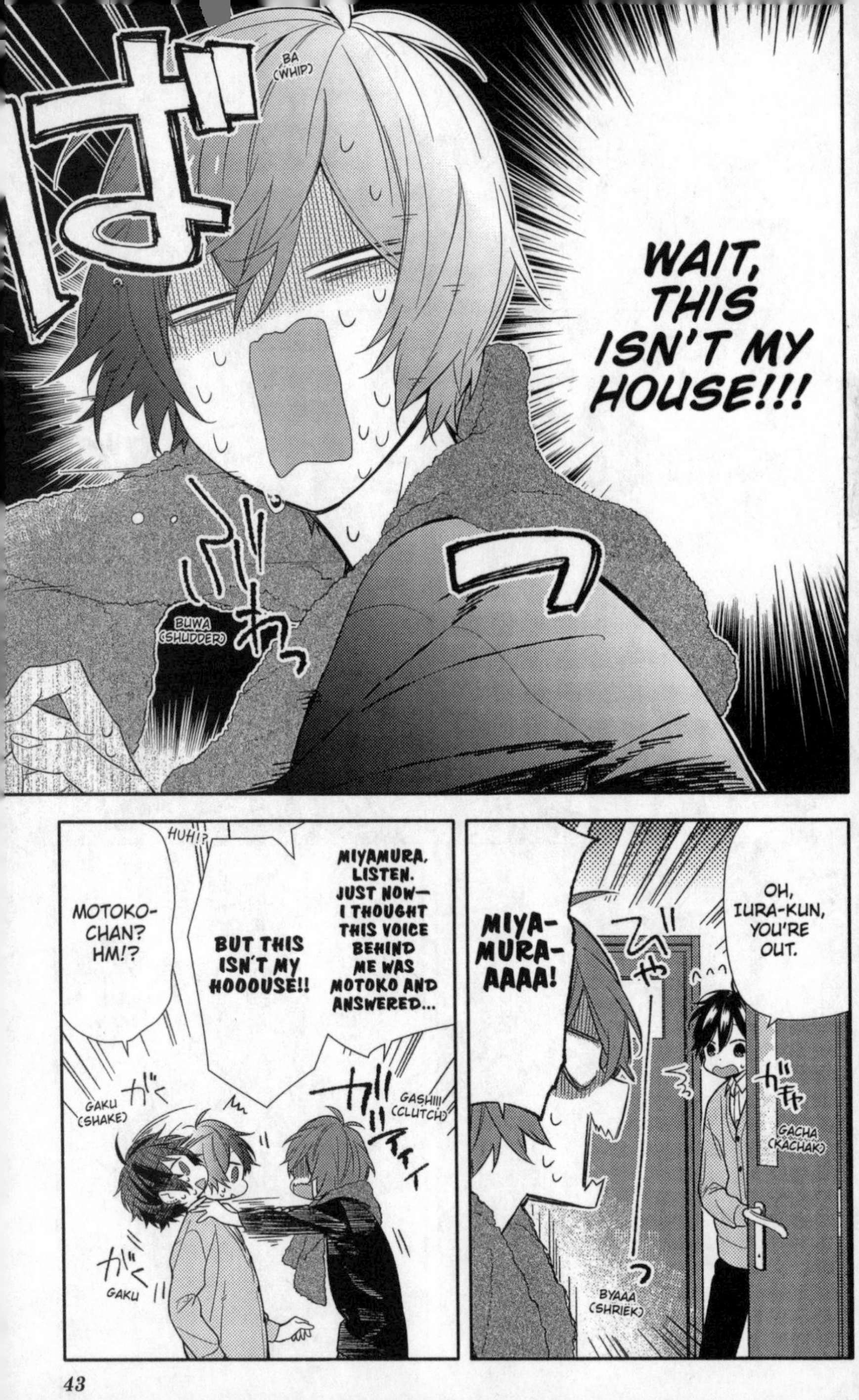
BA (WHIP)
WAIT, THIS ISN'T MY HOUSE!!!
BUWA (SHUDDER)
OH, IURA-KUN, YOU'RE OUT.
GACHA (KACHAK)
MIYA-MURA-AAAA!
BYAAA (SHRIEK)
MIYAMURA, LISTEN. JUST NOW— I THOUGHT THIS VOICE BEHIND ME WAS MOTOKO AND ANSWERED...
GASHIII (CLUTCH)
BUT THIS ISN'T MY HOOOUSE!!
HUH!?
MOTOKO-CHAN? HM!?
GAKU (SHAKE)
GAKU

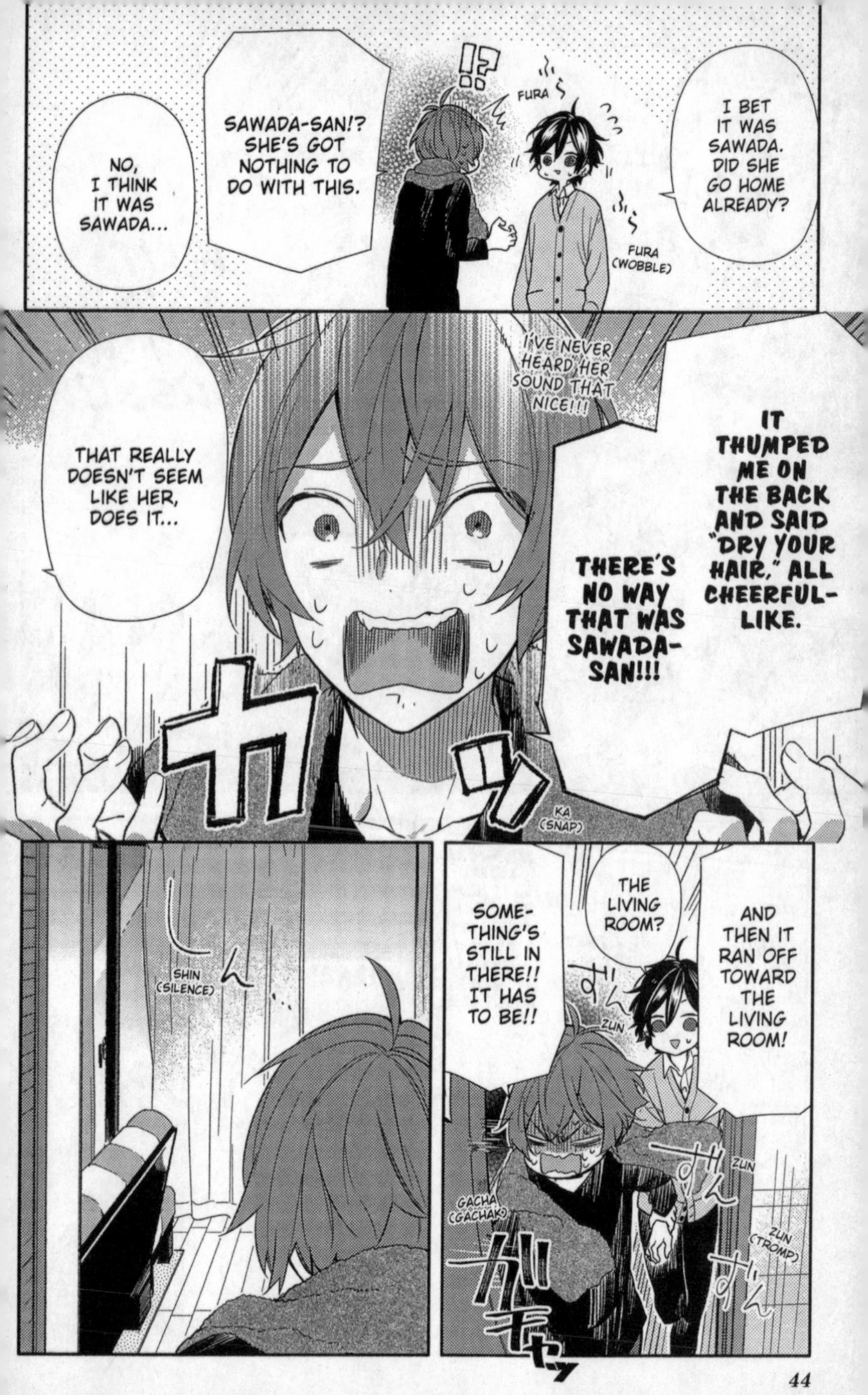
I BET IT WAS SAWADA. DID SHE GO HOME ALREADY?
FURA
FURA (WOBBLE)
!?
SAWADA-SAN!? SHE'S GOT NOTHING TO DO WITH THIS.
NO, I THINK IT WAS SAWADA...
IT THUMPED ME ON THE BACK AND SAID "DRY YOUR HAIR," ALL CHEERFUL-LIKE.
I'VE NEVER HEARD HER SOUND THAT NICE!!!
THERE'S NO WAY THAT WAS SAWADA-SAN!!!
THAT REALLY DOESN'T SEEM LIKE HER, DOES IT...
KA (SNAP)
AND THEN IT RAN OFF TOWARD THE LIVING ROOM!
THE LIVING ROOM?
ZUN
SOME-THING'S STILL IN THERE!! IT HAS TO BE!!
ZUN
ZUN (TROMP)
GACHA (GACHAK)
SHIN (SILENCE)

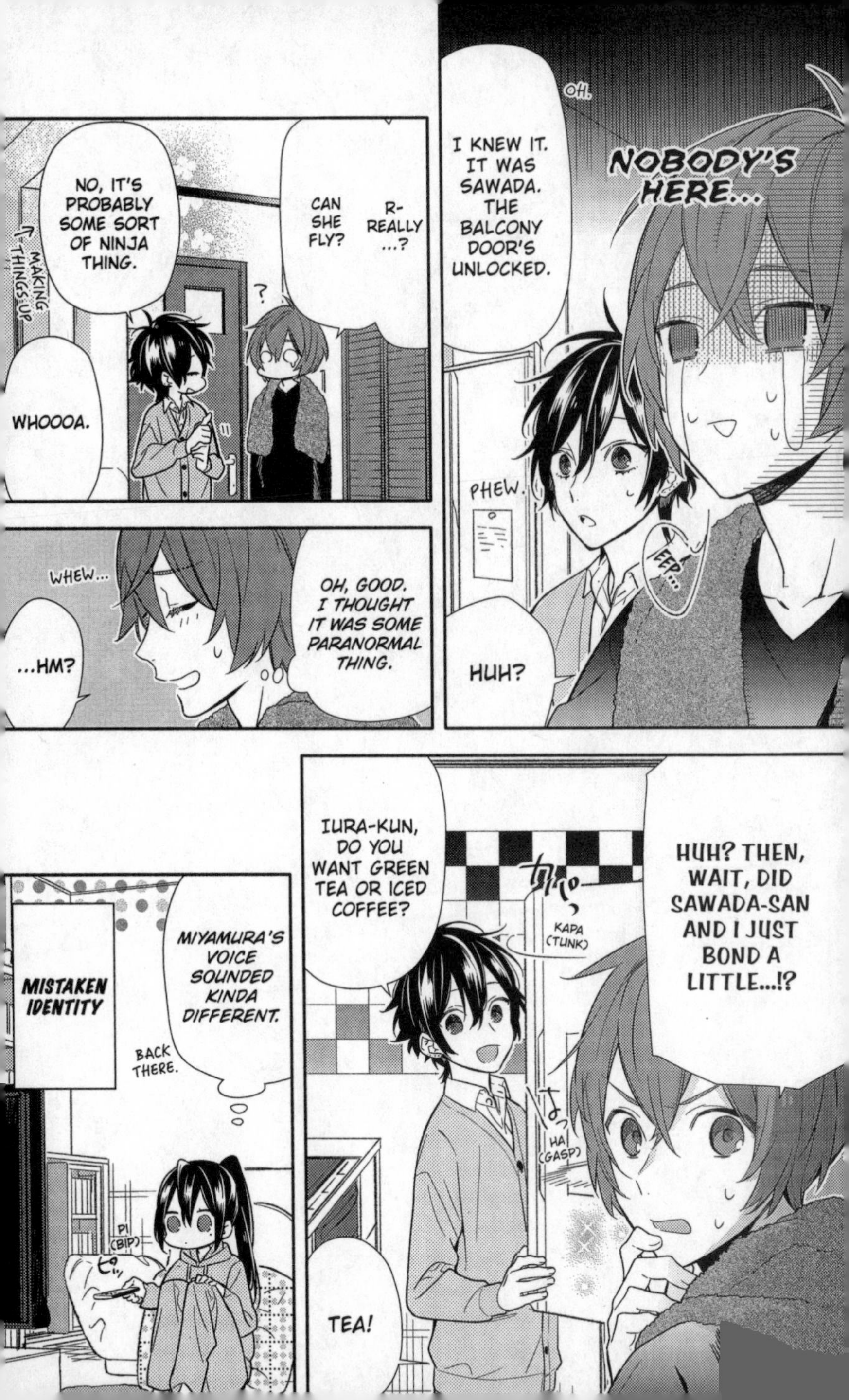
NOBODY'S HERE...
OH.
I KNEW IT. IT WAS SAWADA. THE BALCONY DOOR'S UNLOCKED.
PHEW.
EEP...
HUH?
R-REALLY...?
CAN SHE FLY?
?
NO, IT'S PROBABLY SOME SORT OF NINJA THING.
MAKING THINGS UP
WHOOOA.
OH, GOOD. I THOUGHT IT WAS SOME PARANORMAL THING.
WHEW...
...HM?
HUH? THEN, WAIT, DID SAWADA-SAN AND I JUST BOND A LITTLE...!?
IURA-KUN, DO YOU WANT GREEN TEA OR ICED COFFEE?
KAPA (TUNK)
HA (GASP)
TEA!
MIYAMURA'S VOICE SOUNDED KINDA DIFFERENT.
BACK THERE.
MISTAKEN IDENTITY
PI (BIP)

HORIMIYA

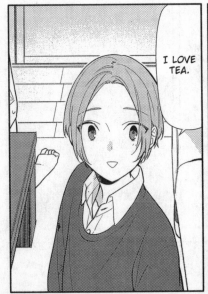

HERE AGAIN, HUH, KITAHARA-KUN?
ARE YOU A TEA DRINKER?
TEA'S ALL WE'VE GOT.
I LOVE TEA.
IT'S EVEN MORE BITTER THAN LAST TIME.
DON (BOOM)
BAN (BAM)
CHALLENGE ACCEPTED, SIR.

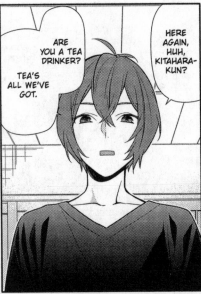

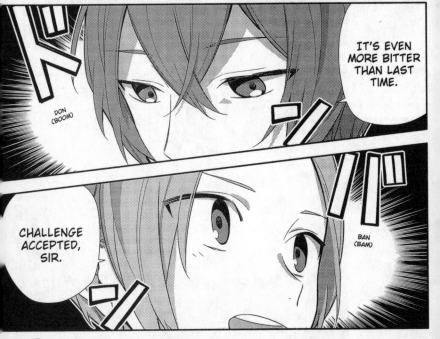

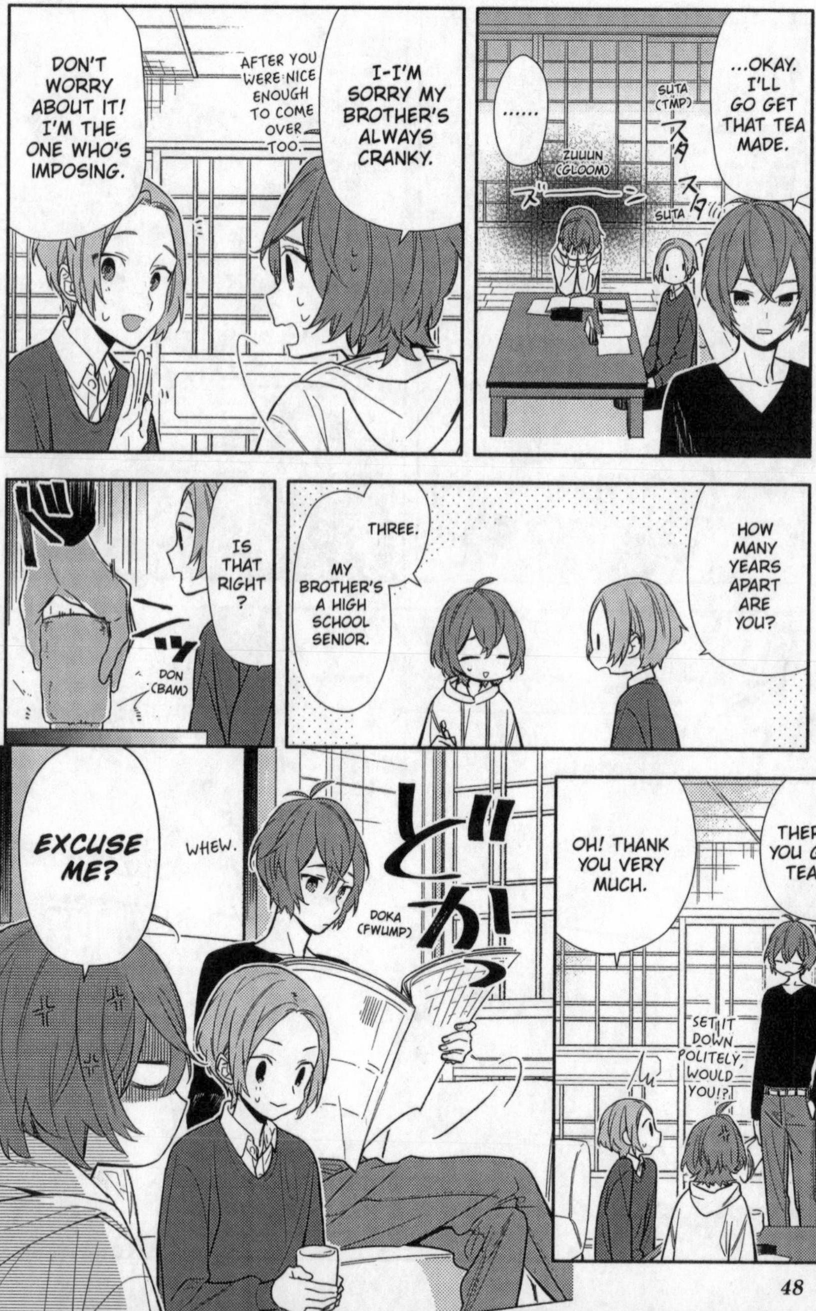
...OKAY. I'LL GO GET THAT TEA MADE.
SUTA (TMP)
SUTA
......
ZUUUN (GLOOM)
I-I'M SORRY MY BROTHER'S ALWAYS CRANKY.
AFTER YOU WERE NICE ENOUGH TO COME OVER TOO.
DON'T WORRY ABOUT IT! I'M THE ONE WHO'S IMPOSING.
HOW MANY YEARS APART ARE YOU?
THREE.
MY BROTHER'S A HIGH SCHOOL SENIOR.
IS THAT RIGHT?
DON (BAM)
THERE YOU GO. TEA.
OH! THANK YOU VERY MUCH.
SET IT DOWN POLITELY, WOULD YOU!?
DOKA (FWUMP)
WHEW.
EXCUSE ME?

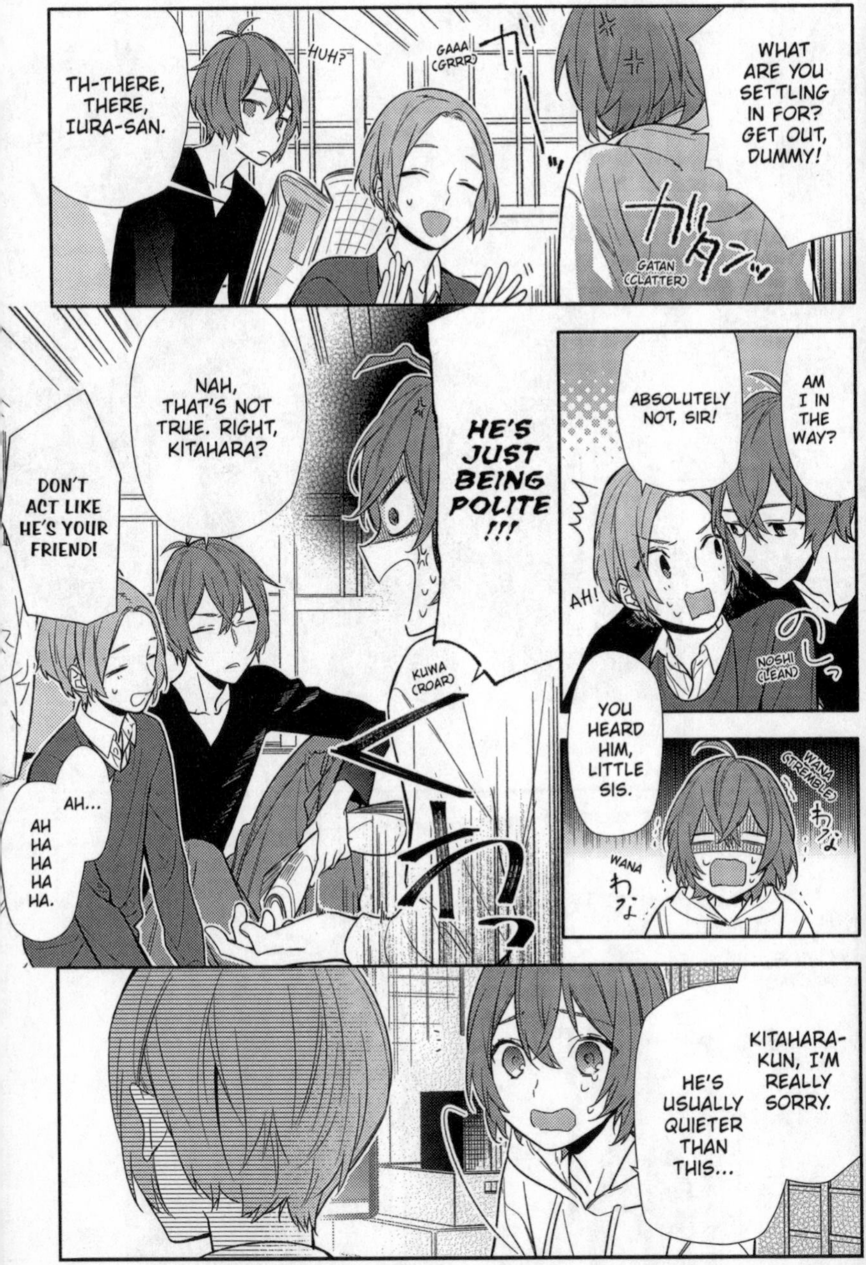
WHAT ARE YOU SETTLING IN FOR? GET OUT, DUMMY!
GATAN (CLATTER)
GAAA (GRRR)
HUH?
TH-THERE, THERE, IURA-SAN.
AM I IN THE WAY?
ABSOLUTELY NOT, SIR!
AH!
NOSHI (LEAN)
YOU HEARD HIM, LITTLE SIS.
WANA (TREMBLE)
WANA
HE'S JUST BEING POLITE!!!
NAH, THAT'S NOT TRUE. RIGHT, KITAHARA?
DON'T ACT LIKE HE'S YOUR FRIEND!
KUWA (ROAR)
AH... AH HA HA HA HA.
KITAHARA-KUN, I'M REALLY SORRY.
HE'S USUALLY QUIETER THAN THIS...

OH...

I'M SORRY. I WASN'T REALLY LISTENING ...

UM...

HA (GASP)

...

JIII (STAAARE)

THAT'S THE LIVING ROOM.

AW, C'MON.

DON'T COME IN HERE AGAIN!!

MOTOOO...

PISHAN (SLAM)

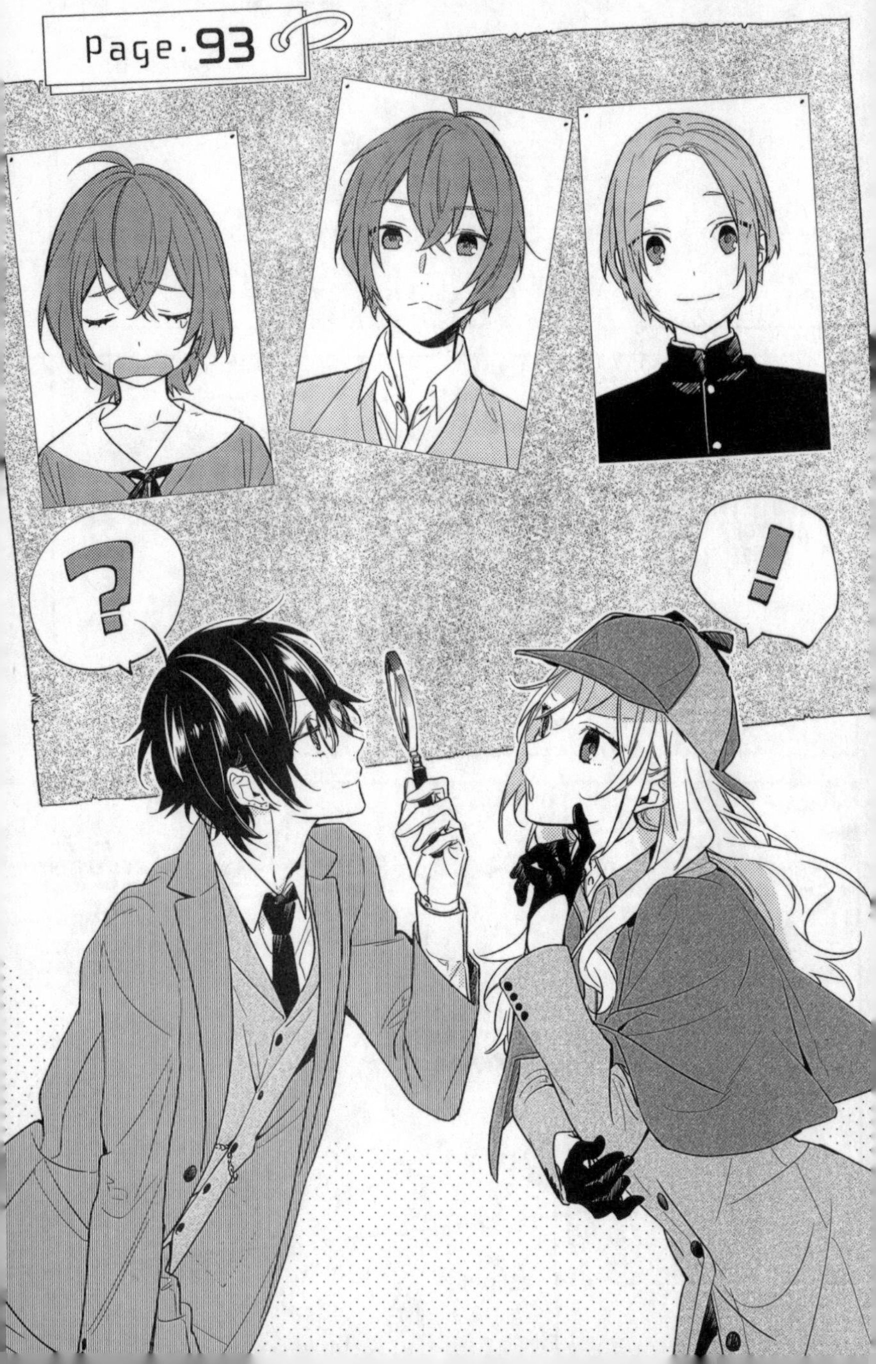
Page.93
?
!

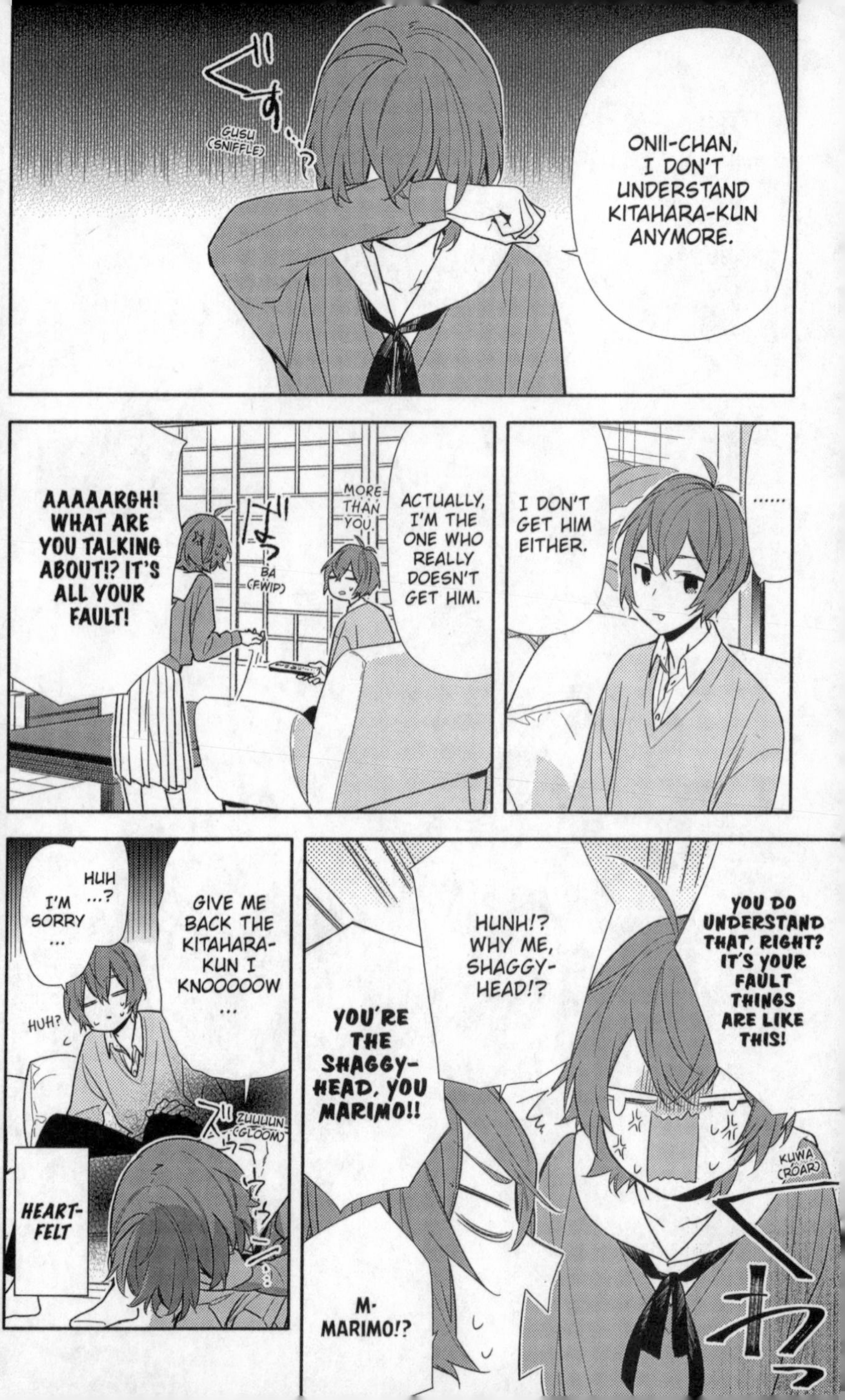
ONII-CHAN, I DON'T UNDERSTAND KITAHARA-KUN ANYMORE.
GUSU (SNIFFLE)
......
I DON'T GET HIM EITHER.
ACTUALLY, I'M THE ONE WHO REALLY DOESN'T GET HIM.
MORE THAN YOU.
BA (FWIP)
AAAAARGH! WHAT ARE YOU TALKING ABOUT!? IT'S ALL YOUR FAULT!
YOU DO UNDERSTAND THAT, RIGHT? IT'S YOUR FAULT THINGS ARE LIKE THIS!
KUWA (ROAR)
HUNH!? WHY ME, SHAGGY-HEAD!?
YOU'RE THE SHAGGY-HEAD, YOU MARIMO!!
M-MARIMO!?
GIVE ME BACK THE KITAHARA-KUN I KNOOOOOW...
HUH ...?
I'M SORRY ...
HUH?
ZUUUUUN (GLOOM)
HEART-FELT

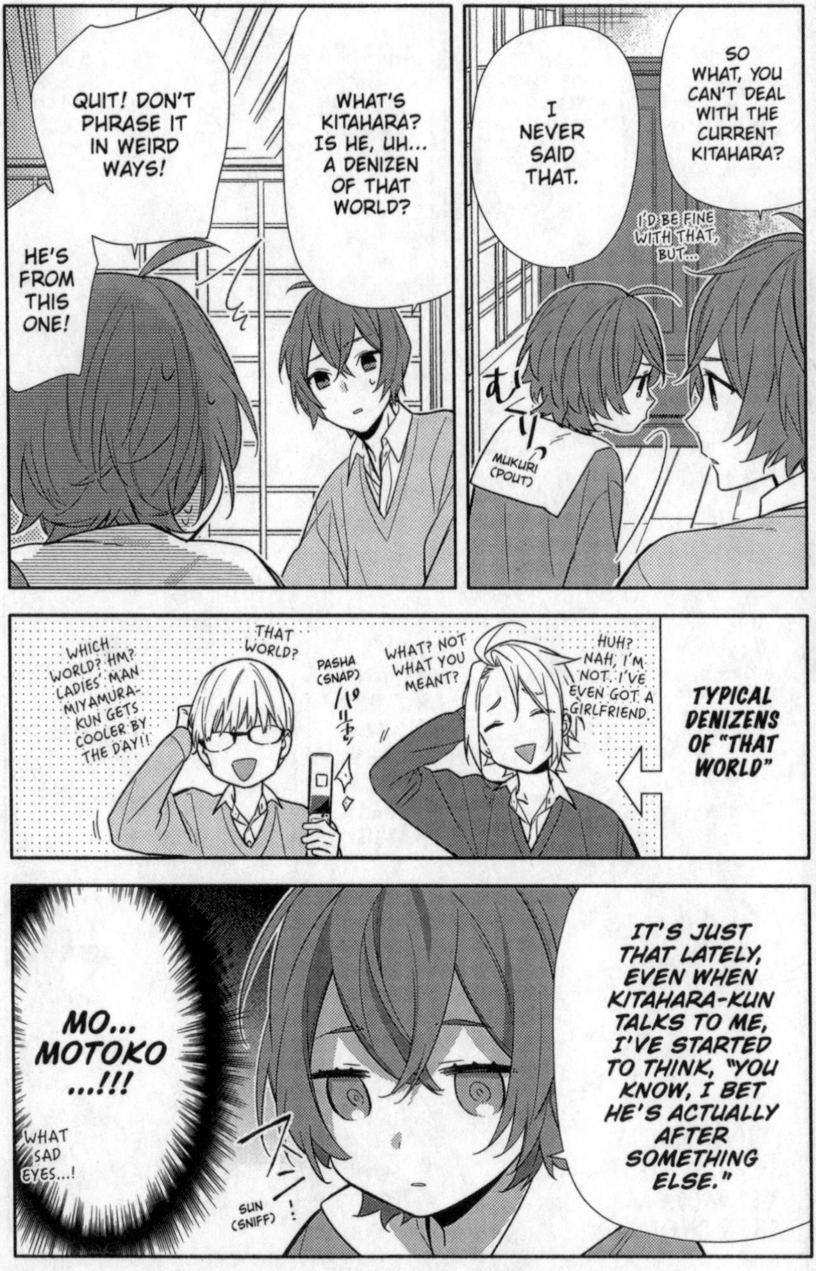
SO WHAT, YOU CAN'T DEAL WITH THE CURRENT KITAHARA?
I'D BE FINE WITH THAT, BUT...
I NEVER SAID THAT.
MUKURI (POUT)
WHAT'S KITAHARA? IS HE, UH... A DENIZEN OF THAT WORLD?
QUIT! DON'T PHRASE IT IN WEIRD WAYS!
HE'S FROM THIS ONE!
TYPICAL DENIZENS OF "THAT WORLD"
HUH? NAH, I'M NOT. I'VE EVEN GOT A GIRLFRIEND.
WHAT? NOT WHAT YOU MEANT?
PASHA (SNAP)
THAT WORLD?
WHICH WORLD? HM? LADIES' MAN MIYAMURA-KUN GETS COOLER BY THE DAY!!
IT'S JUST THAT LATELY, EVEN WHEN KITAHARA-KUN TALKS TO ME, I'VE STARTED TO THINK, "YOU KNOW, I BET HE'S ACTUALLY AFTER SOMETHING ELSE."
MO... MOTOKO ...!!!
WHAT SAD EYES...!
SUN (SNIFF)

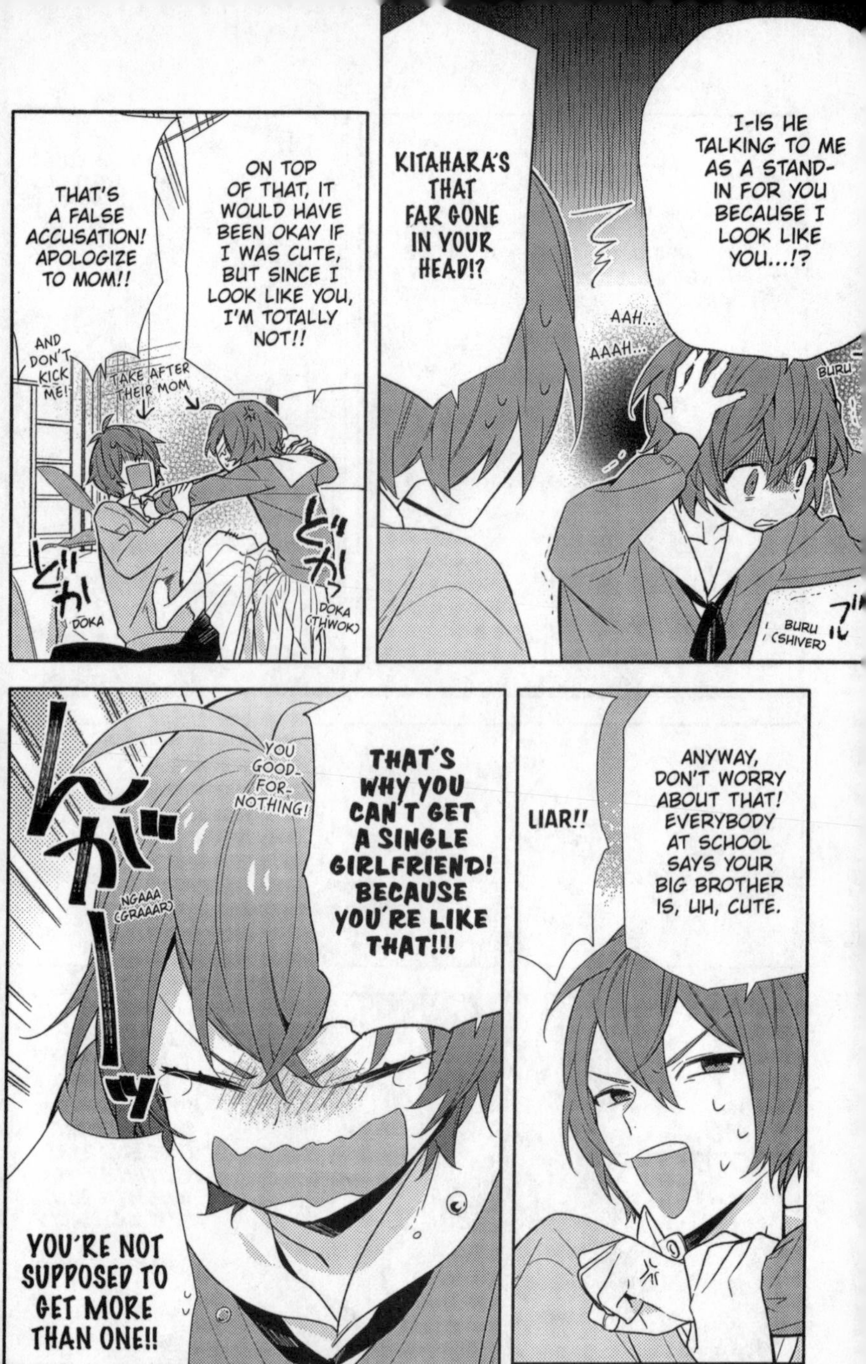
I-IS HE TALKING TO ME AS A STAND-IN FOR YOU BECAUSE I LOOK LIKE YOU...!?
KITAHARA'S THAT FAR GONE IN YOUR HEAD!?
AAH... AAAH...
BURU
BURU (SHIVER)
ON TOP OF THAT, IT WOULD HAVE BEEN OKAY IF I WAS CUTE, BUT SINCE I LOOK LIKE YOU, I'M TOTALLY NOT!!
THAT'S A FALSE ACCUSATION! APOLOGIZE TO MOM!!
AND DON'T KICK ME!
TAKE AFTER THEIR MOM
DOKA (THWOK)
DOKA
ANYWAY, DON'T WORRY ABOUT THAT! EVERYBODY AT SCHOOL SAYS YOUR BIG BROTHER IS, UH, CUTE.
LIAR!!
THAT'S WHY YOU CAN'T GET A SINGLE GIRLFRIEND! BECAUSE YOU'RE LIKE THAT!!!
YOU GOOD-FOR-NOTHING!
NGAAA (GRAAAR)
YOU'RE NOT SUPPOSED TO GET MORE THAN ONE!!

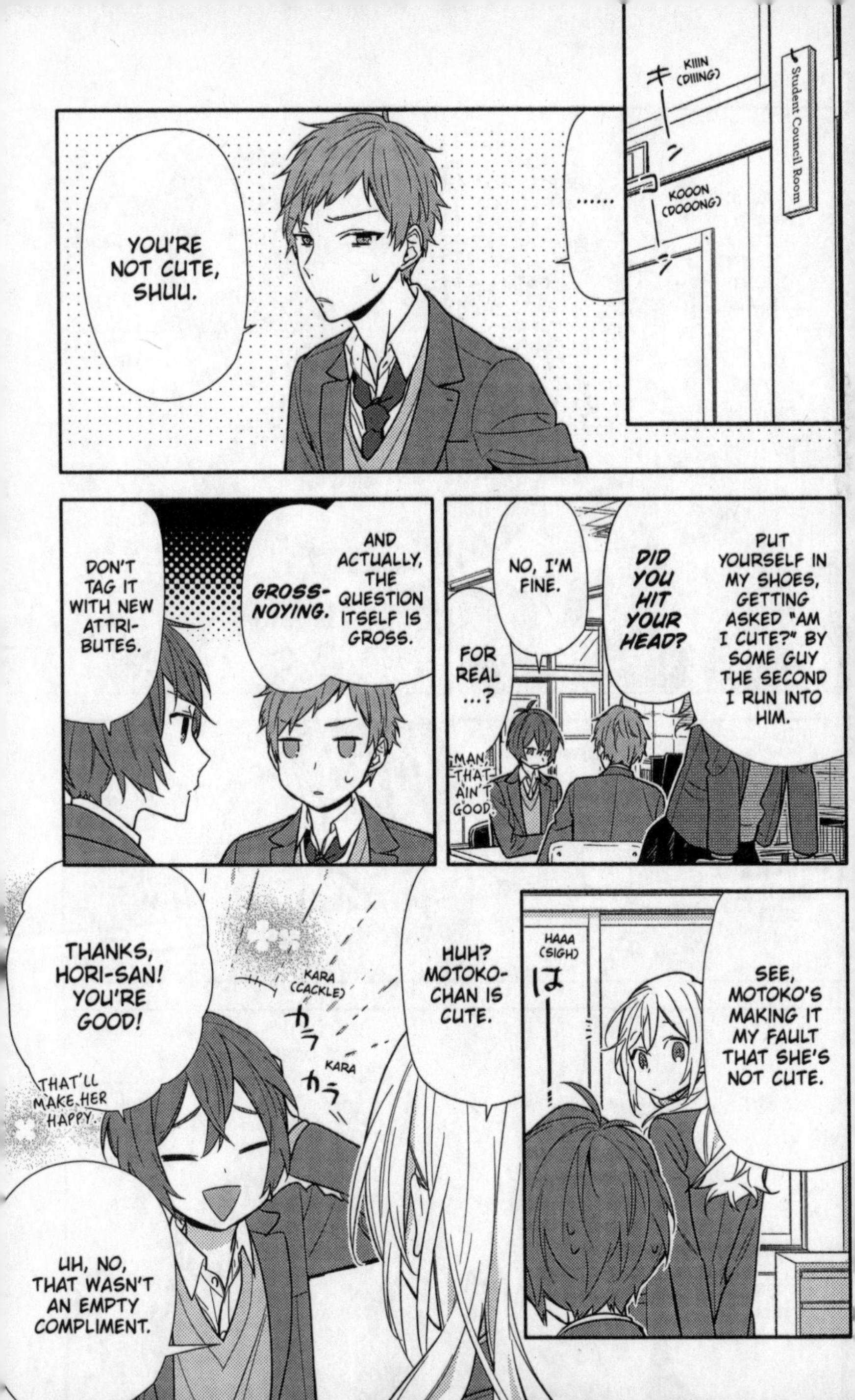
Student Council Room
KIIN (DIIING)
KOOON (DOOONG)
......
YOU'RE NOT CUTE, SHUU.
PUT YOURSELF IN MY SHOES, GETTING ASKED "AM I CUTE?" BY SOME GUY THE SECOND I RUN INTO HIM.
DID YOU HIT YOUR HEAD?
NO, I'M FINE.
FOR REAL ...?
MAN, THAT AIN'T GOOD.
AND ACTUALLY, THE QUESTION ITSELF IS GROSS.
GROSS-NOYING.
DON'T TAG IT WITH NEW ATTRI-BUTES.
SEE, MOTOKO'S MAKING IT MY FAULT THAT SHE'S NOT CUTE.
HAAA (SIGH)
HUH? MOTOKO-CHAN IS CUTE.
KARA (CACKLE)
KARA
THANKS, HORI-SAN! YOU'RE GOOD!
THAT'LL MAKE HER HAPPY.
UH, NO, THAT WASN'T AN EMPTY COMPLIMENT.

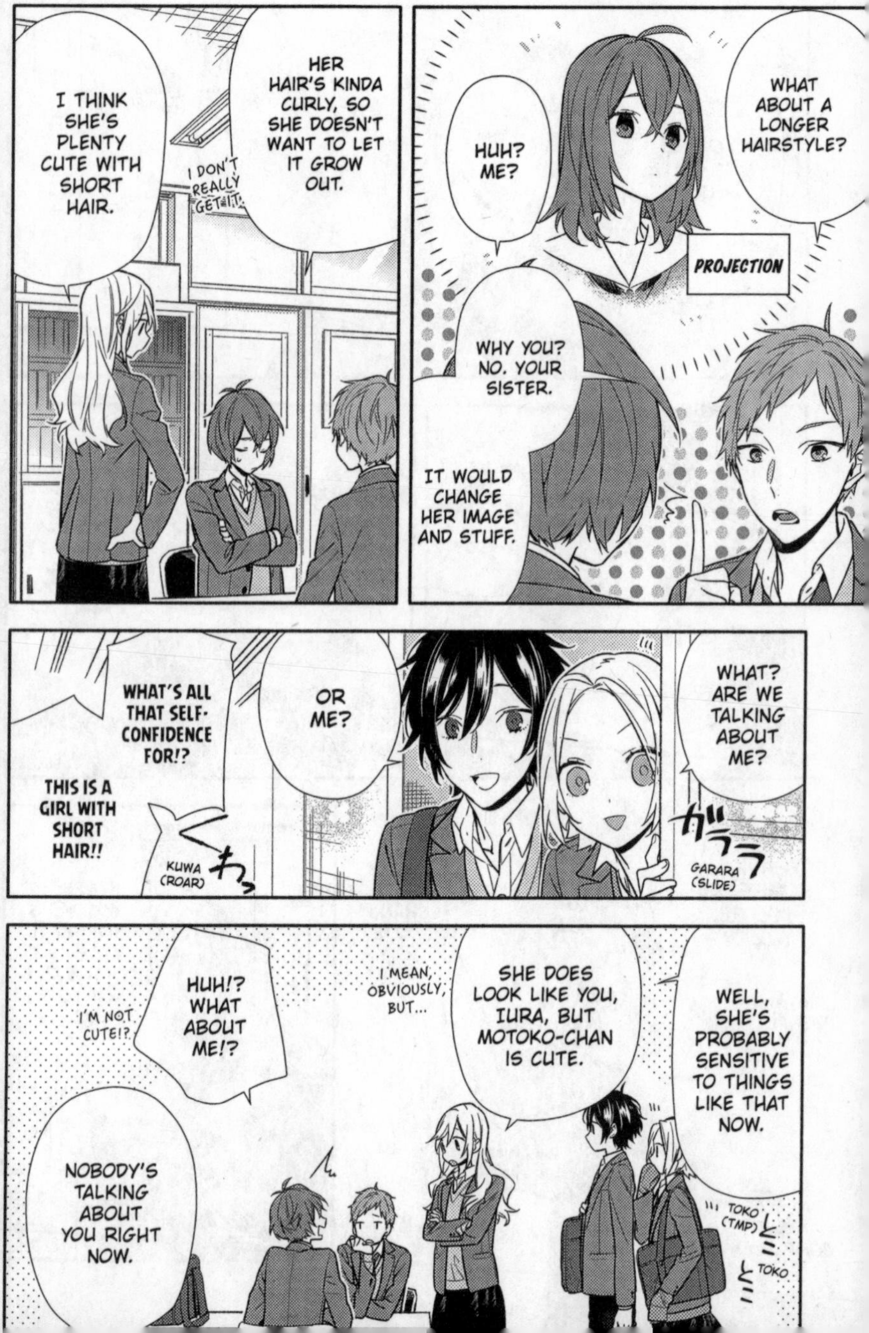
WHAT ABOUT A LONGER HAIRSTYLE?
HUH? ME?
PROJECTION
WHY YOU? NO. YOUR SISTER.
IT WOULD CHANGE HER IMAGE AND STUFF.
HER HAIR'S KINDA CURLY, SO SHE DOESN'T WANT TO LET IT GROW OUT.
I DON'T REALLY GET IT.
I THINK SHE'S PLENTY CUTE WITH SHORT HAIR.
GARARA (SLIDE)
WHAT? ARE WE TALKING ABOUT ME?
OR ME?
WHAT'S ALL THAT SELF-CONFIDENCE FOR!?
THIS IS A GIRL WITH SHORT HAIR!!
KUWA (ROAR)
WELL, SHE'S PROBABLY SENSITIVE TO THINGS LIKE THAT NOW.
TOKO (TMP)
TOKO
SHE DOES LOOK LIKE YOU, IURA, BUT MOTOKO-CHAN IS CUTE.
I MEAN, OBVIOUSLY, BUT...
HUH!? WHAT ABOUT ME!?
I'M NOT CUTE!?
NOBODY'S TALKING ABOUT YOU RIGHT NOW.

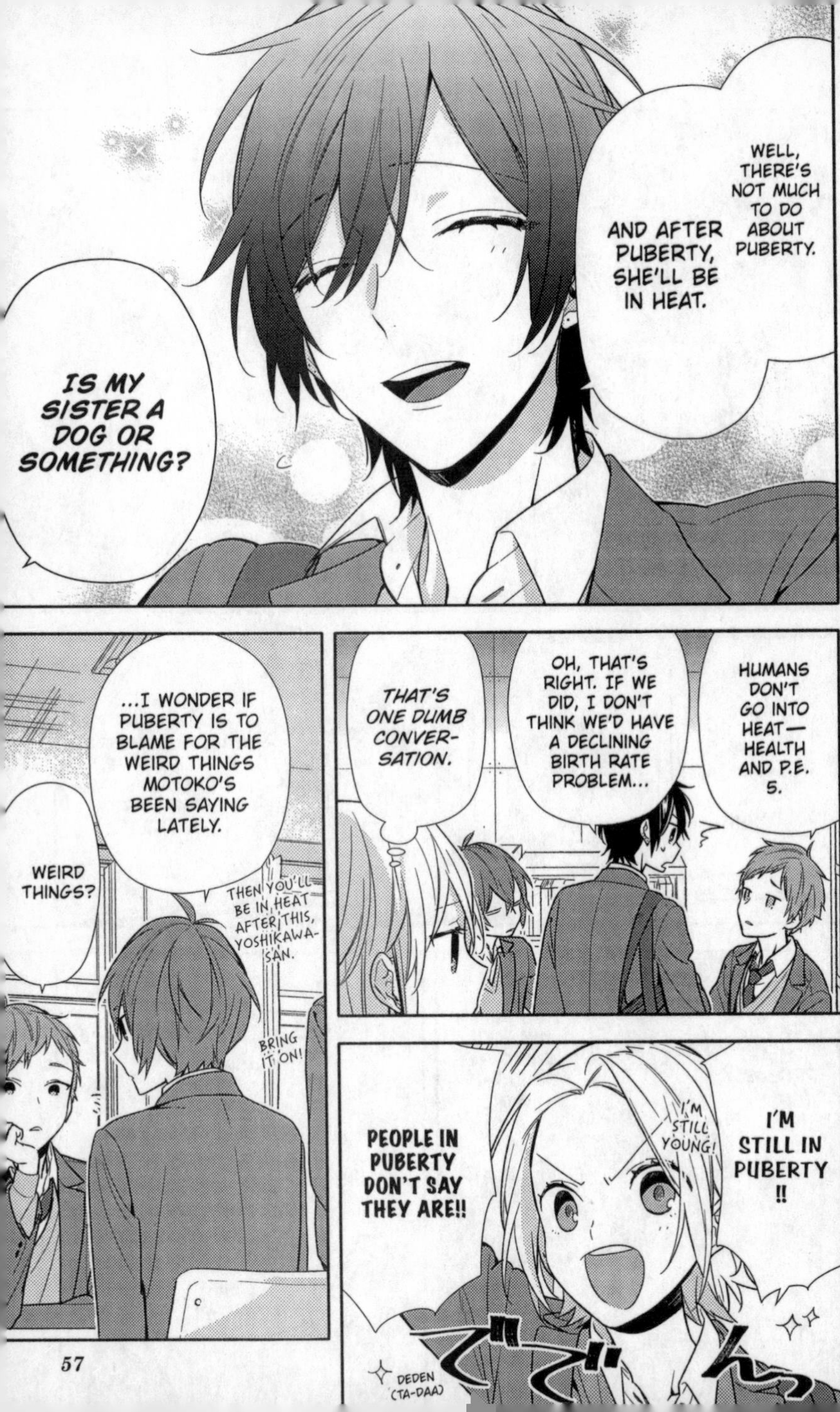
WELL, THERE'S NOT MUCH TO DO ABOUT PUBERTY.
AND AFTER PUBERTY, SHE'LL BE IN HEAT.
IS MY SISTER A DOG OR SOMETHING?
HUMANS DON'T GO INTO HEAT— HEALTH AND P.E. 5.
OH, THAT'S RIGHT. IF WE DID, I DON'T THINK WE'D HAVE A DECLINING BIRTH RATE PROBLEM...
THAT'S ONE DUMB CONVERSATION.
I'M STILL IN PUBERTY !!
I'M STILL YOUNG!
PEOPLE IN PUBERTY DON'T SAY THEY ARE!!
DEDEN (TA-DAA)
...I WONDER IF PUBERTY IS TO BLAME FOR THE WEIRD THINGS MOTOKO'S BEEN SAYING LATELY.
WEIRD THINGS?
THEN YOU'LL BE IN HEAT AFTER THIS, YOSHIKAWA-SAN.
BRING IT ON!

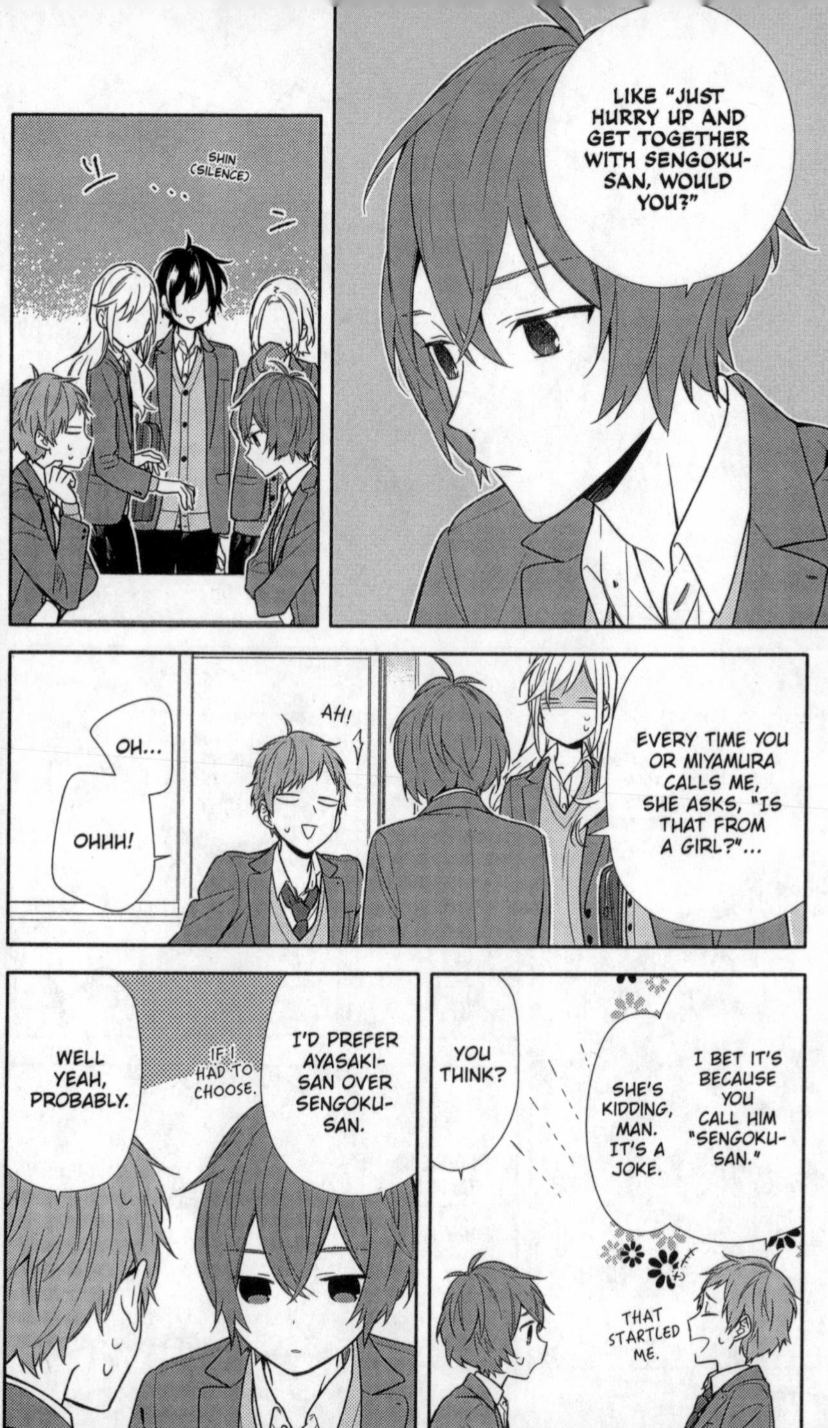
LIKE "JUST HURRY UP AND GET TOGETHER WITH SENGOKU-SAN, WOULD YOU?"
SHIN (SILENCE)
...
EVERY TIME YOU OR MIYAMURA CALLS ME, SHE ASKS, "IS THAT FROM A GIRL?"...
AH!
OH...
OHHH!
I BET IT'S BECAUSE YOU CALL HIM "SENGOKU-SAN."
SHE'S KIDDING, MAN. IT'S A JOKE.
YOU THINK?
THAT STARTLED ME.
I'D PREFER AYASAKI-SAN OVER SENGOKU-SAN.
IF I HAD TO CHOOSE.
WELL YEAH, PROBABLY.

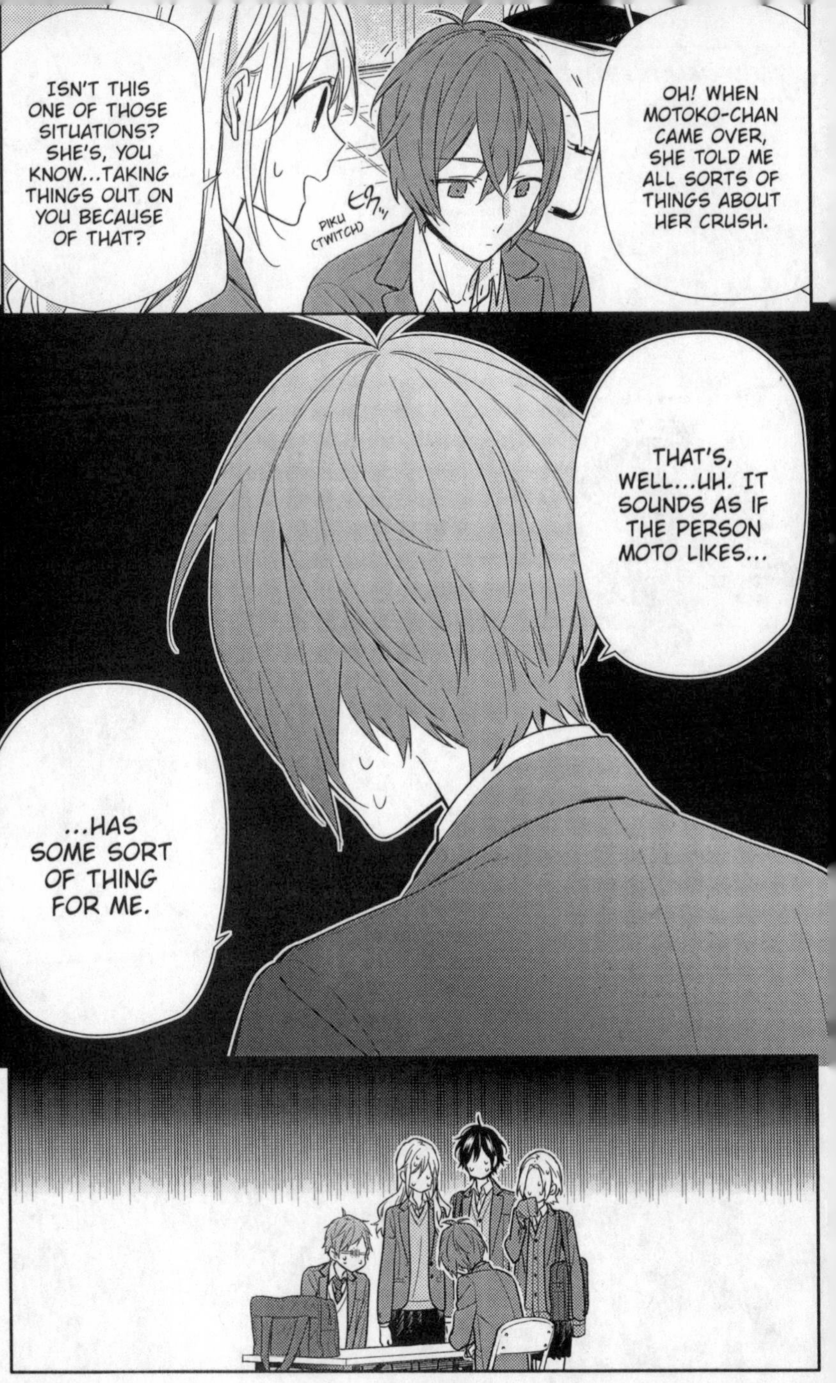
OH! WHEN MOTOKO-CHAN CAME OVER, SHE TOLD ME ALL SORTS OF THINGS ABOUT HER CRUSH.
PIKU (TWITCH)
ISN'T THIS ONE OF THOSE SITUATIONS? SHE'S, YOU KNOW...TAKING THINGS OUT ON YOU BECAUSE OF THAT?
THAT'S, WELL...UH. IT SOUNDS AS IF THE PERSON MOTO LIKES...
...HAS SOME SORT OF THING FOR ME.

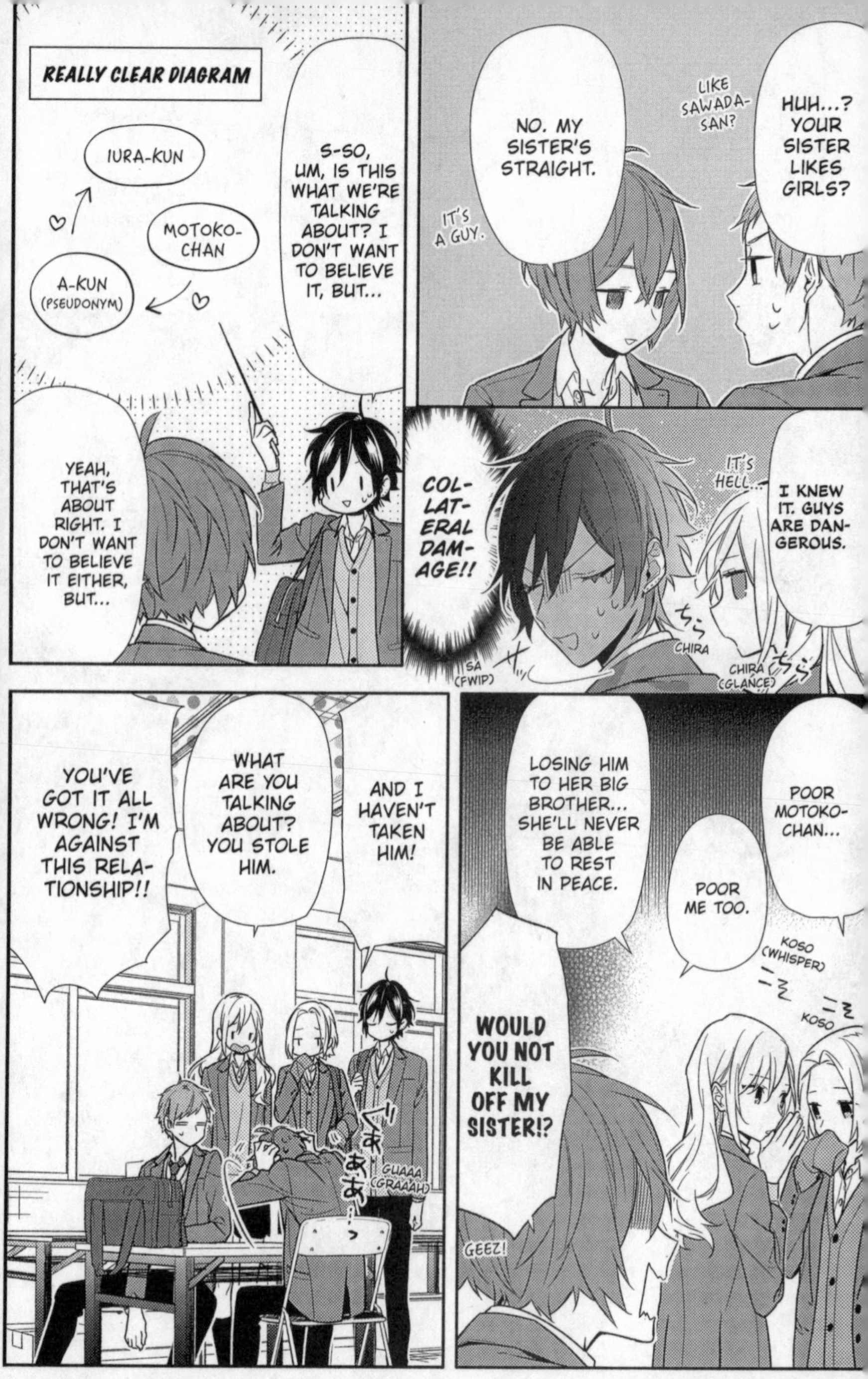
HUH...? YOUR SISTER LIKES GIRLS?
LIKE SAWADA-SAN?
NO. MY SISTER'S STRAIGHT.
IT'S A GUY.
I KNEW IT. GUYS ARE DAN-GEROUS.
IT'S HELL...
COL-LAT-ERAL DAM-AGE!!
CHIRA (GLANCE)
CHIRA
SA (FWIP)
REALLY CLEAR DIAGRAM
IURA-KUN
MOTOKO-CHAN
A-KUN (PSEUDONYM)
S-SO, UM, IS THIS WHAT WE'RE TALKING ABOUT? I DON'T WANT TO BELIEVE IT, BUT...
YEAH, THAT'S ABOUT RIGHT. I DON'T WANT TO BELIEVE IT EITHER, BUT...
POOR MOTOKO-CHAN...
POOR ME TOO.
LOSING HIM TO HER BIG BROTHER... SHE'LL NEVER BE ABLE TO REST IN PEACE.
KOSO (WHISPER)
KOSO
WOULD YOU NOT KILL OFF MY SISTER!?
GEEZ!
AND I HAVEN'T TAKEN HIM!
WHAT ARE YOU TALKING ABOUT? YOU STOLE HIM.
YOU'VE GOT IT ALL WRONG! I'M AGAINST THIS RELA-TIONSHIP!!
GUAAA (GRAAAH)

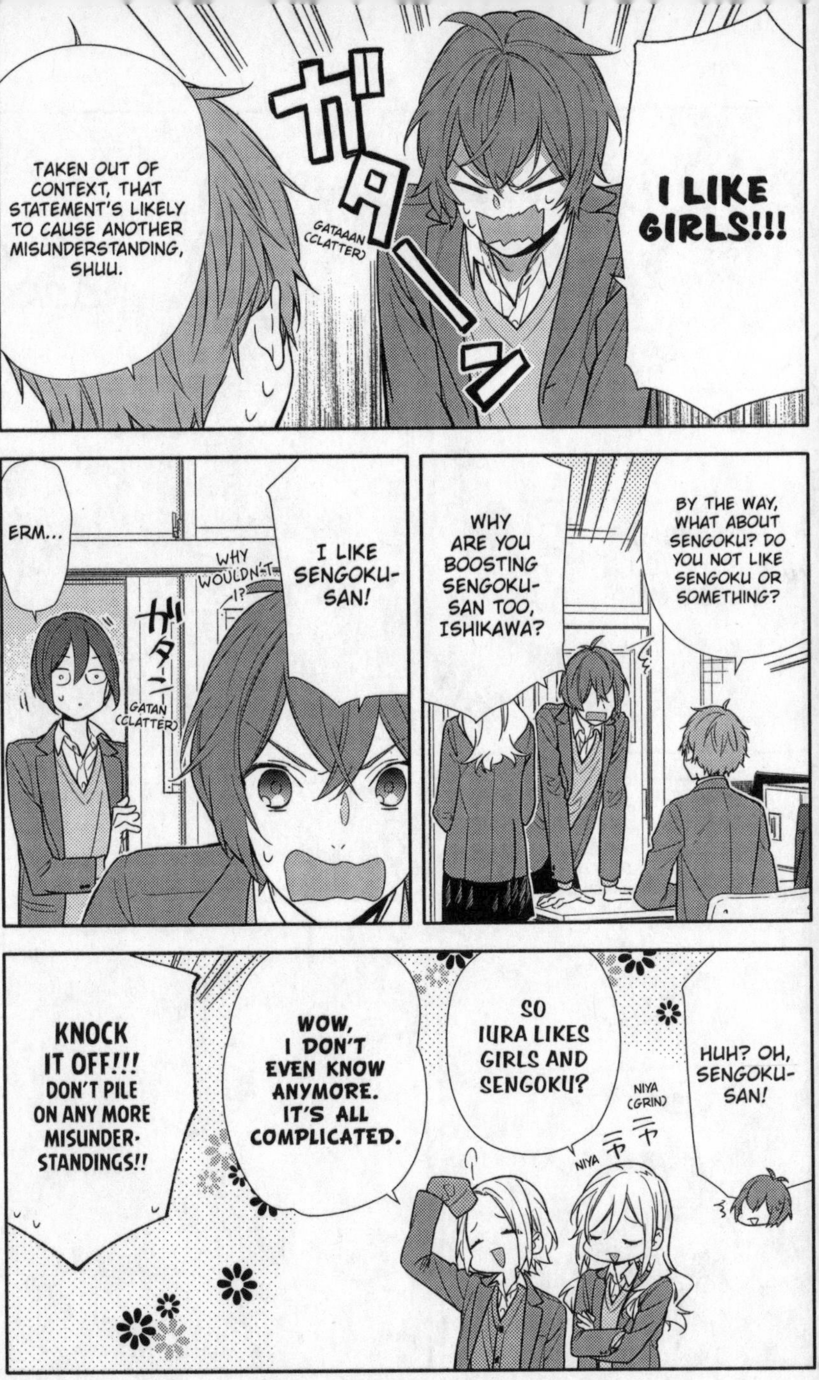
I LIKE GIRLS!!!
GATAAAN (CLATTER)
TAKEN OUT OF CONTEXT, THAT STATEMENT'S LIKELY TO CAUSE ANOTHER MISUNDERSTANDING, SHUU.
BY THE WAY, WHAT ABOUT SENGOKU? DO YOU NOT LIKE SENGOKU OR SOMETHING?
WHY ARE YOU BOOSTING SENGOKU-SAN TOO, ISHIKAWA?
I LIKE SENGOKU-SAN!
WHY WOULDN'T I?
GATAN (CLATTER)
ERM...
HUH? OH, SENGOKU-SAN!
NIYA (GRIN)
NIYA
SO IURA LIKES GIRLS AND SENGOKU?
WOW, I DON'T EVEN KNOW ANYMORE. IT'S ALL COMPLICATED.
KNOCK IT OFF!!! DON'T PILE ON ANY MORE MISUNDER-STANDINGS!!

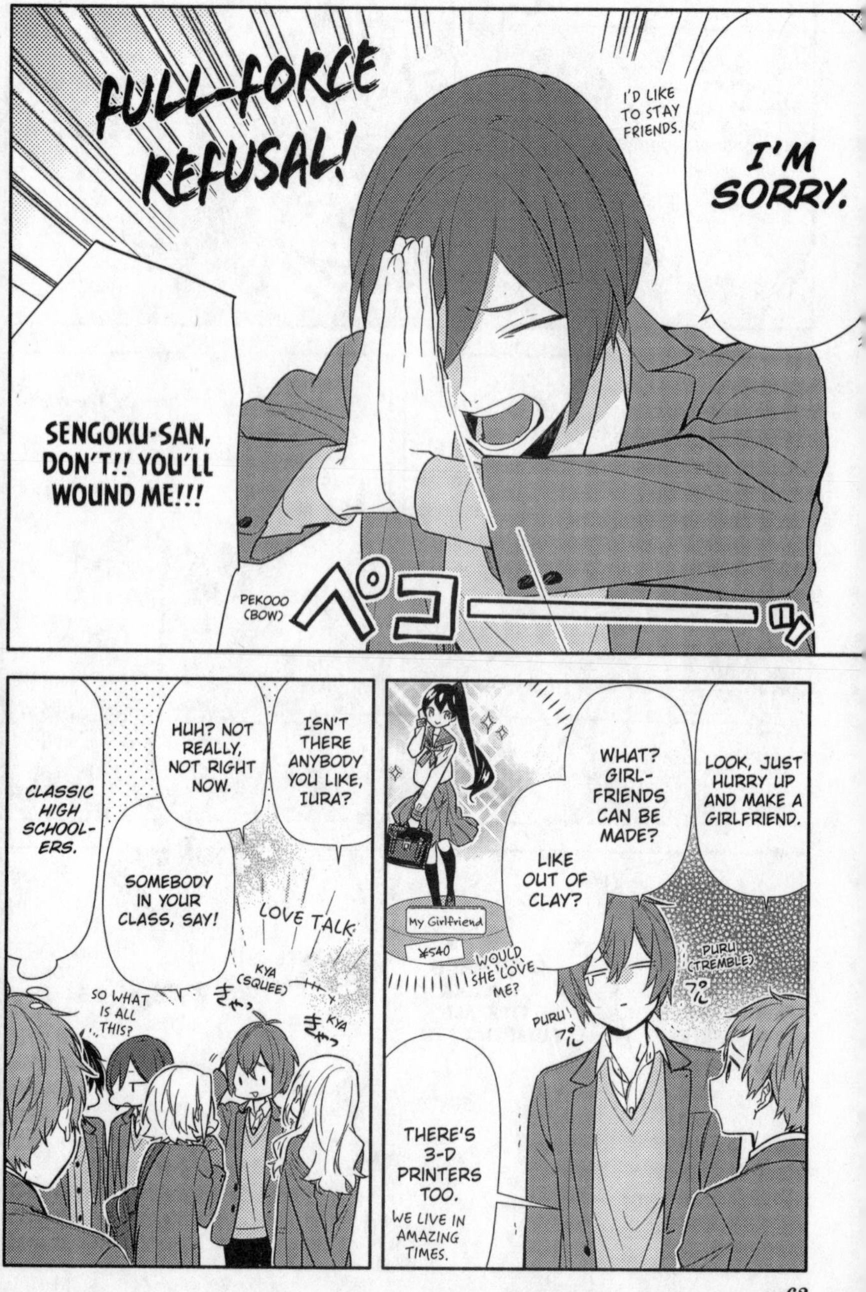
I'M SORRY.
I'D LIKE TO STAY FRIENDS.
FULL-FORCE REFUSAL!
SENGOKU-SAN, DON'T!! YOU'LL WOUND ME!!!
PEKOOO (BOW)
ペコーーッ
LOOK, JUST HURRY UP AND MAKE A GIRLFRIEND.
WHAT? GIRLFRIENDS CAN BE MADE?
LIKE OUT OF CLAY?
My Girlfriend
¥540
WOULD SHE LOVE ME?
PURU (TREMBLE)
PURU
THERE'S 3-D PRINTERS TOO.
WE LIVE IN AMAZING TIMES.
ISN'T THERE ANYBODY YOU LIKE, IURA?
HUH? NOT REALLY, NOT RIGHT NOW.
CLASSIC HIGH SCHOOLERS.
SOMEBODY IN YOUR CLASS, SAY!
LOVE TALK
KYA (SQUEE)
KYA
SO WHAT IS ALL THIS?

HORIMIYA

HORIMIYA

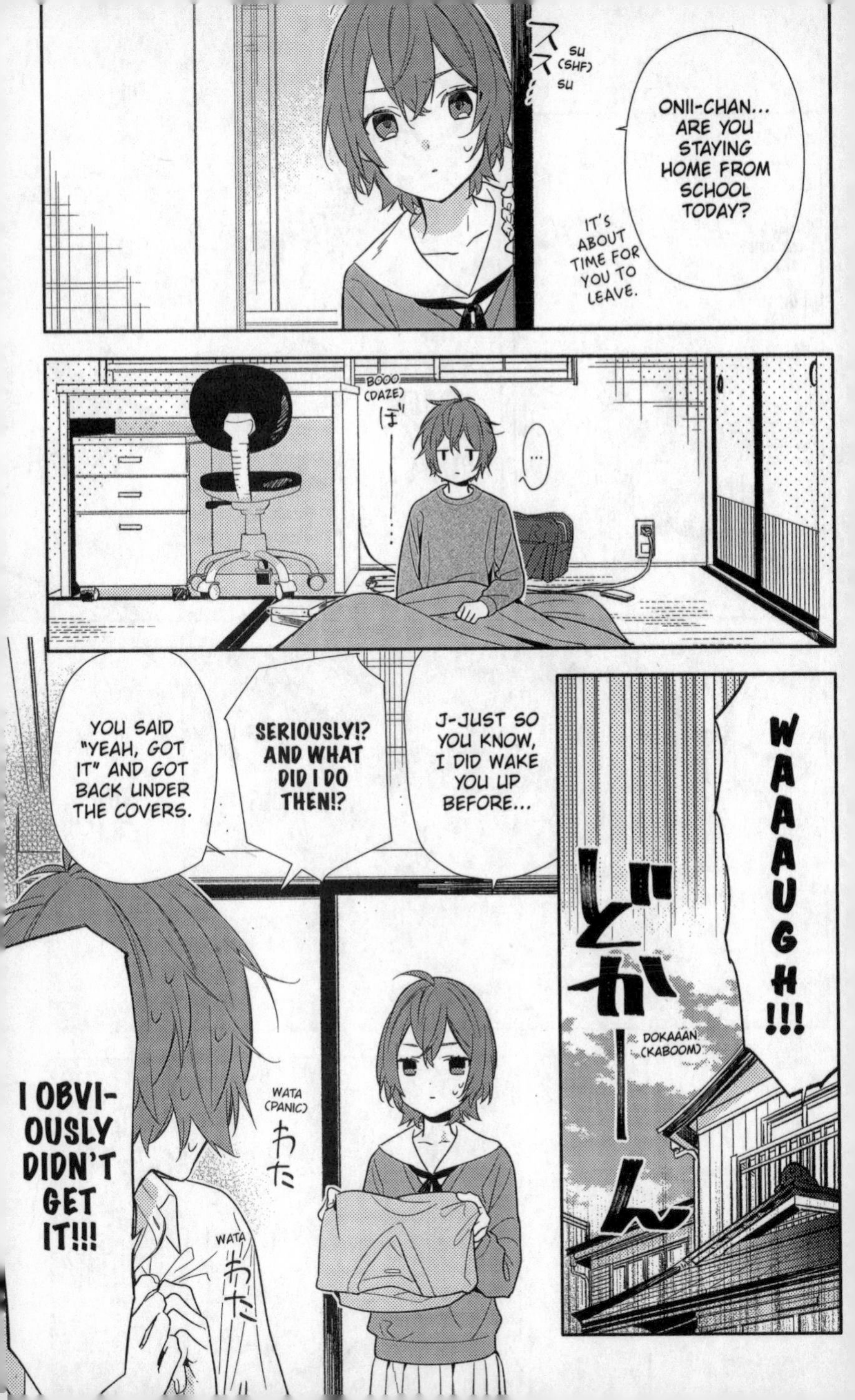
SU (SHF) SU
ONII-CHAN... ARE YOU STAYING HOME FROM SCHOOL TODAY?
IT'S ABOUT TIME FOR YOU TO LEAVE.
BOOO (DAZE)
...
WAAAAUGH!!!
DOKAAAN (KABOOM)
J-JUST SO YOU KNOW, I DID WAKE YOU UP BEFORE...
SERIOUSLY!? AND WHAT DID I DO THEN!?
YOU SAID "YEAH, GOT IT" AND GOT BACK UNDER THE COVERS.
WATA (PANIC)
WATA
I OBVI-OUSLY DIDN'T GET IT!!!

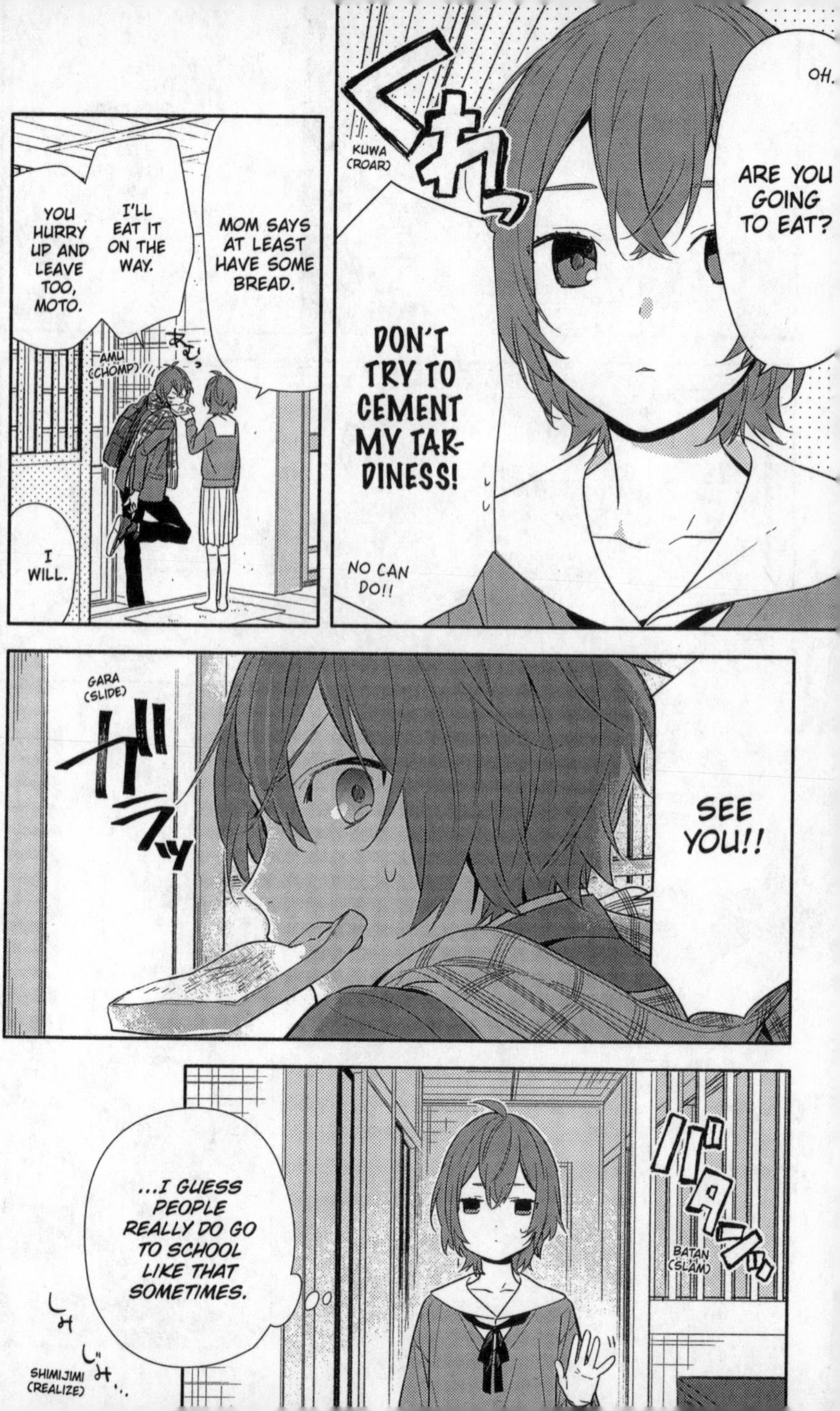
OH.
ARE YOU GOING TO EAT?
KUWA (ROAR)
DON'T TRY TO CEMENT MY TARDINESS!
NO CAN DO!!
MOM SAYS AT LEAST HAVE SOME BREAD.
I'LL EAT IT ON THE WAY.
YOU HURRY UP AND LEAVE TOO, MOTO.
AMU (CHOMP)
I WILL.
SEE YOU!!
GARA (SLIDE)
BATAN (SLAM)
...I GUESS PEOPLE REALLY DO GO TO SCHOOL LIKE THAT SOMETIMES.
SHIMIJIMI (REALIZE)

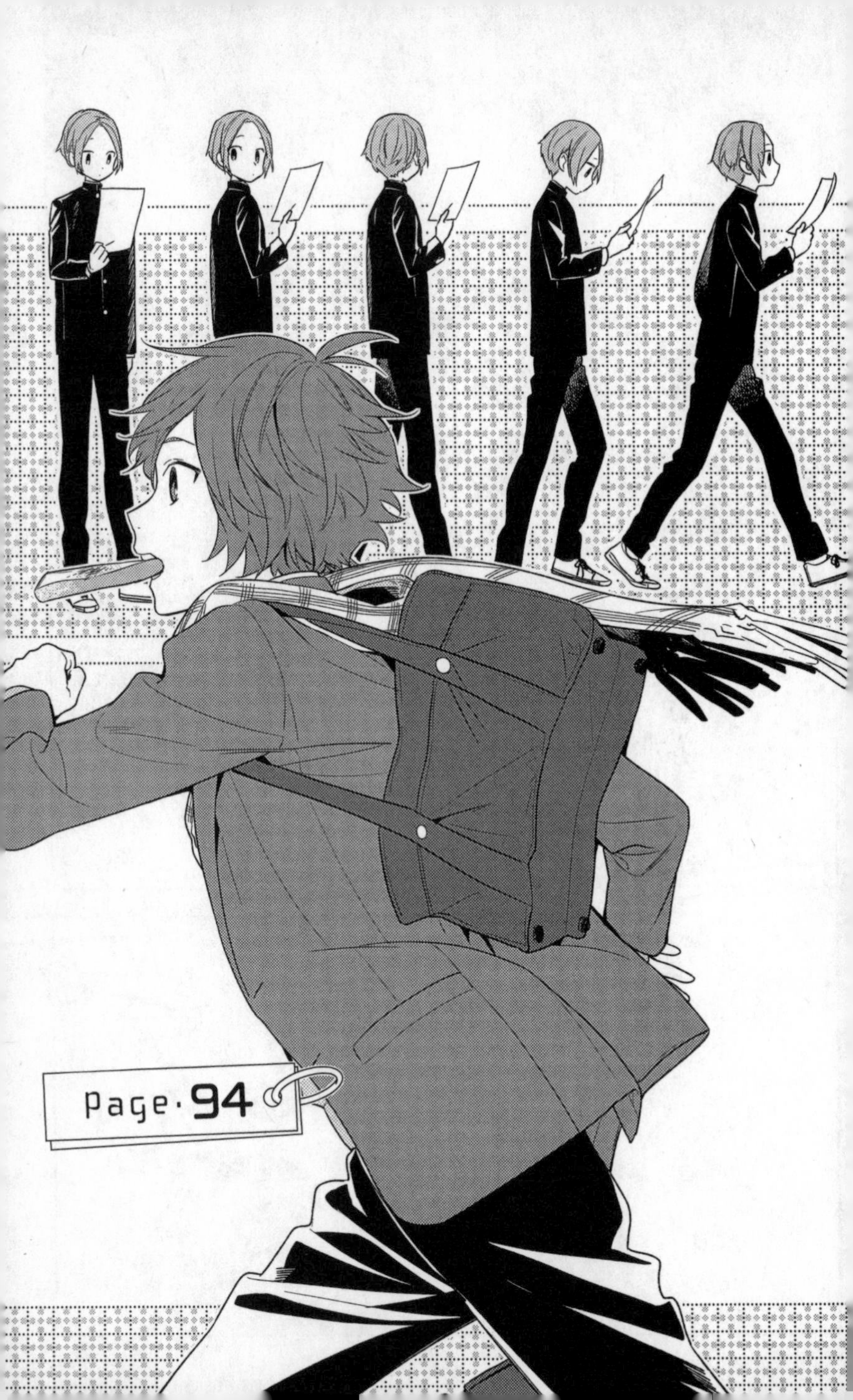
Page・94

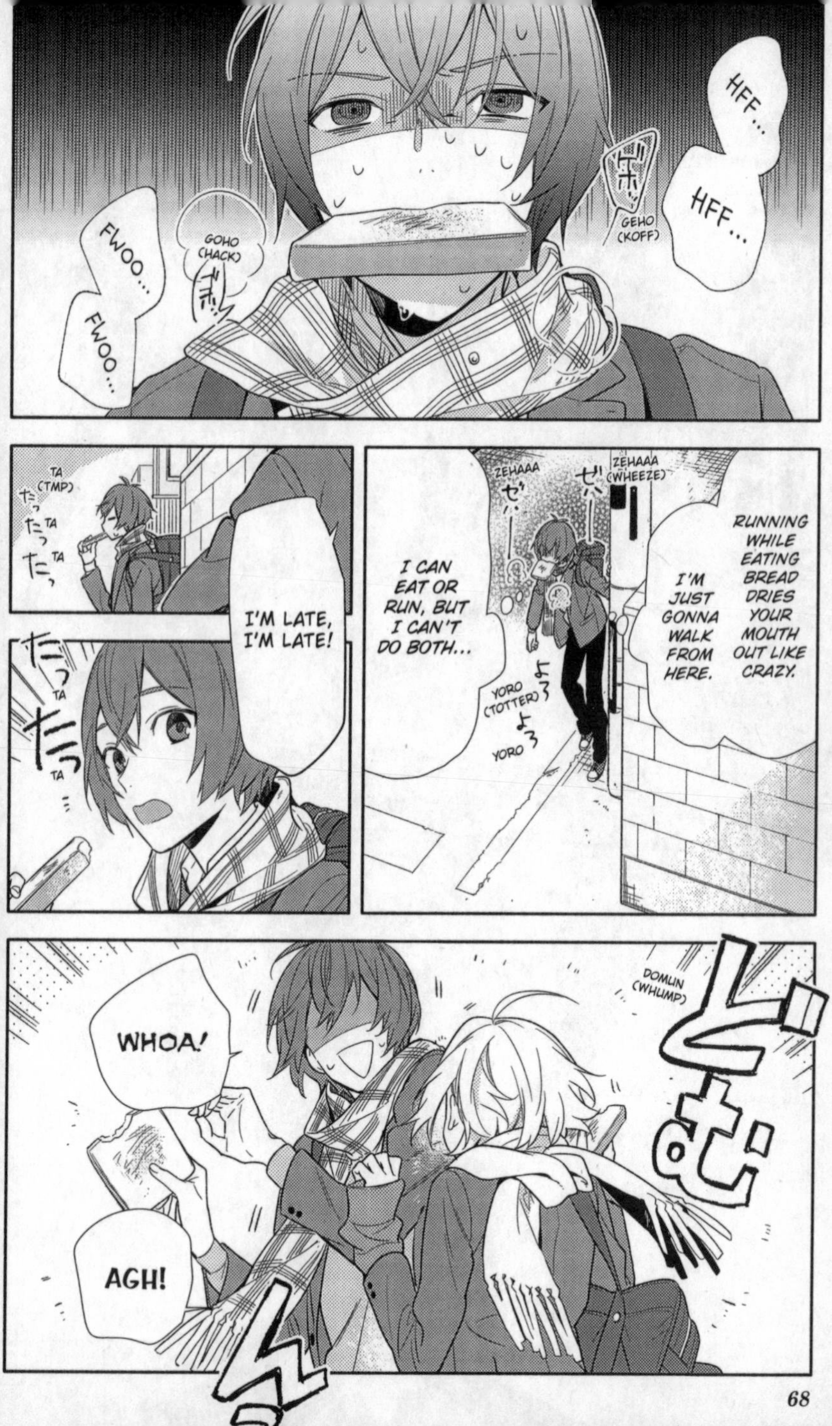
HFF...
HFF...
GEHO (KOFF)
GOHO (HACK)
FWOO...
FWOO...
RUNNING WHILE EATING BREAD DRIES YOUR MOUTH OUT LIKE CRAZY.
I'M JUST GONNA WALK FROM HERE.
ZEHAAA (WHEEZE)
ZEHAAA
I CAN EAT OR RUN, BUT I CAN'T DO BOTH...
YORO (TOTTER)
YORO
TA (TMP)
TA
TA
I'M LATE, I'M LATE!
TA
TA
DOMUN (WHUMP)
WHOA!
AGH!

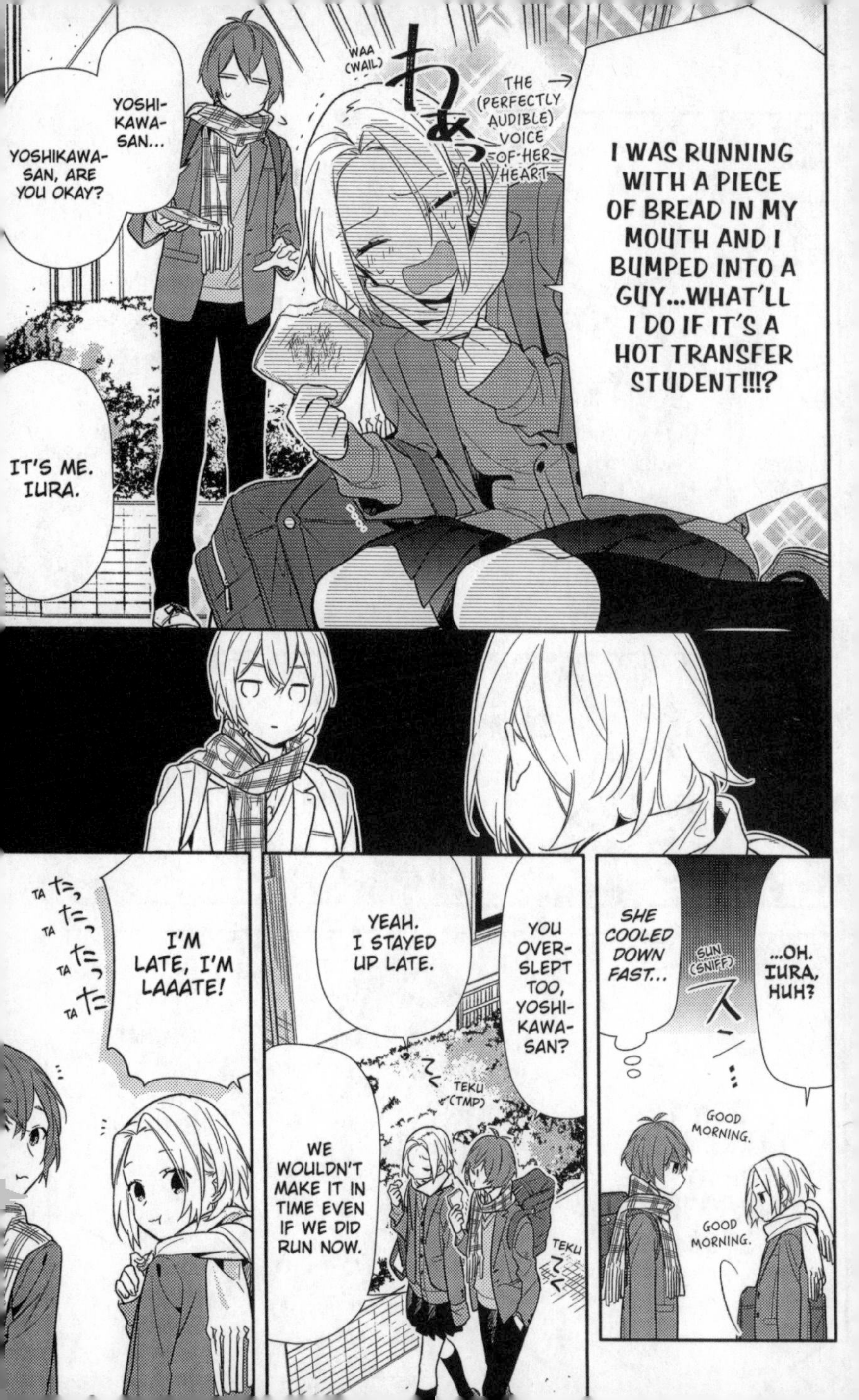
I WAS RUNNING WITH A PIECE OF BREAD IN MY MOUTH AND I BUMPED INTO A GUY...WHAT'LL I DO IF IT'S A HOT TRANSFER STUDENT!!!?
WAA (WAIL)
THE (PERFECTLY AUDIBLE) VOICE OF HER HEART
YOSHI-KAWA-SAN...
YOSHIKAWA-SAN, ARE YOU OKAY?
IT'S ME. IURA.
...OH. IURA, HUH?
SHE COOLED DOWN FAST...
SUN (SNIFF)
GOOD MORNING.
GOOD MORNING.
YOU OVER-SLEPT TOO, YOSHI-KAWA-SAN?
YEAH. I STAYED UP LATE.
TEKU (TMP)
WE WOULDN'T MAKE IT IN TIME EVEN IF WE DID RUN NOW.
TEKU
I'M LATE, I'M LAAATE!
TA TA TA TA

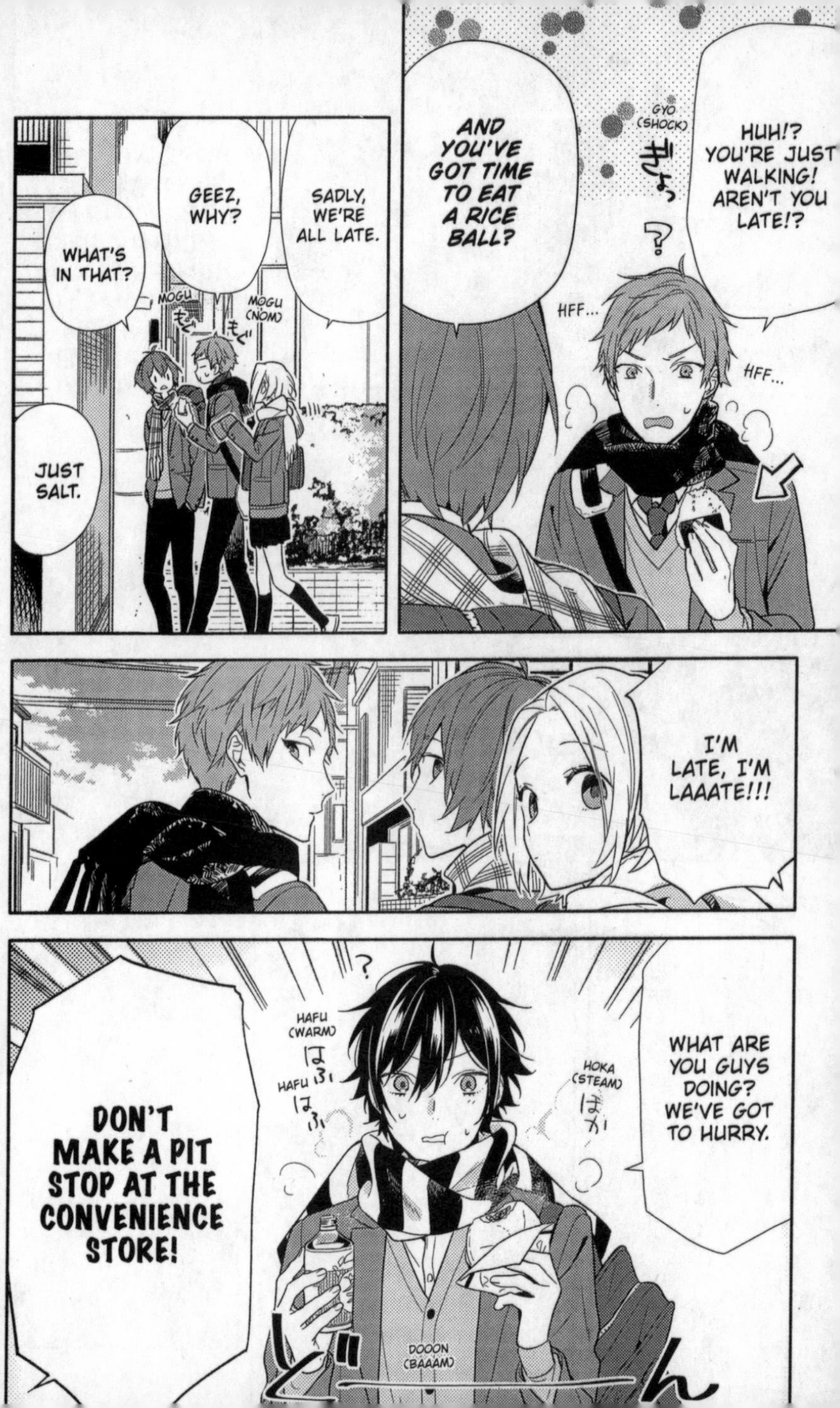
GYO (SHOCK)
ぎょっ
HUH!? YOU'RE JUST WALKING! AREN'T YOU LATE!?
?
HFF...
HFF...
AND YOU'VE GOT TIME TO EAT A RICE BALL?
SADLY, WE'RE ALL LATE.
MOGU (NOM)
もぐ
GEEZ, WHY?
MOGU
もぐ
WHAT'S IN THAT?
JUST SALT.
I'M LATE, I'M LAAATE!!!
WHAT ARE YOU GUYS DOING? WE'VE GOT TO HURRY.
HOKA (STEAM)
ほか
?
HAFU (WARM)
はふ
HAFU
はふ
DON'T MAKE A PIT STOP AT THE CONVENIENCE STORE!
DOOON (BAAAM)

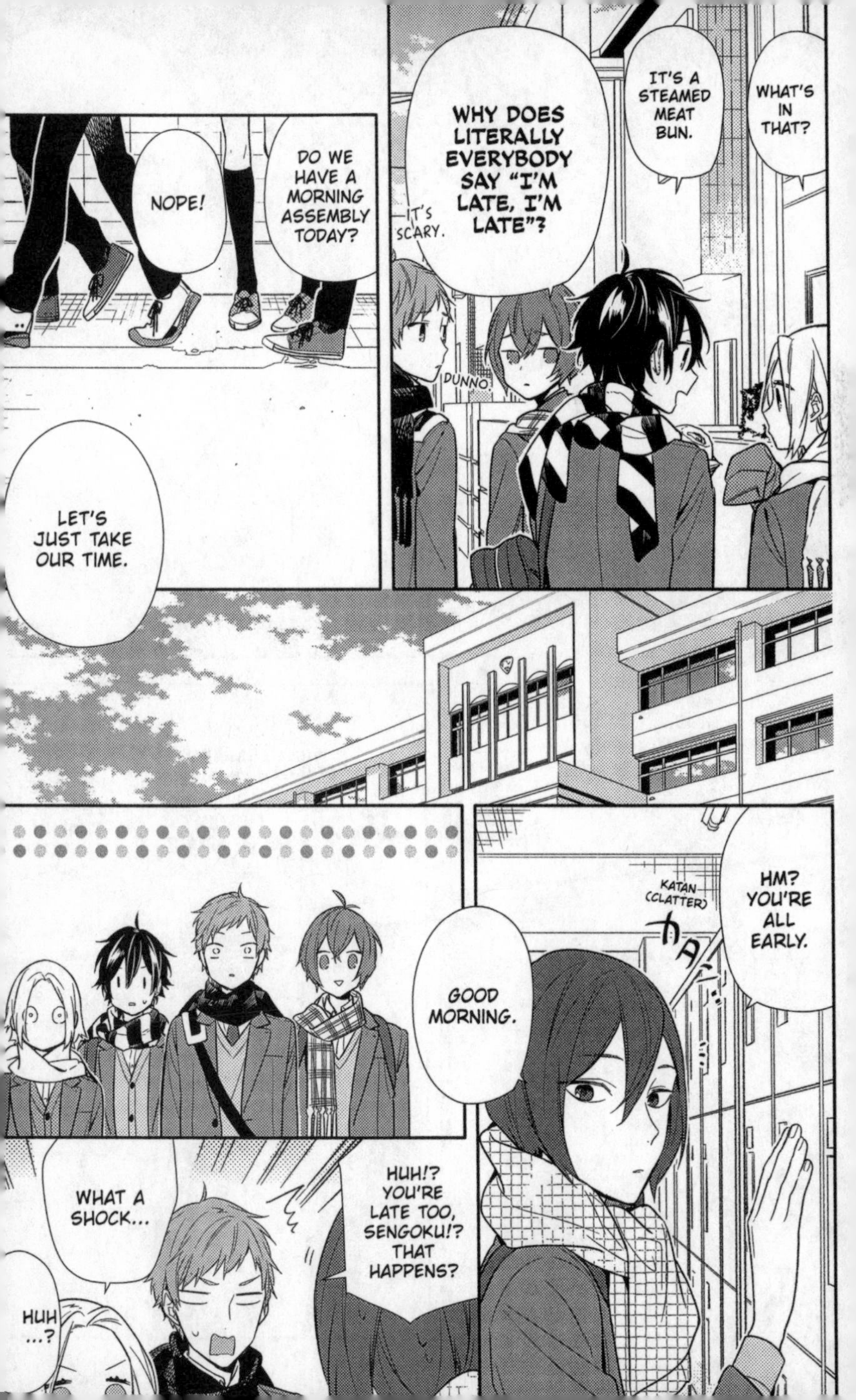

WHAT'S IN THAT?
IT'S A STEAMED MEAT BUN.
WHY DOES LITERALLY EVERYBODY SAY "I'M LATE, I'M LATE"?
IT'S SCARY.
DUNNO.
DO WE HAVE A MORNING ASSEMBLY TODAY?
NOPE!
LET'S JUST TAKE OUR TIME.
HM? YOU'RE ALL EARLY.
KATAN (CLATTER)
GOOD MORNING.
HUH!? YOU'RE LATE TOO, SENGOKU!? THAT HAPPENS?
WHAT A SHOCK...
HUH ...?

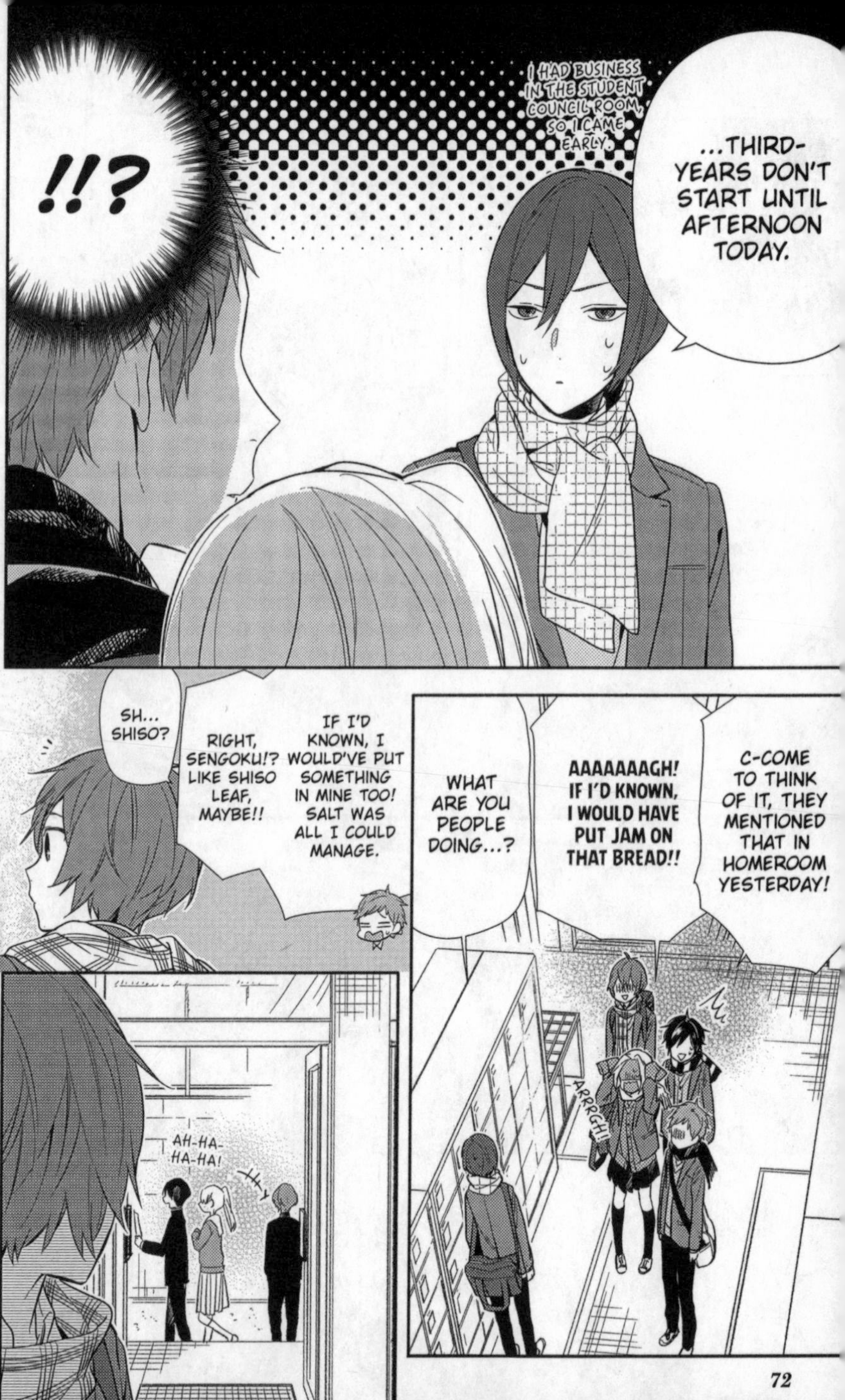
...THIRD-YEARS DON'T START UNTIL AFTERNOON TODAY.
I HAD BUSINESS IN THE STUDENT COUNCIL ROOM, SO I CAME EARLY.
!!?
C-COME TO THINK OF IT, THEY MENTIONED THAT IN HOMEROOM YESTERDAY!
AAAAAAAGH! IF I'D KNOWN, I WOULD HAVE PUT JAM ON THAT BREAD!!
ARRRGH!
WHAT ARE YOU PEOPLE DOING...?
IF I'D KNOWN, I WOULD'VE PUT SOMETHING IN MINE TOO! SALT WAS ALL I COULD MANAGE.
RIGHT, SENGOKU!? LIKE SHISO LEAF, MAYBE!!
SH... SHISO?
AH-HA-HA-HA!

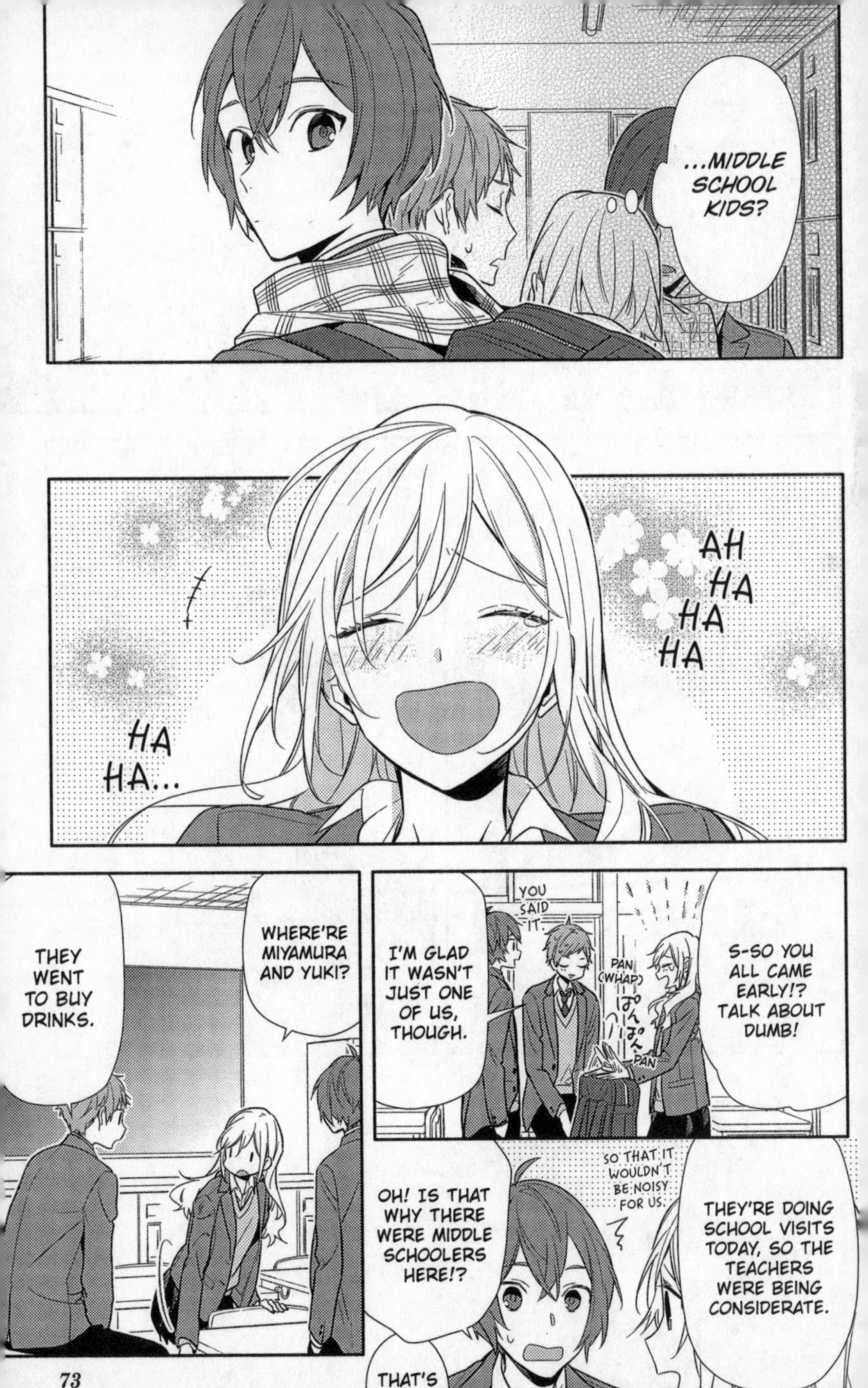
...MIDDLE SCHOOL KIDS?
AH HA HA HA
HA HA...
S-SO YOU ALL CAME EARLY!? TALK ABOUT DUMB!
PAN (WHAP) ぱん ぱん PAN
YOU SAID IT.
I'M GLAD IT WASN'T JUST ONE OF US, THOUGH.
THEY'RE DOING SCHOOL VISITS TODAY, SO THE TEACHERS WERE BEING CONSIDERATE.
SO THAT IT WOULDN'T BE NOISY FOR US.
OH! IS THAT WHY THERE WERE MIDDLE SCHOOLERS HERE!?
THAT'S RIGHT.
WHERE'RE MIYAMURA AND YUKI?
THEY WENT TO BUY DRINKS.

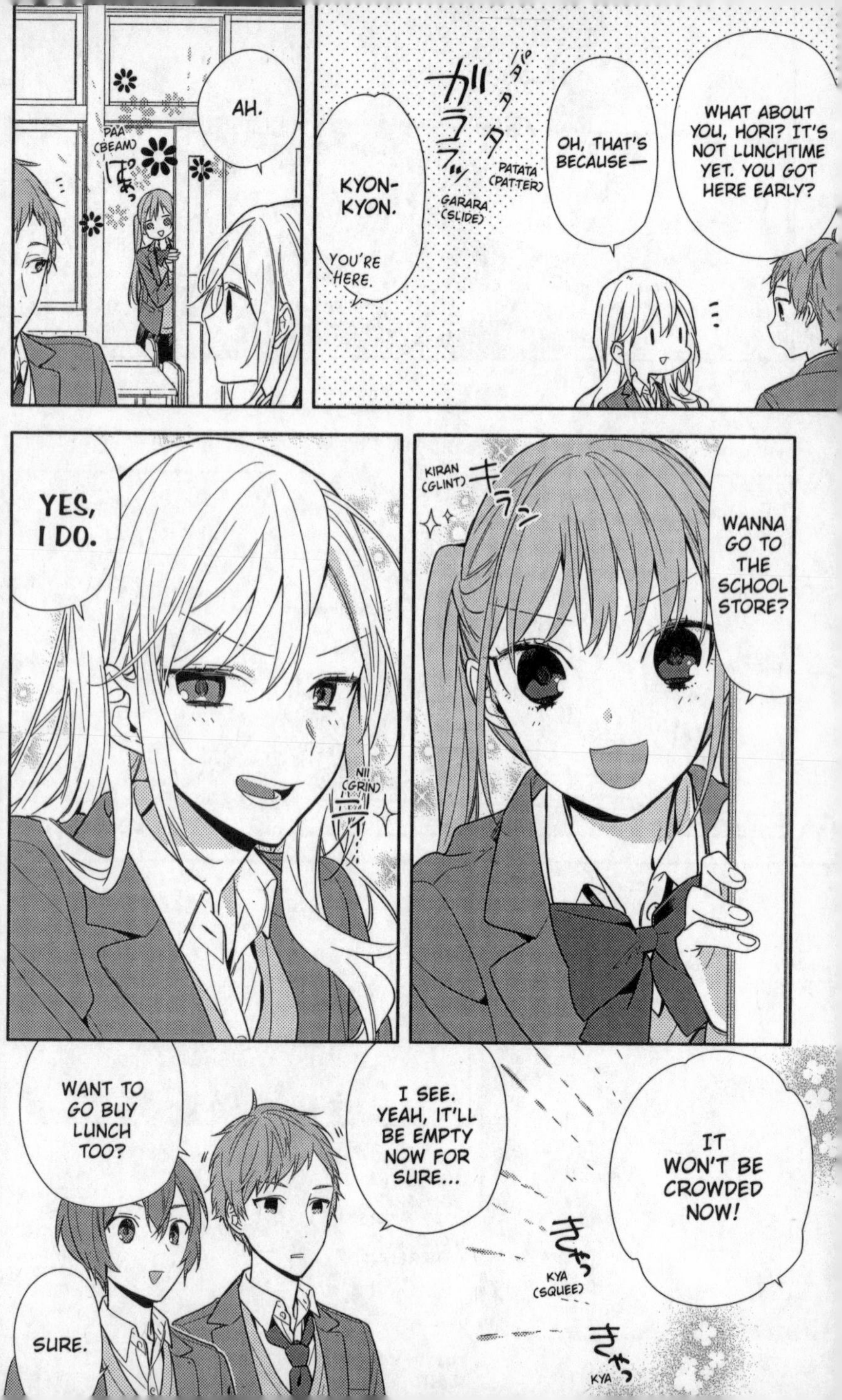
WHAT ABOUT YOU, HORI? IT'S NOT LUNCHTIME YET. YOU GOT HERE EARLY?
OH, THAT'S BECAUSE—
PATATA (PATTER)
GARARA (SLIDE)
KYON-KYON.
YOU'RE HERE.
AH.
PAA (BEAM)
KIRAN (GLINT)
WANNA GO TO THE SCHOOL STORE?
YES, I DO.
NII (GRIN)
IT WON'T BE CROWDED NOW!
KYA (SQUEE)
KYA
I SEE. YEAH, IT'LL BE EMPTY NOW FOR SURE...
WANT TO GO BUY LUNCH TOO?
SURE.

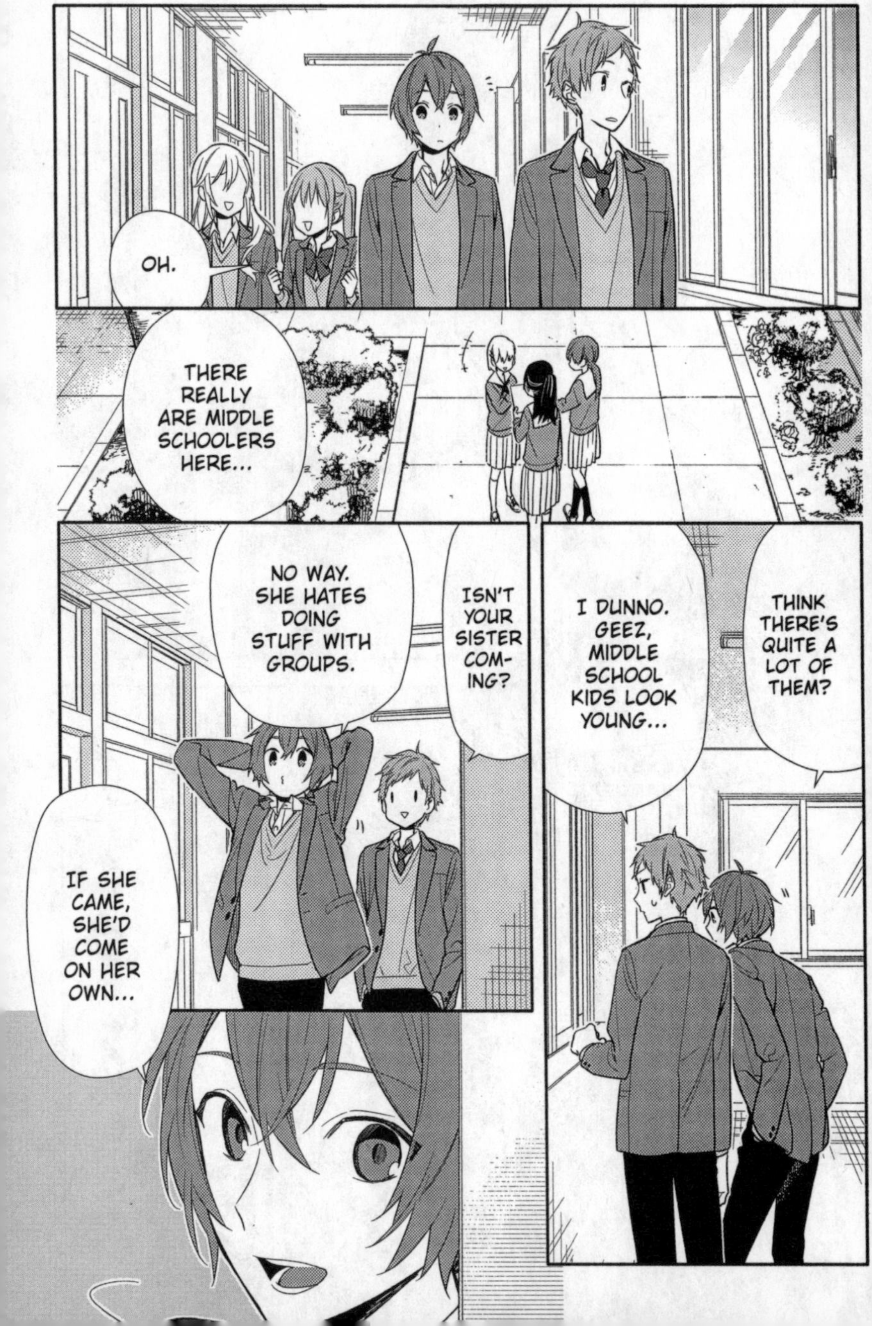
OH.
THERE REALLY ARE MIDDLE SCHOOLERS HERE...
THINK THERE'S QUITE A LOT OF THEM?
I DUNNO. GEEZ, MIDDLE SCHOOL KIDS LOOK YOUNG...
ISN'T YOUR SISTER COM-ING?
NO WAY. SHE HATES DOING STUFF WITH GROUPS.
IF SHE CAME, SHE'D COME ON HER OWN...

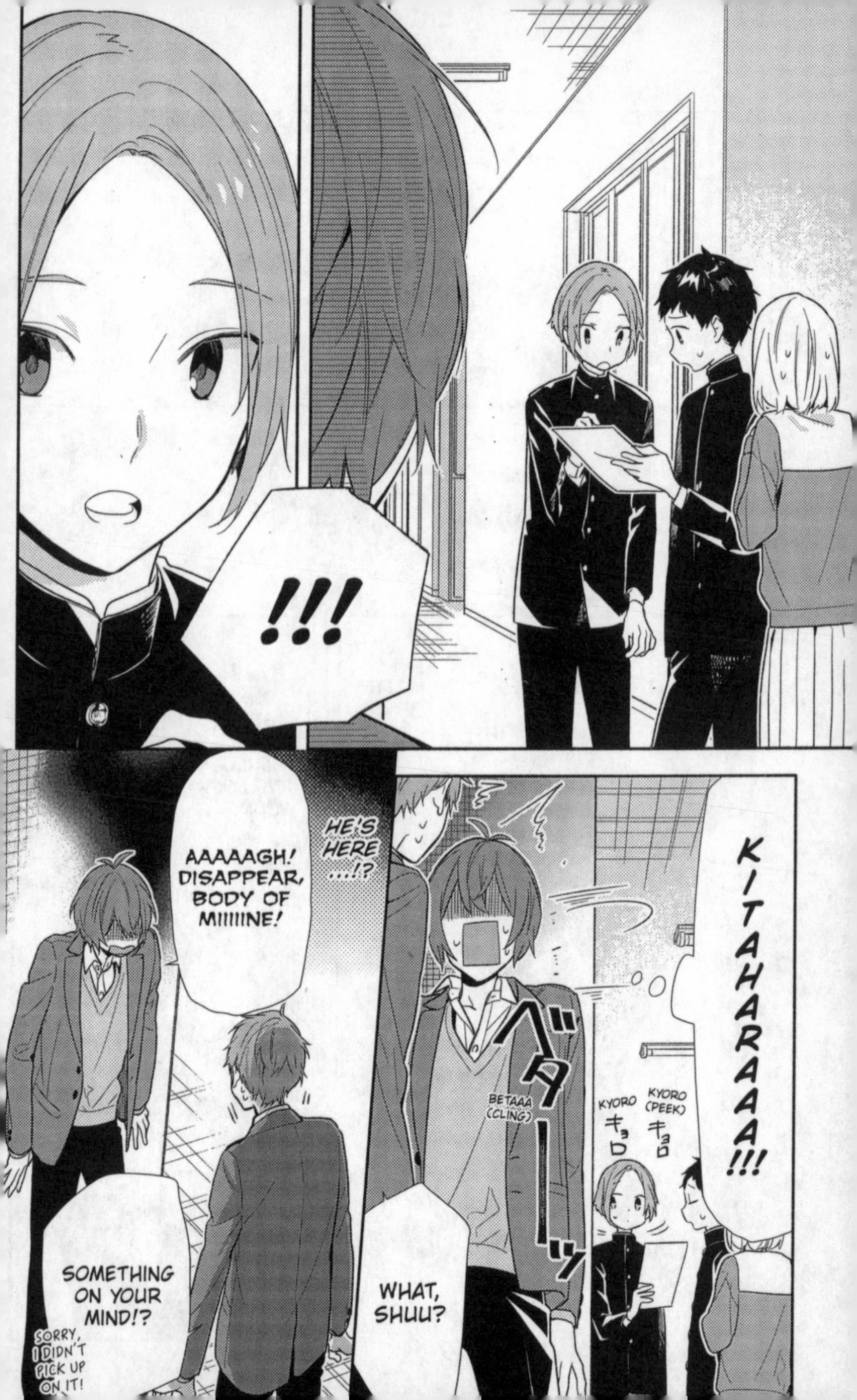
!!!
KITAHARAAAA!!!
KYORO KYORO (PEEK)
HE'S HERE ...!?
BETAAA (CLING)
WHAT, SHUU?
AAAAAGH! DISAPPEAR, BODY OF MIIIIINE!
SOMETHING ON YOUR MIND!?
SORRY, I DIDN'T PICK UP ON IT!

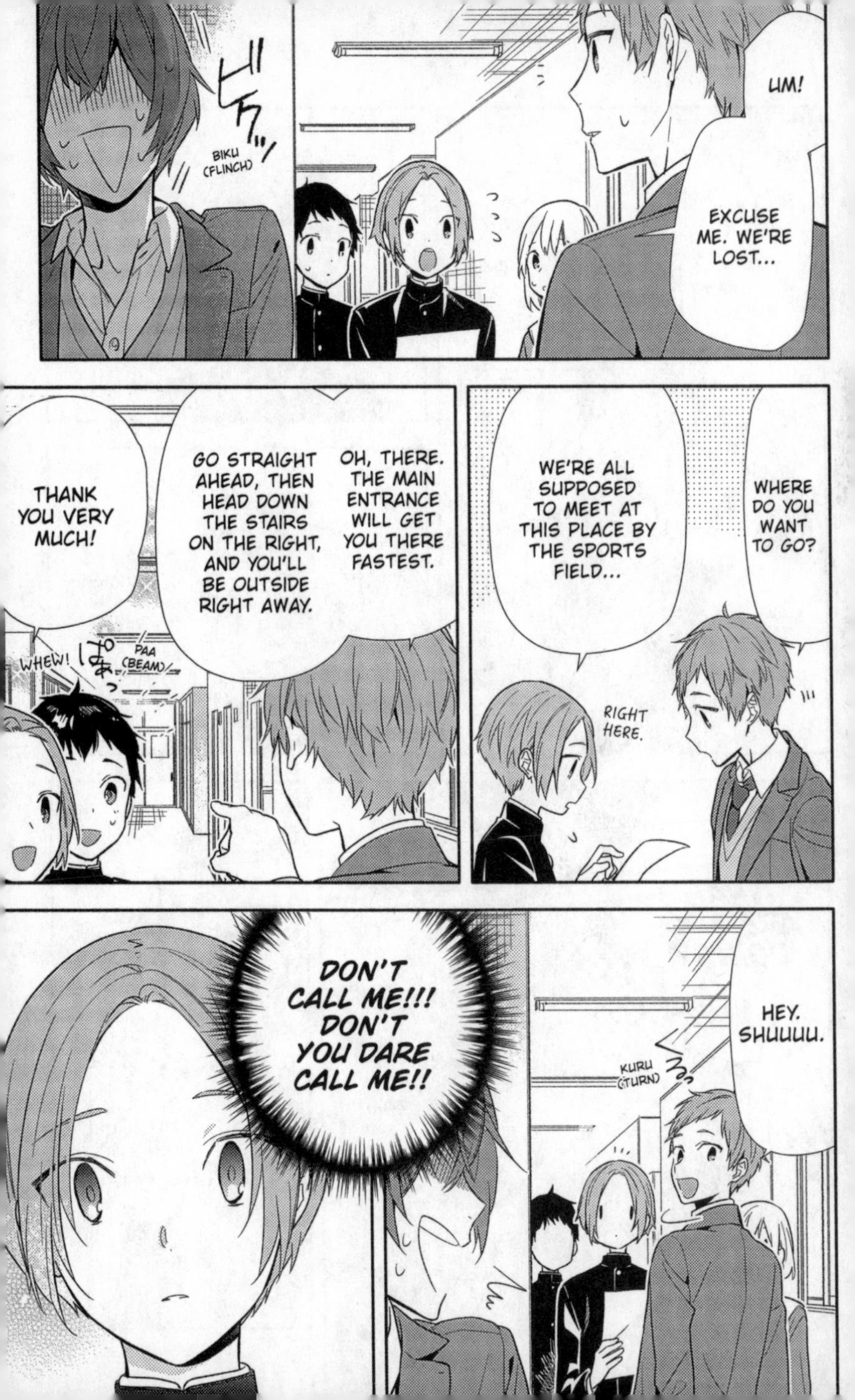
UM!
EXCUSE ME. WE'RE LOST...
BIKU (FLINCH)
WHERE DO YOU WANT TO GO?
WE'RE ALL SUPPOSED TO MEET AT THIS PLACE BY THE SPORTS FIELD...
RIGHT HERE.
OH, THERE. THE MAIN ENTRANCE WILL GET YOU THERE FASTEST.
GO STRAIGHT AHEAD, THEN HEAD DOWN THE STAIRS ON THE RIGHT, AND YOU'LL BE OUTSIDE RIGHT AWAY.
THANK YOU VERY MUCH!
PAA (BEAM)
WHEW!
HEY. SHUUUU.
KURU (TURN)
DON'T CALL ME!!! DON'T YOU DARE CALL ME!!

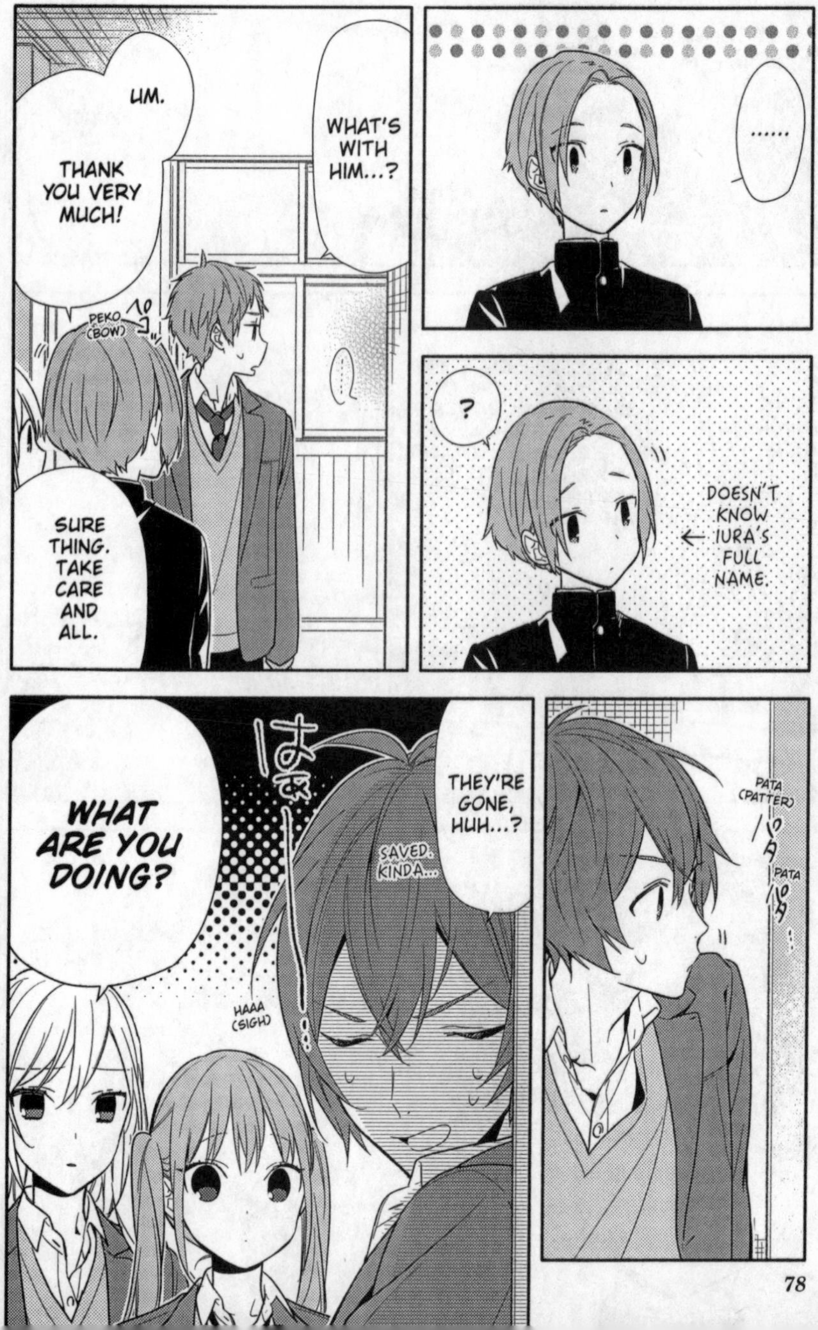
......
?
DOESN'T KNOW IURA'S FULL NAME.
WHAT'S WITH HIM...?
UM.
THANK YOU VERY MUCH!
PEKO (BOW)
SURE THING. TAKE CARE AND ALL.
PATA (PATTER)
PATA
THEY'RE GONE, HUH...?
SAVED. KINDA...
HAAA (SIGH)
WHAT ARE YOU DOING?

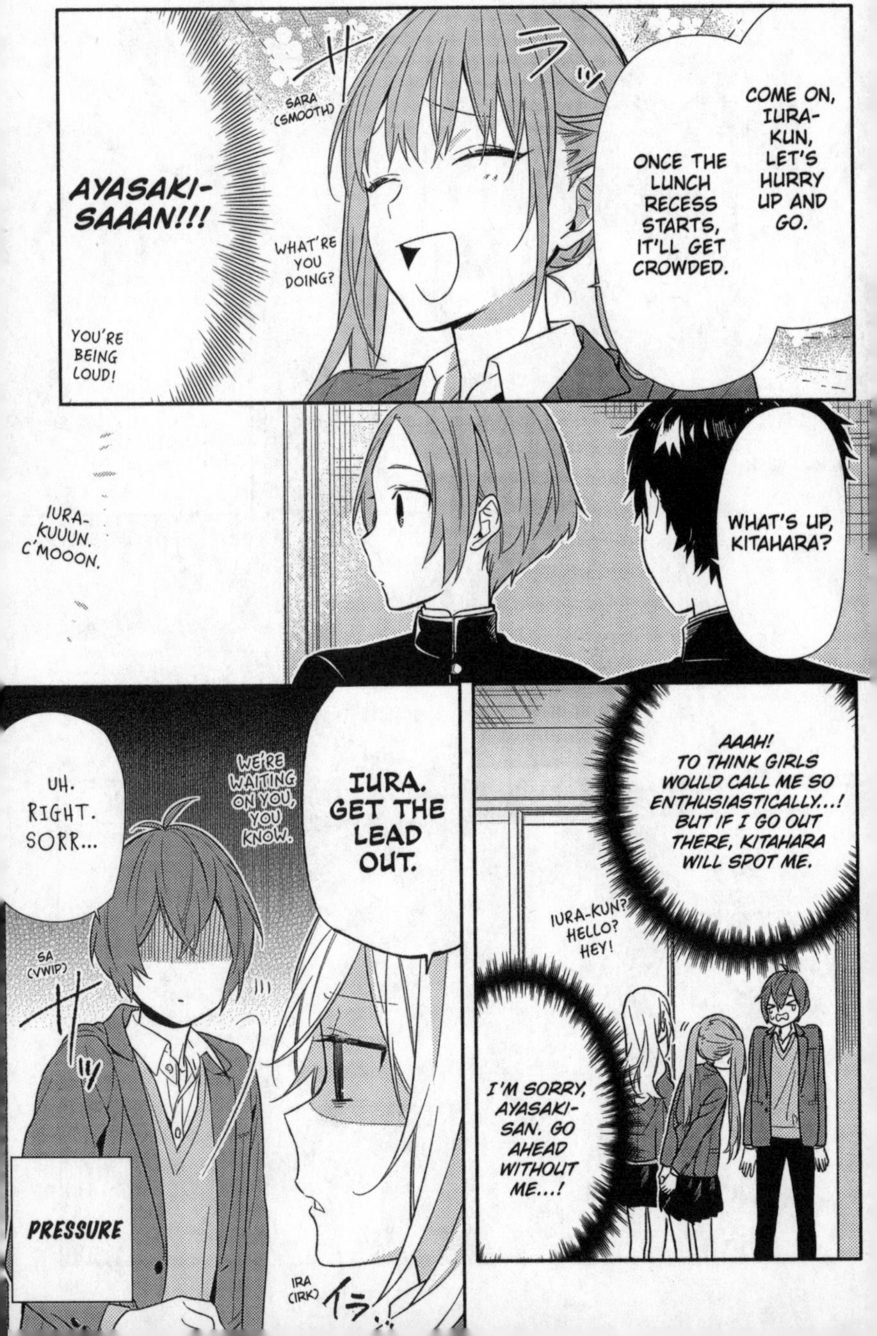
COME ON, IURA-KUN, LET'S HURRY UP AND GO.
ONCE THE LUNCH RECESS STARTS, IT'LL GET CROWDED.
SARA (SMOOTH)
WHAT'RE YOU DOING?
AYASAKI-SAAAN!!!
YOU'RE BEING LOUD!
WHAT'S UP, KITAHARA?
IURA-KUUUN. C'MOOON.
AAAH! TO THINK GIRLS WOULD CALL ME SO ENTHUSIASTICALLY...! BUT IF I GO OUT THERE, KITAHARA WILL SPOT ME.
IURA-KUN? HELLO? HEY!
I'M SORRY, AYASAKI-SAN. GO AHEAD WITHOUT ME...!
IURA. GET THE LEAD OUT.
WE'RE WAITING ON YOU, YOU KNOW.
UH. RIGHT. SORR...
SA (VWIP)
PRESSURE
IRA (IRK)

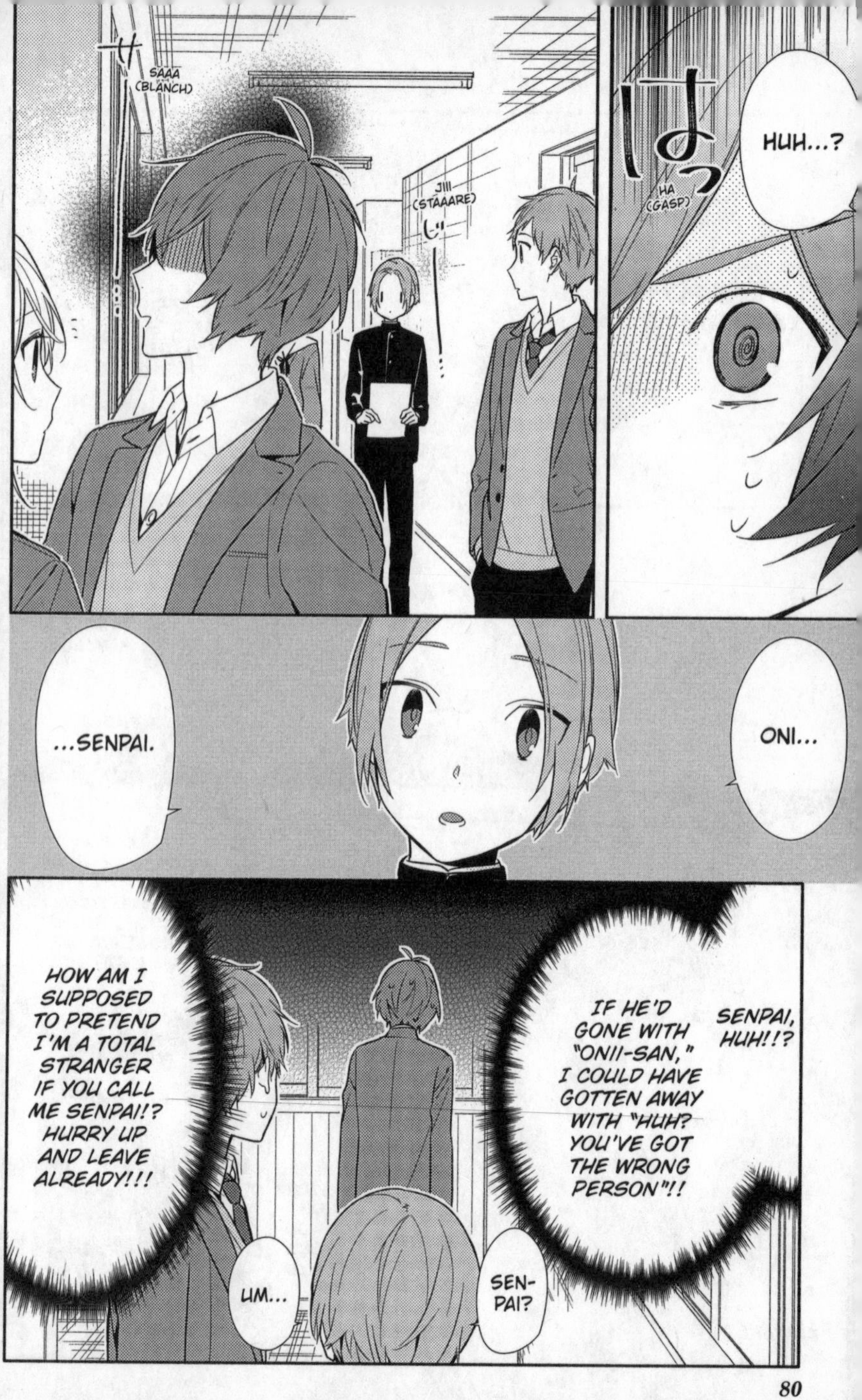
HUH...?
HA (GASP)
JIII (STAAARE)
SAAA (BLANCH)
ONI...
...SENPAI.
SENPAI, HUH!!?
IF HE'D GONE WITH "ONII-SAN," I COULD HAVE GOTTEN AWAY WITH "HUH? YOU'VE GOT THE WRONG PERSON"!!
HOW AM I SUPPOSED TO PRETEND I'M A TOTAL STRANGER IF YOU CALL ME SENPAI!? HURRY UP AND LEAVE ALREADY!!!
SEN-PAI?
UM...

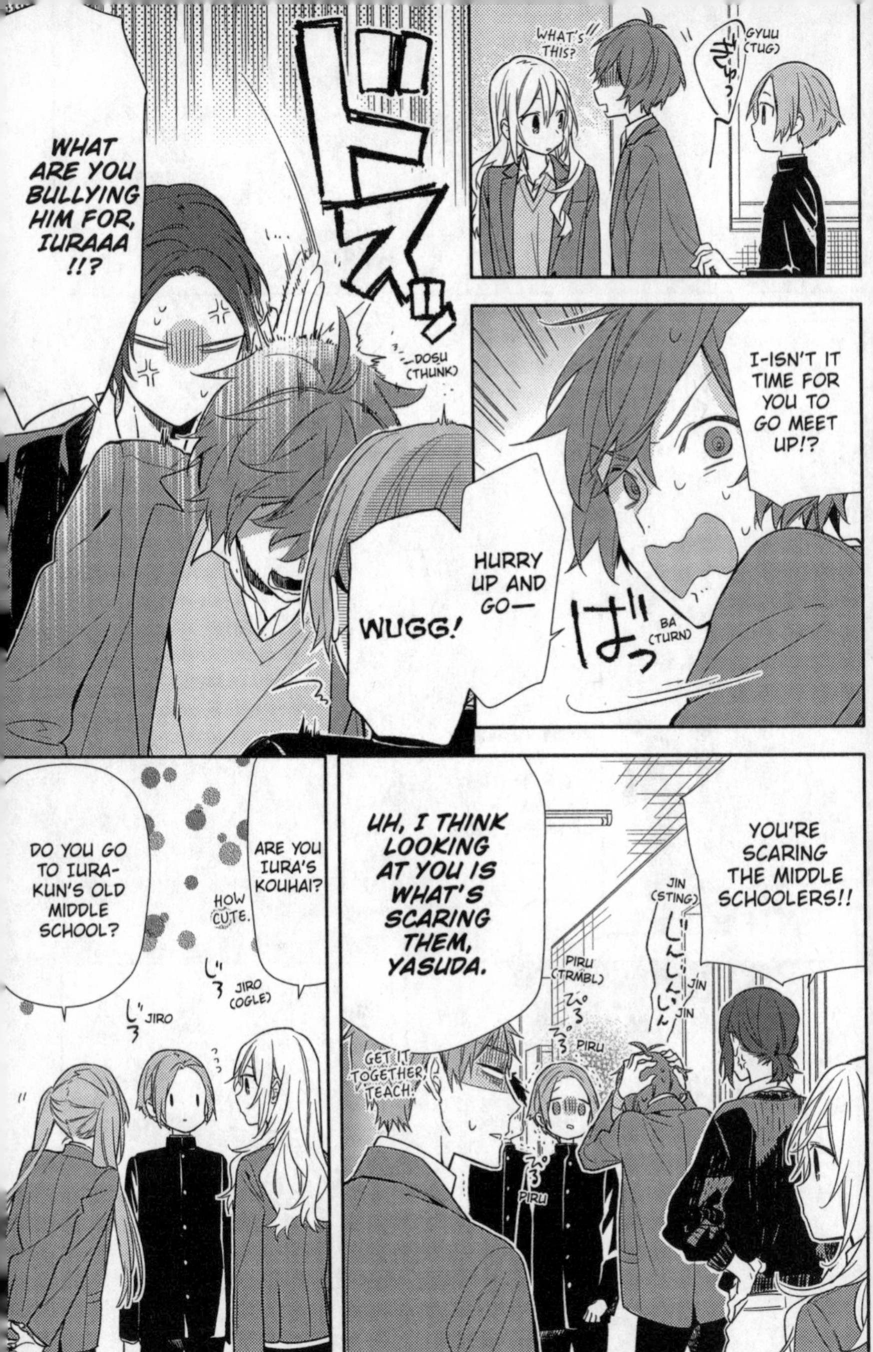
WHAT'S THIS?
GYUU (TUG)
I-ISN'T IT TIME FOR YOU TO GO MEET UP!?
BA (TURN)
HURRY UP AND GO— WUGG!
DOSU (THUNK)
WHAT ARE YOU BULLYING HIM FOR, IURAAA!!?
YOU'RE SCARING THE MIDDLE SCHOOLERS!!
JIN (STING)
JIN JIN
PIRU (TRMBL)
PIRU
UH, I THINK LOOKING AT YOU IS WHAT'S SCARING THEM, YASUDA.
GET IT TOGETHER, TEACH.
PIRU
ARE YOU IURA'S KOUHAI?
HOW CUTE.
JIRO (OGLE)
DO YOU GO TO IURA-KUN'S OLD MIDDLE SCHOOL?
JIRO

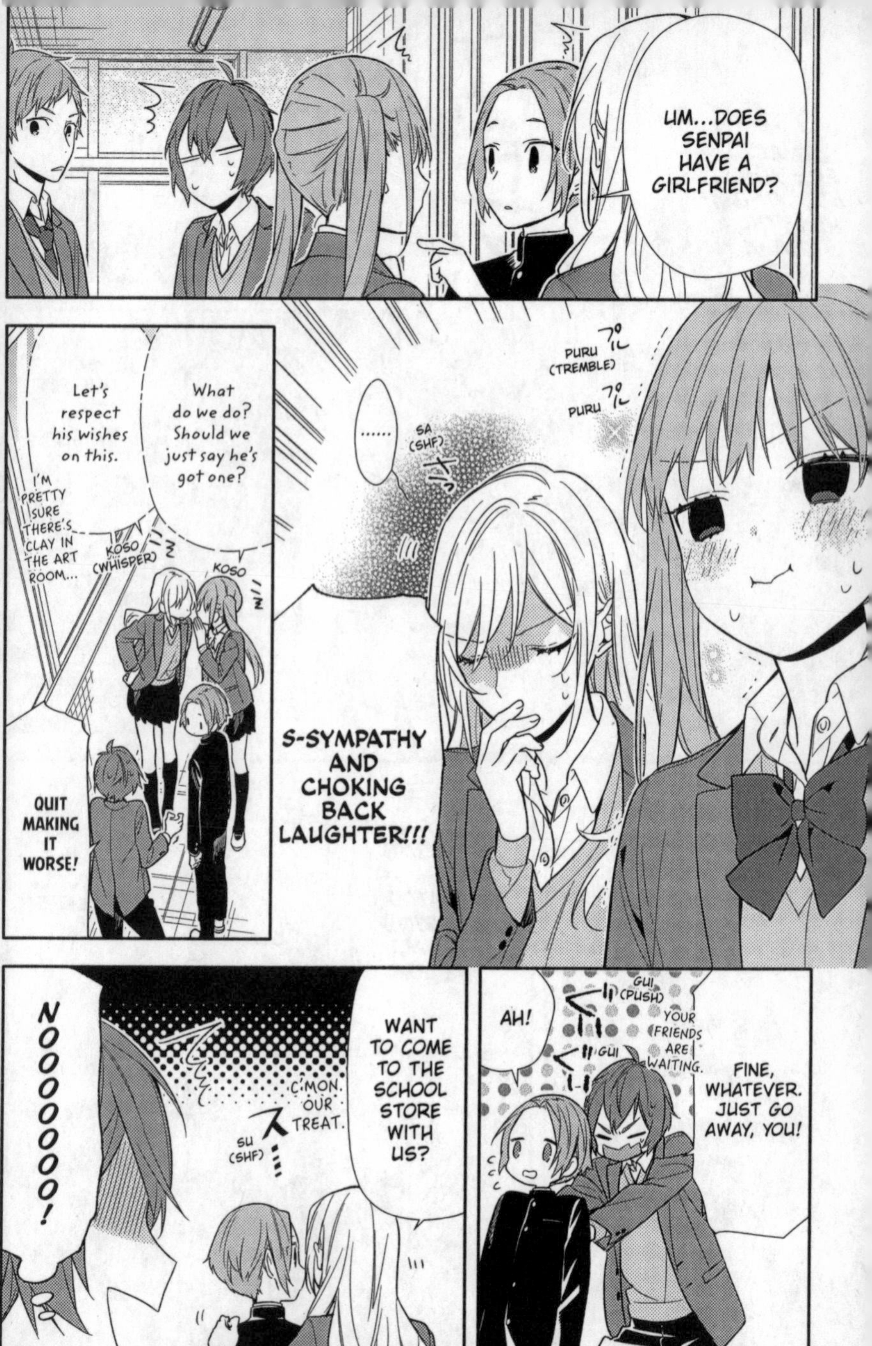
UM...DOES SENPAI HAVE A GIRLFRIEND?
PURU (TREMBLE)
PURU
SA (SHF)
......
S-SYMPATHY AND CHOKING BACK LAUGHTER!!!
What do we do? Should we just say he's got one?
Let's respect his wishes on this.
KOSO (WHISPER)
KOSO
I'M PRETTY SURE THERE'S CLAY IN THE ART ROOM...
QUIT MAKING IT WORSE!
AH!
GUI (PUSH)
GUI
YOUR FRIENDS ARE WAITING.
FINE, WHATEVER. JUST GO AWAY, YOU!
WANT TO COME TO THE SCHOOL STORE WITH US?
C'MON. OUR TREAT.
SU (SHF)
NOOOOOOOO!

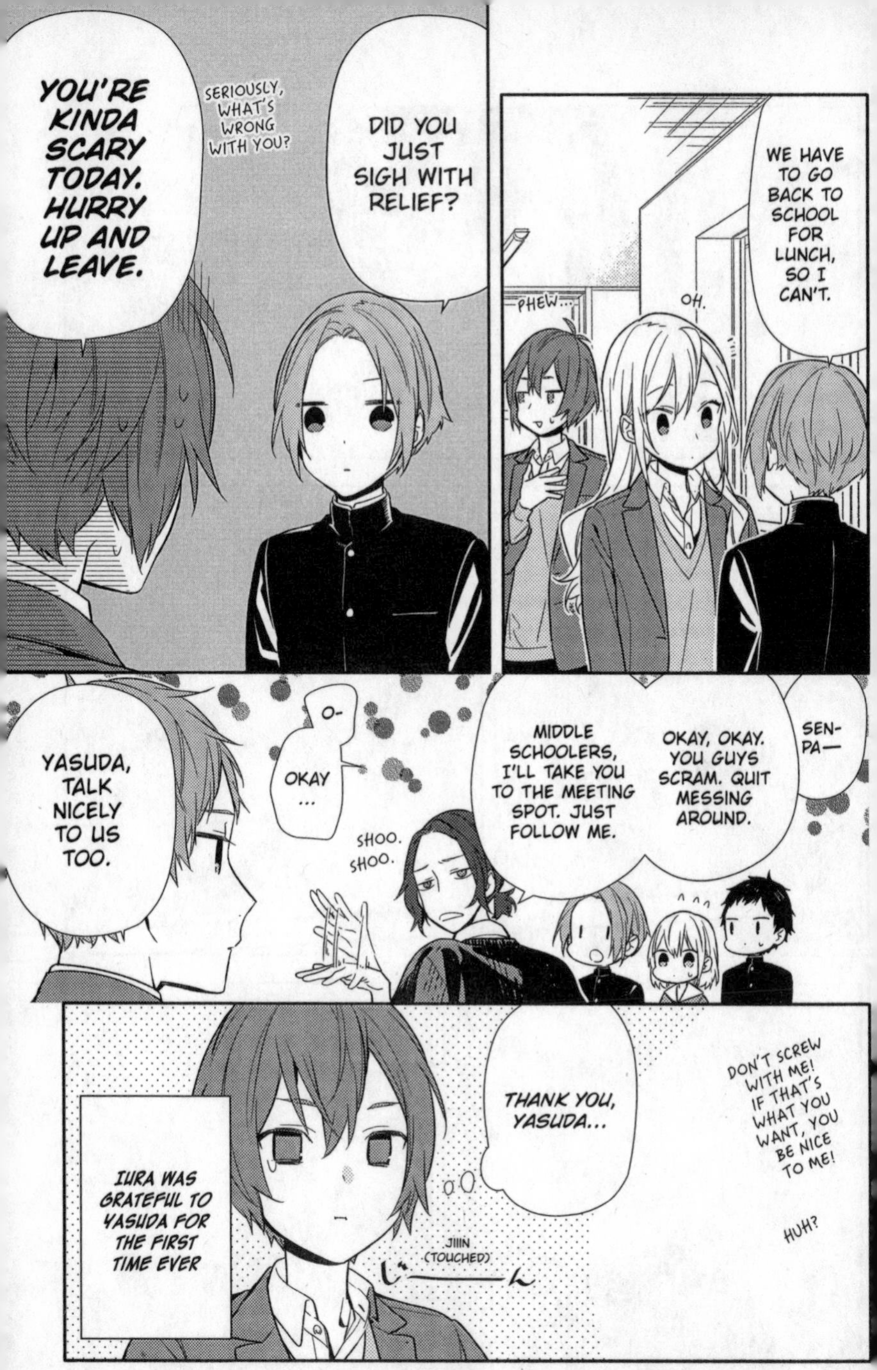
WE HAVE TO GO BACK TO SCHOOL FOR LUNCH, SO I CAN'T.
OH.
PHEW...
DID YOU JUST SIGH WITH RELIEF?
SERIOUSLY, WHAT'S WRONG WITH YOU?
YOU'RE KINDA SCARY TODAY. HURRY UP AND LEAVE.
SEN-PA—
OKAY, OKAY. YOU GUYS SCRAM. QUIT MESSING AROUND.
MIDDLE SCHOOLERS, I'LL TAKE YOU TO THE MEETING SPOT. JUST FOLLOW ME.
SHOO. SHOO.
O- OKAY...
YASUDA, TALK NICELY TO US TOO.
DON'T SCREW WITH ME! IF THAT'S WHAT YOU WANT, YOU BE NICE TO ME!
HUH?
THANK YOU, YASUDA...
JIIIN (TOUCHED)
IURA WAS GRATEFUL TO YASUDA FOR THE FIRST TIME EVER

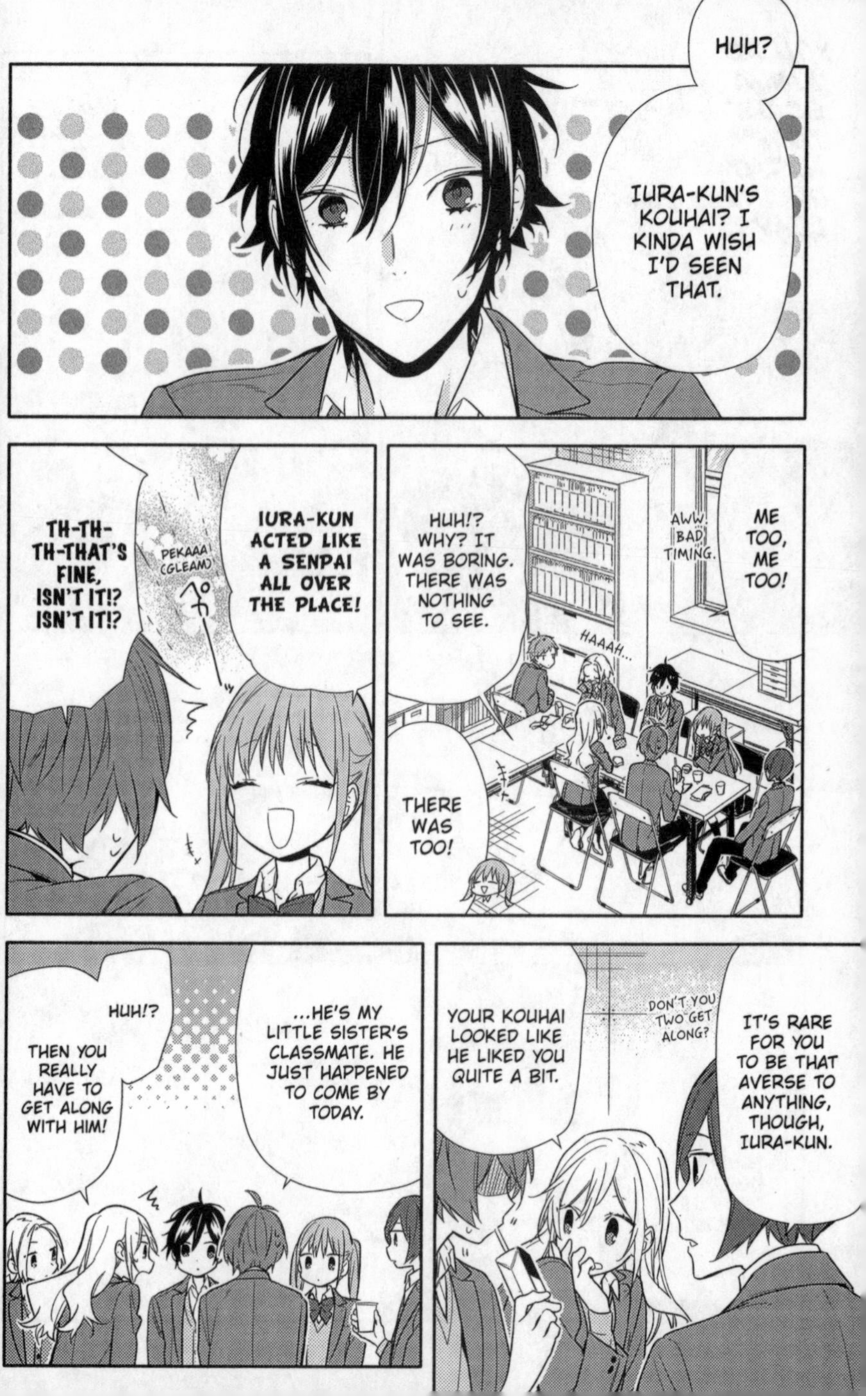
HUH?
IURA-KUN'S KOUHAI? I KINDA WISH I'D SEEN THAT.
ME TOO, ME TOO!
AWW! BAD TIMING.
HUH!? WHY? IT WAS BORING. THERE WAS NOTHING TO SEE.
HAAAH...
THERE WAS TOO!
IURA-KUN ACTED LIKE A SENPAI ALL OVER THE PLACE!
PEKAAA (GLEAM)
TH-TH-TH-THAT'S FINE, ISN'T IT!? ISN'T IT!?
IT'S RARE FOR YOU TO BE THAT AVERSE TO ANYTHING, THOUGH, IURA-KUN.
DON'T YOU TWO GET ALONG?
YOUR KOUHAI LOOKED LIKE HE LIKED YOU QUITE A BIT.
...HE'S MY LITTLE SISTER'S CLASSMATE. HE JUST HAPPENED TO COME BY TODAY.
HUH!?
THEN YOU REALLY HAVE TO GET ALONG WITH HIM!

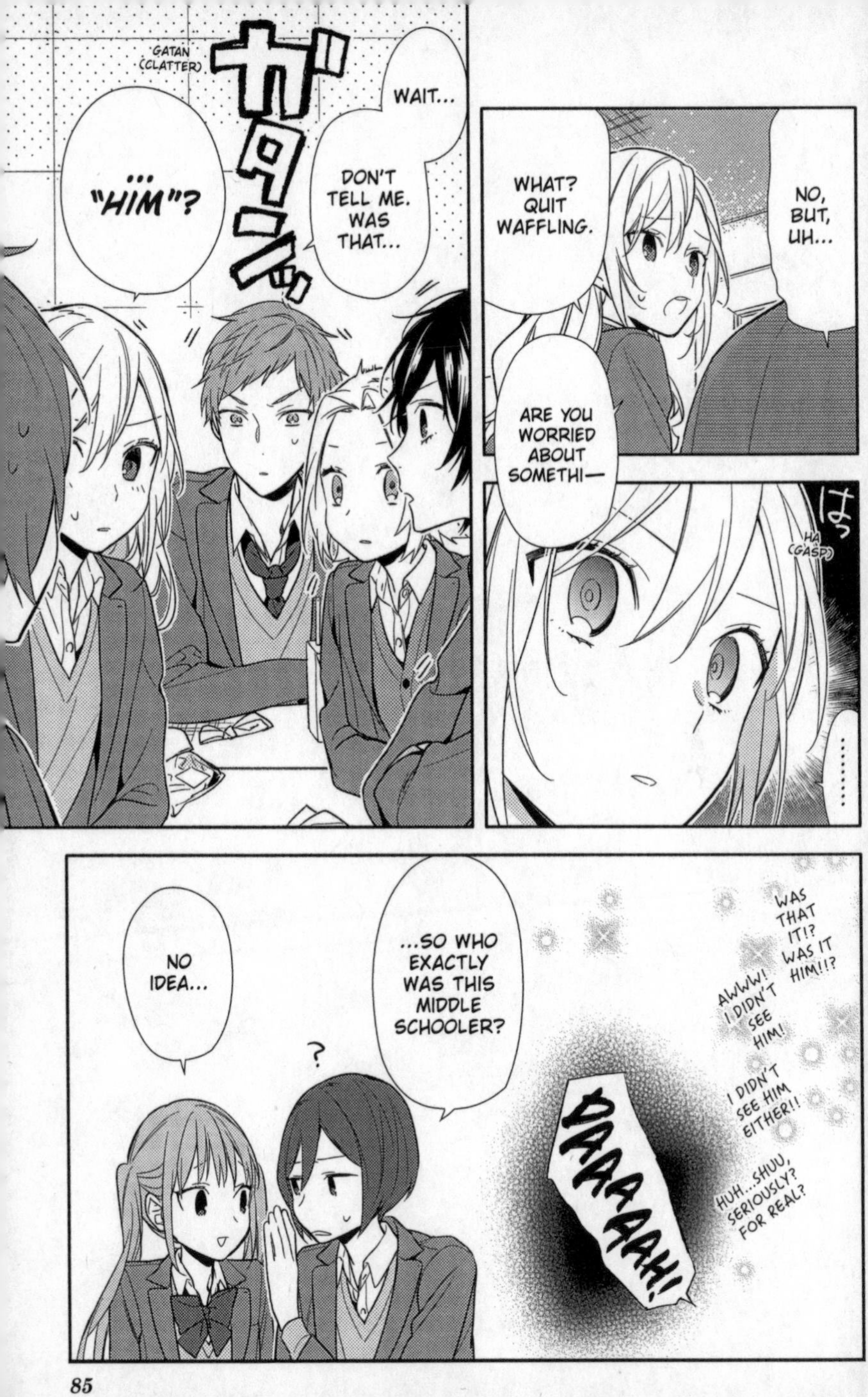

NO, BUT, UH...
WHAT? QUIT WAFFLING.
ARE YOU WORRIED ABOUT SOMETHI—
は
HA (GASP)
......
ガタッ
GATAN (CLATTER)
WAIT...
DON'T TELL ME. WAS THAT...
..."HIM"?
WAS THAT IT!? WAS IT HIM!!?
AWWW! I DIDN'T SEE HIM!
I DIDN'T SEE HIM EITHER!!
HUH...SHUU, SERIOUSLY? FOR REAL?
DAAAAAH!
...SO WHO EXACTLY WAS THIS MIDDLE SCHOOLER?
?
NO IDEA...

HORIMIYA

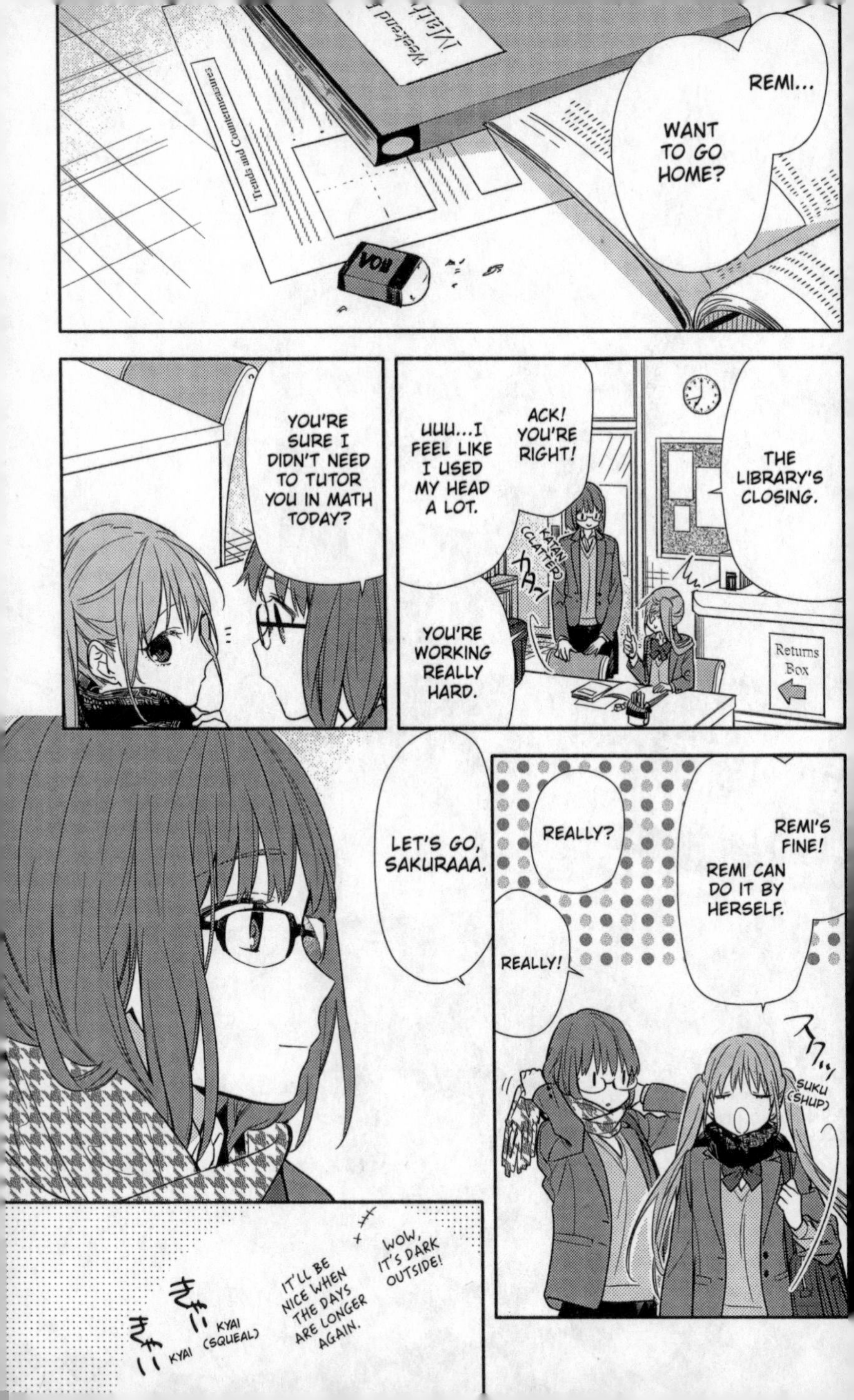

Trends and Countermeasures
REMI...
WANT TO GO HOME?
THE LIBRARY'S CLOSING.
ACK! YOU'RE RIGHT!
KATAN (CLATTER)
UUU...I FEEL LIKE I USED MY HEAD A LOT.
YOU'RE WORKING REALLY HARD.
Returns Box
YOU'RE SURE I DIDN'T NEED TO TUTOR YOU IN MATH TODAY?
REMI'S FINE!
REMI CAN DO IT BY HERSELF.
REALLY?
REALLY!
SUKU (SHUP)
LET'S GO, SAKURAAA.
WOW, IT'S DARK OUTSIDE!
IT'LL BE NICE WHEN THE DAYS ARE LONGER AGAIN.
KYAI (SQUEAL)
KYAI

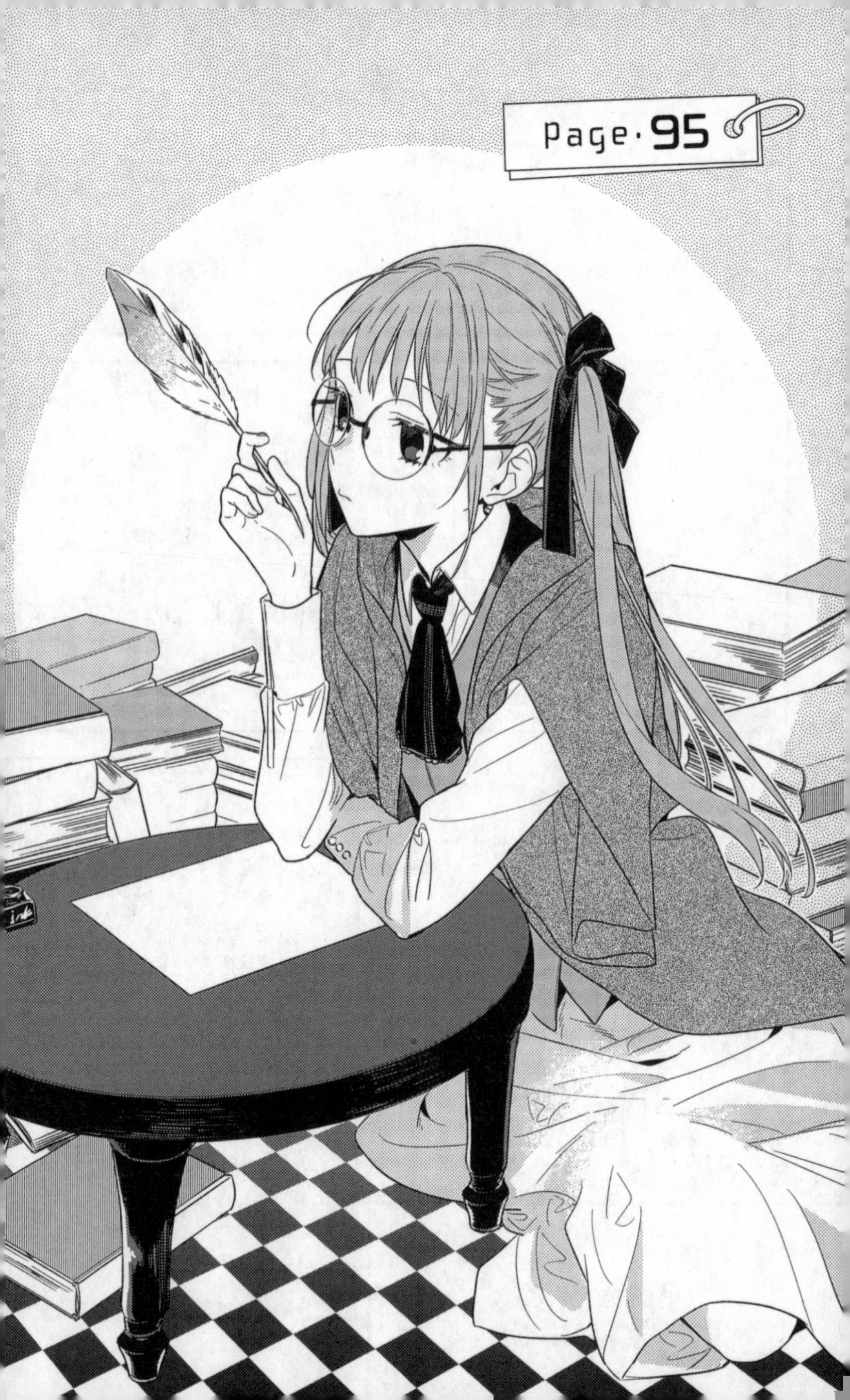
Page·95
ink

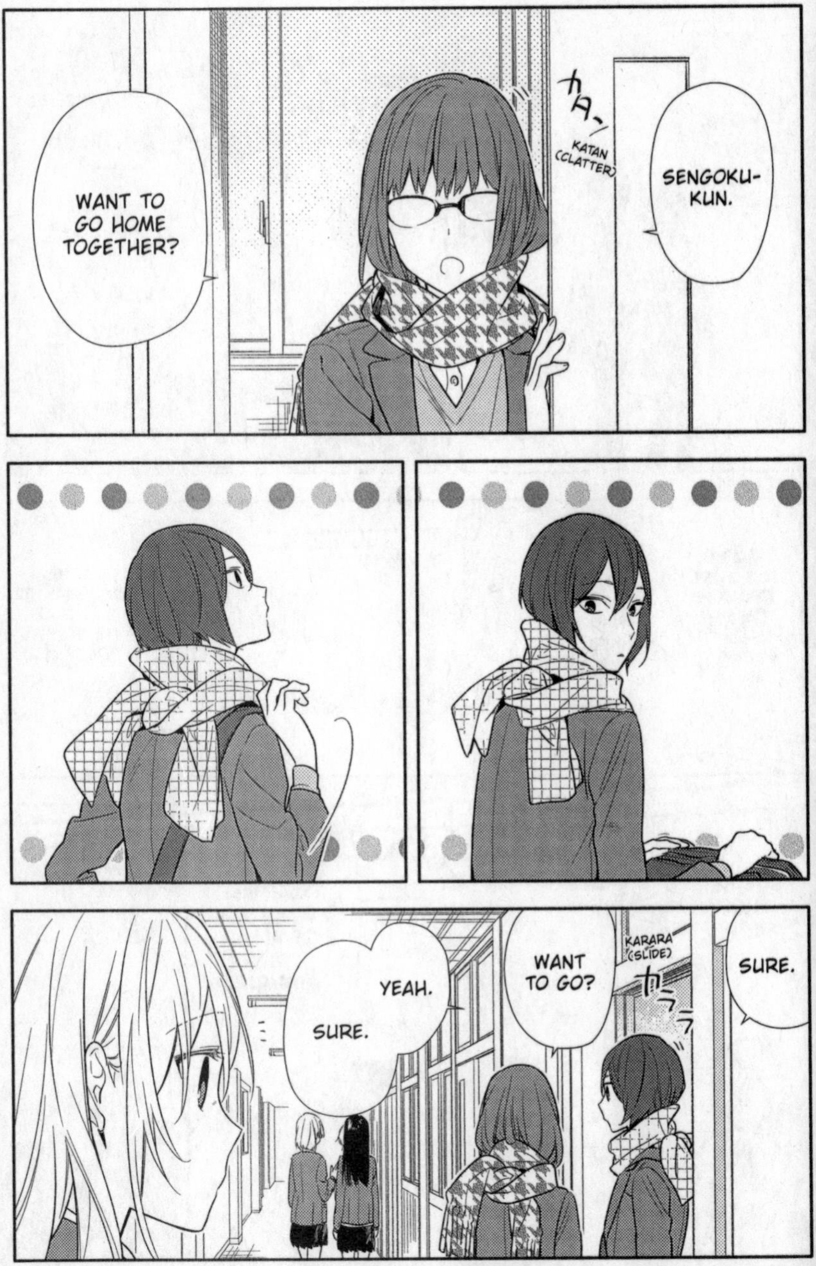
SENGOKU-KUN.
カタン
KATAN (CLATTER)
WANT TO GO HOME TOGETHER?
SURE.
ガラ
KARARA (SLIDE)
WANT TO GO?
YEAH.
SURE.

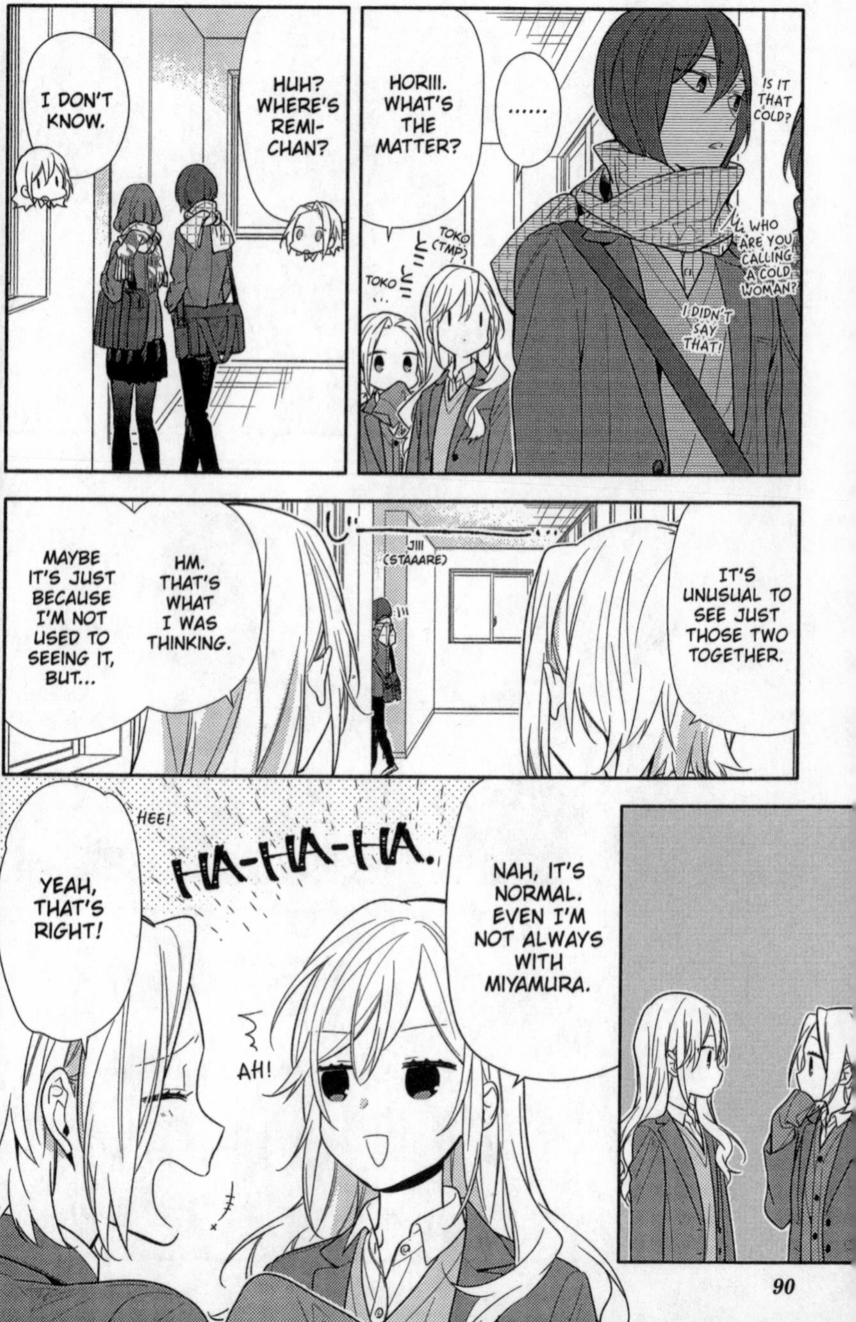
IS IT THAT COLD?
......
HORIII. WHAT'S THE MATTER?
WHO ARE YOU CALLING A COLD WOMAN?
I DIDN'T SAY THAT!
TOKO (TMP)
TOKO
HUH? WHERE'S REMI-CHAN?
I DON'T KNOW.
IT'S UNUSUAL TO SEE JUST THOSE TWO TOGETHER.
JIII (STAAARE)
HM. THAT'S WHAT I WAS THINKING.
MAYBE IT'S JUST BECAUSE I'M NOT USED TO SEEING IT, BUT...
NAH, IT'S NORMAL. EVEN I'M NOT ALWAYS WITH MIYAMURA.
HA-HA-HA.
HEE!
AH!
YEAH, THAT'S RIGHT!

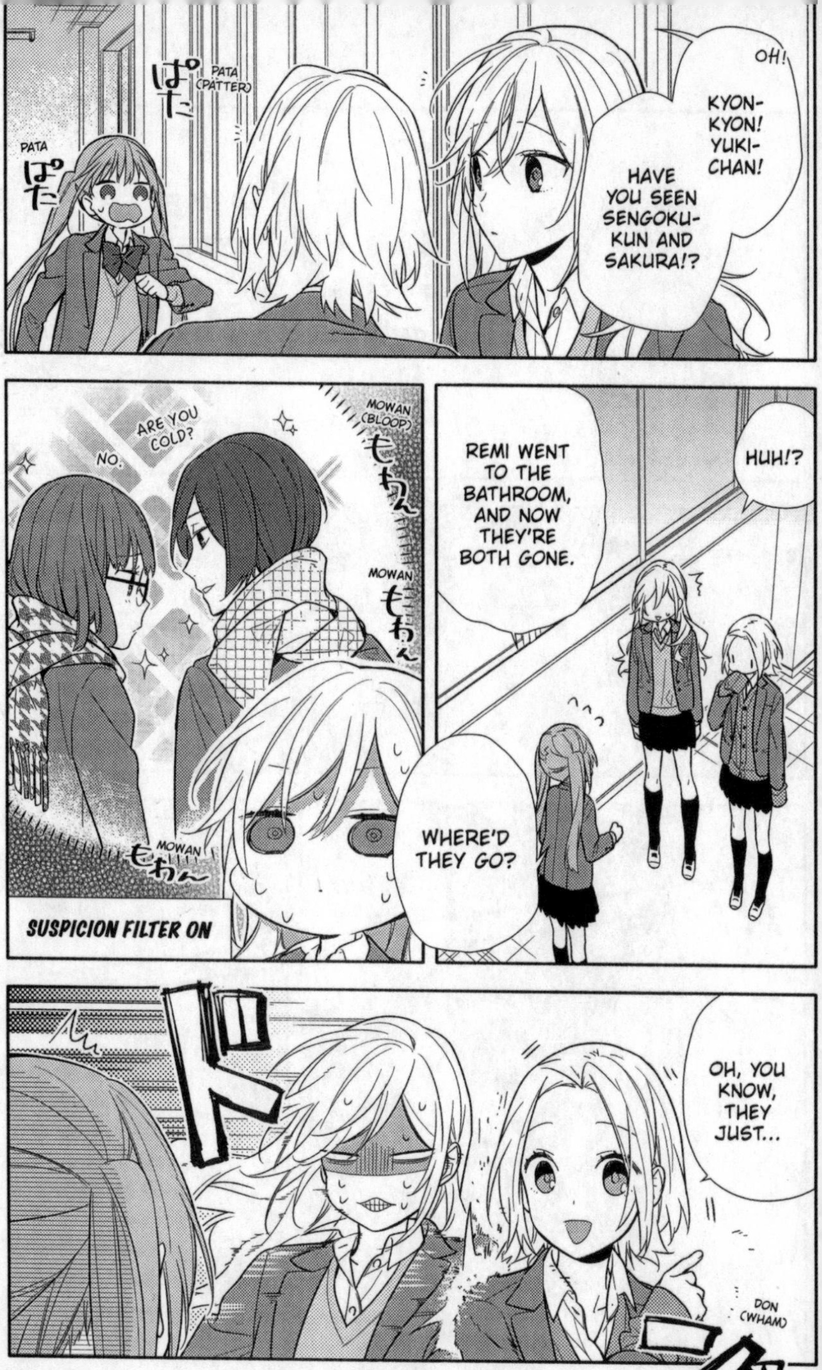
OH!
KYON-KYON! YUKI-CHAN!
HAVE YOU SEEN SENGOKU-KUN AND SAKURA!?
ぱた PATA (PATTER)
ぱた PATA
HUH!?
REMI WENT TO THE BATHROOM, AND NOW THEY'RE BOTH GONE.
WHERE'D THEY GO?
もわん MOWAN (BLOOP)
もわん MOWAN
ARE YOU COLD?
NO.
もわん〜 MOWAN
SUSPICION FILTER ON
OH, YOU KNOW, THEY JUST...
DON (WHAM)

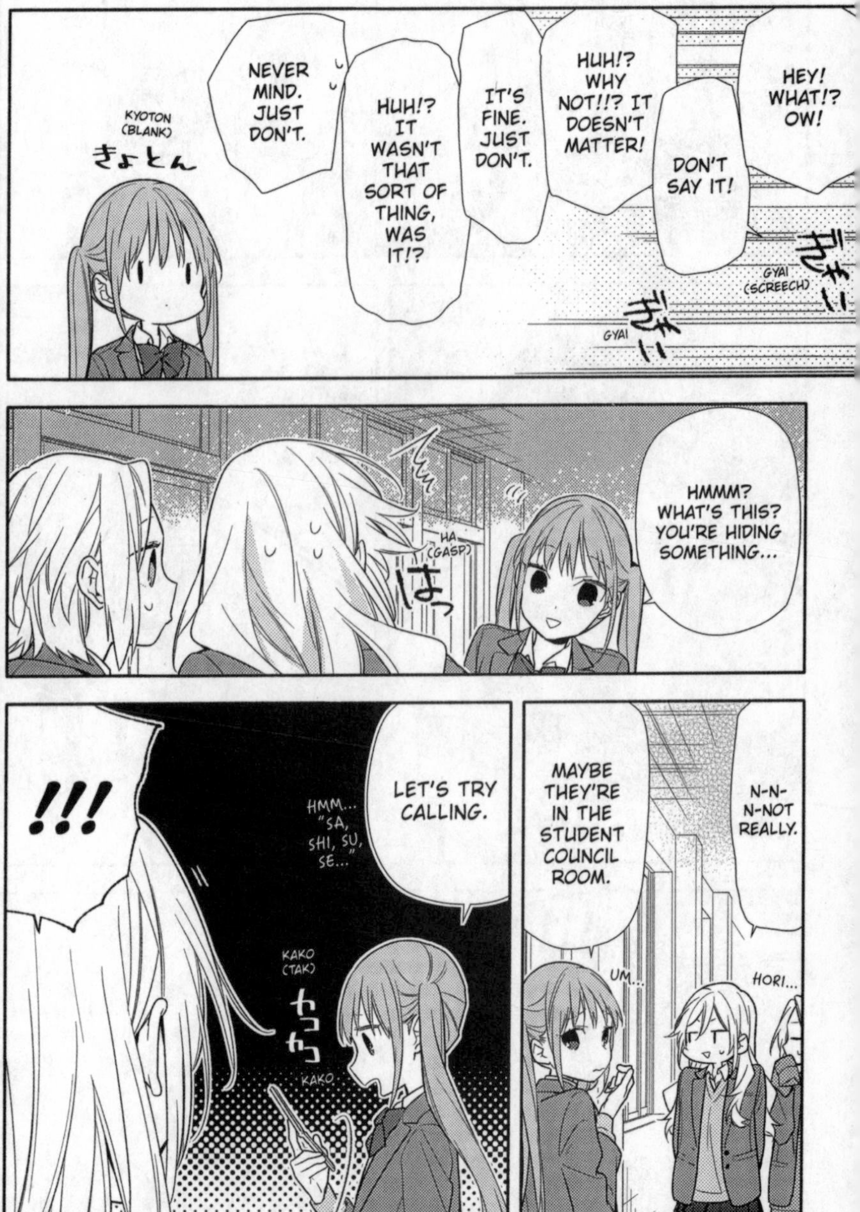
HEY! WHAT!? OW!
DON'T SAY IT!
HUH!? WHY NOT!!? IT DOESN'T MATTER!
IT'S FINE. JUST DON'T.
HUH!? IT WASN'T THAT SORT OF THING, WAS IT!?
NEVER MIND. JUST DON'T.
GYAI (SCREECH)
GYAI
KYOTON (BLANK)
HMMM? WHAT'S THIS? YOU'RE HIDING SOMETHING...
HA (GASP)
N-N-N-NOT REALLY.
MAYBE THEY'RE IN THE STUDENT COUNCIL ROOM.
HORI...
UM...
LET'S TRY CALLING.
HMM... "SA, SHI, SU, SE..."
KAKO (TAK)
KAKO
!!!

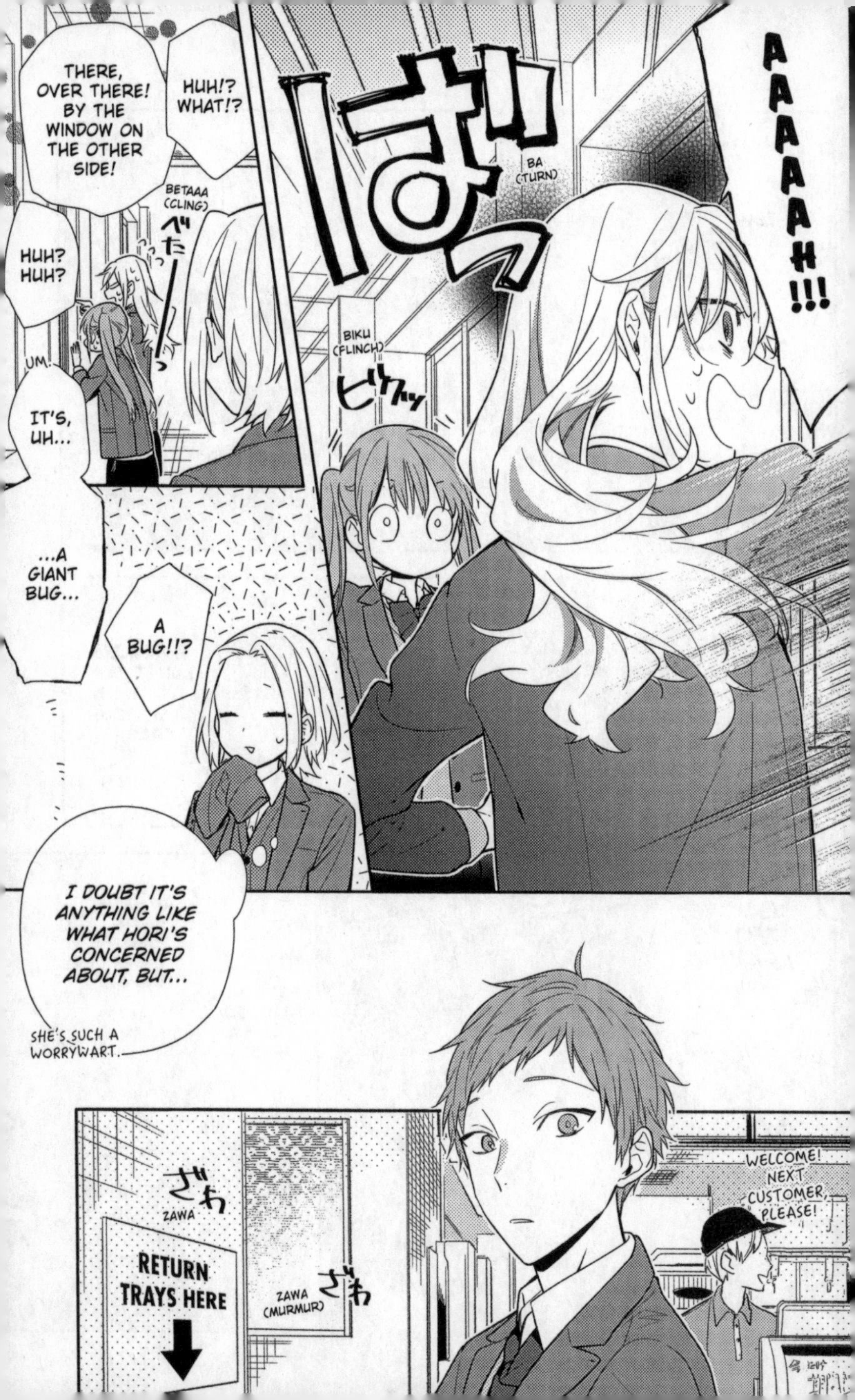
AAAAAH!!!
はっ
BA (TURN)
BIKU (FLINCH)
ビクッ
THERE, OVER THERE! BY THE WINDOW ON THE OTHER SIDE!
HUH!? WHAT!?
BETAAA (CLING)
べたっ
HUH? HUH?
UM!
IT'S, UH...
...A GIANT BUG...
A BUG!!?
I DOUBT IT'S ANYTHING LIKE WHAT HORI'S CONCERNED ABOUT, BUT...
SHE'S SUCH A WORRYWART.
WELCOME! NEXT CUSTOMER, PLEASE!
ざわ
ZAWA
ざわ
ZAWA (MURMUR)
RETURN TRAYS HERE

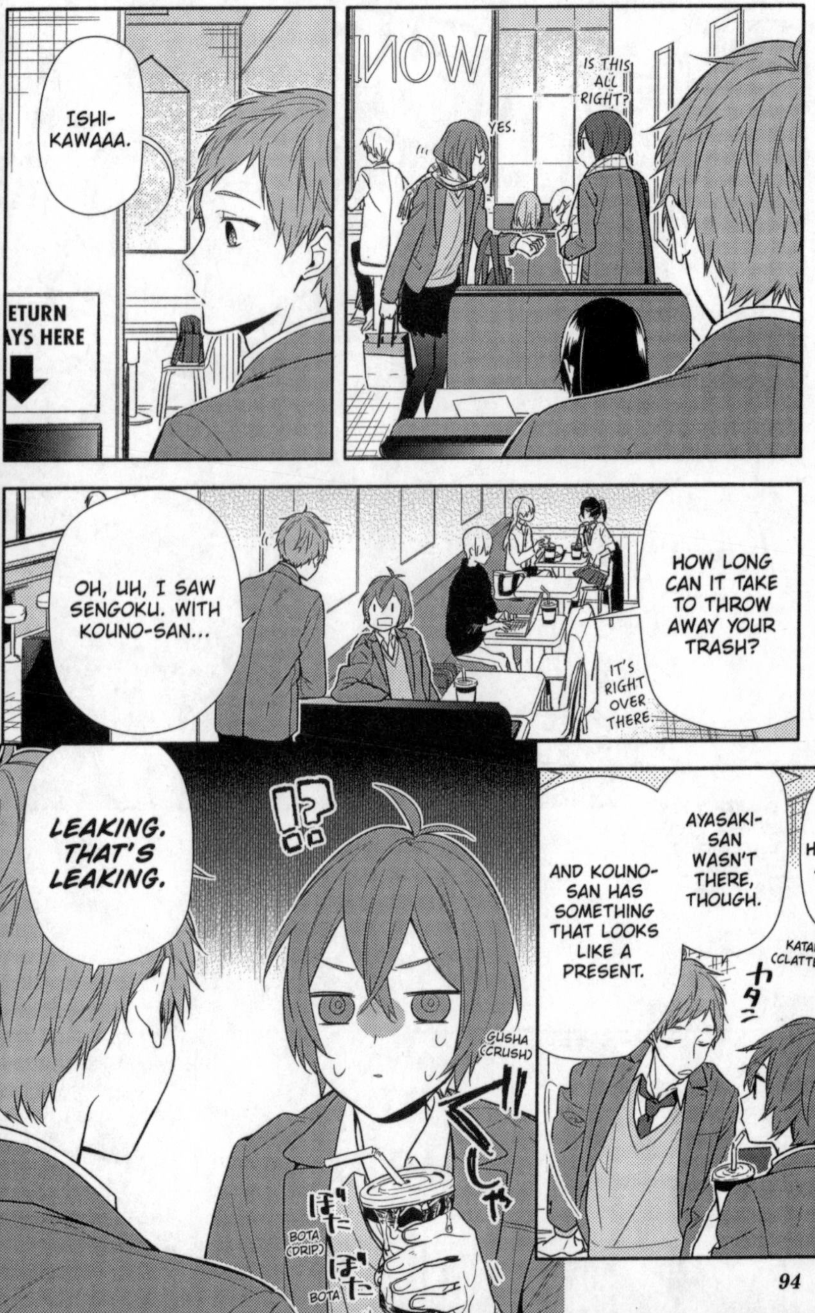
IS THIS ALL RIGHT?
YES.
ISHI-KAWAAA.
ETURN
AYS HERE
HOW LONG CAN IT TAKE TO THROW AWAY YOUR TRASH?
IT'S RIGHT OVER THERE.
OH, UH, I SAW SENGOKU. WITH KOUNO-SAN...
HUH...
AYASAKI-SAN WASN'T THERE, THOUGH.
AND KOUNO-SAN HAS SOMETHING THAT LOOKS LIKE A PRESENT.
KATAN (CLATTER)
カタン
LEAKING. THAT'S LEAKING.
!?
GUSHA (CRUSH)
ぐしゃ
BOTA (DRIP)
ぼた
BOTA
ぼた

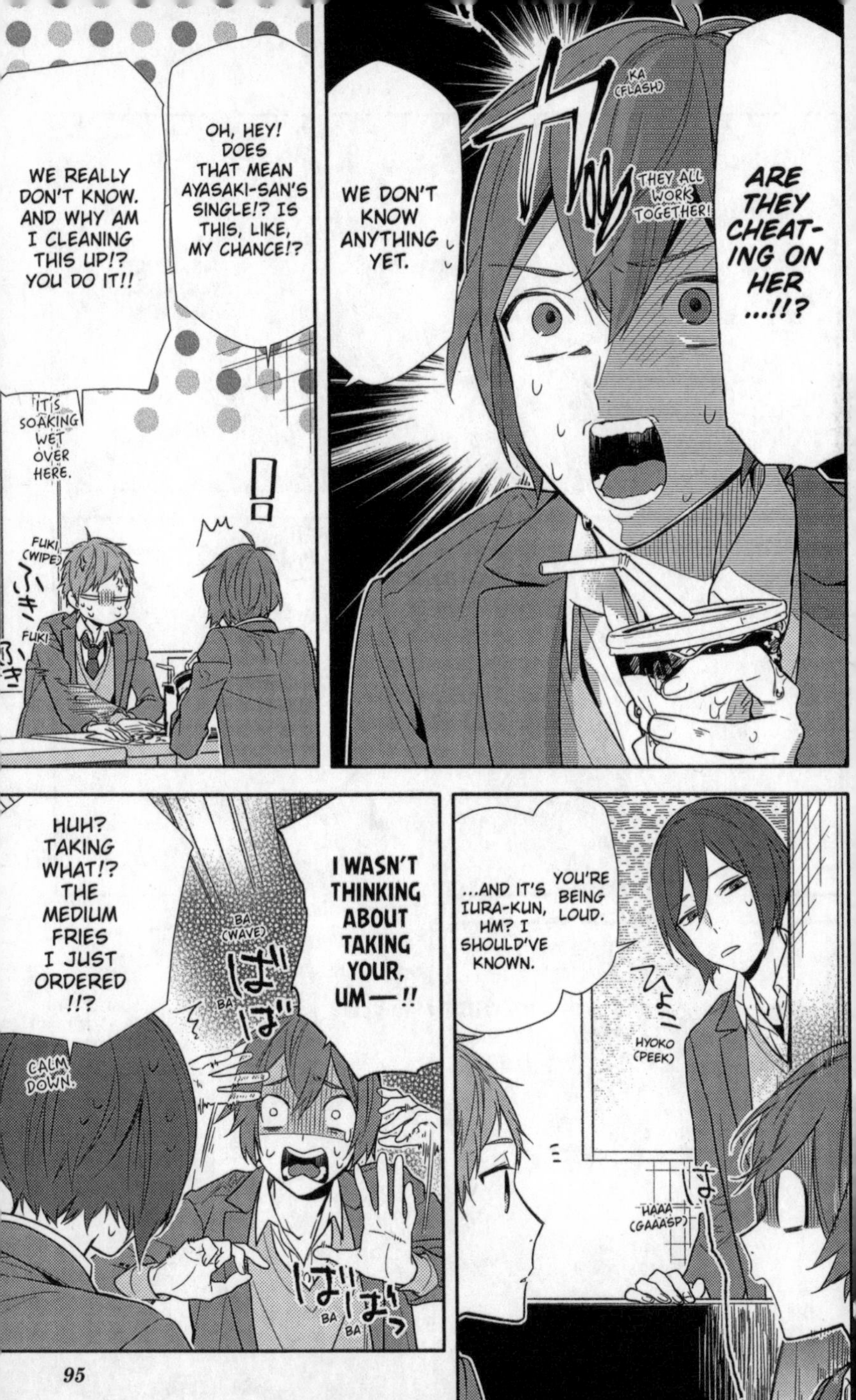
ARE THEY CHEAT-ING ON HER ...!!?
KA (FLASH)
THEY ALL WORK TOGETHER!
WE DON'T KNOW ANYTHING YET.
OH, HEY! DOES THAT MEAN AYASAKI-SAN'S SINGLE!? IS THIS, LIKE, MY CHANCE!?
WE REALLY DON'T KNOW. AND WHY AM I CLEANING THIS UP!? YOU DO IT!!
IT'S SOAKING WET OVER HERE.
FUKI (WIPE)
FUKI
YOU'RE BEING LOUD.
...AND IT'S IURA-KUN, HM? I SHOULD'VE KNOWN.
HYOKO (PEEK)
HAAA (GAAASP)
I WASN'T THINKING ABOUT TAKING YOUR, UM—!!
HUH? TAKING WHAT!? THE MEDIUM FRIES I JUST ORDERED !!?
BA (WAVE)
BA
CALM DOWN.
BA
BA

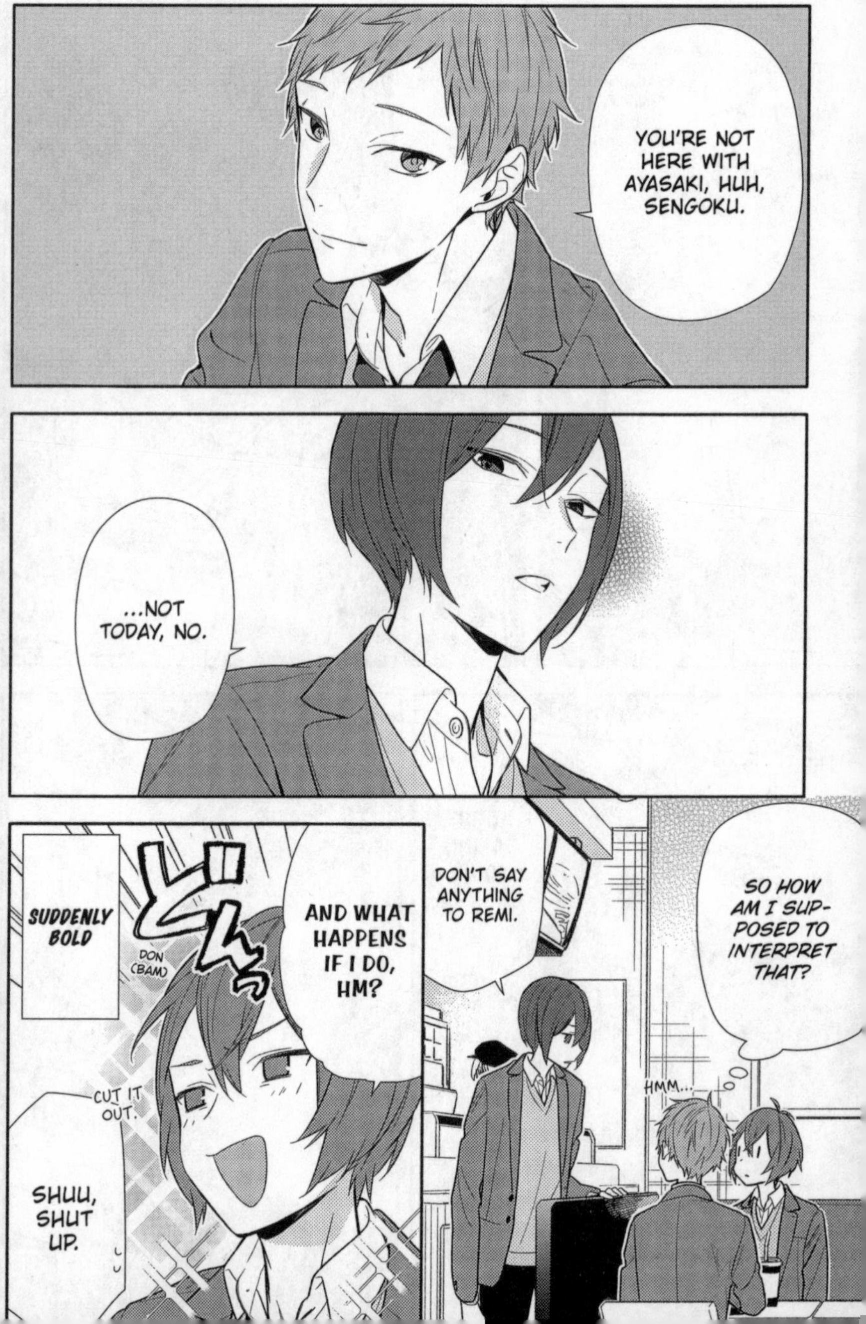
YOU'RE NOT HERE WITH AYASAKI, HUH, SENGOKU.
...NOT TODAY, NO.
SO HOW AM I SUP-POSED TO INTERPRET THAT?
DON'T SAY ANYTHING TO REMI.
HMM...
AND WHAT HAPPENS IF I DO, HM?
SUDDENLY BOLD
DON (BAM)
CUT IT OUT.
SHUU, SHUT UP.

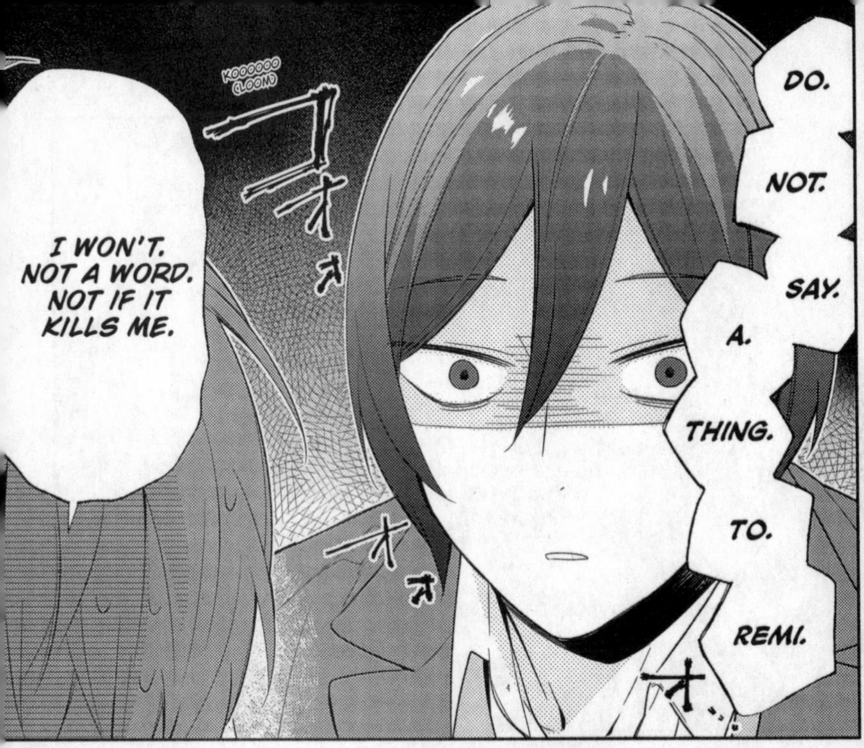
DO. NOT. SAY. A. THING. TO. REMI.
KOOOOOO (GLOOM)
I WON'T. NOT A WORD. NOT IF IT KILLS ME.
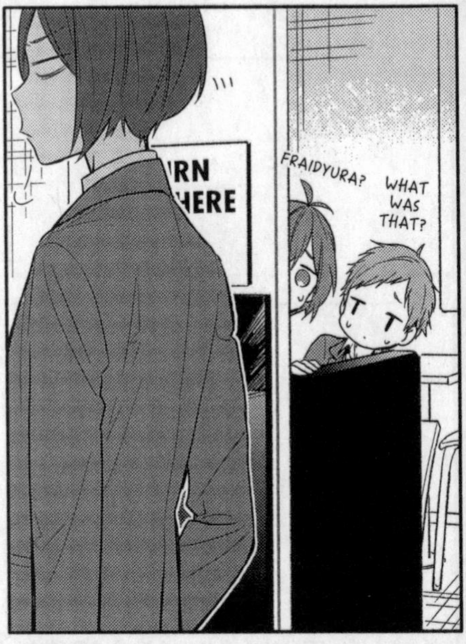
FRAIDYURA?
WHAT WAS THAT?
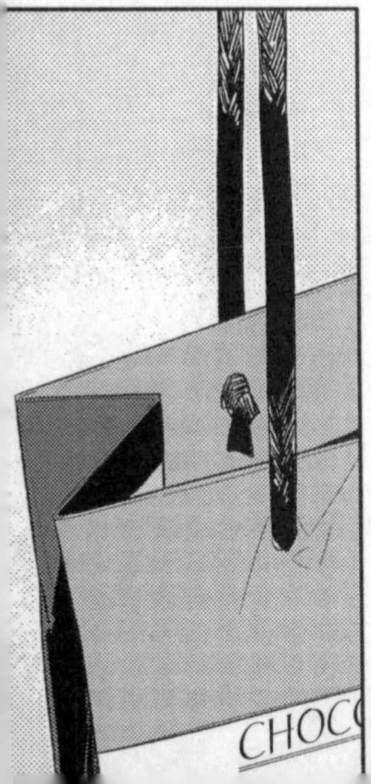

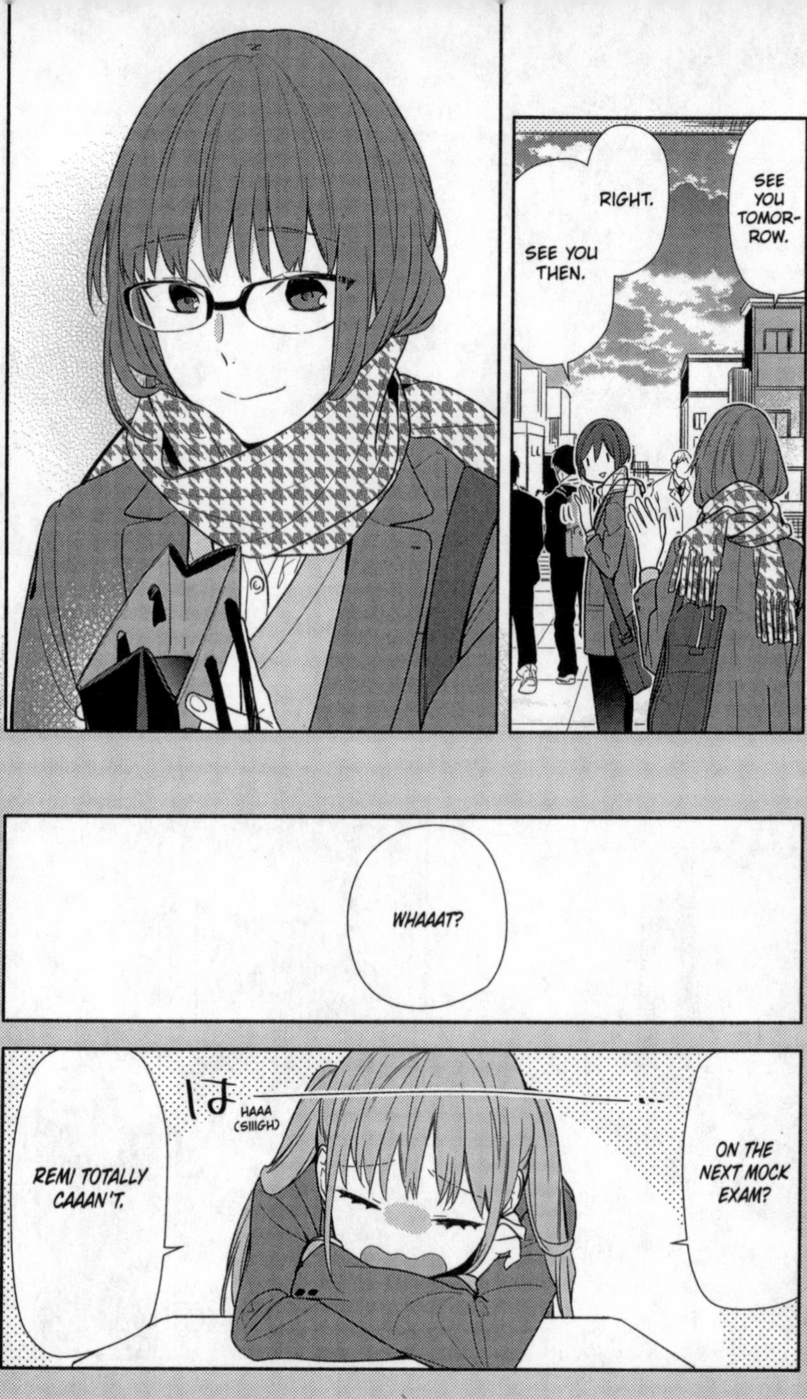
SEE YOU TOMOR-ROW.
RIGHT.
SEE YOU THEN.
WHAAAT?
ON THE NEXT MOCK EXAM?
は HAAA (SIIIGH)
REMI TOTALLY CAAAN'T.

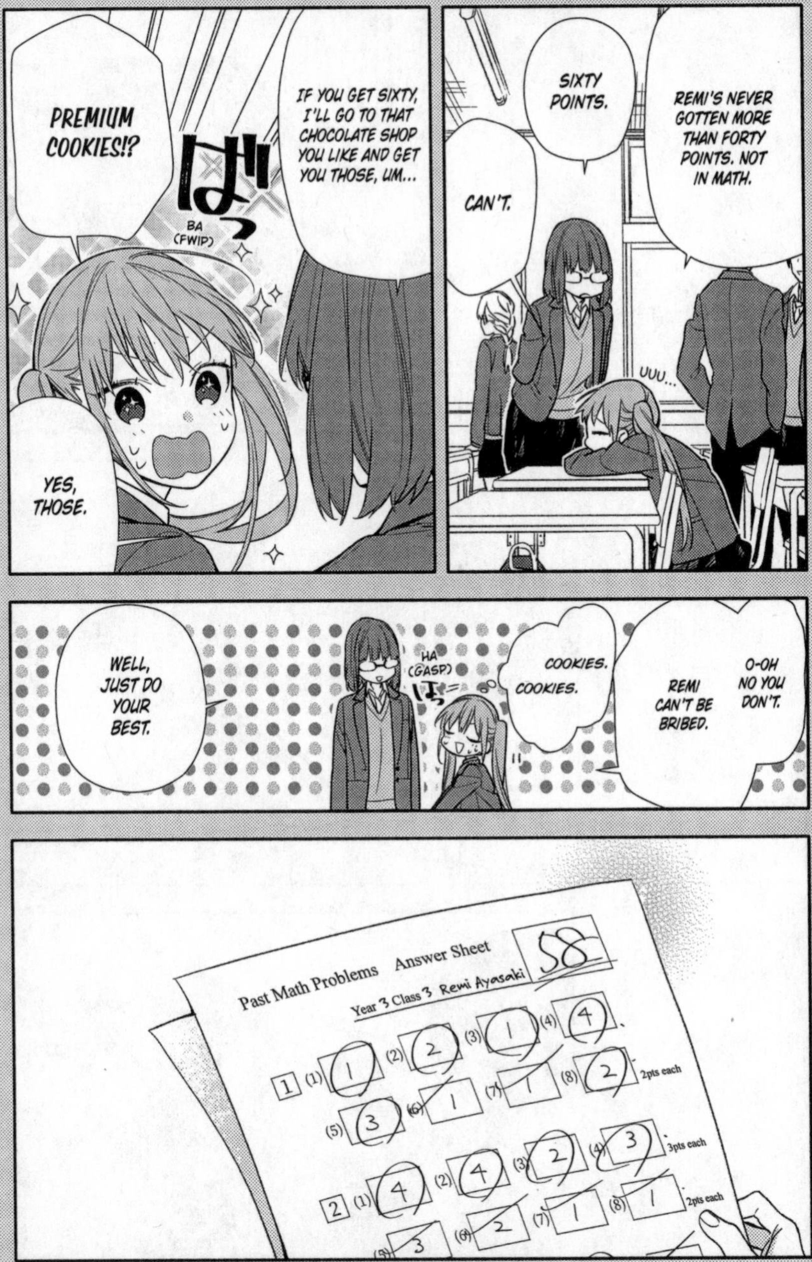
REMI'S NEVER GOTTEN MORE THAN FORTY POINTS. NOT IN MATH.
SIXTY POINTS.
CAN'T.
UUU...
IF YOU GET SIXTY, I'LL GO TO THAT CHOCOLATE SHOP YOU LIKE AND GET YOU THOSE, UM...
PREMIUM COOKIES!?
ばっ
BA (FWIP)
YES, THOSE.
O-OH NO YOU DON'T.
REMI CAN'T BE BRIBED.
COOKIES.
COOKIES.
はっ
HA (GASP)
WELL, JUST DO YOUR BEST.
Past Math Problems Answer Sheet
58
Year 3 Class 3 Remi Ayasaki
2pts each
3pts each
2pts each

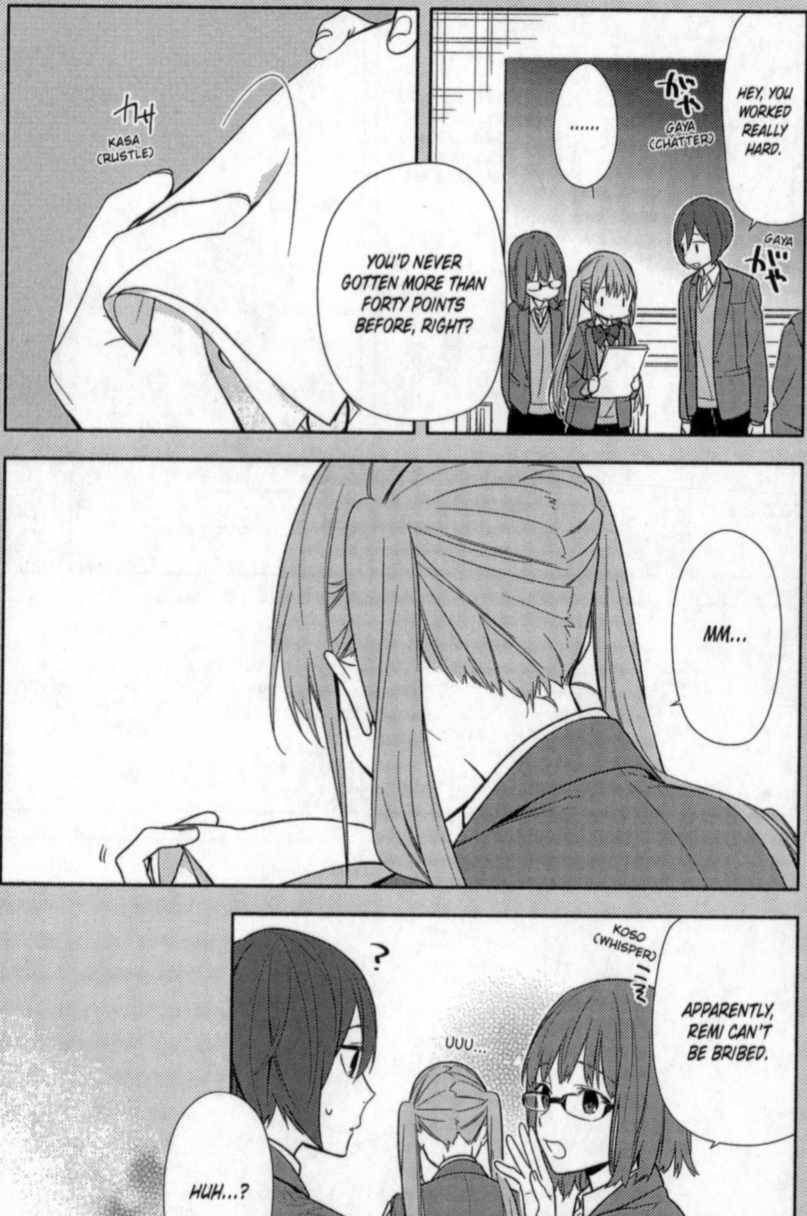

HEY, YOU WORKED REALLY HARD.
GAYA (CHATTER)
......
GAYA
YOU'D NEVER GOTTEN MORE THAN FORTY POINTS BEFORE, RIGHT?
KASA (RUSTLE)
MM...
KOSO (WHISPER)
APPARENTLY, REMI CAN'T BE BRIBED.
UUU...
?
HUH...?

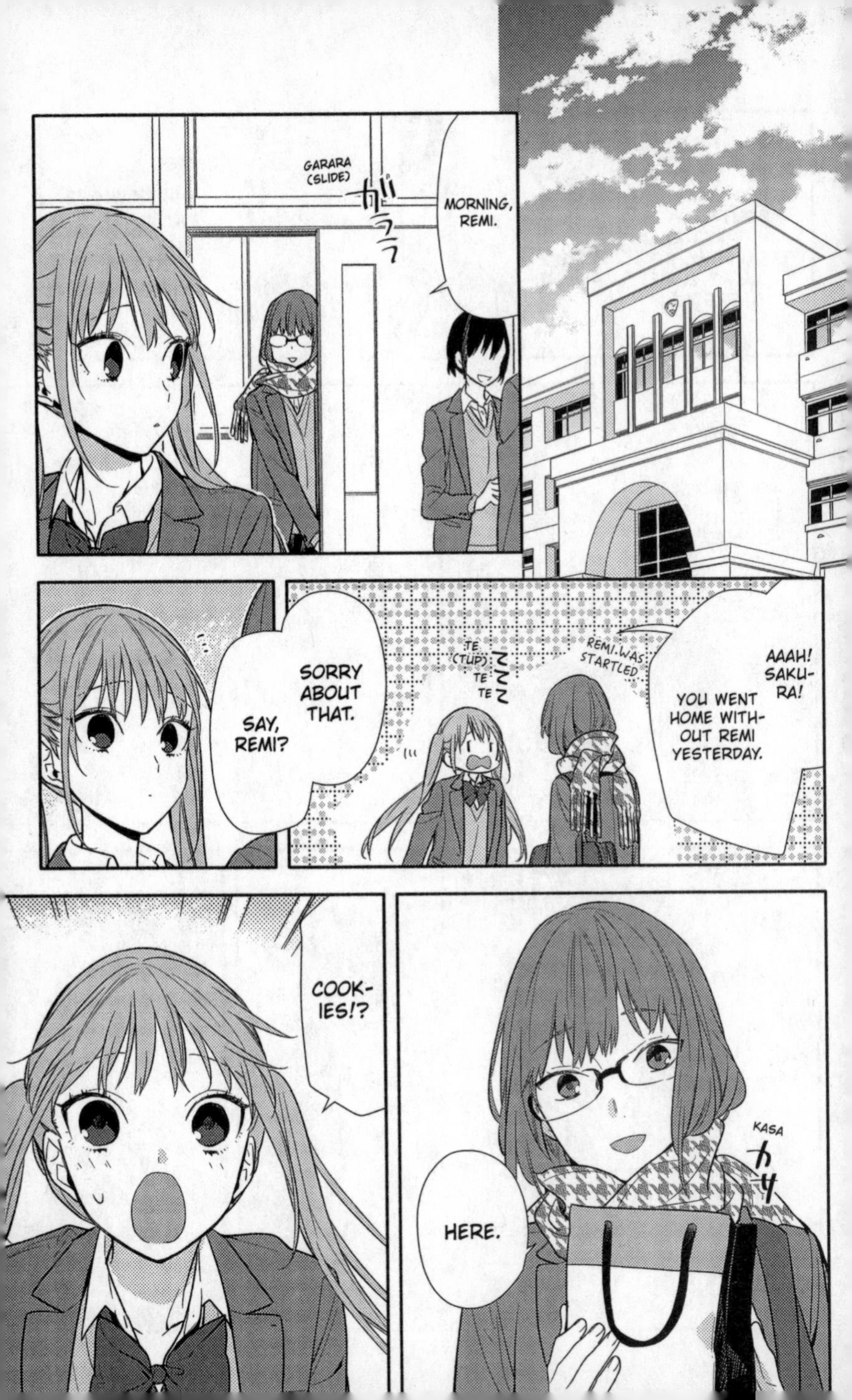
MORNING, REMI.
GARARA (SLIDE)
AAAH! SAKURA!
YOU WENT HOME WITHOUT REMI YESTERDAY.
REMI WAS STARTLED
TE (TUP) TE TE
SORRY ABOUT THAT.
SAY, REMI?
KASA
HERE.
COOKIES!?

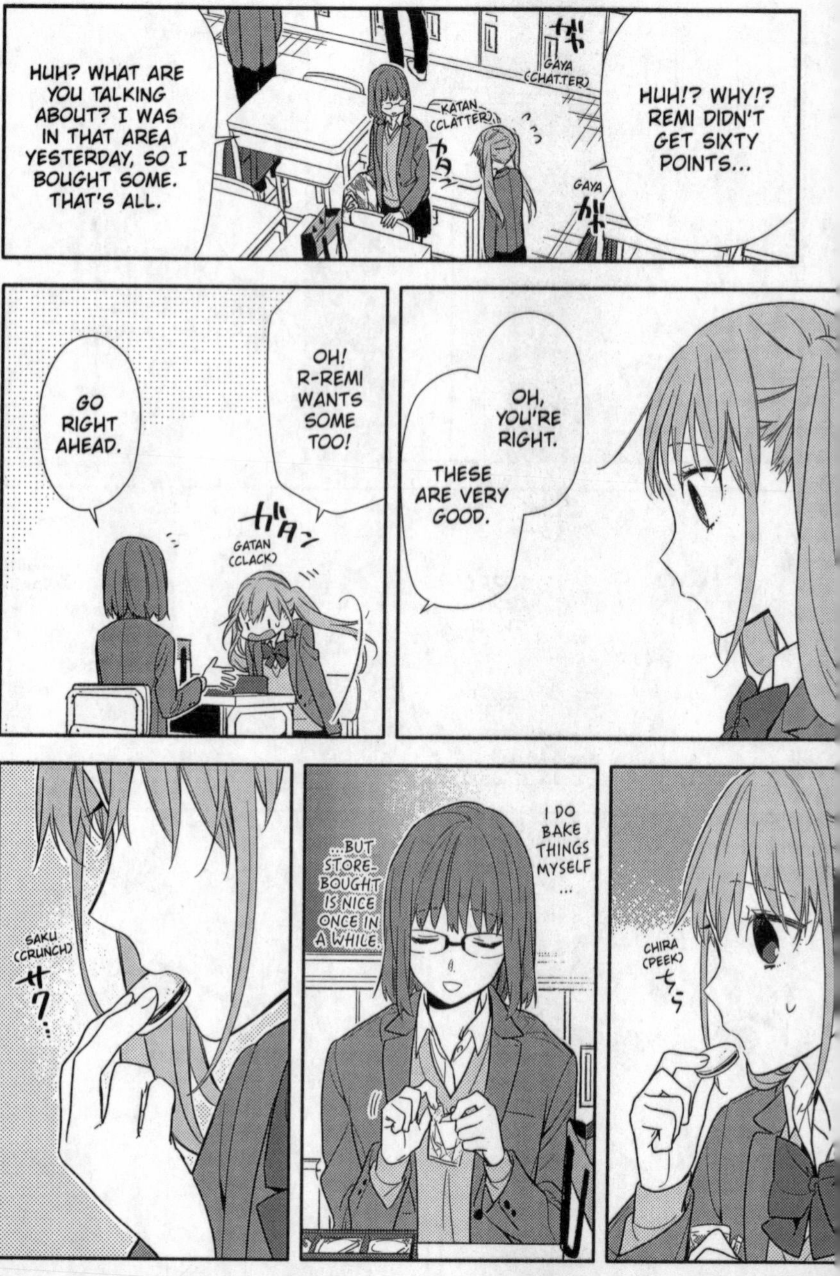
HUH!? WHY!? REMI DIDN'T GET SIXTY POINTS...
GAYA (CHATTER)
KATAN (CLATTER)
GAYA
HUH? WHAT ARE YOU TALKING ABOUT? I WAS IN THAT AREA YESTERDAY, SO I BOUGHT SOME. THAT'S ALL.
OH, YOU'RE RIGHT.
THESE ARE VERY GOOD.
OH! R-REMI WANTS SOME TOO!
GATAN (CLACK)
GO RIGHT AHEAD.
CHIRA (PEEK)
I DO BAKE THINGS MYSELF...
...BUT STORE-BOUGHT IS NICE ONCE IN A WHILE.
SAKU (CRUNCH)

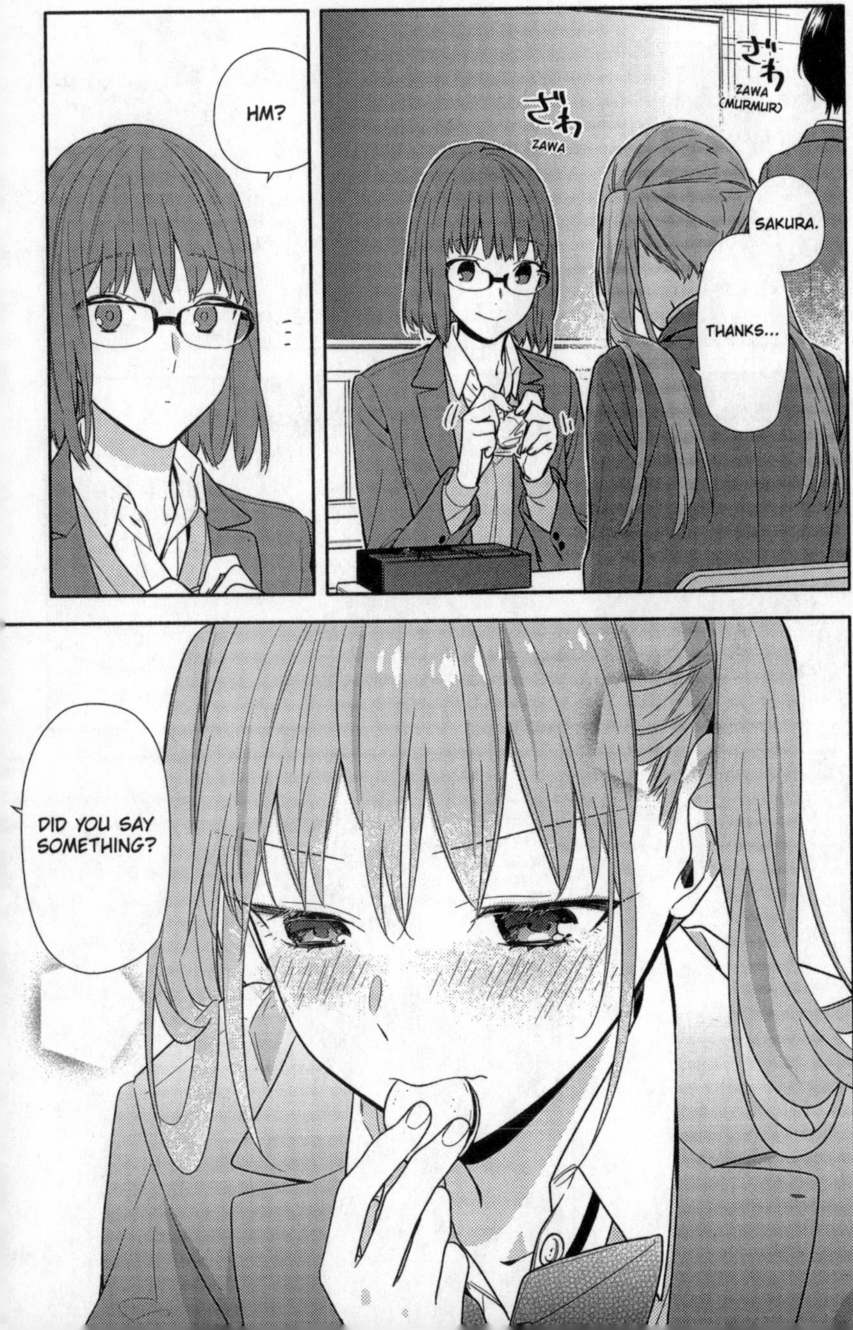
ざわ
ZAWA (MURMUR)
ざわ
ZAWA
SAKURA.
THANKS...
HM?
DID YOU SAY SOMETHING?

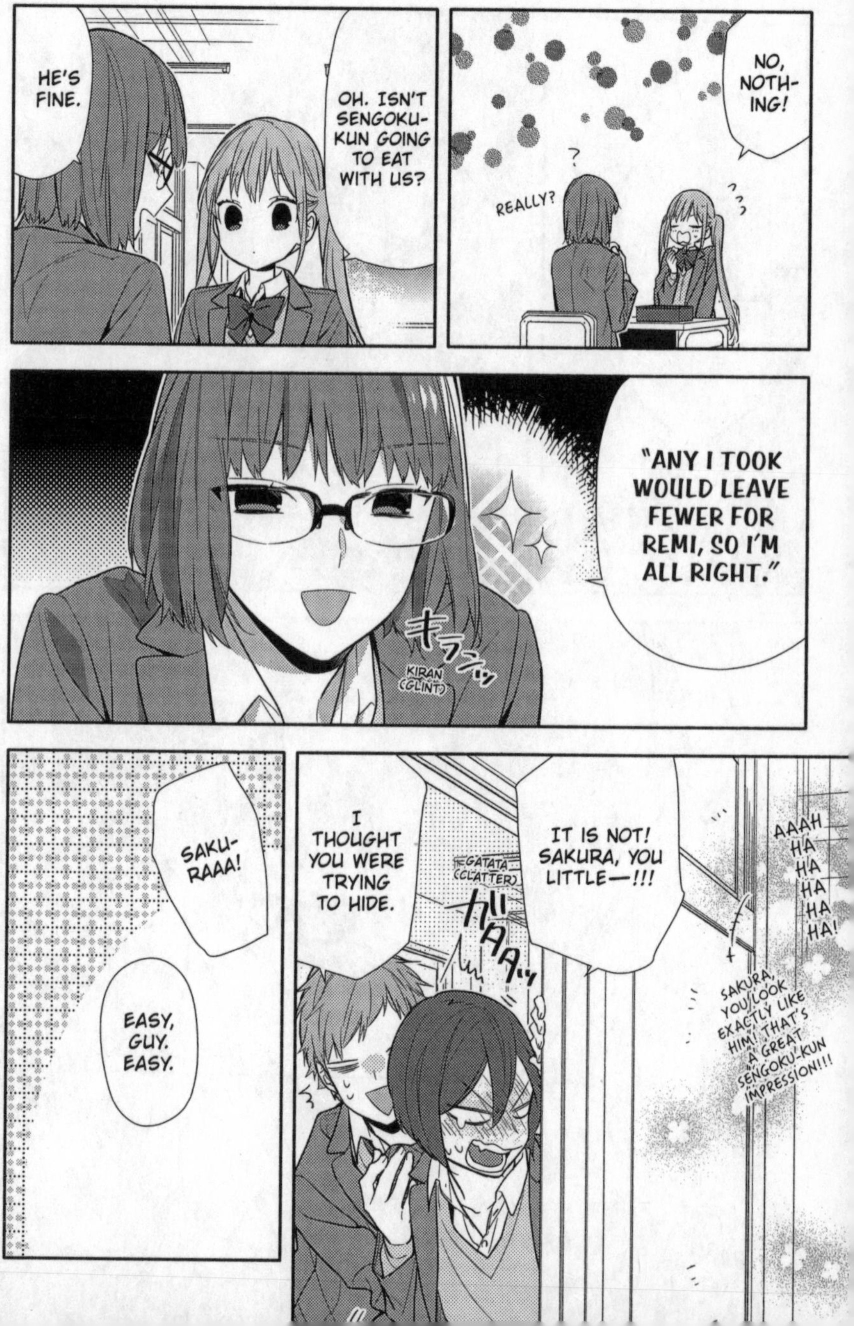
NO, NOTHING!
REALLY?
OH. ISN'T SENGOKU-KUN GOING TO EAT WITH US?
HE'S FINE.
"ANY I TOOK WOULD LEAVE FEWER FOR REMI, SO I'M ALL RIGHT."
KIRAN (GLINT)
AAAH HA HA HA HA HA!
SAKURA, YOU LOOK EXACTLY LIKE HIM! THAT'S A GREAT SENGOKU-KUN IMPRESSION!!!
IT IS NOT! SAKURA, YOU LITTLE—!!!
GATATA (CLATTER)
I THOUGHT YOU WERE TRYING TO HIDE.
SAKU-RAAA!
EASY, GUY. EASY.

HORIMIYA

HORIMIYA

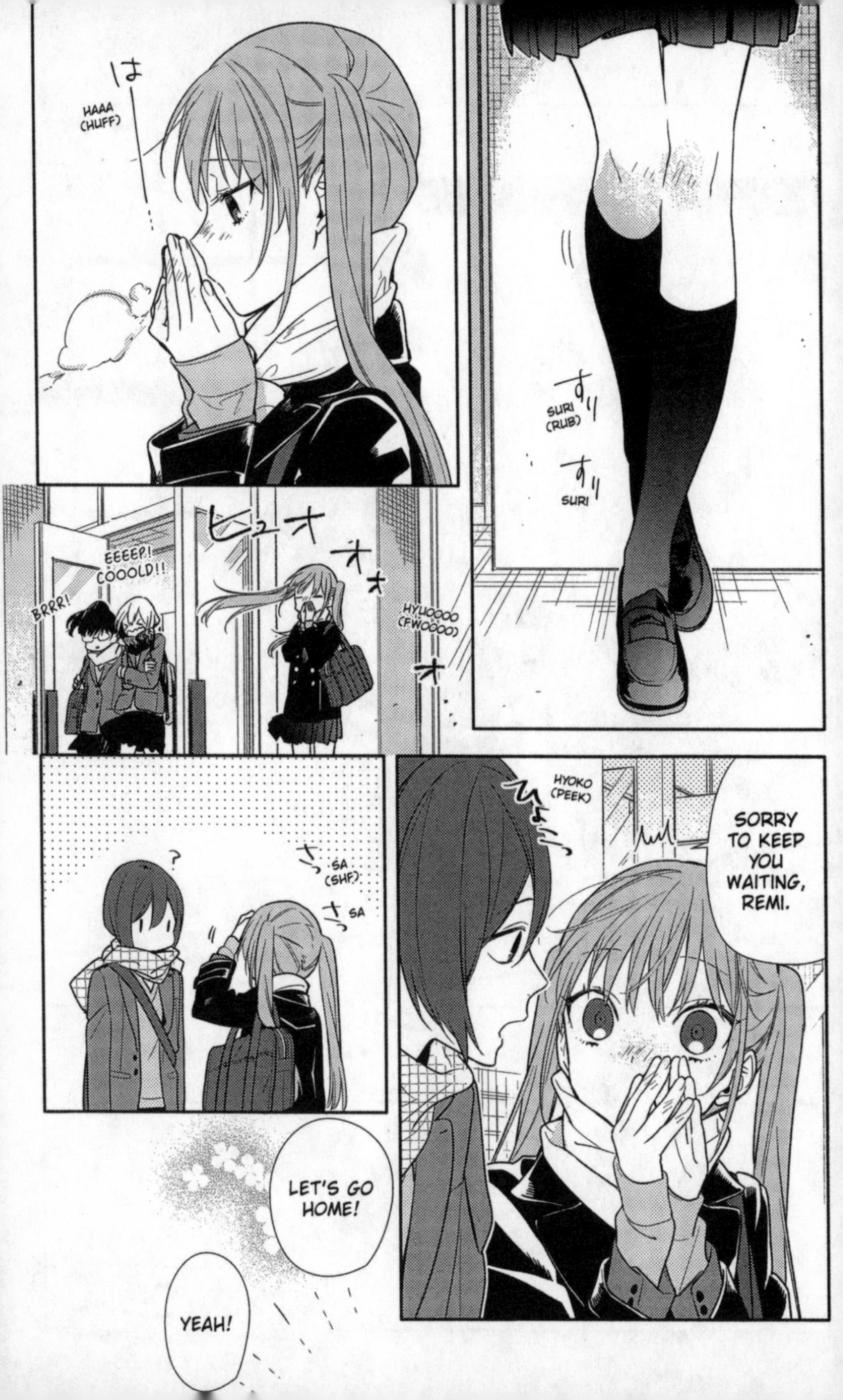
すり
SURI (RUB)
すり
SURI
は
HAAA (HUFF)
ヒュオオオ
EEEEP! COOOLD!!
BRRR!
HYUOOOO (FWOOOO)
ひょこ
HYOKO (PEEK)
SORRY TO KEEP YOU WAITING, REMI.
?
さっ
SA (SHF)
さっ
SA
LET'S GO HOME!
YEAH!

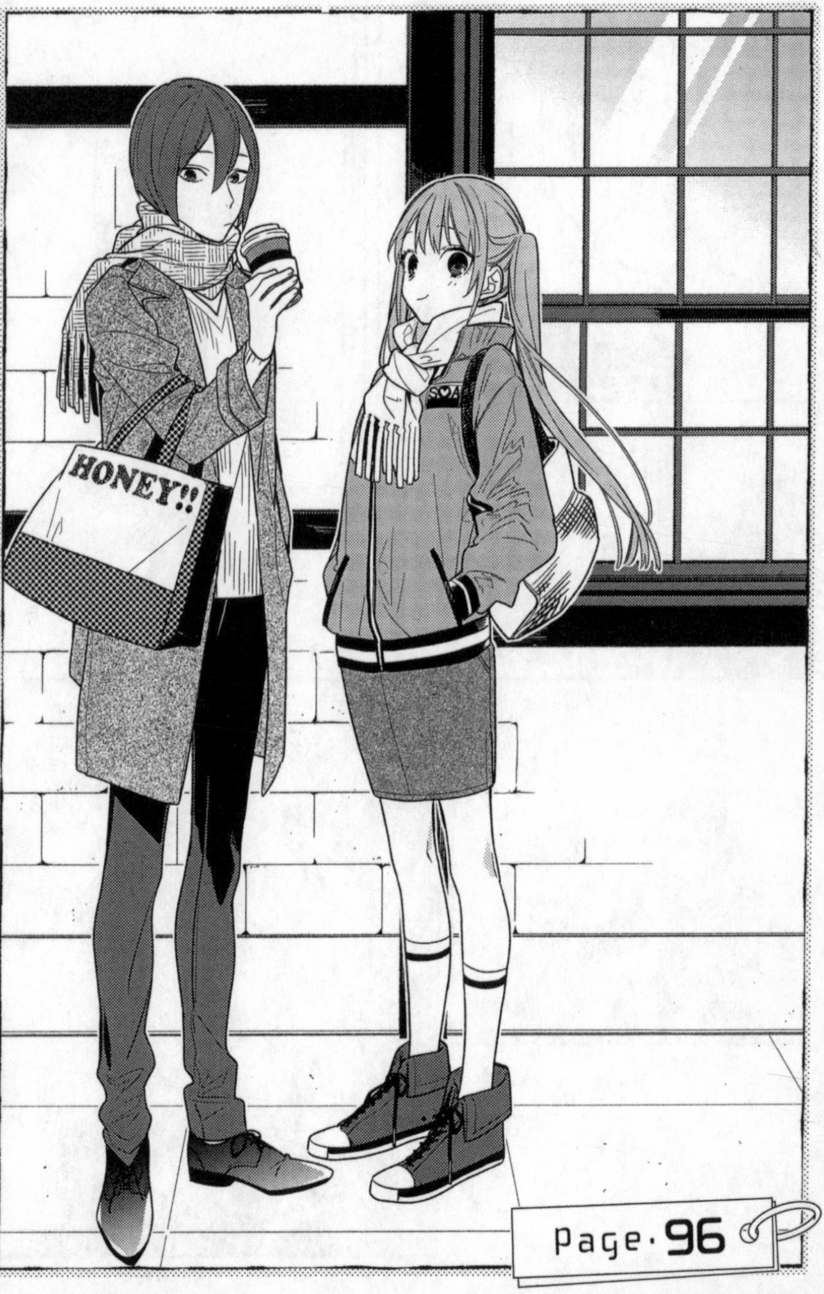
HONEY!!
Page.96

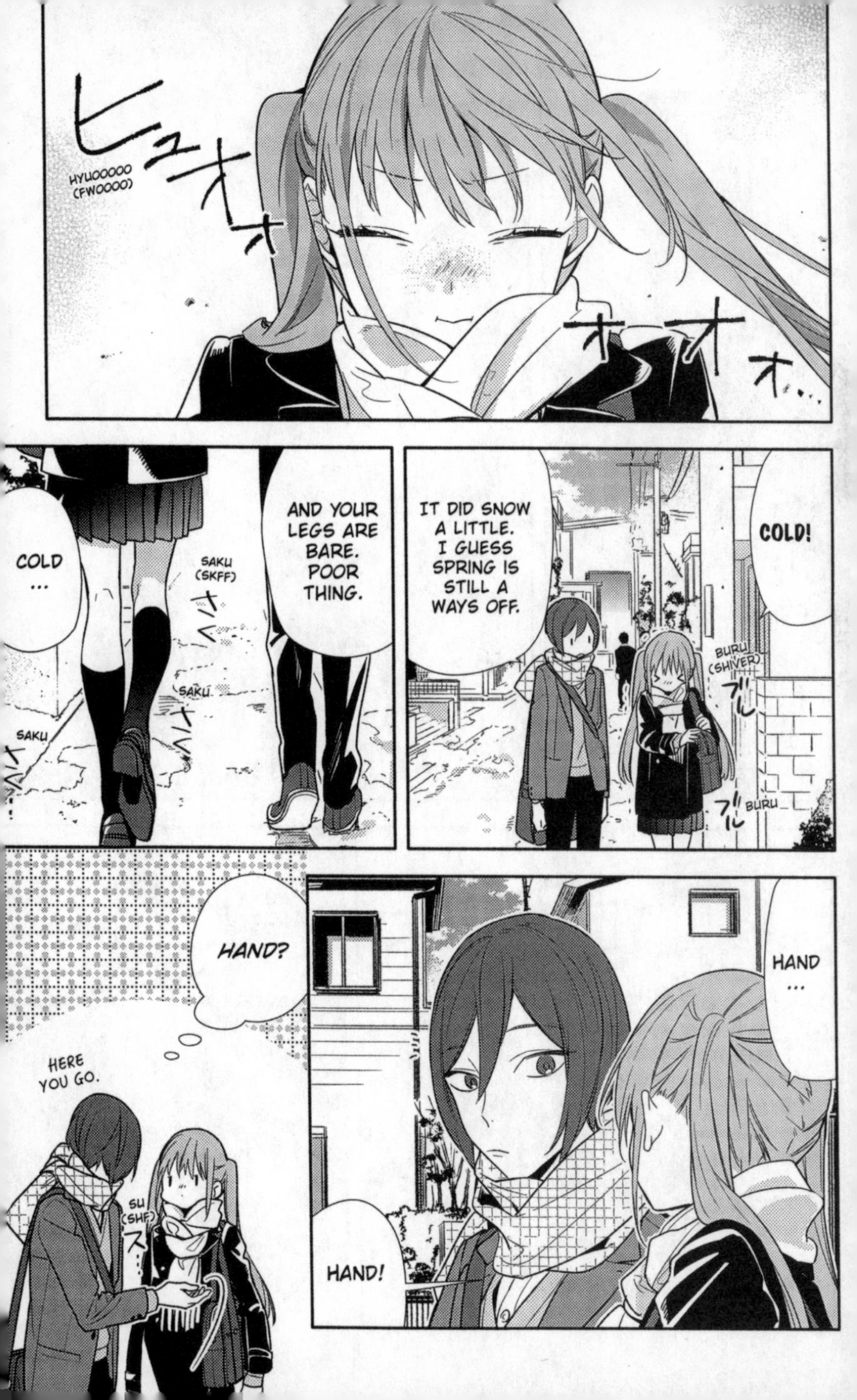
HYUOOOO (FWOOOO)
COLD!
BURU (SHIVER)
BURU
IT DID SNOW A LITTLE. I GUESS SPRING IS STILL A WAYS OFF.
AND YOUR LEGS ARE BARE. POOR THING.
SAKU (SKFF)
SAKU
COLD...
SAKU
HAND...
HAND?
HAND!
HERE YOU GO.
SU (SHF)

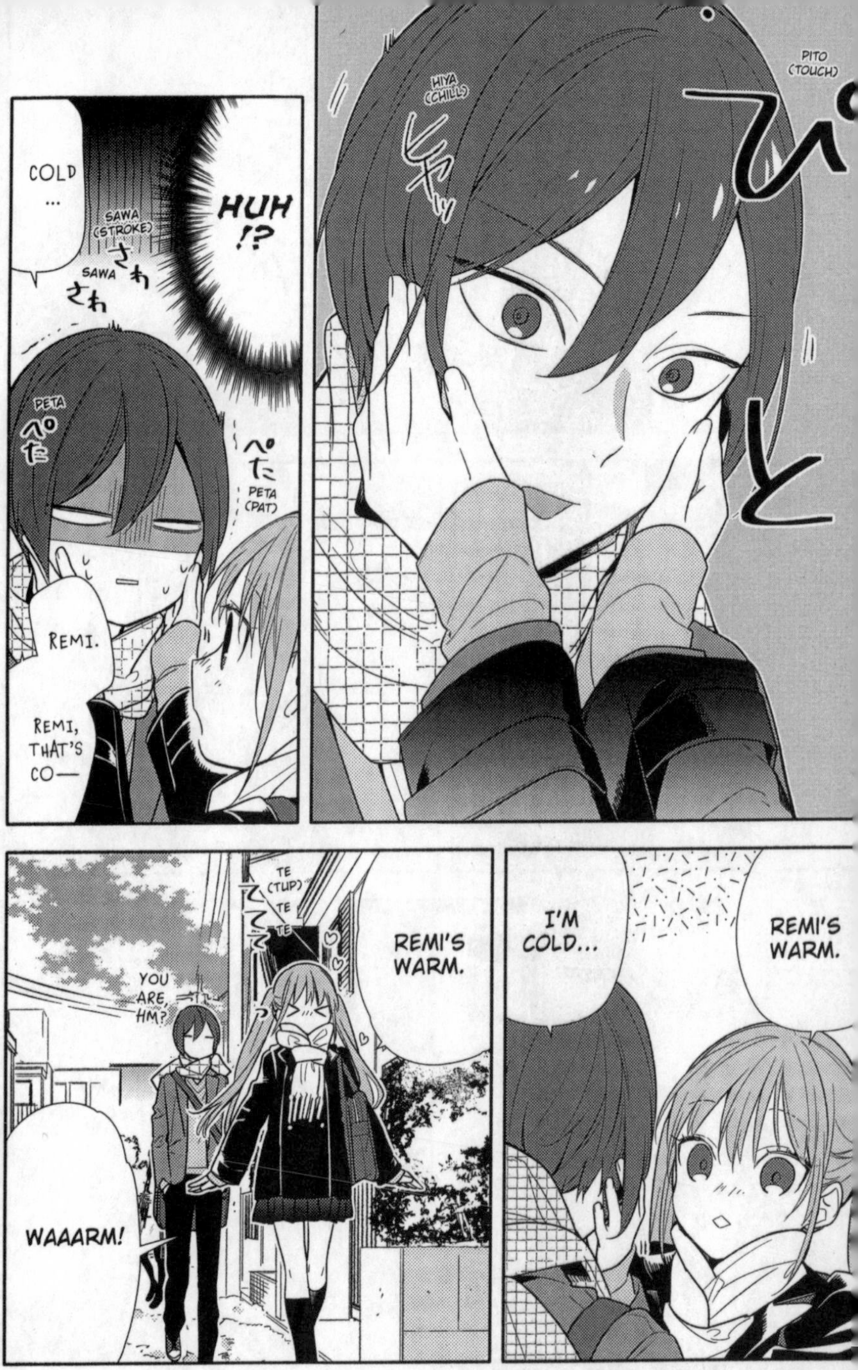
PITO (TOUCH)
ぴと
HIYA (CHILL)
ひやッ
HUH !?
COLD ...
SAWA (STROKE)
さわ
SAWA
さわ
PETA
ぺた
ぺた
PETA (PAT)
REMI.
REMI, THAT'S CO—
REMI'S WARM.
I'M COLD...
REMI'S WARM.
TE (TUP) TE TE
てててー
YOU ARE, HM?
WAAARM!

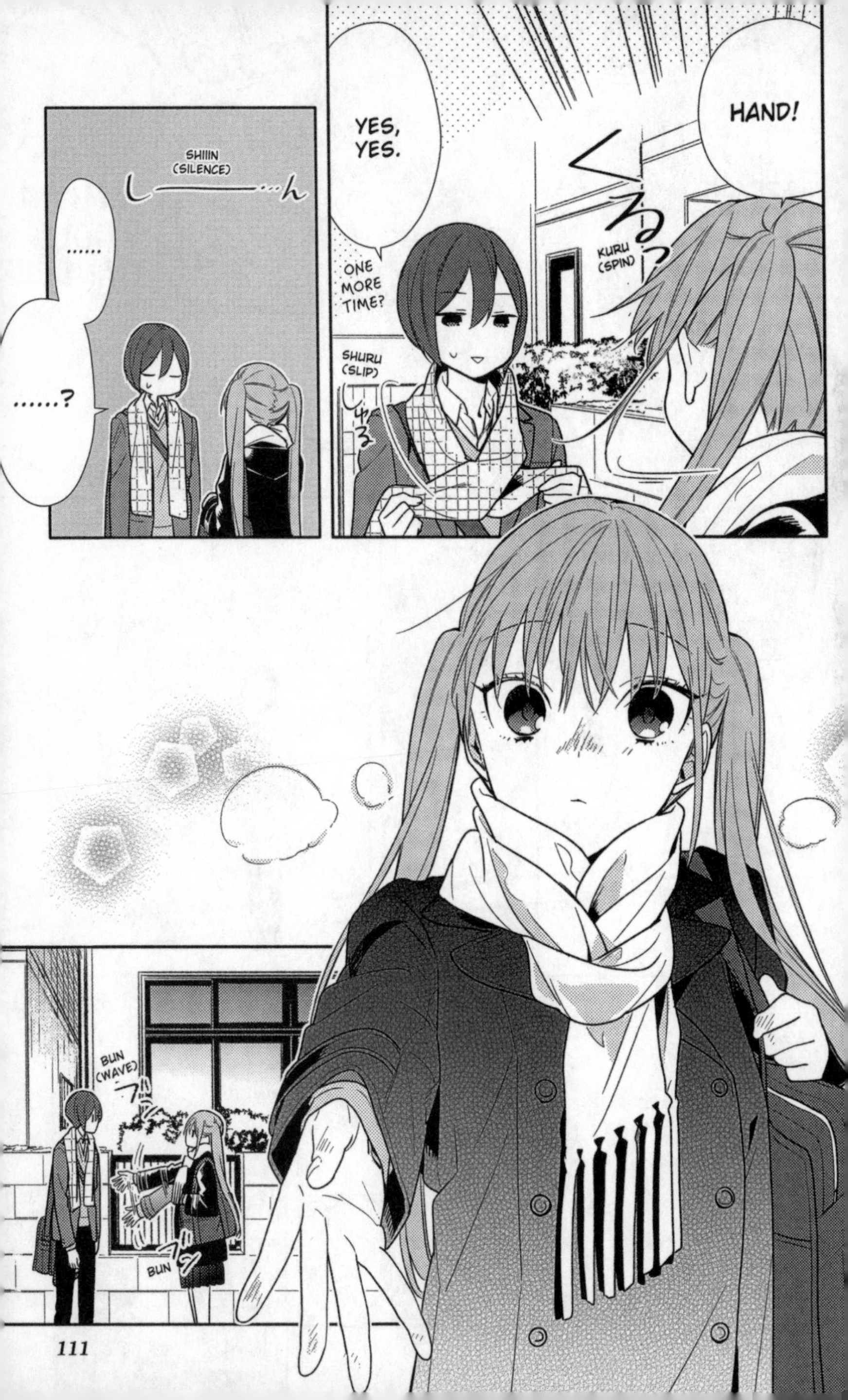

HAND!
KURU (SPIN)
YES, YES.
ONE MORE TIME?
SHURU (SLIP)
SHIIN (SILENCE)
......
......?
BUN (WAVE)
BUN

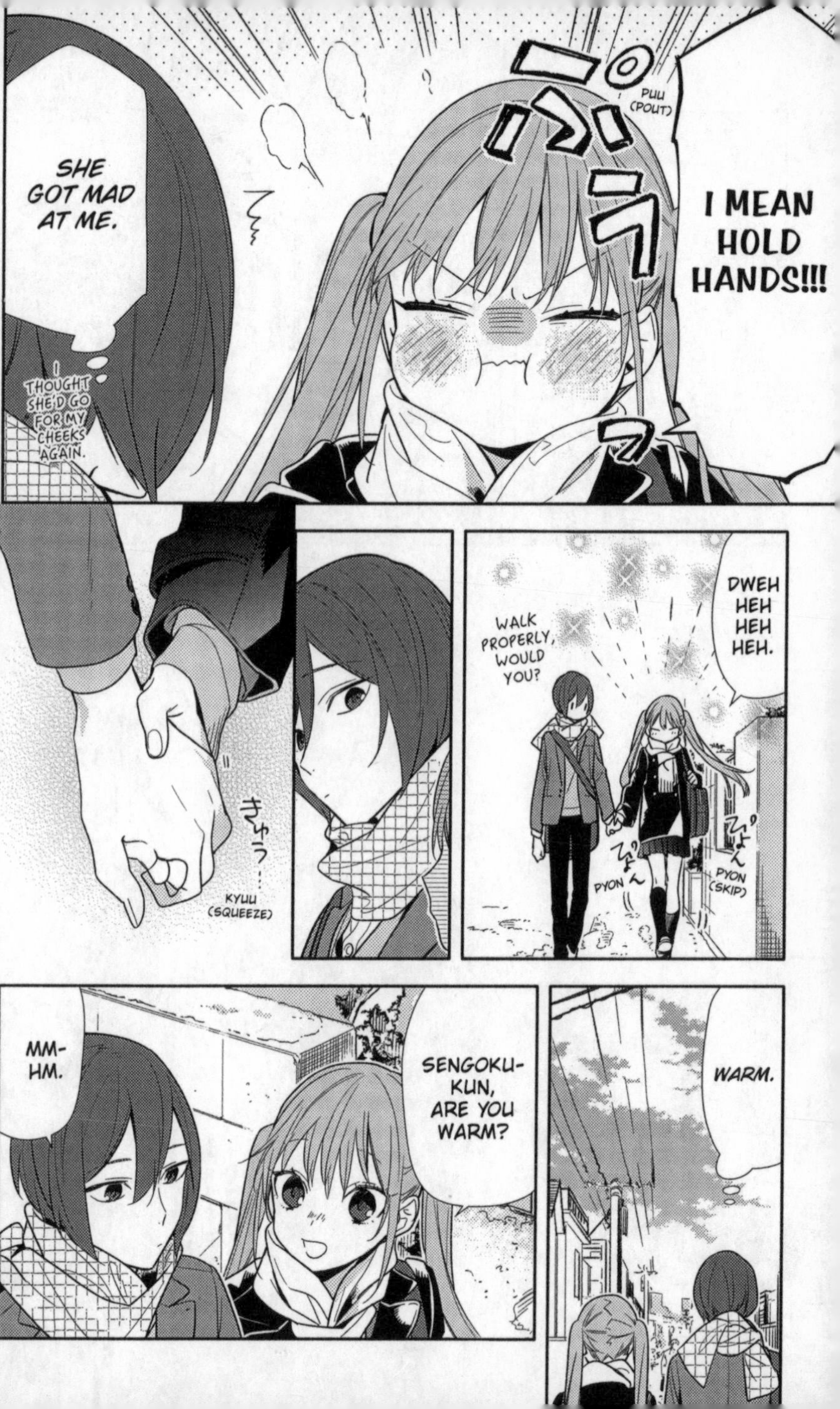
I MEAN HOLD HANDS!!!
PUU (POUT)
SHE GOT MAD AT ME.
I THOUGHT SHE'D GO FOR MY CHEEKS AGAIN.
DWEH HEH HEH HEH.
WALK PROPERLY, WOULD YOU?
PYON (SKIP)
PYON
KYUU (SQUEEZE)
WARM.
SENGOKU-KUN, ARE YOU WARM?
MM-HM.

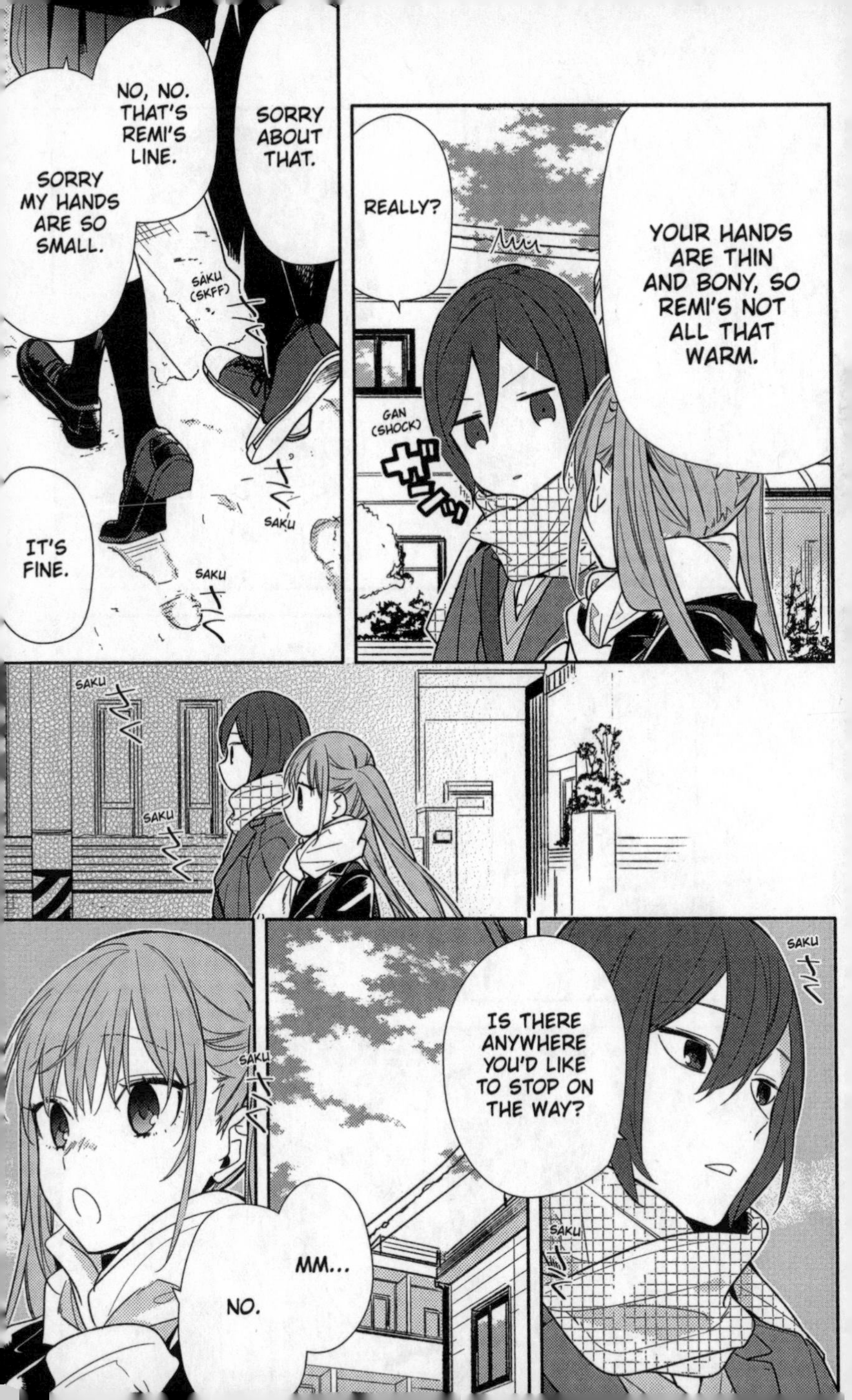
YOUR HANDS ARE THIN AND BONY, SO REMI'S NOT ALL THAT WARM.
REALLY?
GAN (SHOCK)
SORRY ABOUT THAT.
NO, NO. THAT'S REMI'S LINE.
SORRY MY HANDS ARE SO SMALL.
SAKU (SKFF)
SAKU
SAKU
IT'S FINE.
SAKU
SAKU
SAKU
IS THERE ANYWHERE YOU'D LIKE TO STOP ON THE WAY?
SAKU
SAKU
MM...
NO.

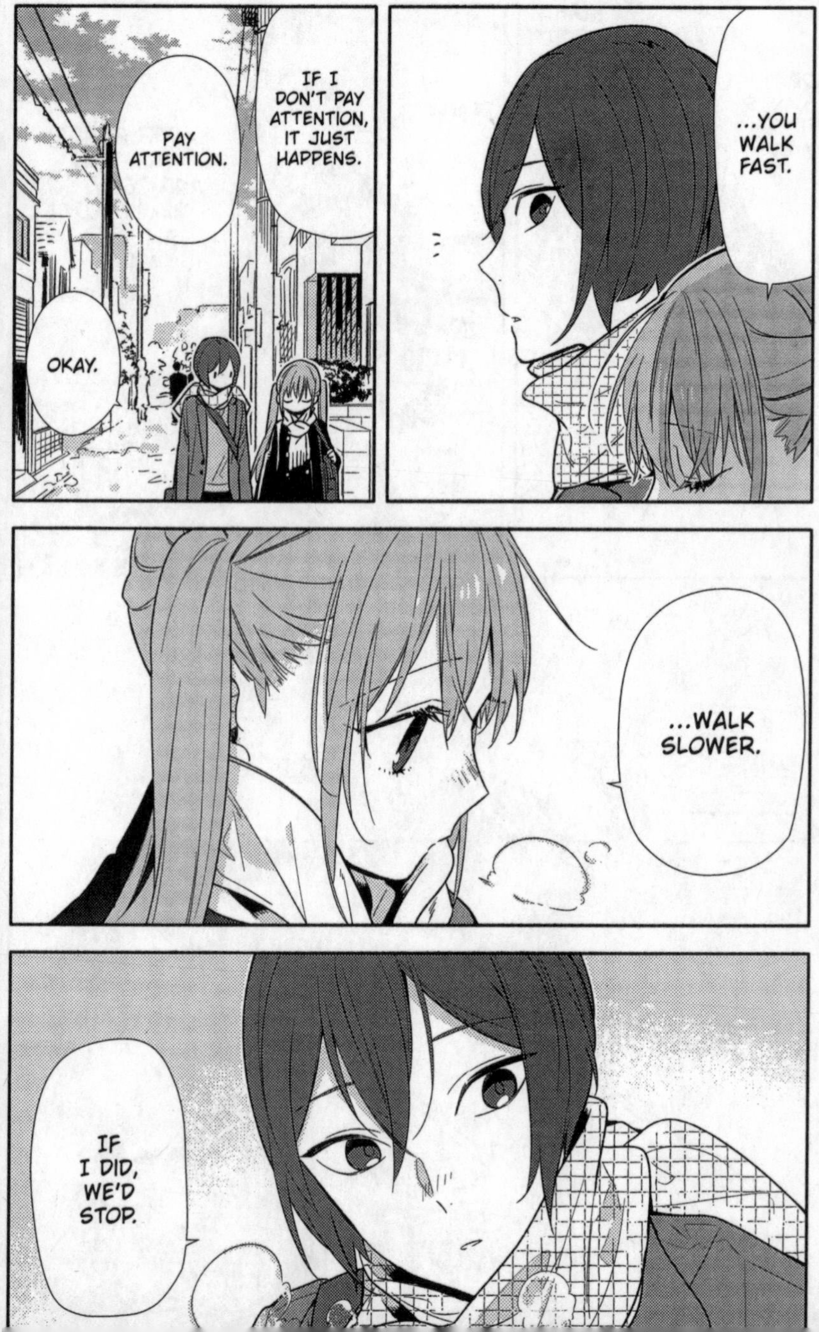
...YOU WALK FAST.
IF I DON'T PAY ATTENTION, IT JUST HAPPENS.
PAY ATTENTION.
OKAY.
...WALK SLOWER.
IF I DID, WE'D STOP.

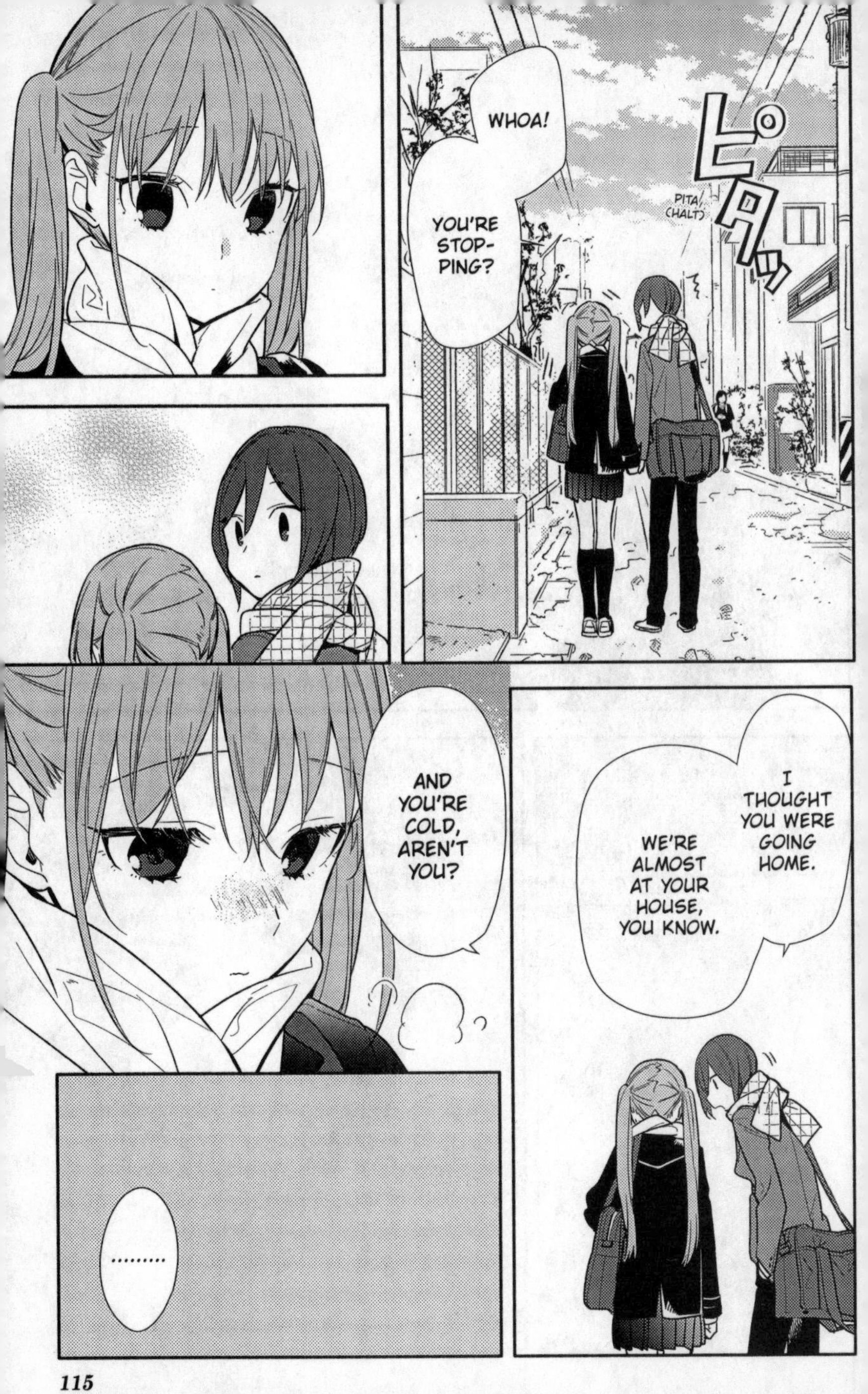
WHOA!
YOU'RE STOP-PING?
ピタッ
PITA (HALT)
I THOUGHT YOU WERE GOING HOME.
WE'RE ALMOST AT YOUR HOUSE, YOU KNOW.
AND YOU'RE COLD, AREN'T YOU?
....

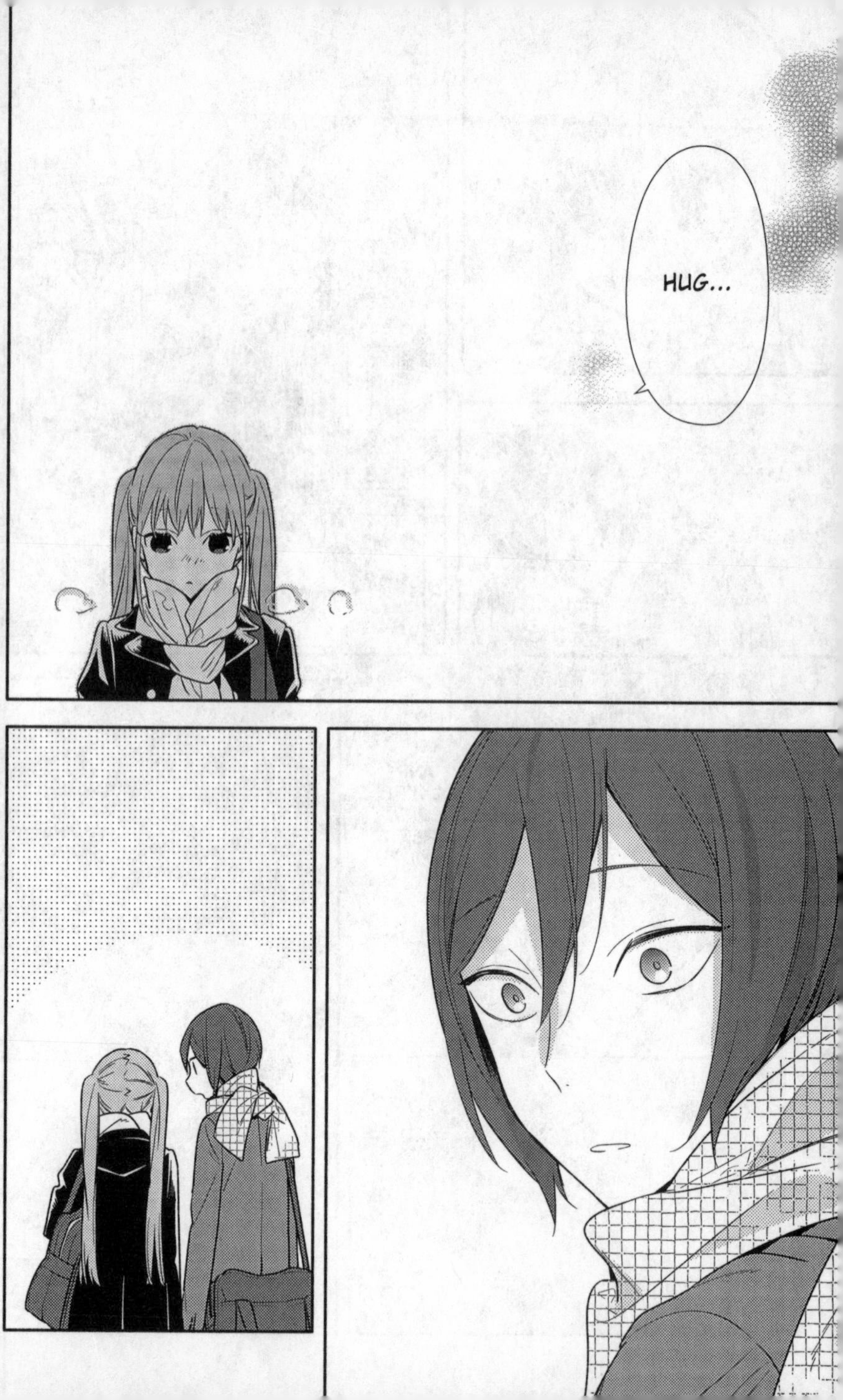
HUG...

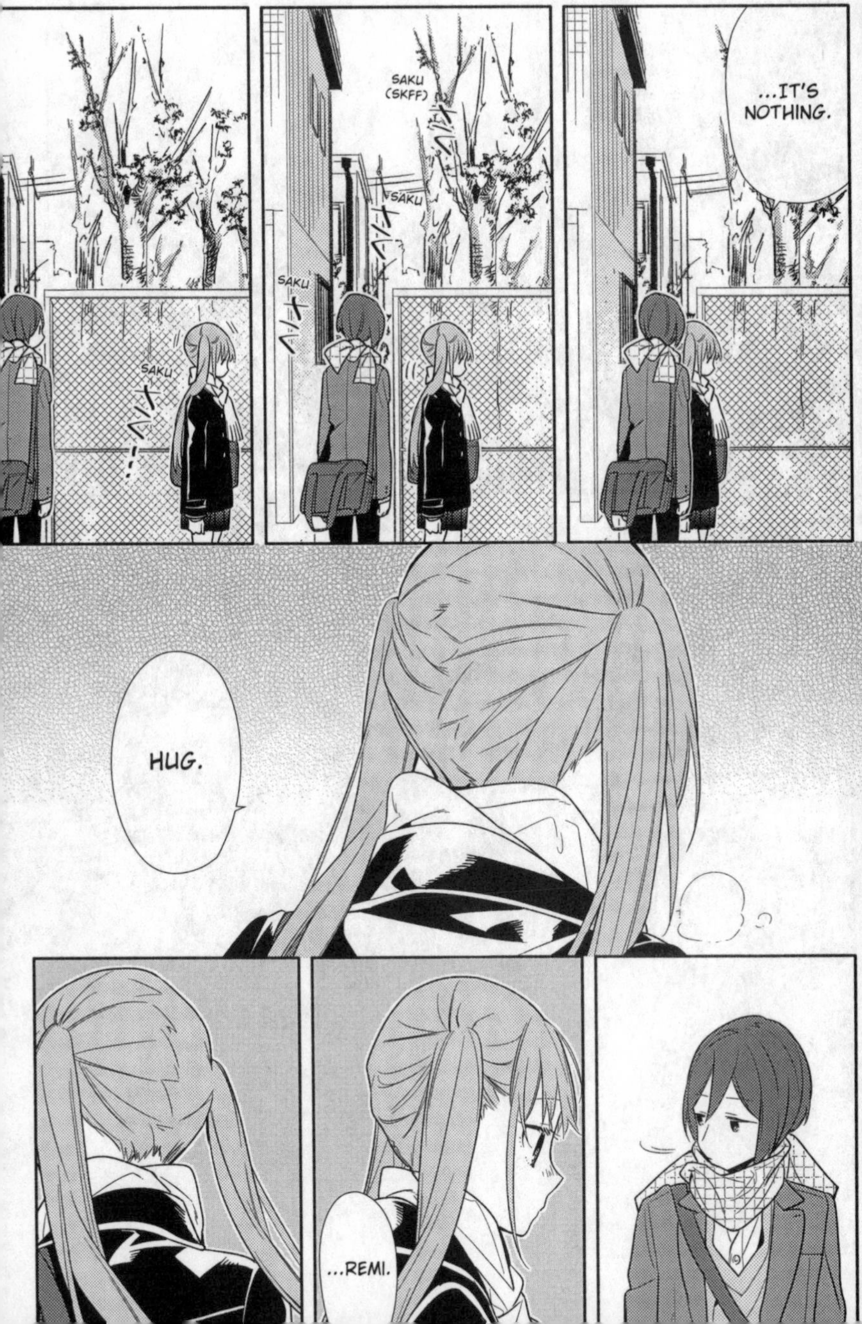
...IT'S NOTHING.
SAKU (SKFF)
SAKU
SAKU
SAKU
HUG.
...REMI.

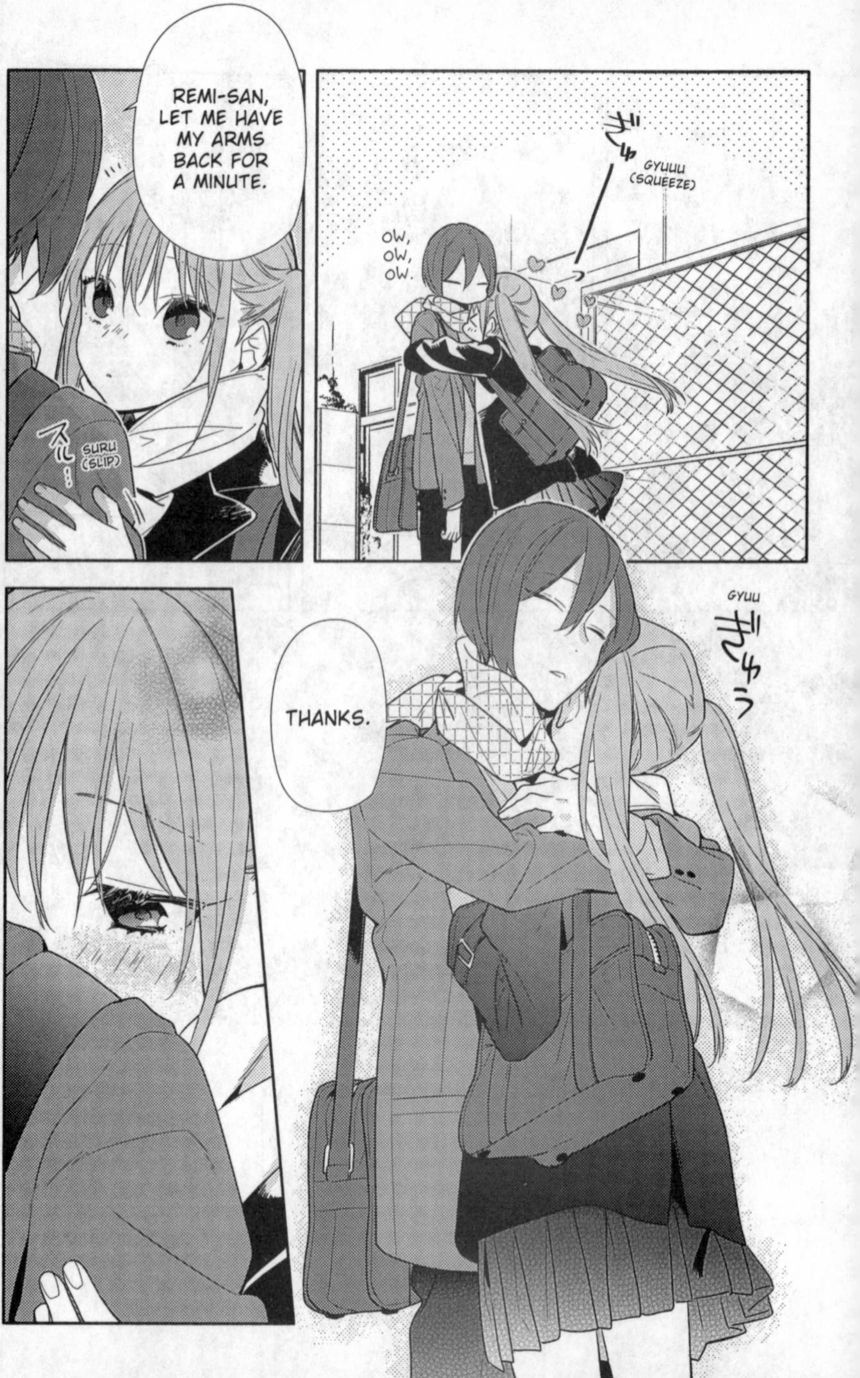
ぎゅー
GYUUU (SQUEEZE)
OW, OW, OW.
REMI-SAN, LET ME HAVE MY ARMS BACK FOR A MINUTE.
スル…
SURU (SLIP)
GYUU
ぎゅう
THANKS.

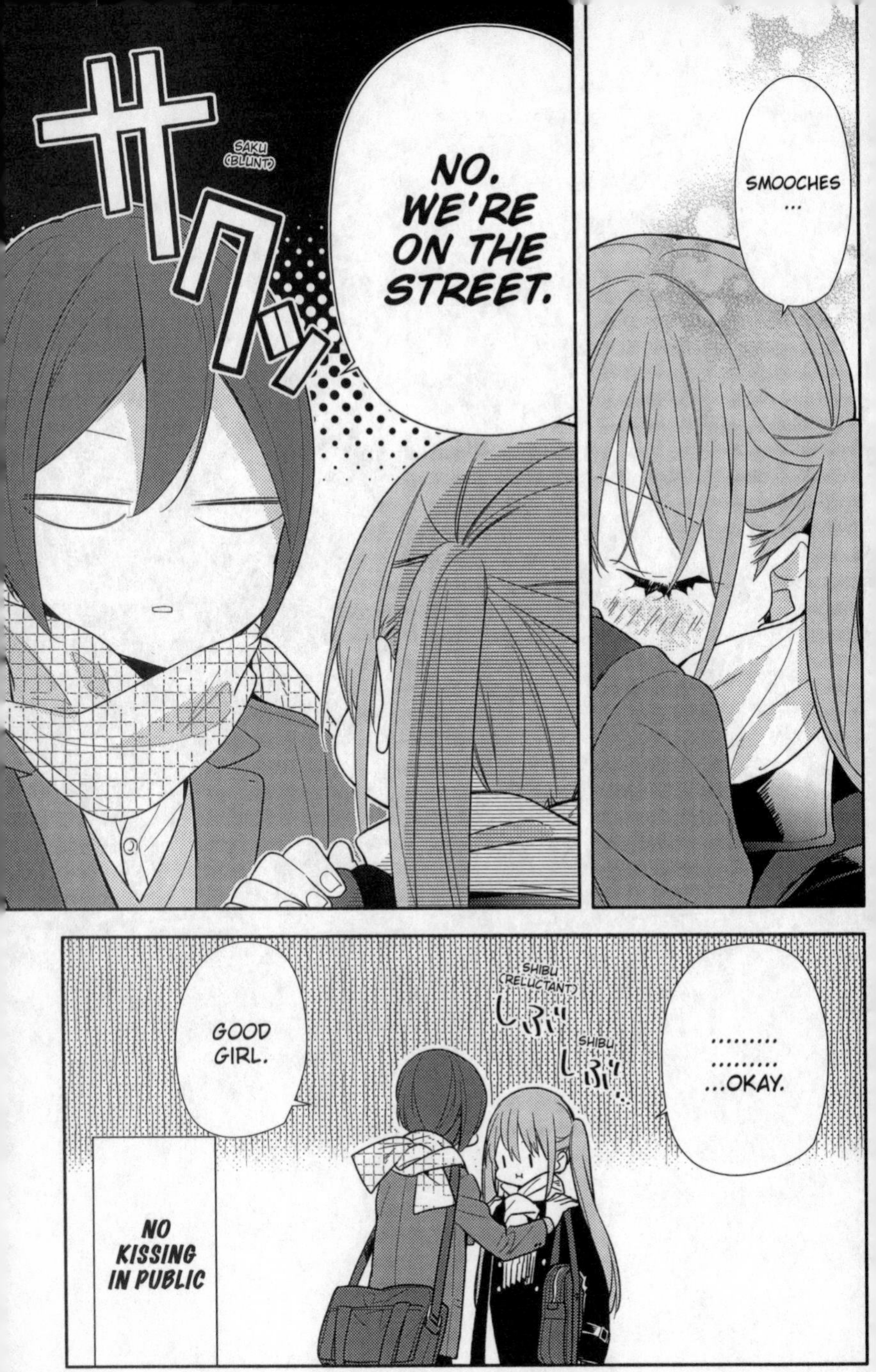
SMOOCHES ...
NO. WE'RE ON THE STREET.
SAKU (BLUNT)
....
....
...OKAY.
SHIBU (RELUCTANT)
SHIBU
GOOD GIRL.
NO KISSING IN PUBLIC

HORIMIYA

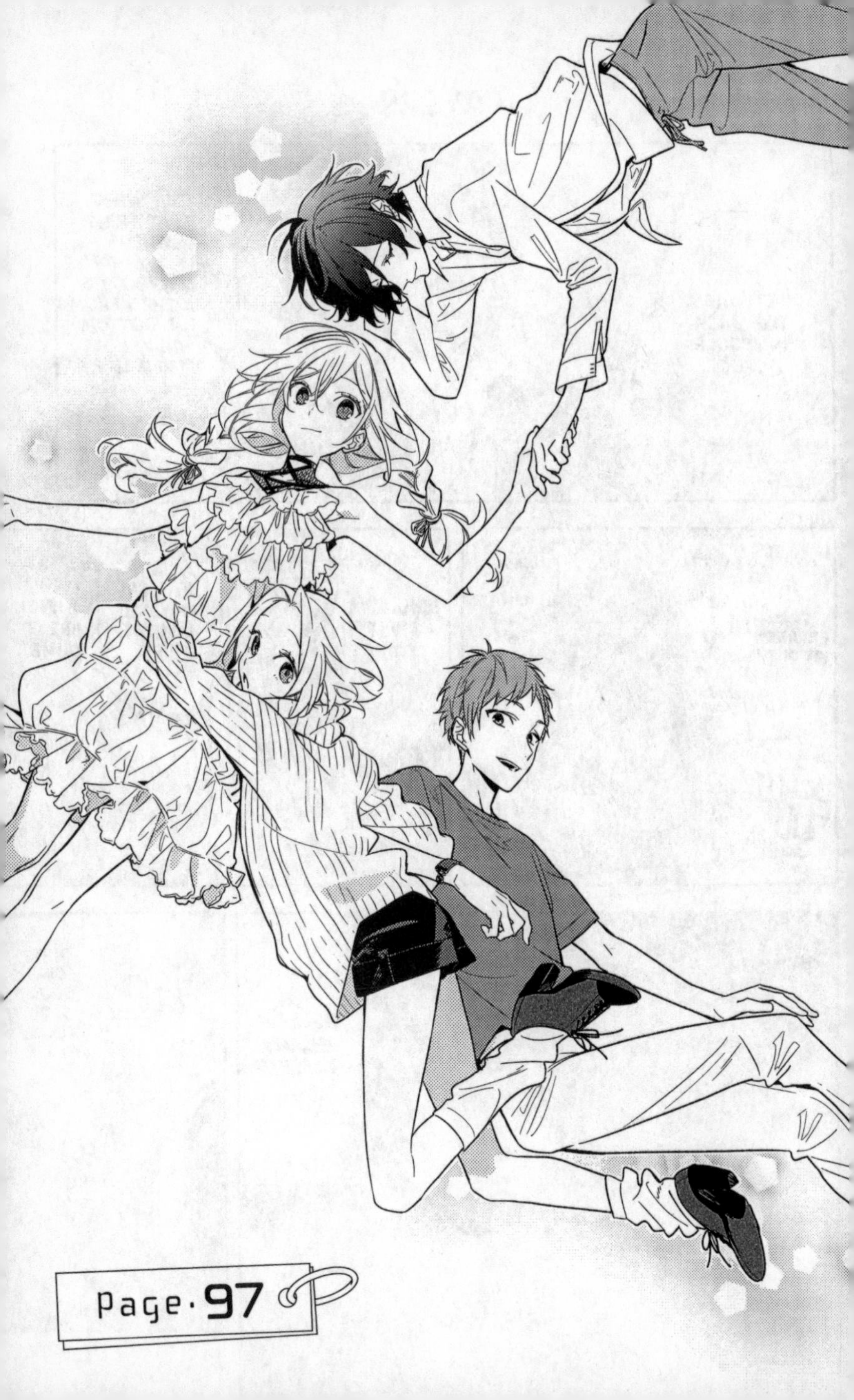

page·97

LAYERS

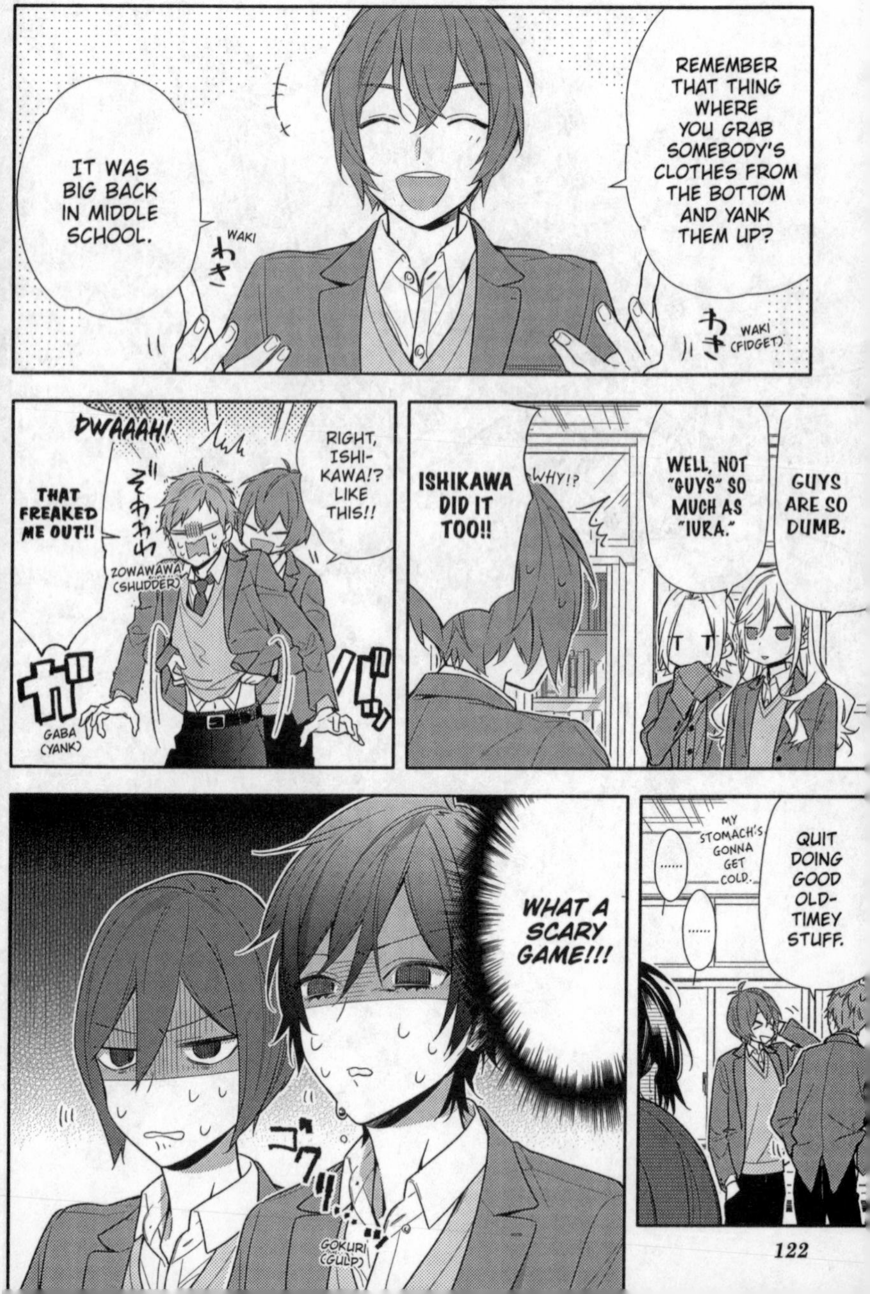

REMEMBER THAT THING WHERE YOU GRAB SOMEBODY'S CLOTHES FROM THE BOTTOM AND YANK THEM UP?
WAKI (FIDGET)
IT WAS BIG BACK IN MIDDLE SCHOOL.
WAKI
GUYS ARE SO DUMB.
WELL, NOT "GUYS" SO MUCH AS "IURA."
WHY!?
ISHIKAWA DID IT TOO!!
RIGHT, ISHIKAWA!? LIKE THIS!!
DWAAAH!
THAT FREAKED ME OUT!!
ZOWAWAWA! (SHUDDER)
GABA (YANK)
QUIT DOING GOOD OLD-TIMEY STUFF.
MY STOMACH'S GONNA GET COLD.
......
......
WHAT A SCARY GAME!!!
GOKURI (GULP)

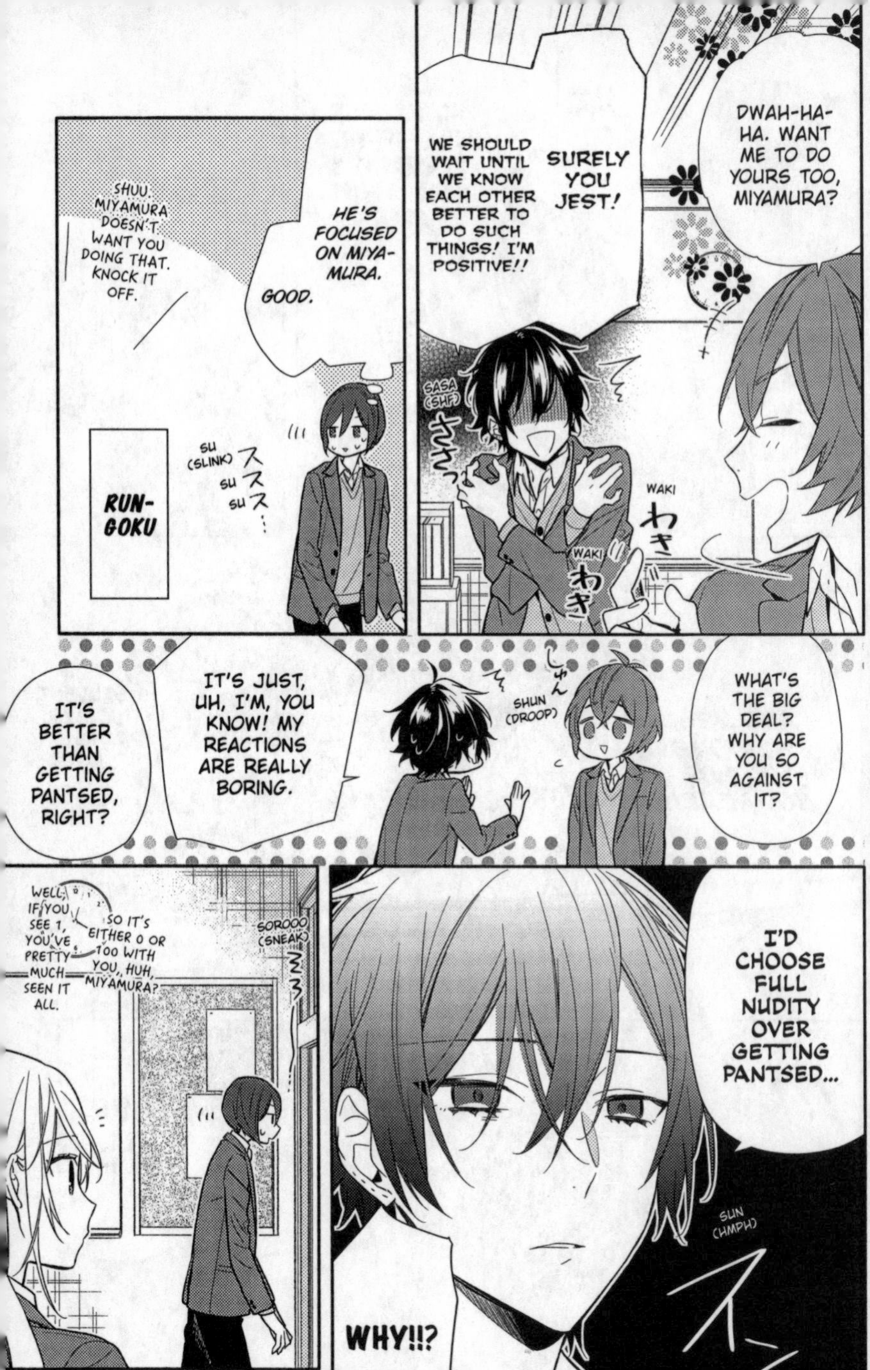
DWAH-HA-HA. WANT ME TO DO YOURS TOO, MIYAMURA?
SURELY YOU JEST!
WE SHOULD WAIT UNTIL WE KNOW EACH OTHER BETTER TO DO SUCH THINGS! I'M POSITIVE!!
SASA (SHF)
ささっ
WAKI
わき
WAKI
わき
HE'S FOCUSED ON MIYA-MURA.
GOOD.
SHUU. MIYAMURA DOESN'T WANT YOU DOING THAT. KNOCK IT OFF.
SU (SLINK)
SU
SU
RUN-GOKU
WHAT'S THE BIG DEAL? WHY ARE YOU SO AGAINST IT?
SHUN (DROOP)
しゅん
IT'S JUST, UH, I'M, YOU KNOW! MY REACTIONS ARE REALLY BORING.
IT'S BETTER THAN GETTING PANTSED, RIGHT?
I'D CHOOSE FULL NUDITY OVER GETTING PANTSED...
SUN (HMPH)
WHY!!?
SOROOO (SNEAK)
SO IT'S EITHER 0 OR 100 WITH YOU, HUH, MIYAMURA?
WELL, IF YOU SEE 1, YOU'VE PRETTY MUCH SEEN IT ALL.

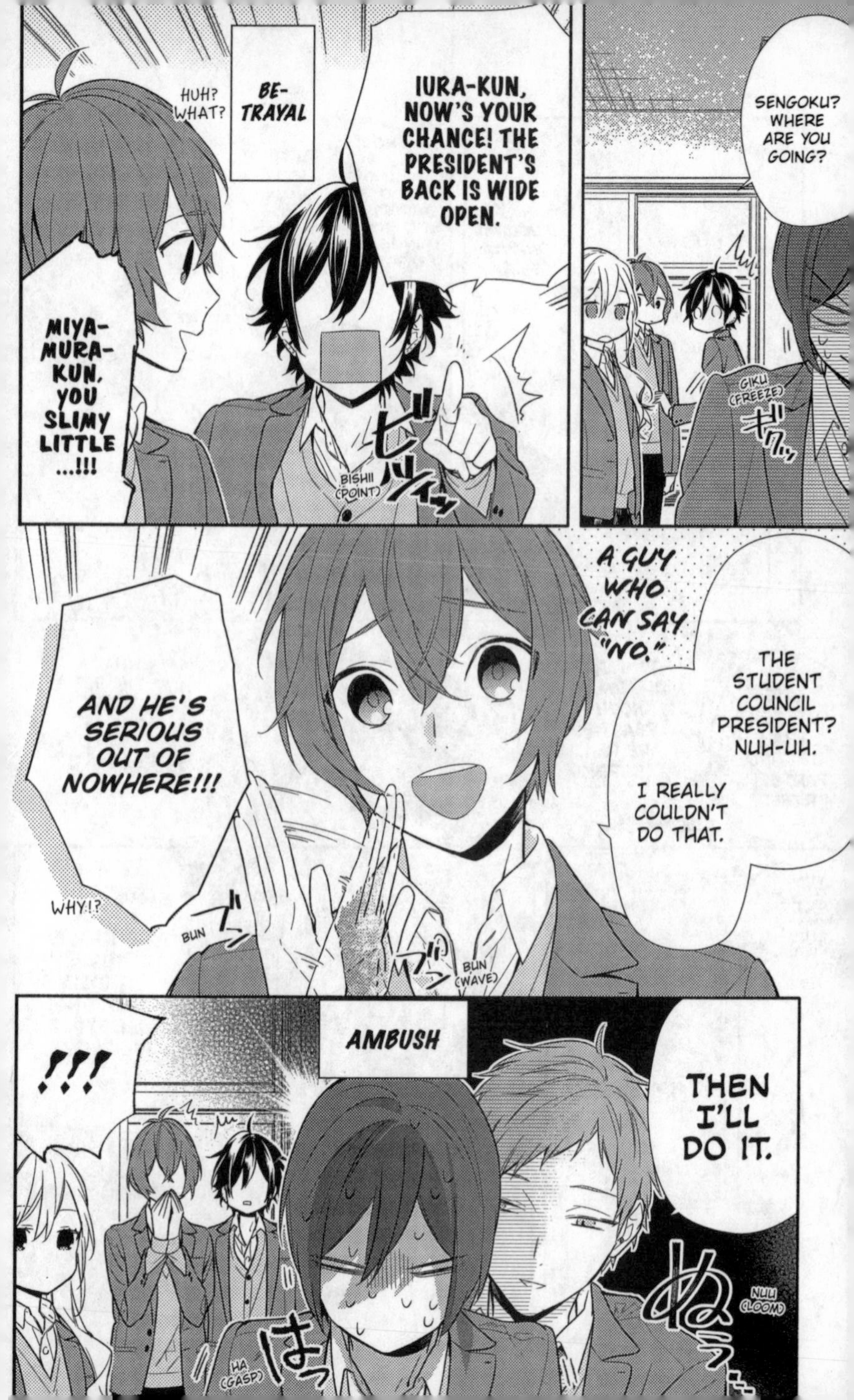
SENGOKU? WHERE ARE YOU GOING?
GIKU (FREEZE)
IURA-KUN, NOW'S YOUR CHANCE! THE PRESIDENT'S BACK IS WIDE OPEN.
BE-TRAYAL
HUH? WHAT?
MIYAMURA-KUN, YOU SLIMY LITTLE ...!!!
BISHII (POINT)
THE STUDENT COUNCIL PRESIDENT? NUH-UH.
I REALLY COULDN'T DO THAT.
A GUY WHO CAN SAY "NO."
AND HE'S SERIOUS OUT OF NOWHERE!!!
BUN (WAVE)
BUN
WHY!?
THEN I'LL DO IT.
AMBUSH
!!!
NUU (LOOM)
HA (GASP)

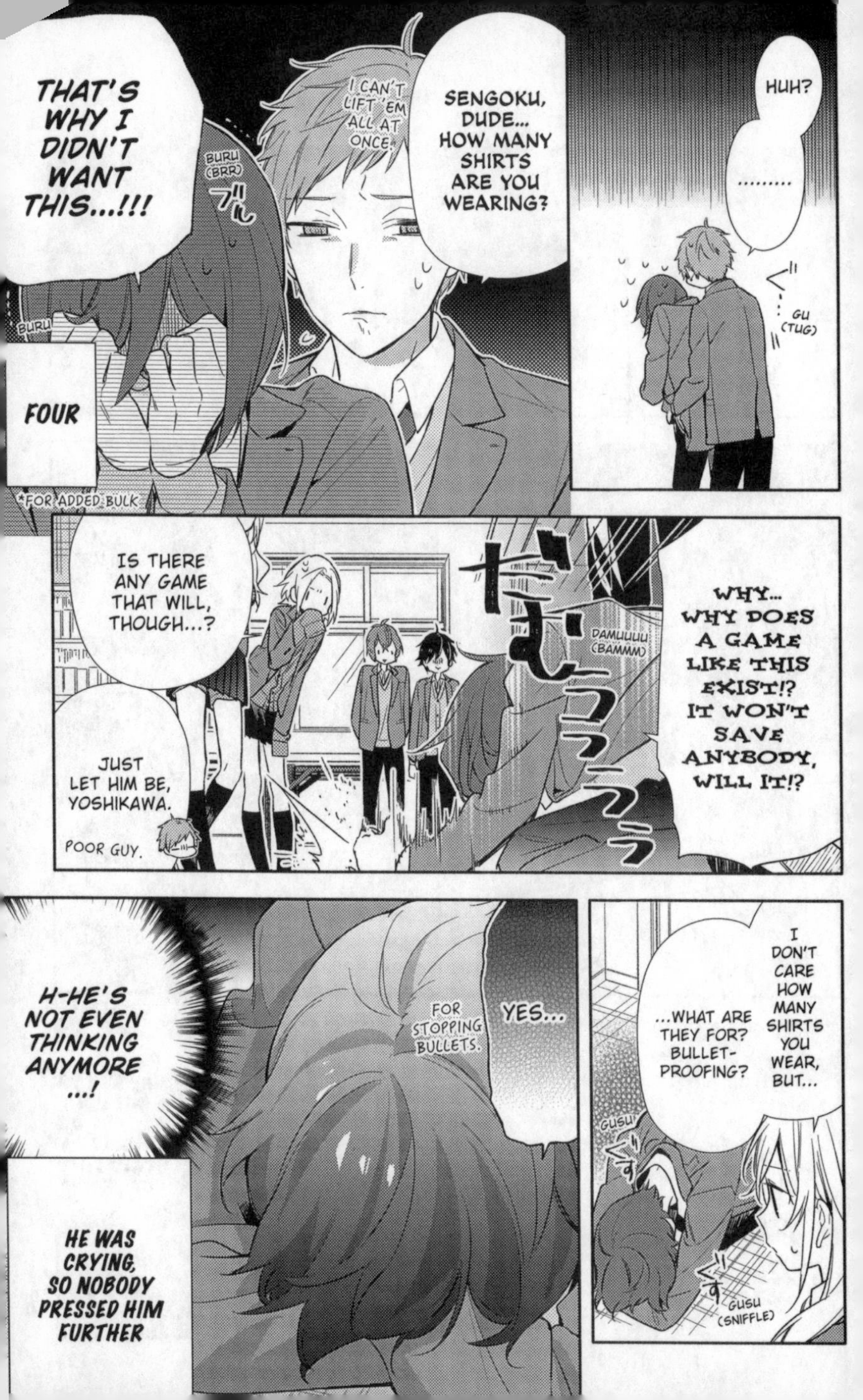
HUH?
....
GU (TUG)
SENGOKU, DUDE... HOW MANY SHIRTS ARE YOU WEARING?
I CAN'T LIFT 'EM ALL AT ONCE.
BURU (BRR)
THAT'S WHY I DIDN'T WANT THIS...!!!
BURU
FOUR
*FOR ADDED BULK
WHY... WHY DOES A GAME LIKE THIS EXIST!? IT WON'T SAVE ANYBODY, WILL IT!?
DAMUUUU (BAMMM)
IS THERE ANY GAME THAT WILL, THOUGH...?
JUST LET HIM BE, YOSHIKAWA.
POOR GUY.
I DON'T CARE HOW MANY SHIRTS YOU WEAR, BUT...
...WHAT ARE THEY FOR? BULLET-PROOFING?
GUSU
GUSU (SNIFFLE)
YES...
FOR STOPPING BULLETS.
H-HE'S NOT EVEN THINKING ANYMORE ...!
HE WAS CRYING, SO NOBODY PRESSED HIM FURTHER

TEST OF COURAGE

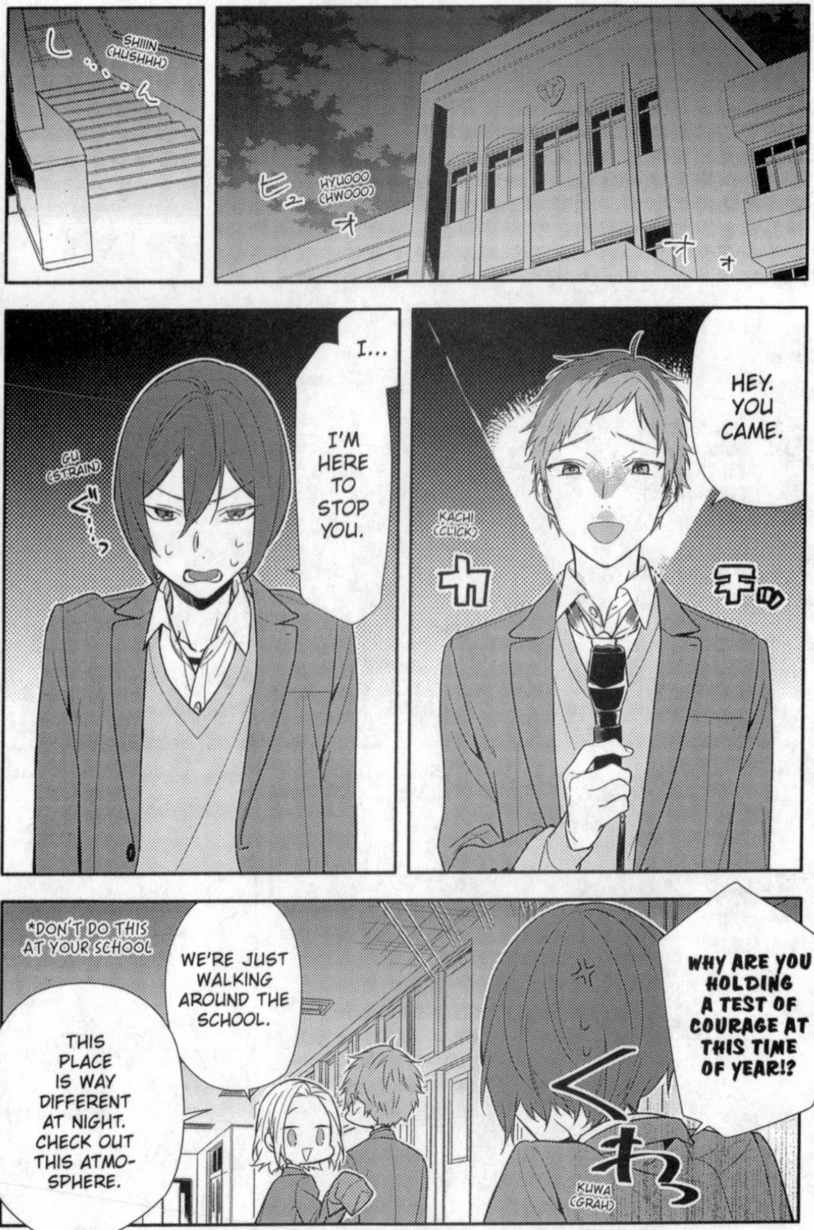
HYUOOO (HWOOO)
SHIIN (HUSHHH)
HEY. YOU CAME.
KACHI (CLICK)
I...
I'M HERE TO STOP YOU.
GU (STRAIN)
WHY ARE YOU HOLDING A TEST OF COURAGE AT THIS TIME OF YEAR!?
KUWA (GRAH)
WE'RE JUST WALKING AROUND THE SCHOOL.
THIS PLACE IS WAY DIFFERENT AT NIGHT. CHECK OUT THIS ATMO-SPHERE.
*DON'T DO THIS AT YOUR SCHOOL

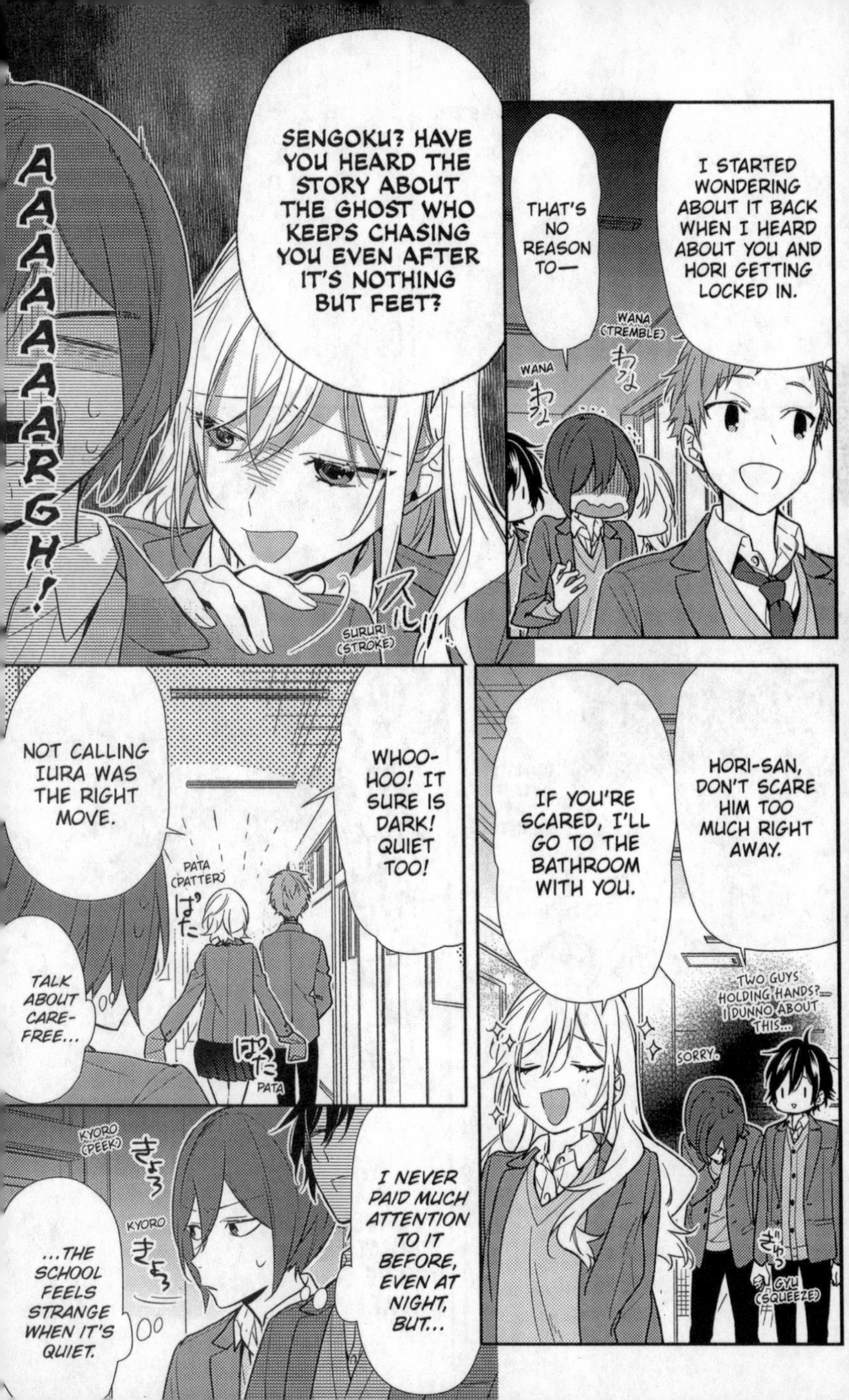
I STARTED WONDERING ABOUT IT BACK WHEN I HEARD ABOUT YOU AND HORI GETTING LOCKED IN.
WANA (TREMBLE)
THAT'S NO REASON TO—
WANA
SENGOKU? HAVE YOU HEARD THE STORY ABOUT THE GHOST WHO KEEPS CHASING YOU EVEN AFTER IT'S NOTHING BUT FEET?
SURURI (STROKE)
AAAAAAARGH!
HORI-SAN, DON'T SCARE HIM TOO MUCH RIGHT AWAY.
IF YOU'RE SCARED, I'LL GO TO THE BATHROOM WITH YOU.
TWO GUYS HOLDING HANDS? I DUNNO ABOUT THIS...
SORRY.
GYU (SQUEEZE)
WHOO-HOO! IT SURE IS DARK! QUIET TOO!
NOT CALLING IURA WAS THE RIGHT MOVE.
PATA (PATTER)
PATA
TALK ABOUT CARE-FREE...
I NEVER PAID MUCH ATTENTION TO IT BEFORE, EVEN AT NIGHT, BUT...
KYORO (PEEK)
KYORO
...THE SCHOOL FEELS STRANGE WHEN IT'S QUIET.

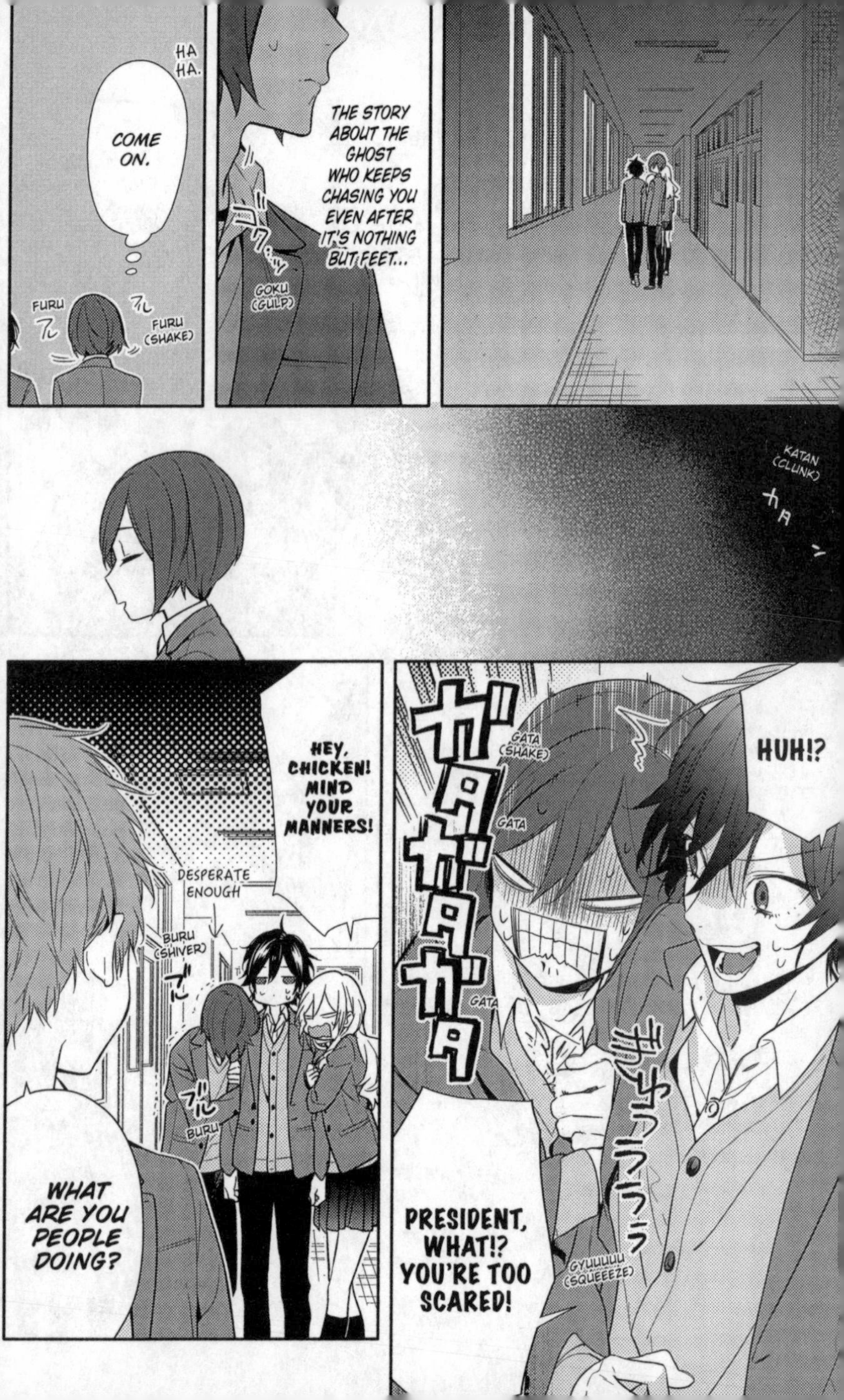
THE STORY ABOUT THE GHOST WHO KEEPS CHASING YOU EVEN AFTER IT'S NOTHING BUT FEET...
GOKU (GULP)
HA HA.
COME ON.
FURU
FURU (SHAKE)
KATAN (CLUNK)
GATA (SHAKE)
GATA
GATA
HUH!?
GYUUUUU (SQUEEEZE)
PRESIDENT, WHAT!? YOU'RE TOO SCARED!
HEY, CHICKEN! MIND YOUR MANNERS!
DESPERATE ENOUGH
BURU (SHIVER)
BURU
WHAT ARE YOU PEOPLE DOING?

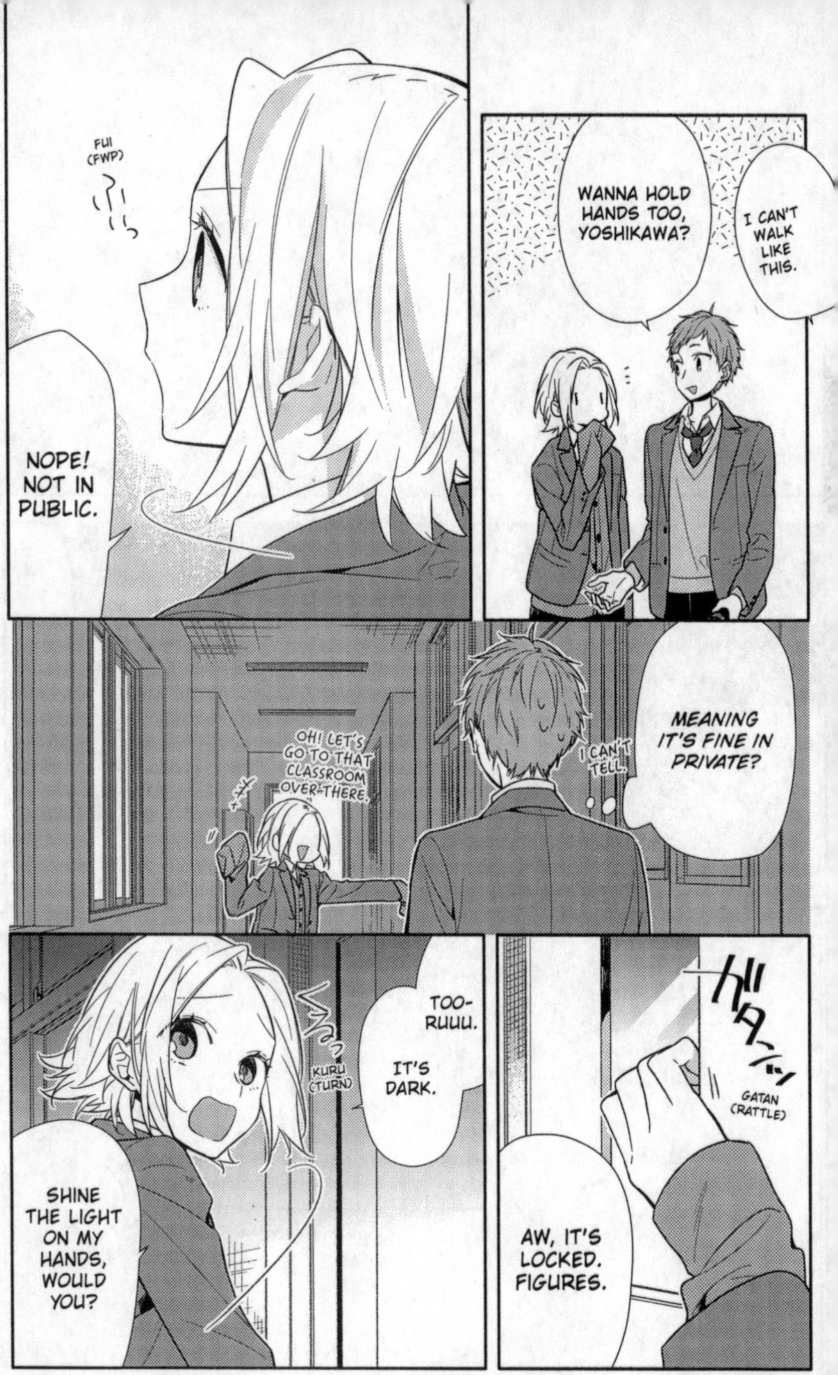
I CAN'T WALK LIKE THIS.
WANNA HOLD HANDS TOO, YOSHIKAWA?
FUI (FWP)
NOPE! NOT IN PUBLIC.
MEANING IT'S FINE IN PRIVATE?
I CAN'T TELL.
OH! LET'S GO TO THAT CLASSROOM OVER THERE.
GATAN (RATTLE)
AW, IT'S LOCKED. FIGURES.
TOO-RUUU.
IT'S DARK.
KURU (TURN)
SHINE THE LIGHT ON MY HANDS, WOULD YOU?

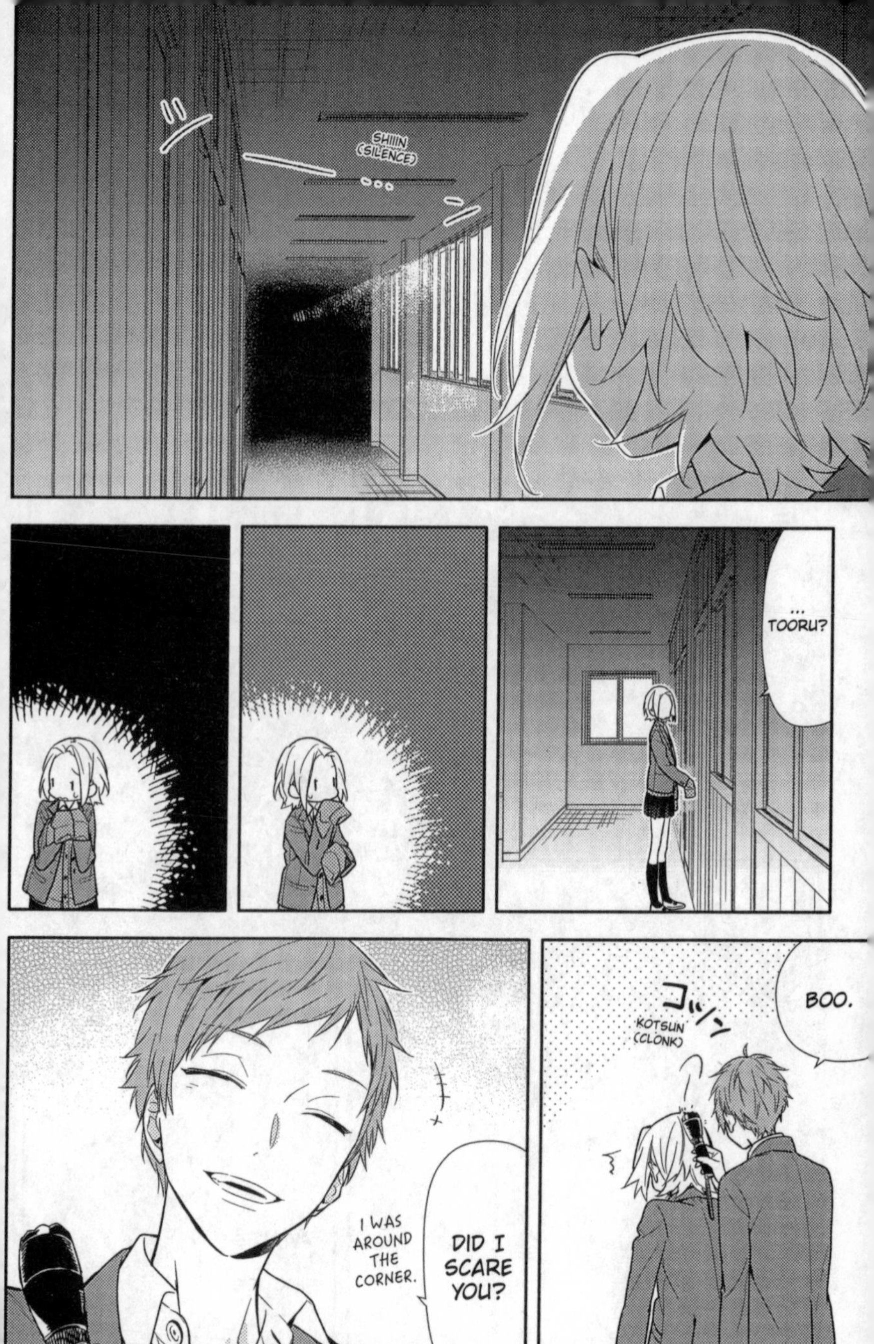
SHIIN (SILENCE)
...TOORU?
BOO.
KOTSUN (CLONK)
DID I SCARE YOU?
I WAS AROUND THE CORNER.

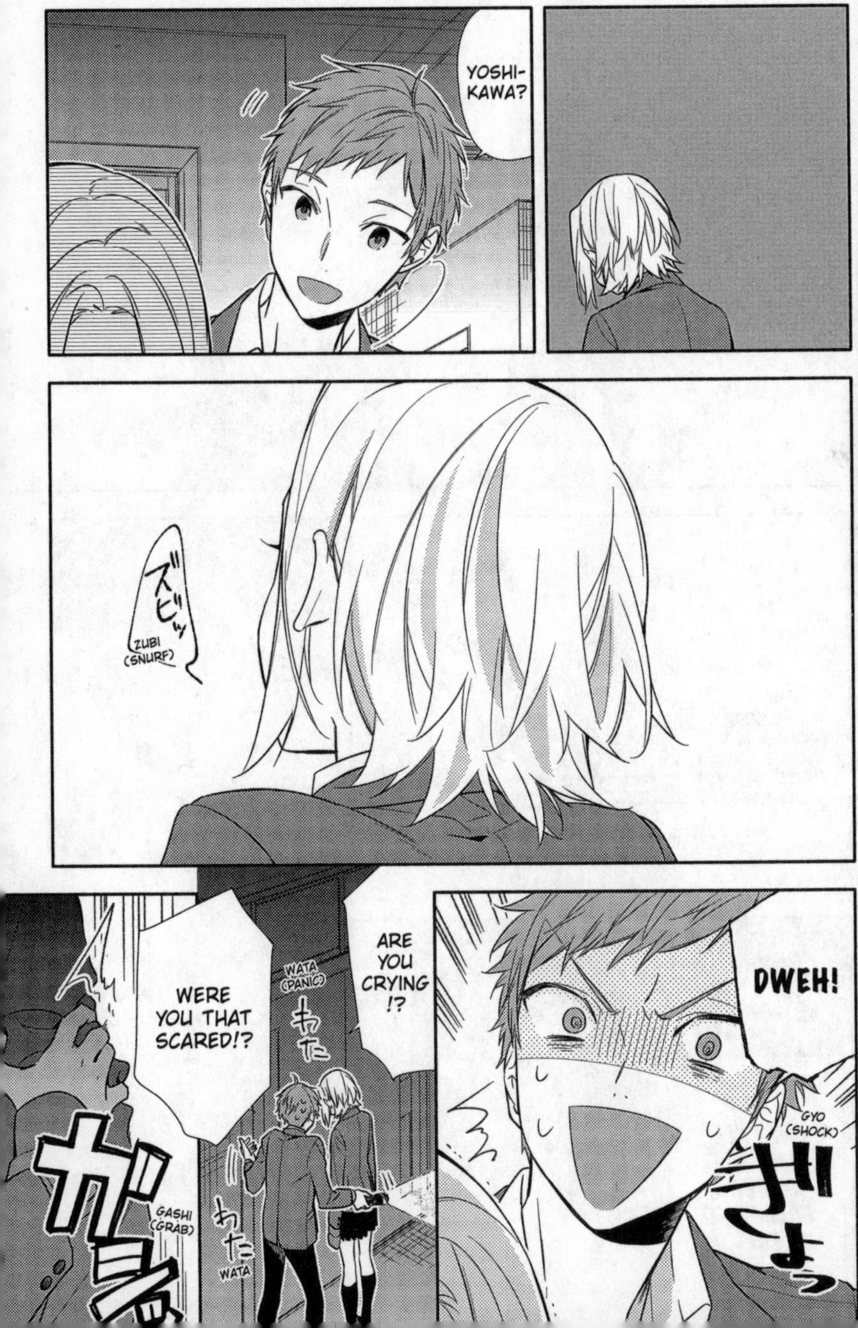
YOSHI-KAWA?
ズビッ
ZUBI (SNURF)
DWEH!
GYO (SHOCK)
ARE YOU CRYING!?
WATA (PANIC)
WERE YOU THAT SCARED!?
WATA
GASHI (GRAB)

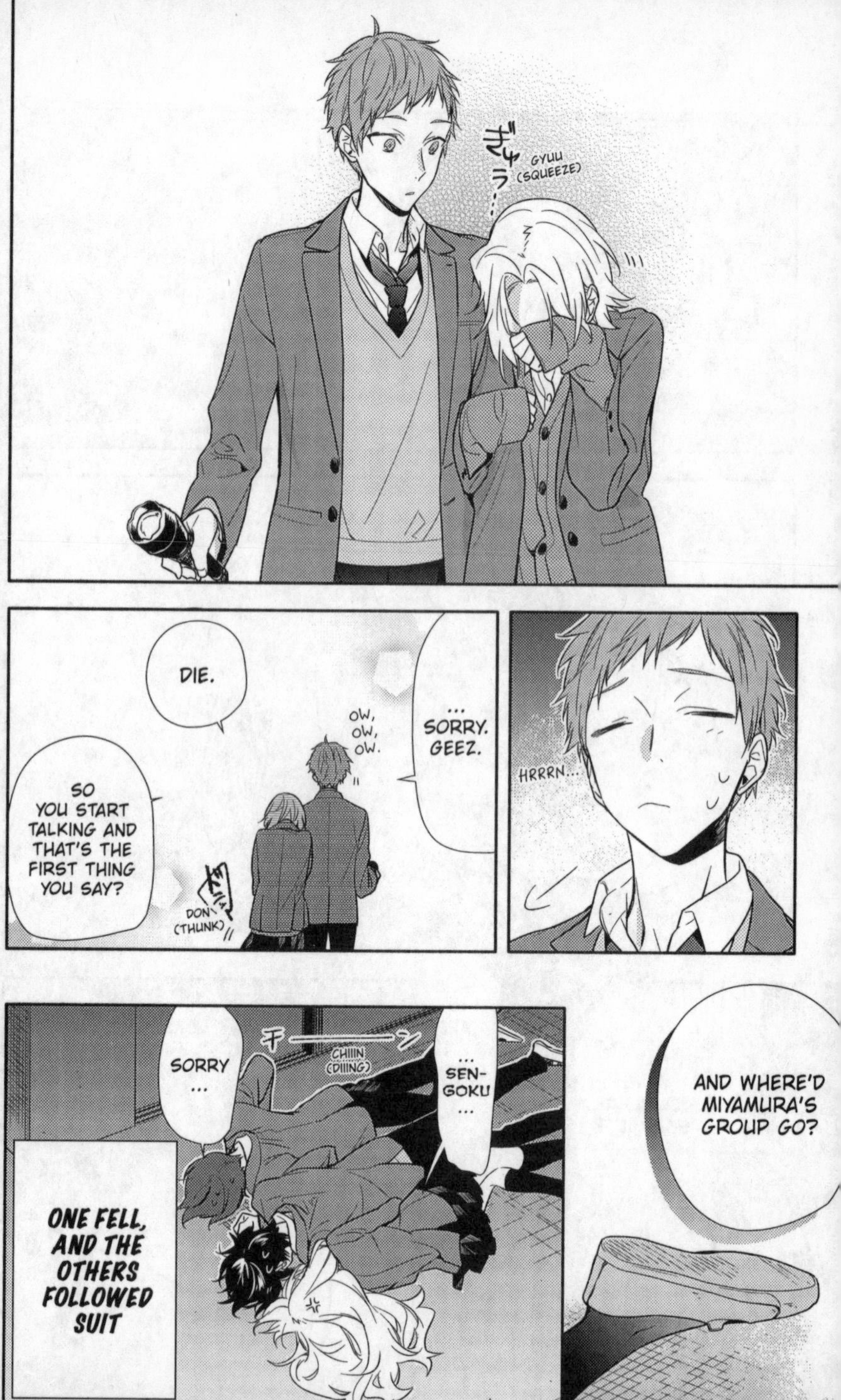
ぎゅう…
GYUU (SQUEEZE)
HRRRN...
... SORRY. GEEZ.
OW, OW, OW.
DIE.
SO YOU START TALKING AND THAT'S THE FIRST THING YOU SAY?
DON (THUNK)
AND WHERE'D MIYAMURA'S GROUP GO?
... SEN-GOKU ...
チーン
CHIIIN (DIIING)
SORRY ...
ONE FELL, AND THE OTHERS FOLLOWED SUIT

HORIMIYA

HORIMIYA

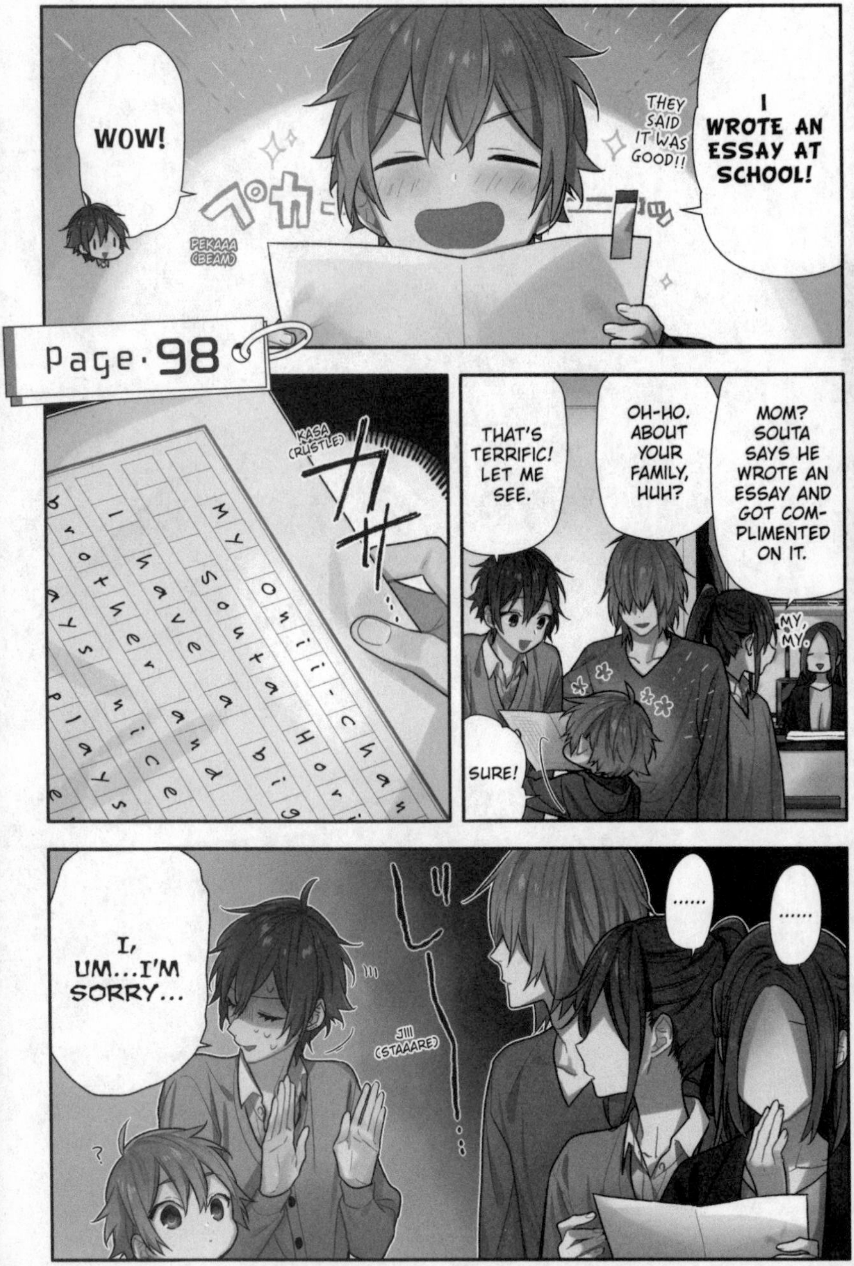
I WROTE AN ESSAY AT SCHOOL!
THEY SAID IT WAS GOOD!!
PEKAAA (BEAM)
WOW!
page·98
MOM? SOUTA SAYS HE WROTE AN ESSAY AND GOT COMPLIMENTED ON IT.
MY, MY
OH-HO. ABOUT YOUR FAMILY, HUH?
THAT'S TERRIFIC! LET ME SEE.
SURE!
KASA (RUSTLE)
......
......
JIII (STAAARE)
I, UM...I'M SORRY...

HORIMIYA

THE HORI COLLECTION

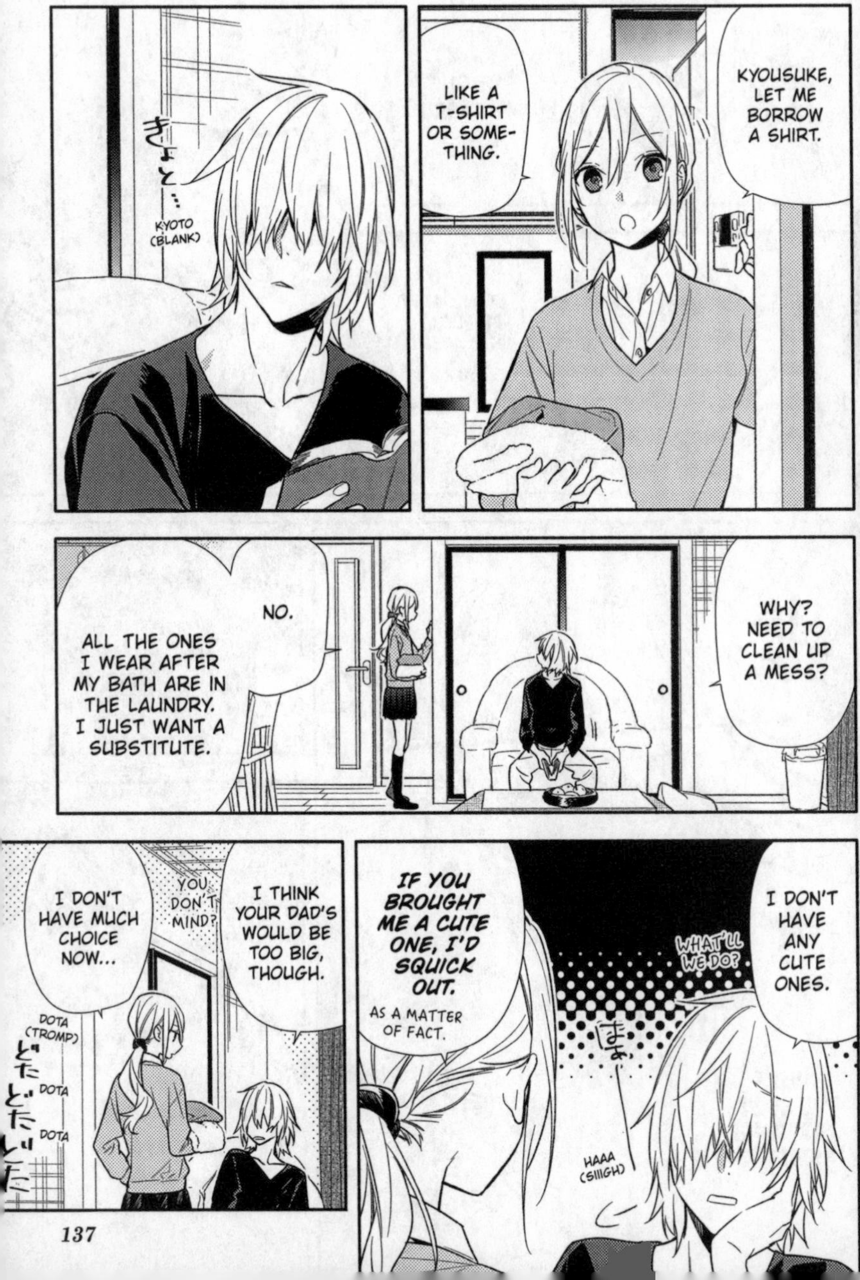
KYOUSUKE, LET ME BORROW A SHIRT.
LIKE A T-SHIRT OR SOMETHING.
きょと…
KYOTO (BLANK)
WHY? NEED TO CLEAN UP A MESS?
NO.
ALL THE ONES I WEAR AFTER MY BATH ARE IN THE LAUNDRY. I JUST WANT A SUBSTITUTE.
I DON'T HAVE ANY CUTE ONES.
WHAT'LL WE DO?
はぁ
HAAA (SIIIGH)
IF YOU BROUGHT ME A CUTE ONE, I'D SQUICK OUT.
AS A MATTER OF FACT.
I THINK YOUR DAD'S WOULD BE TOO BIG, THOUGH.
YOU DON'T MIND?
I DON'T HAVE MUCH CHOICE NOW...
どたどたどた
DOTA (TROMP)
DOTA
DOTA

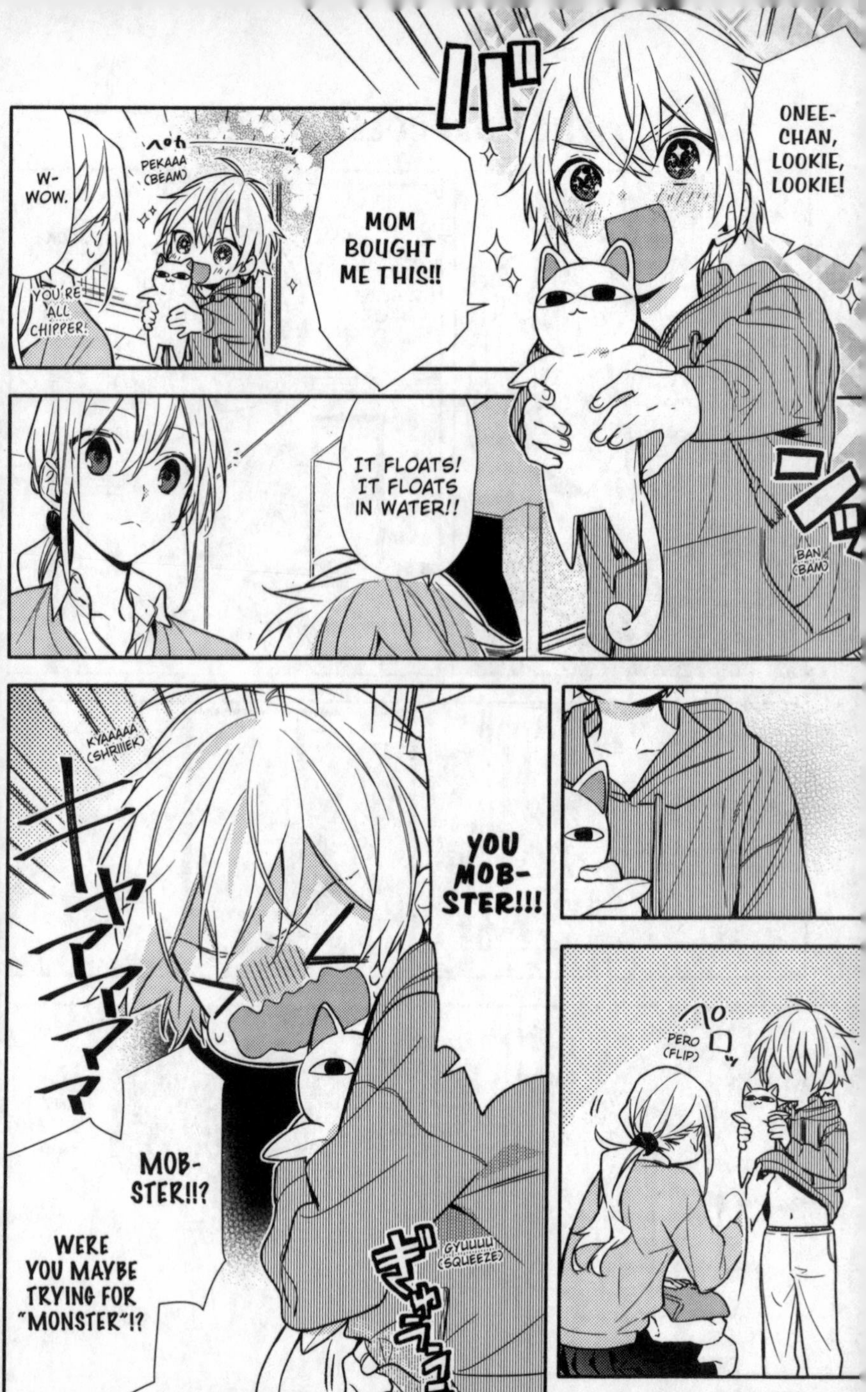
BAN (BAM)
ONEE-CHAN, LOOKIE, LOOKIE!
MOM BOUGHT ME THIS!!
PEKAAA (BEAM)
W-WOW.
YOU'RE ALL CHIPPER!
IT FLOATS! IT FLOATS IN WATER!!
YOU MOB-STER!!!
PERO (FLIP)
KYAAAAA (SHRIIIEK)
MOB-STER!!?
WERE YOU MAYBE TRYING FOR "MONSTER"!?
GYUUUU (SQUEEZE)

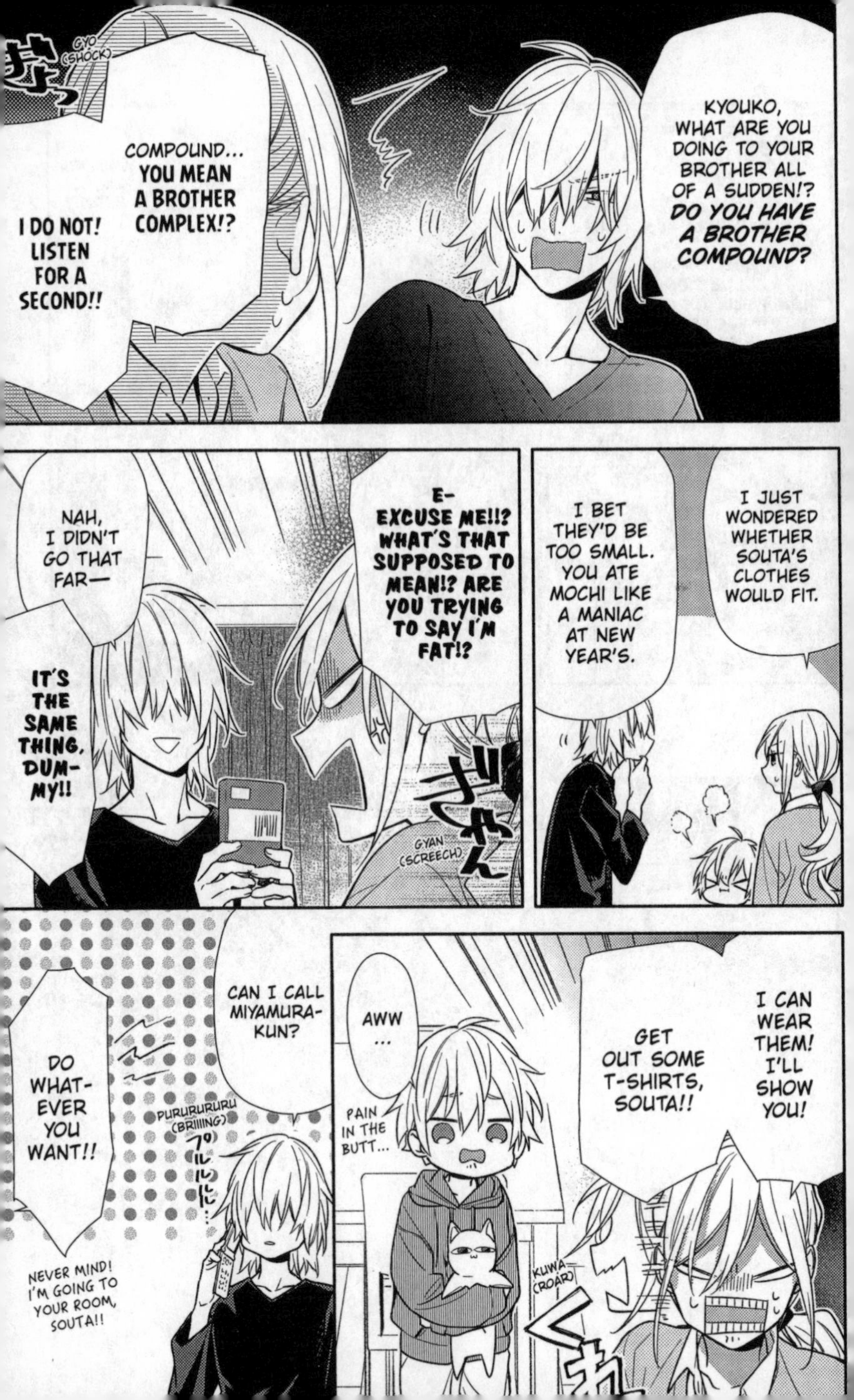
KYOUKO, WHAT ARE YOU DOING TO YOUR BROTHER ALL OF A SUDDEN!? DO YOU HAVE A BROTHER COMPOUND?
GYO (SHOCK)
COMPOUND... YOU MEAN A BROTHER COMPLEX!?
I DO NOT! LISTEN FOR A SECOND!!
I JUST WONDERED WHETHER SOUTA'S CLOTHES WOULD FIT.
I BET THEY'D BE TOO SMALL. YOU ATE MOCHI LIKE A MANIAC AT NEW YEAR'S.
E- EXCUSE ME!!? WHAT'S THAT SUPPOSED TO MEAN!? ARE YOU TRYING TO SAY I'M FAT!?
GYAN (SCREECH)
NAH, I DIDN'T GO THAT FAR—
IT'S THE SAME THING, DUMMY!!
I CAN WEAR THEM! I'LL SHOW YOU!
GET OUT SOME T-SHIRTS, SOUTA!!
KUWA (ROAR)
AWW...
PAIN IN THE BUTT...
CAN I CALL MIYAMURA-KUN?
PURURURURU (BRIIIING)
DO WHATEVER YOU WANT!!
NEVER MIND! I'M GOING TO YOUR ROOM, SOUTA!!

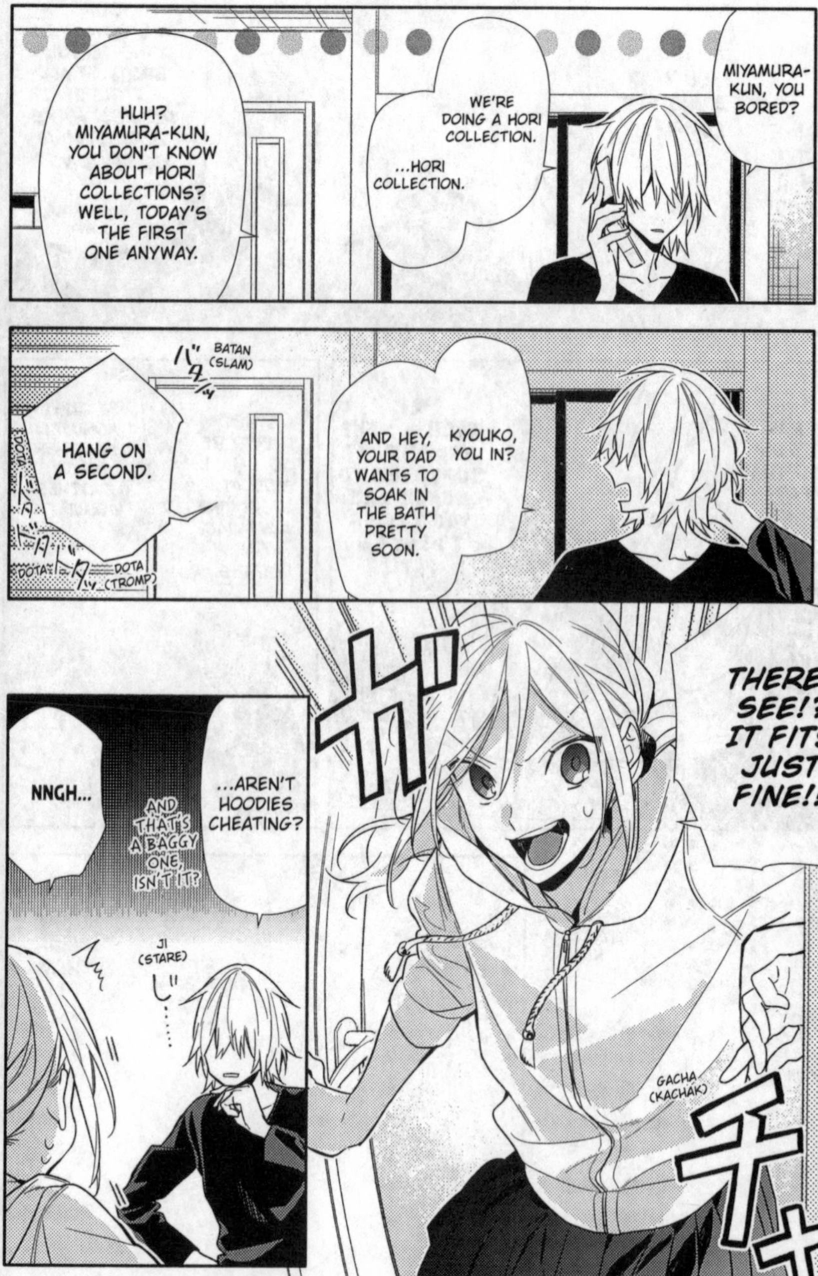
MIYAMURA-KUN, YOU BORED?
WE'RE DOING A HORI COLLECTION.
...HORI COLLECTION.
HUH? MIYAMURA-KUN, YOU DON'T KNOW ABOUT HORI COLLECTIONS? WELL, TODAY'S THE FIRST ONE ANYWAY.
KYOUKO, YOU IN?
AND HEY, YOUR DAD WANTS TO SOAK IN THE BATH PRETTY SOON.
BATAN (SLAM)
HANG ON A SECOND.
DOTA DOTA DOTA (TROMP)
THERE! SEE!? IT FITS JUST FINE!!
GACHA (KACHAK)
...AREN'T HOODIES CHEATING?
AND THAT'S A BAGGY ONE, ISN'T IT?
NNGH...
JI (STARE)

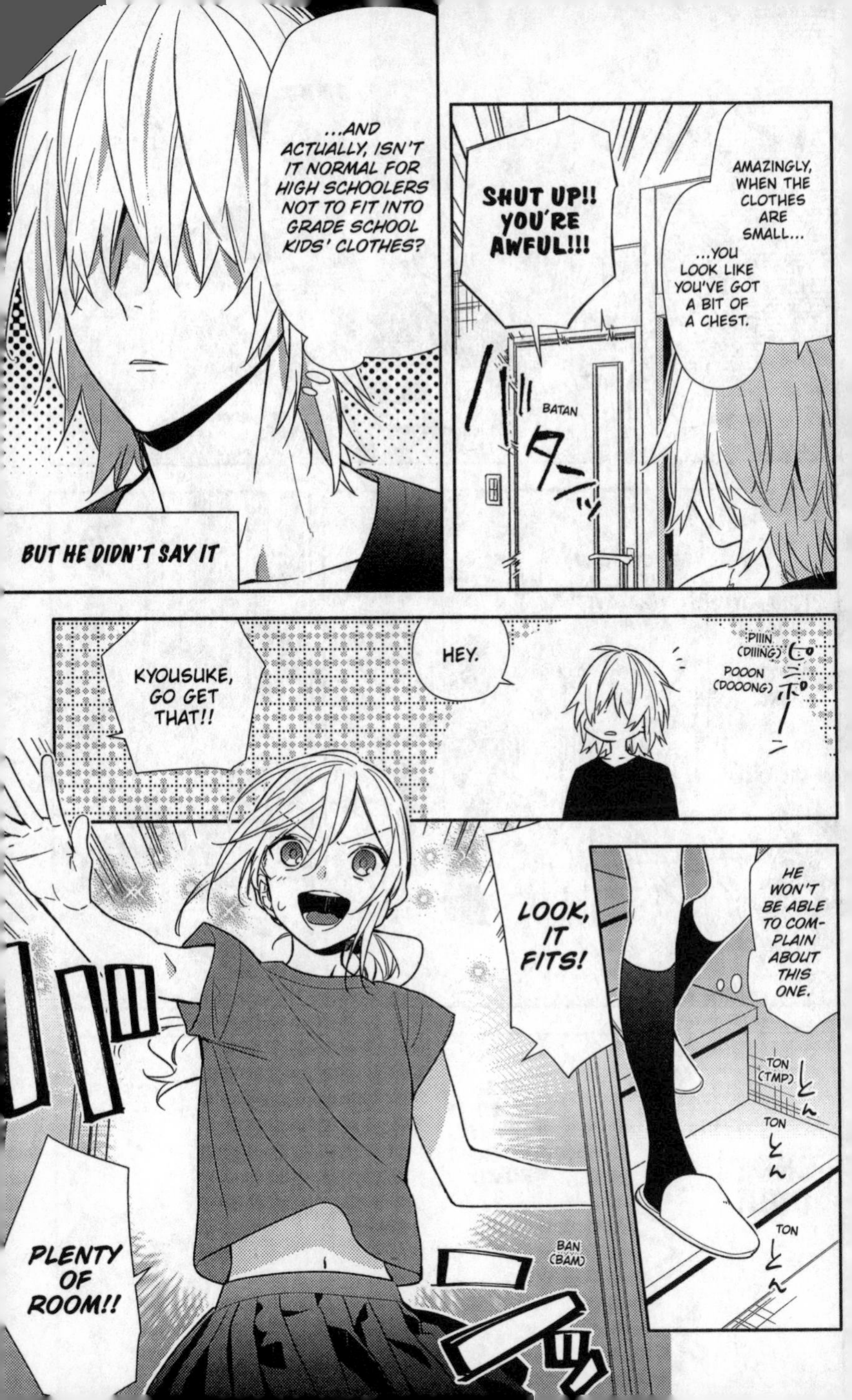
AMAZINGLY, WHEN THE CLOTHES ARE SMALL...
...YOU LOOK LIKE YOU'VE GOT A BIT OF A CHEST.
SHUT UP!! YOU'RE AWFUL!!!
BATAN
...AND ACTUALLY, ISN'T IT NORMAL FOR HIGH SCHOOLERS NOT TO FIT INTO GRADE SCHOOL KIDS' CLOTHES?
BUT HE DIDN'T SAY IT
PIIN (DIIING)
POOON (DOOONG)
HEY.
KYOUSUKE, GO GET THAT!!
HE WON'T BE ABLE TO COMPLAIN ABOUT THIS ONE.
TON (TMP)
TON
TON
LOOK, IT FITS!
BAN (BAM)
PLENTY OF ROOM!!

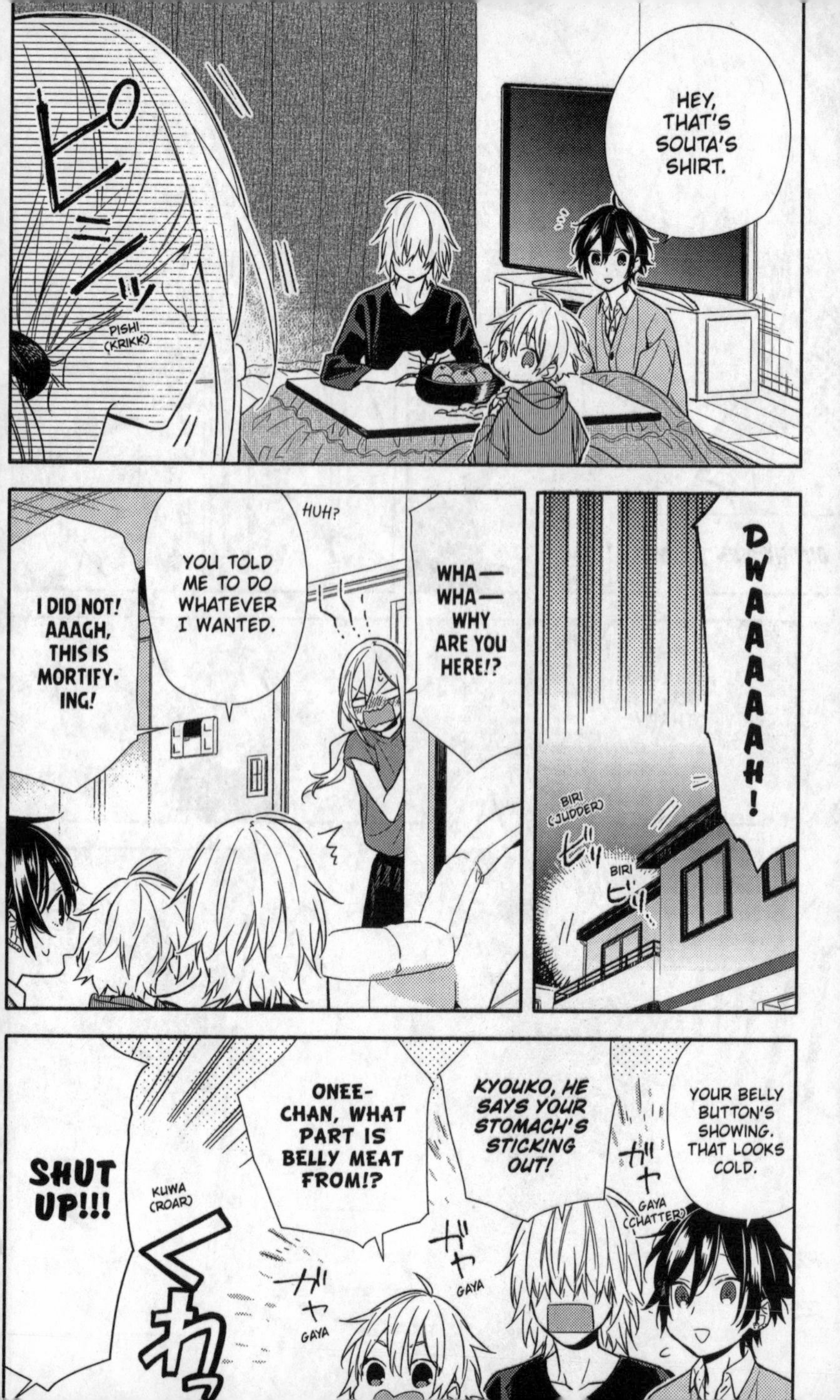
HEY, THAT'S SOUTA'S SHIRT.
...
PISHI (KRIKK)
DWAAAAAAH!
BIRI (JUDDER)
BIRI
WHA— WHA— WHY ARE YOU HERE!?
HUH?
YOU TOLD ME TO DO WHATEVER I WANTED.
I DID NOT! AAAGH, THIS IS MORTIFYING!
YOUR BELLY BUTTON'S SHOWING. THAT LOOKS COLD.
GAYA (CHATTER)
KYOUKO, HE SAYS YOUR STOMACH'S STICKING OUT!
ONEE-CHAN, WHAT PART IS BELLY MEAT FROM!?
GAYA
GAYA
KUWA (ROAR)
SHUT UP!!!

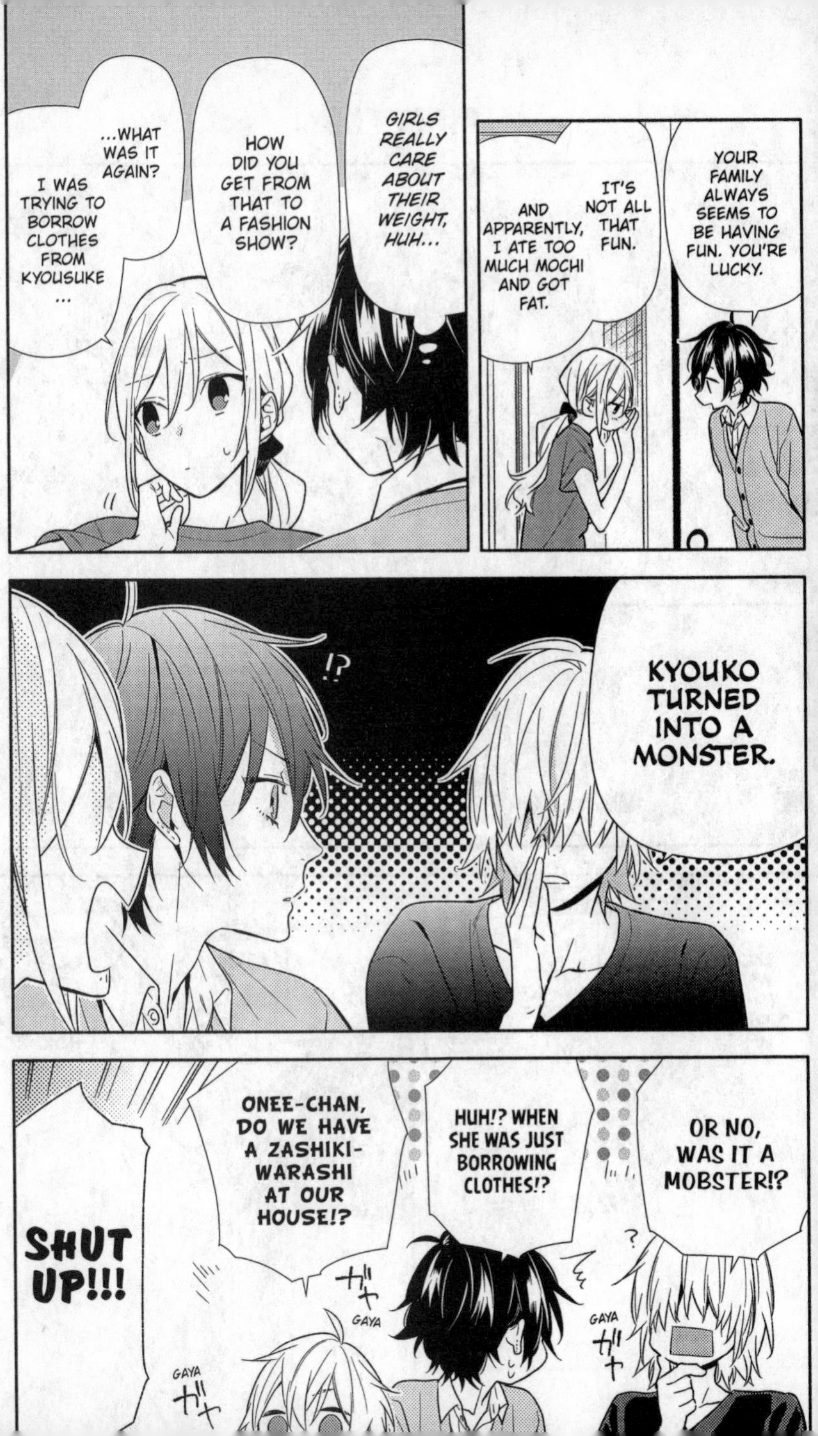
YOUR FAMILY ALWAYS SEEMS TO BE HAVING FUN. YOU'RE LUCKY.
IT'S NOT ALL THAT FUN.
AND APPARENTLY, I ATE TOO MUCH MOCHI AND GOT FAT.
GIRLS REALLY CARE ABOUT THEIR WEIGHT, HUH...
HOW DID YOU GET FROM THAT TO A FASHION SHOW?
...WHAT WAS IT AGAIN?
I WAS TRYING TO BORROW CLOTHES FROM KYOUSUKE ...
KYOUKO TURNED INTO A MONSTER.
!?
OR NO, WAS IT A MOBSTER!?
HUH!? WHEN SHE WAS JUST BORROWING CLOTHES!?
ONEE-CHAN, DO WE HAVE A ZASHIKI-WARASHI AT OUR HOUSE!?
?
ガヤ
GAYA
ガヤ
GAYA
ガヤ
GAYA
SHUT UP!!!

SHUTTLE

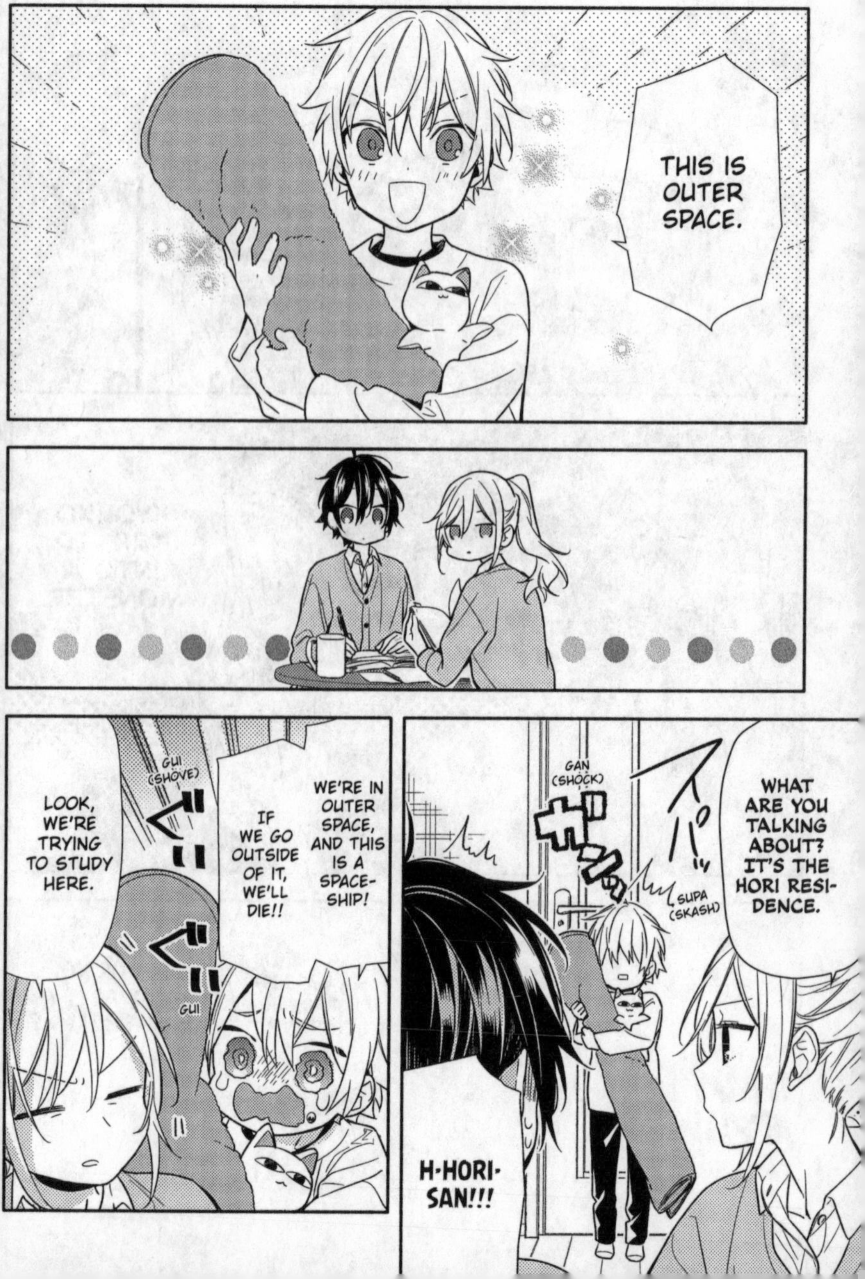
THIS IS OUTER SPACE.
WHAT ARE YOU TALKING ABOUT? IT'S THE HORI RESIDENCE.
SUPA (SKASH)
GAN (SHOCK)
H-HORI-SAN!!!
WE'RE IN OUTER SPACE, AND THIS IS A SPACESHIP!
IF WE GO OUTSIDE OF IT, WE'LL DIE!!
GUI (SHOVE)
LOOK, WE'RE TRYING TO STUDY HERE.
GUI

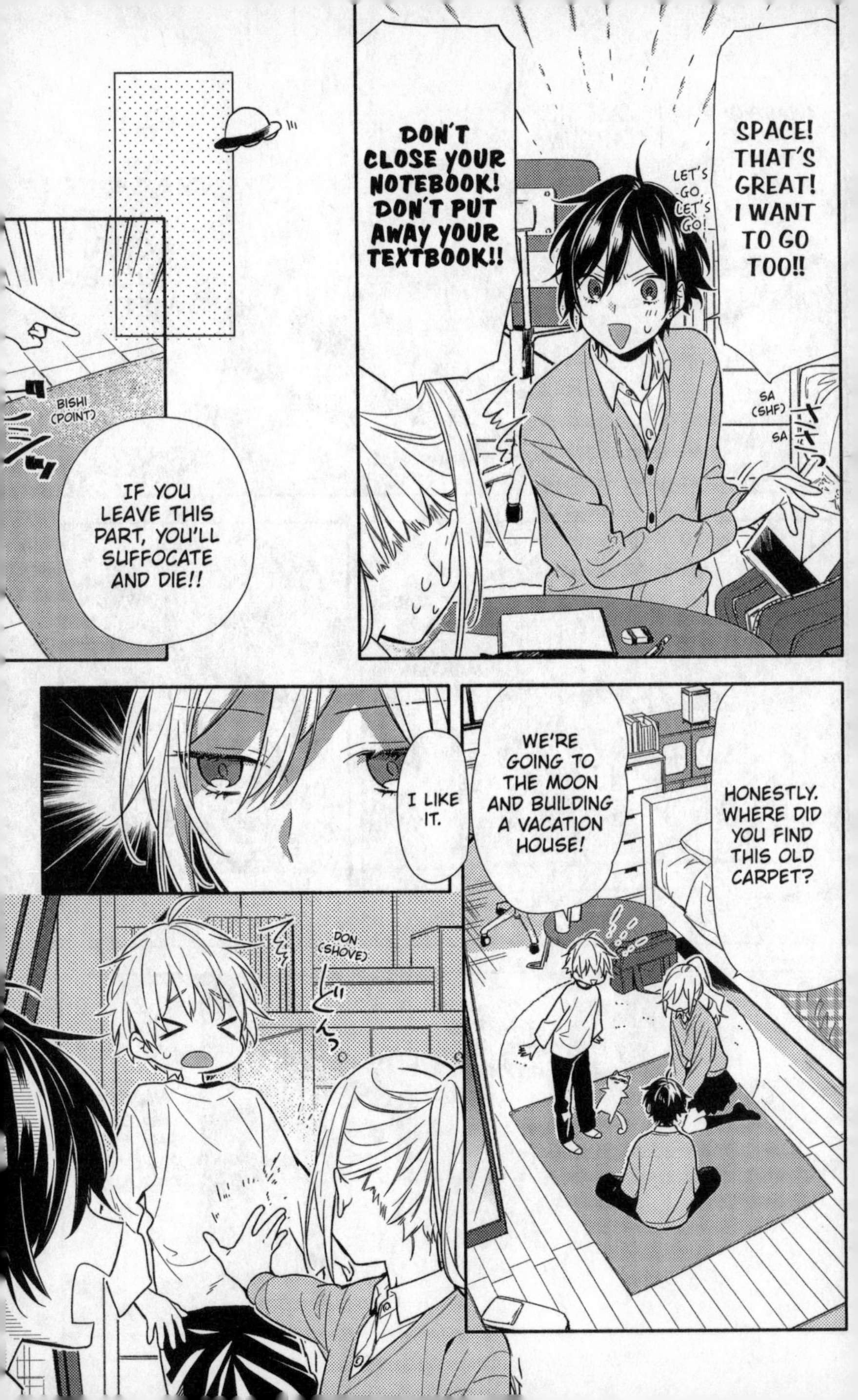
SPACE! THAT'S GREAT! I WANT TO GO TOO!!
LET'S GO, LET'S GO!
DON'T CLOSE YOUR NOTEBOOK! DON'T PUT AWAY YOUR TEXTBOOK!!
SA (SHF) SA
BISHI (POINT)
IF YOU LEAVE THIS PART, YOU'LL SUFFOCATE AND DIE!!
HONESTLY. WHERE DID YOU FIND THIS OLD CARPET?
WE'RE GOING TO THE MOON AND BUILDING A VACATION HOUSE!
I LIKE IT.
DON (SHOVE)

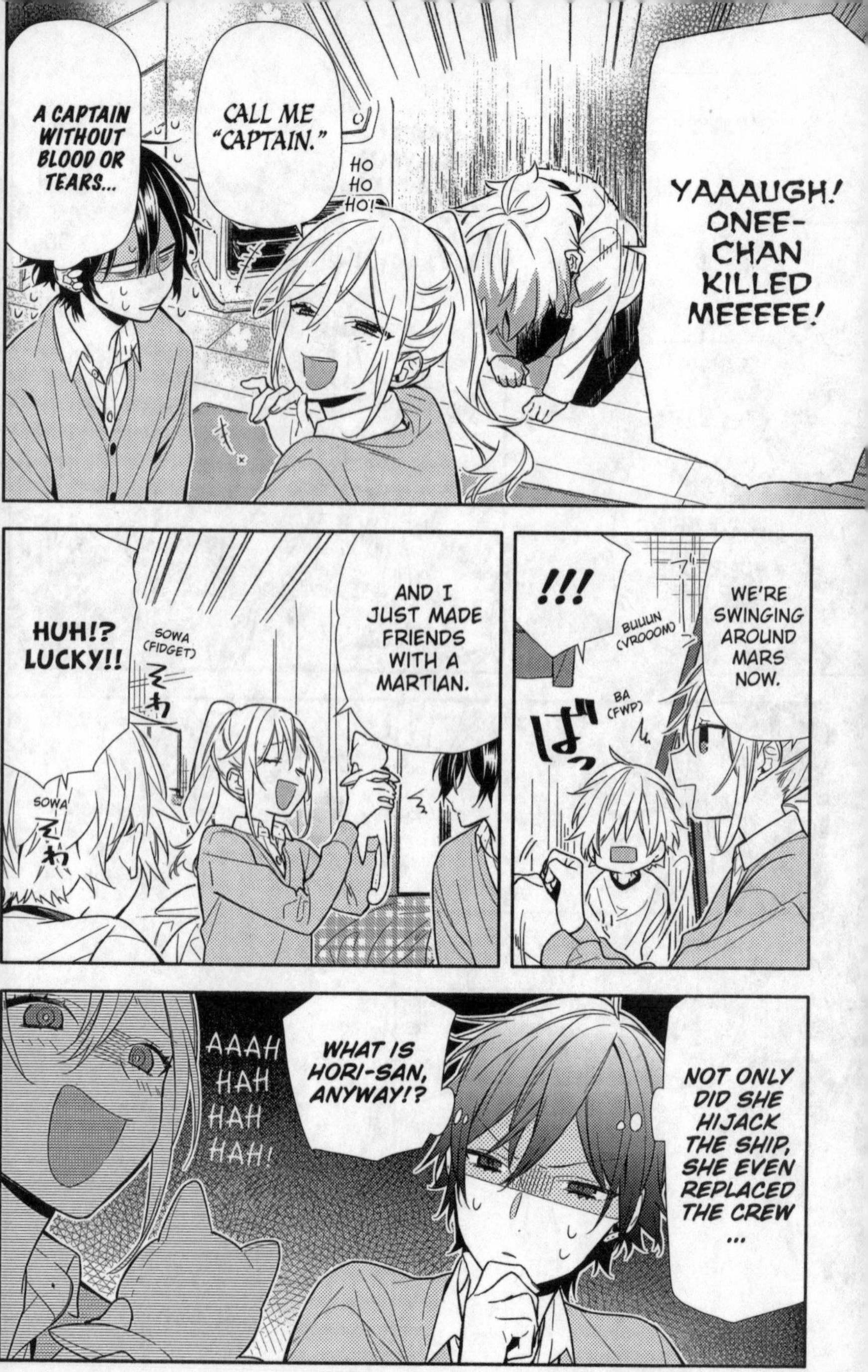
YAAAUGH! ONEE-CHAN KILLED MEEEEE!
HO HO HO!
CALL ME "CAPTAIN."
A CAPTAIN WITHOUT BLOOD OR TEARS...
WE'RE SWINGING AROUND MARS NOW.
BUUUN (VROOOM)
!!!
BA (FWP)
AND I JUST MADE FRIENDS WITH A MARTIAN.
SOWA (FIDGET)
HUH!? LUCKY!!
SOWA
NOT ONLY DID SHE HIJACK THE SHIP, SHE EVEN REPLACED THE CREW ...
WHAT IS HORI-SAN, ANYWAY!?
AAAH HAH HAH HAH!

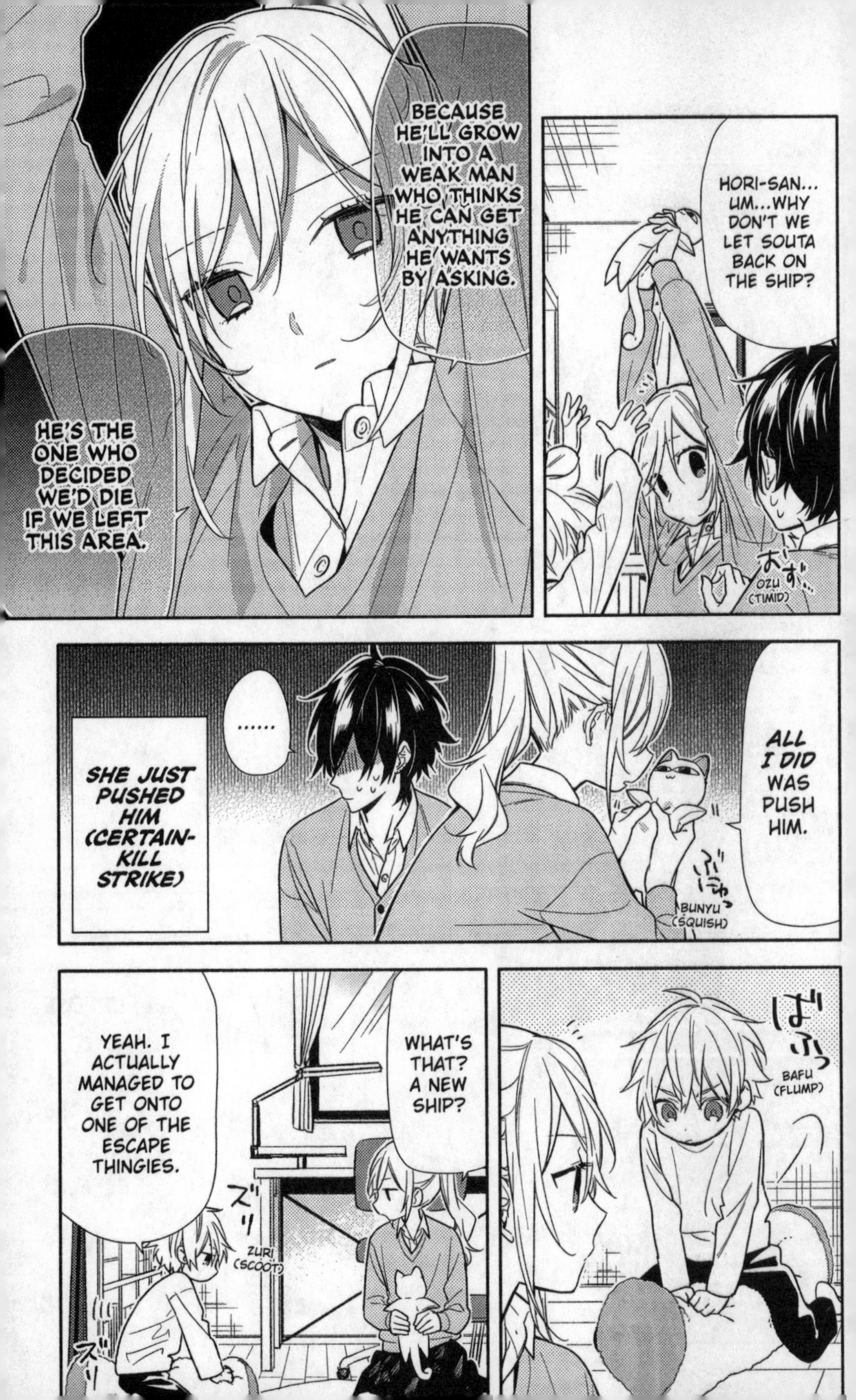
HORI-SAN... UM...WHY DON'T WE LET SOUTA BACK ON THE SHIP?
おず…
OZU (TIMID)
BECAUSE HE'LL GROW INTO A WEAK MAN WHO THINKS HE CAN GET ANYTHING HE WANTS BY ASKING.
HE'S THE ONE WHO DECIDED WE'D DIE IF WE LEFT THIS AREA.
ALL I DID WAS PUSH HIM.
ぶにゅっ
BUNYU (SQUISH)
......
SHE JUST PUSHED HIM (CERTAIN-KILL STRIKE)
ばふっ
BAFU (FLUMP)
WHAT'S THAT? A NEW SHIP?
YEAH. I ACTUALLY MANAGED TO GET ONTO ONE OF THE ESCAPE THINGIES.
ズリ
ZURI (SCOOT)
ズリ

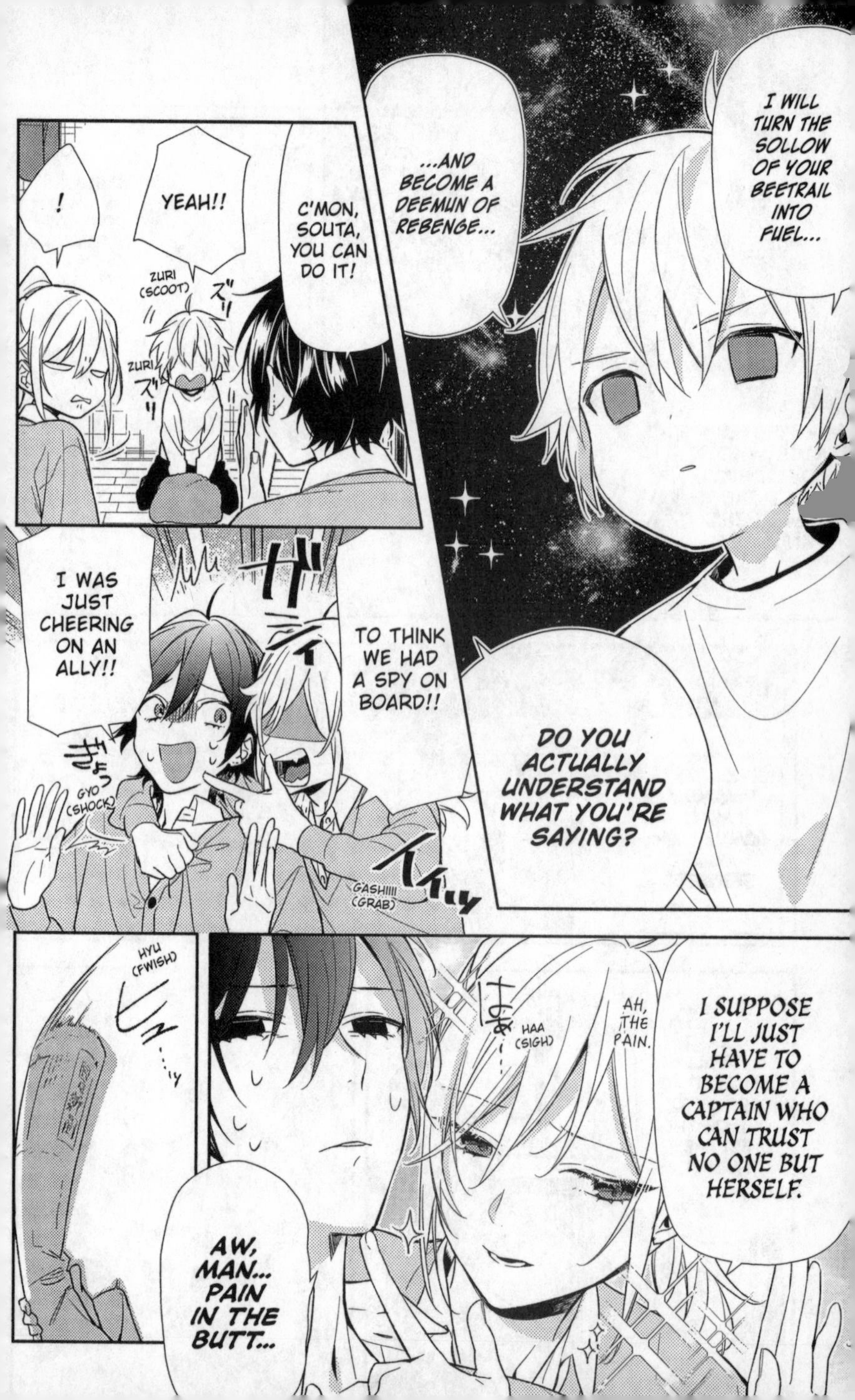

I WILL TURN THE SOLLOW OF YOUR BEETRAIL INTO FUEL...
...AND BECOME A DEEMUN OF REBENGE...
DO YOU ACTUALLY UNDERSTAND WHAT YOU'RE SAYING?
C'MON, SOUTA, YOU CAN DO IT!
YEAH!!
!
ZURI (SCOOT)
ZURI
TO THINK WE HAD A SPY ON BOARD!!
I WAS JUST CHEERING ON AN ALLY!!
GYO (SHOCK)
GASHIIII (GRAB)
I SUPPOSE I'LL JUST HAVE TO BECOME A CAPTAIN WHO CAN TRUST NO ONE BUT HERSELF.
AH, THE PAIN.
HAA (SIGH)
AW, MAN... PAIN IN THE BUTT...
HYU (FWISH)

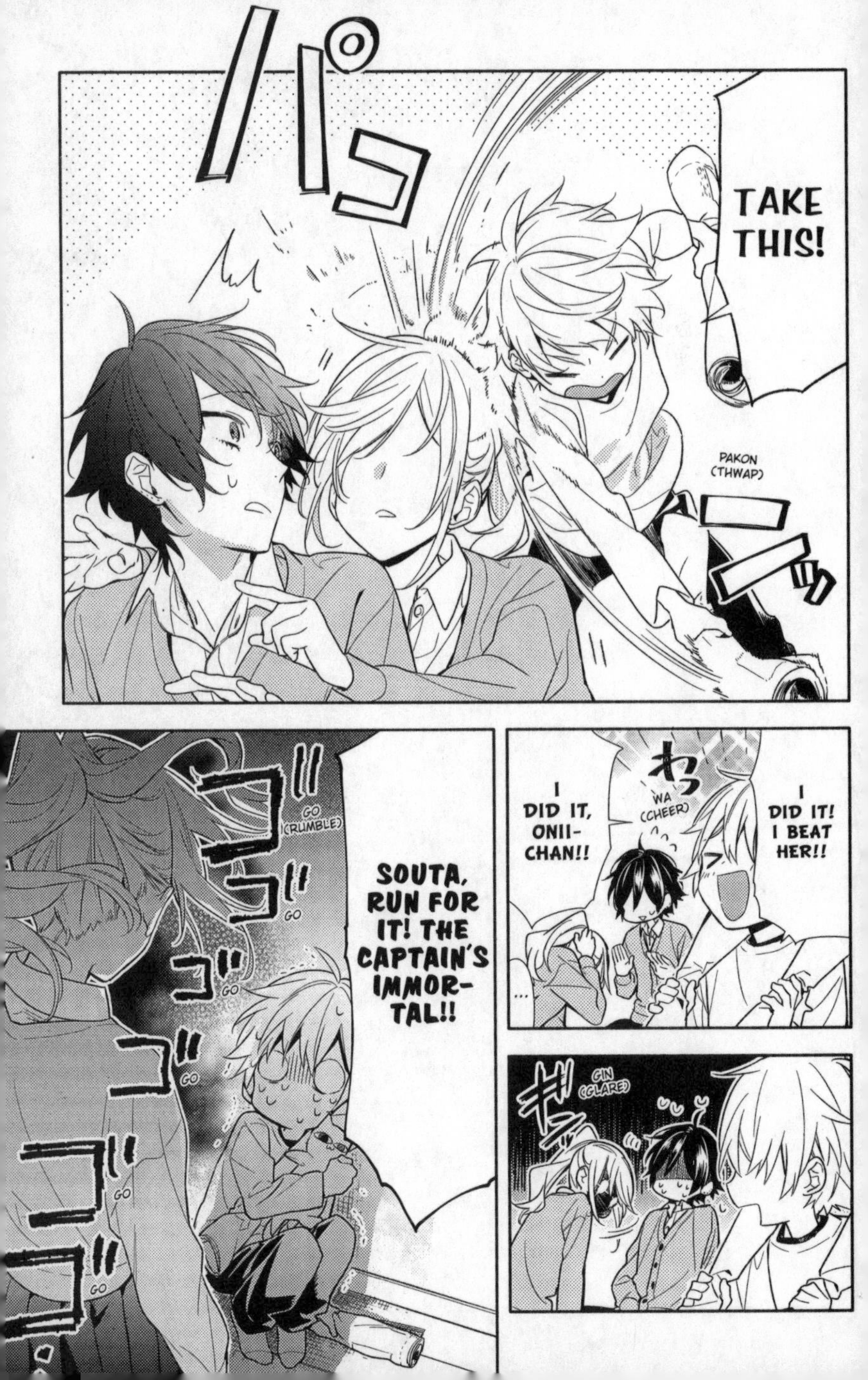
TAKE THIS!
PAKON (THWAP)
I DID IT! I BEAT HER!!
WA (CHEER)
I DID IT, ONII-CHAN!!
...
GIN (GLARE)
SOUTA, RUN FOR IT! THE CAPTAIN'S IMMORTAL!!
GO (RUMBLE)
GO
GO
GO
GO

HORIMIYA

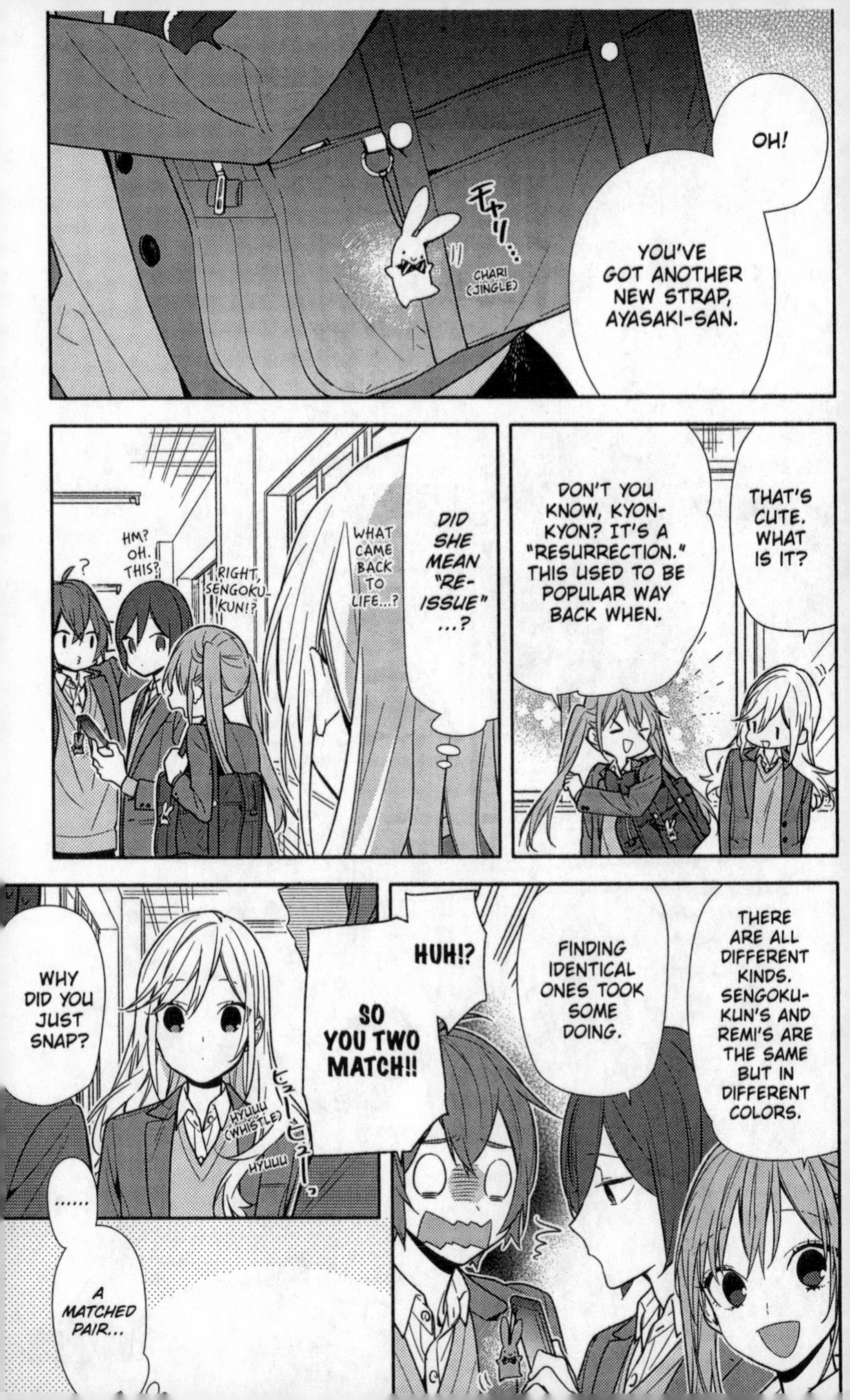
OH!
YOU'VE GOT ANOTHER NEW STRAP, AYASAKI-SAN.
チャリ…
CHARI (JINGLE)
THAT'S CUTE. WHAT IS IT?
DON'T YOU KNOW, KYON-KYON? IT'S A "RESURRECTION." THIS USED TO BE POPULAR WAY BACK WHEN.
DID SHE MEAN "RE-ISSUE"...?
WHAT CAME BACK TO LIFE...?
RIGHT, SENGOKU-KUN!?
HM? OH. THIS?
?
THERE ARE ALL DIFFERENT KINDS. SENGOKU-KUN'S AND REMI'S ARE THE SAME BUT IN DIFFERENT COLORS.
FINDING IDENTICAL ONES TOOK SOME DOING.
HUH!?
SO YOU TWO MATCH!!
WHY DID YOU JUST SNAP?
HYUUU (WHISTLE)
HYUUU
......
A MATCHED PAIR...

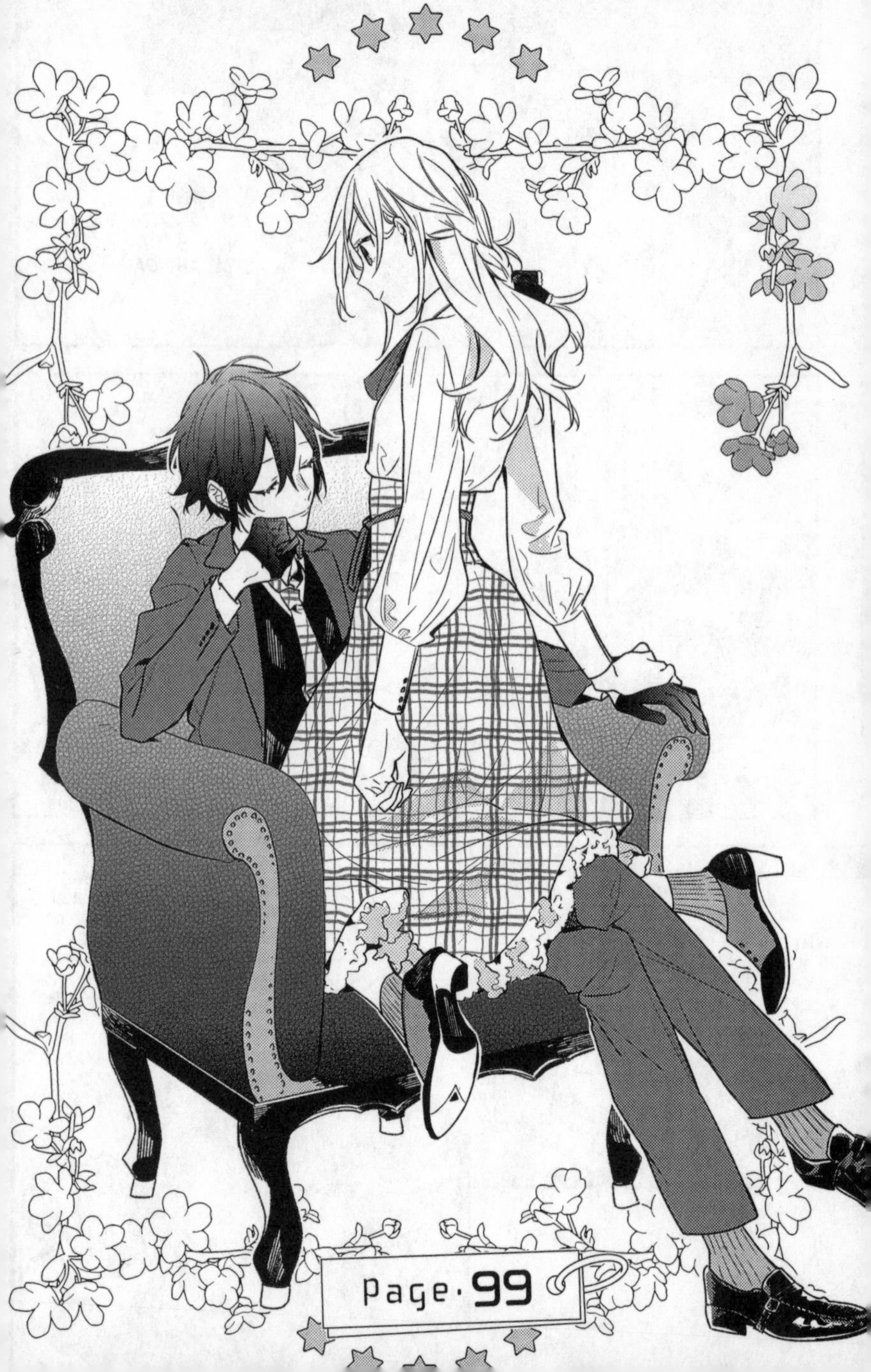
page·99

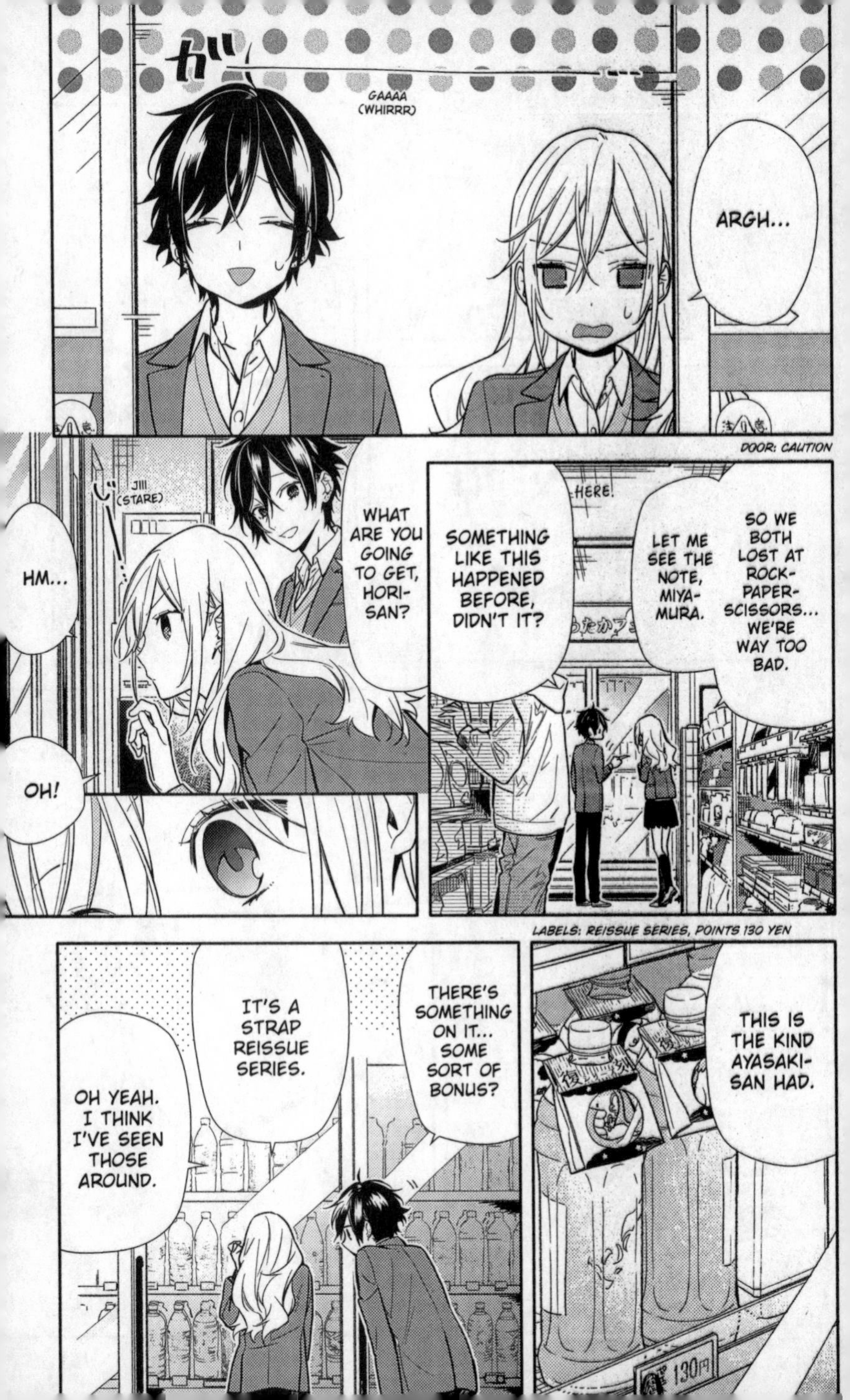
GAAAA (WHIRRR)
ARGH...
DOOR: CAUTION
SO WE BOTH LOST AT ROCK-PAPER-SCISSORS... WE'RE WAY TOO BAD.
LET ME SEE THE NOTE, MIYAMURA.
HERE!
SOMETHING LIKE THIS HAPPENED BEFORE, DIDN'T IT?
WHAT ARE YOU GOING TO GET, HORI-SAN?
JIII (STARE)
HM...
OH!
LABELS: REISSUE SERIES, POINTS 130 YEN
THIS IS THE KIND AYASAKI-SAN HAD.
THERE'S SOMETHING ON IT... SOME SORT OF BONUS?
IT'S A STRAP REISSUE SERIES.
OH YEAH. I THINK I'VE SEEN THOSE AROUND.

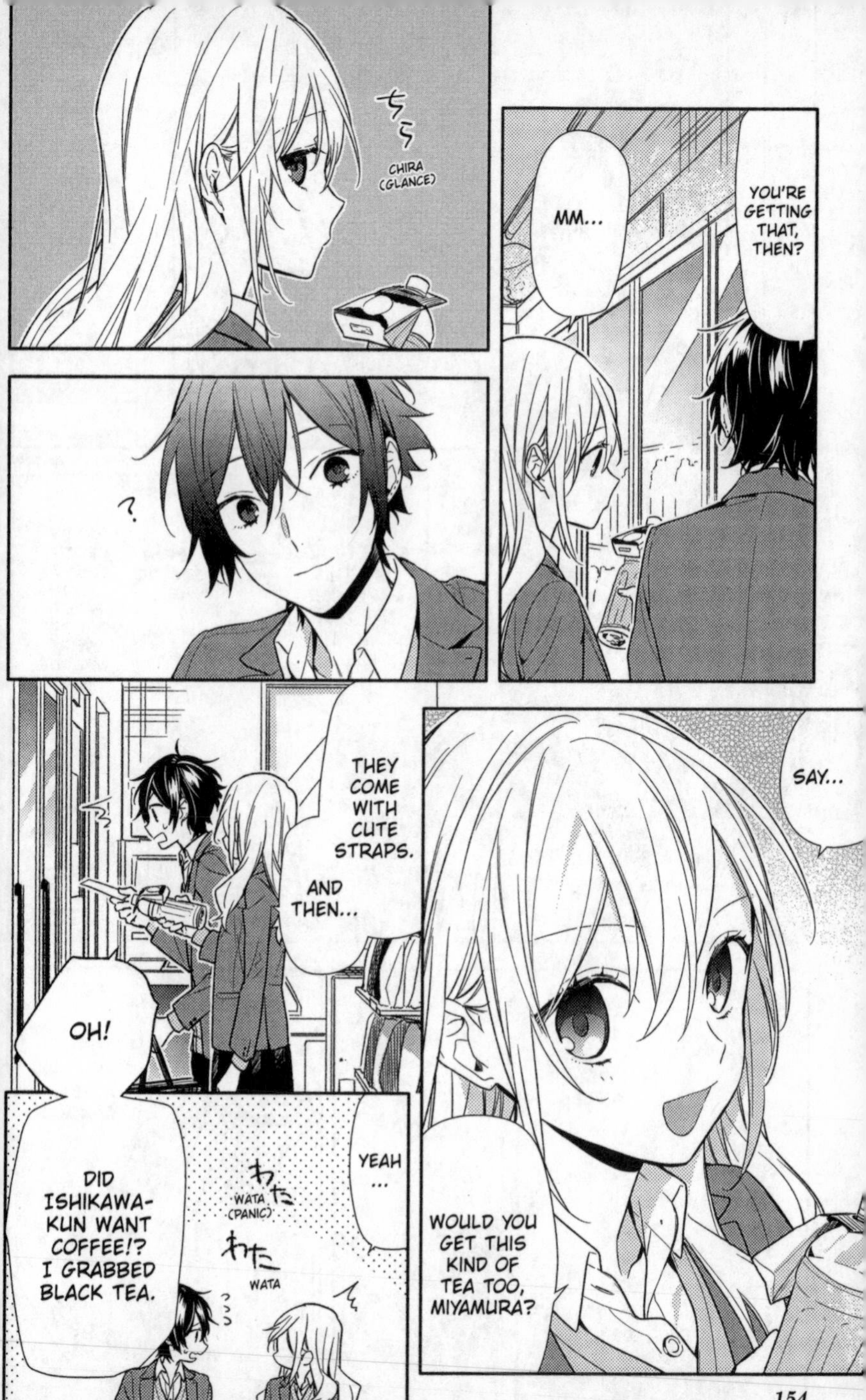
YOU'RE GETTING THAT, THEN?
MM...
CHIRA (GLANCE)
?
SAY...
WOULD YOU GET THIS KIND OF TEA TOO, MIYAMURA?
THEY COME WITH CUTE STRAPS.
AND THEN...
OH!
YEAH ...
WATA (PANIC)
WATA
DID ISHIKAWA-KUN WANT COFFEE!? I GRABBED BLACK TEA.

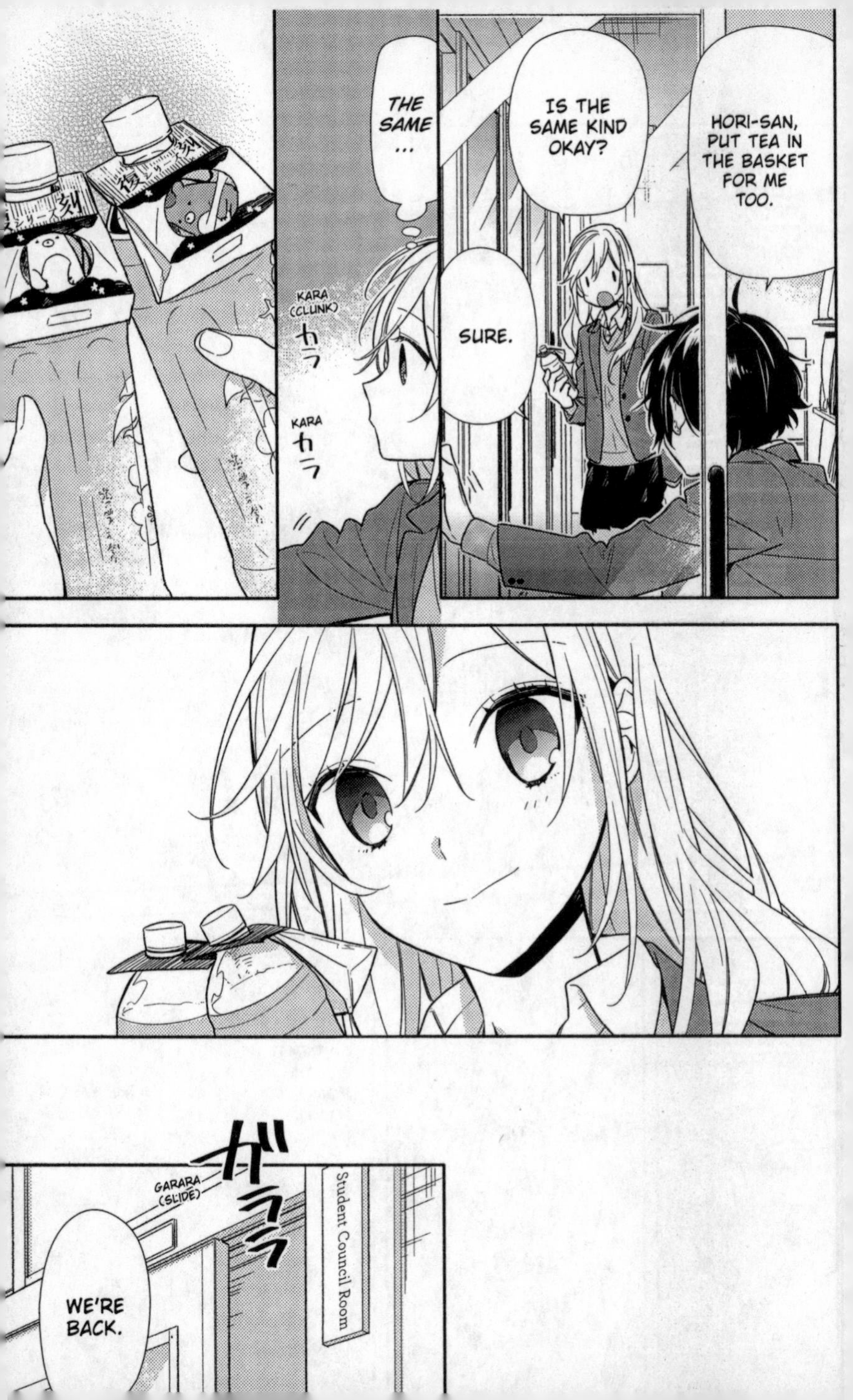
HORI-SAN, PUT TEA IN THE BASKET FOR ME TOO.
IS THE SAME KIND OKAY?
SURE.
THE SAME ...
KARA (CLUNK)
カラ
KARA
カラ
ガラッ
GARARA (SLIDE)
Student Council Room
WE'RE BACK.

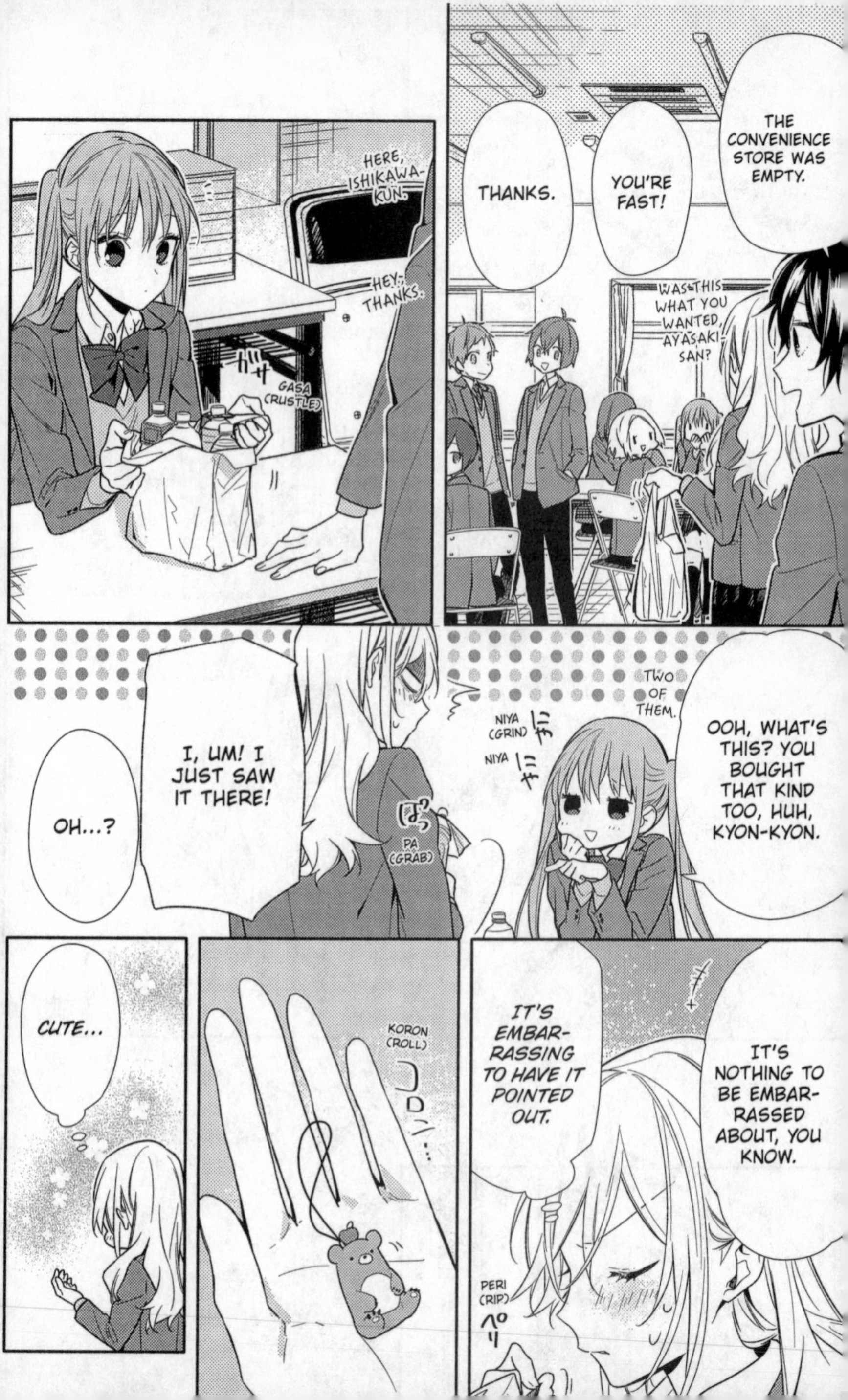
THE CONVENIENCE STORE WAS EMPTY.
YOU'RE FAST!
THANKS.
WAS THIS WHAT YOU WANTED, AYASAKI-SAN?
HERE, ISHIKAWA-KUN.
HEY-THANKS.
GASA (RUSTLE)
OOH, WHAT'S THIS? YOU BOUGHT THAT KIND TOO, HUH, KYON-KYON.
TWO OF THEM.
NIYA (GRIN)
NIYA
PA (GRAB)
I, UM! I JUST SAW IT THERE!
OH...?
IT'S NOTHING TO BE EMBARRASSED ABOUT, YOU KNOW.
IT'S EMBARRASSING TO HAVE IT POINTED OUT.
PERI (RIP)
KORON (ROLL)
CUTE...

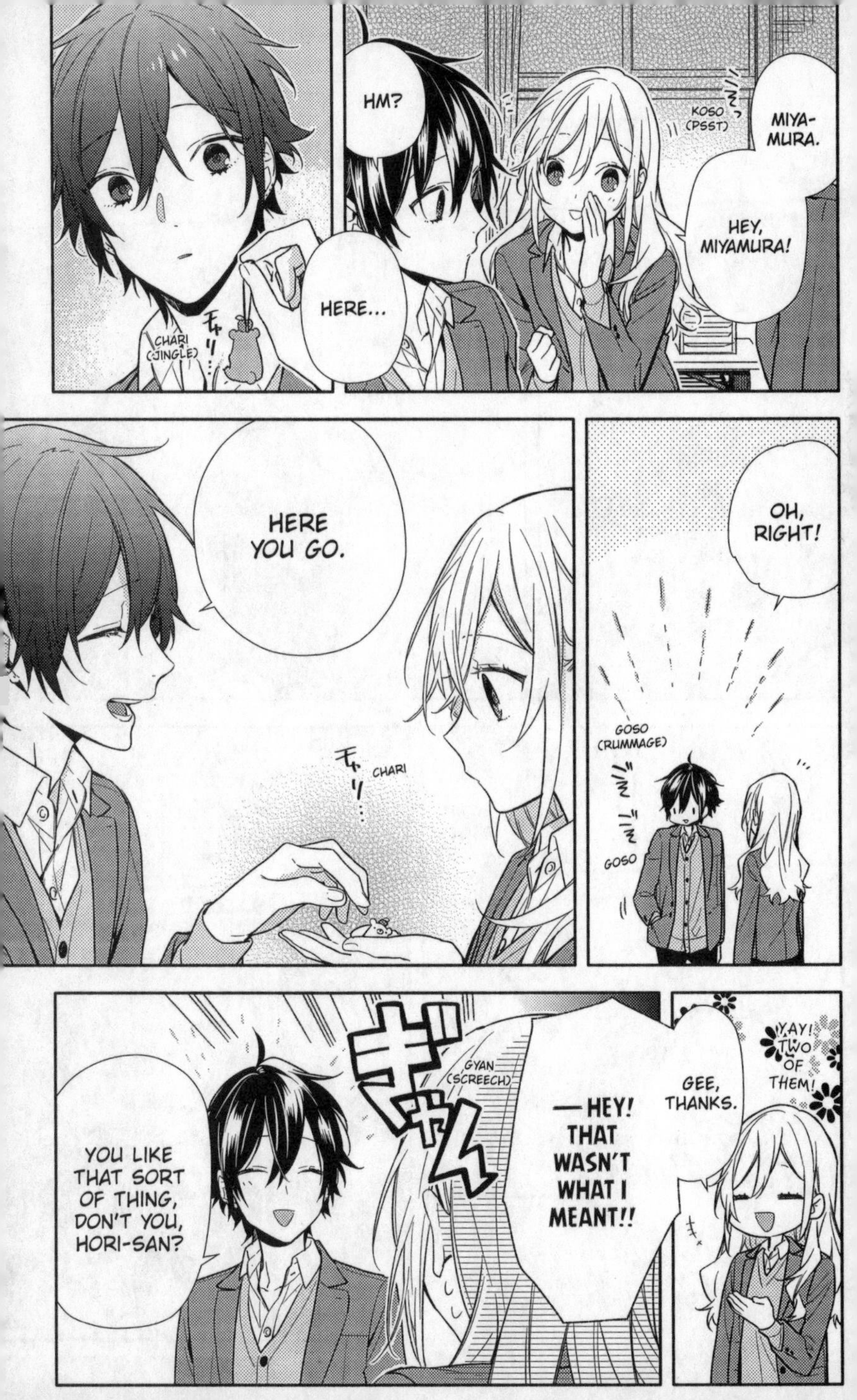
MIYA-MURA.
HEY, MIYAMURA!
KOSO (PSST)
HM?
HERE...
CHARI (JINGLE)
OH, RIGHT!
GOSO (RUMMAGE)
GOSO
HERE YOU GO.
CHARI
YAY! TWO OF THEM!
GEE, THANKS.
—HEY! THAT WASN'T WHAT I MEANT!!
GYAN (SCREECH)
YOU LIKE THAT SORT OF THING, DON'T YOU, HORI-SAN?

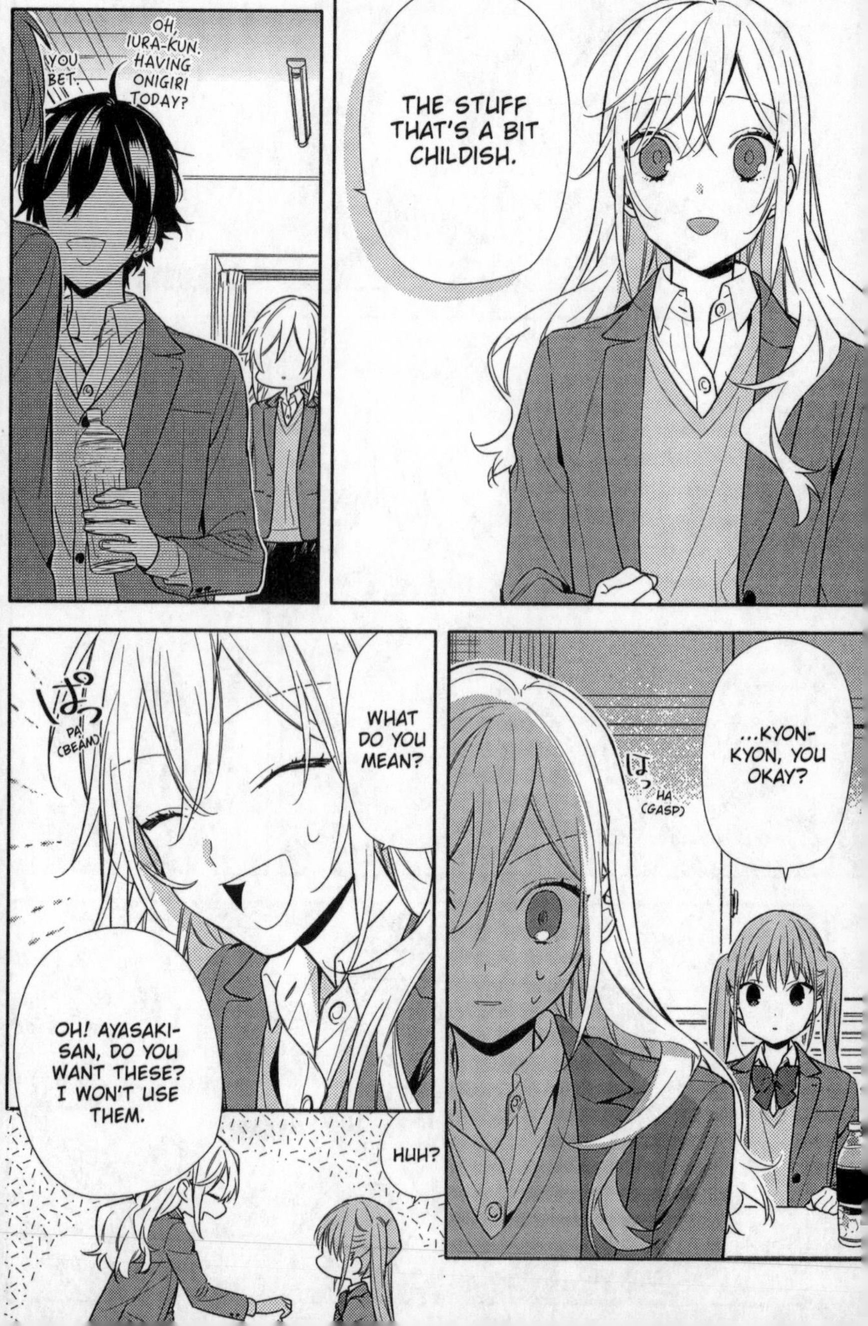
THE STUFF THAT'S A BIT CHILDISH.
OH, IURA-KUN. HAVING ONIGIRI TODAY?
YOU BET.
...KYON-KYON, YOU OKAY?
はっ
HA (GASP)
WHAT DO YOU MEAN?
ぱっ
PA (BEAM)
OH! AYASAKI-SAN, DO YOU WANT THESE? I WON'T USE THEM.
HUH?

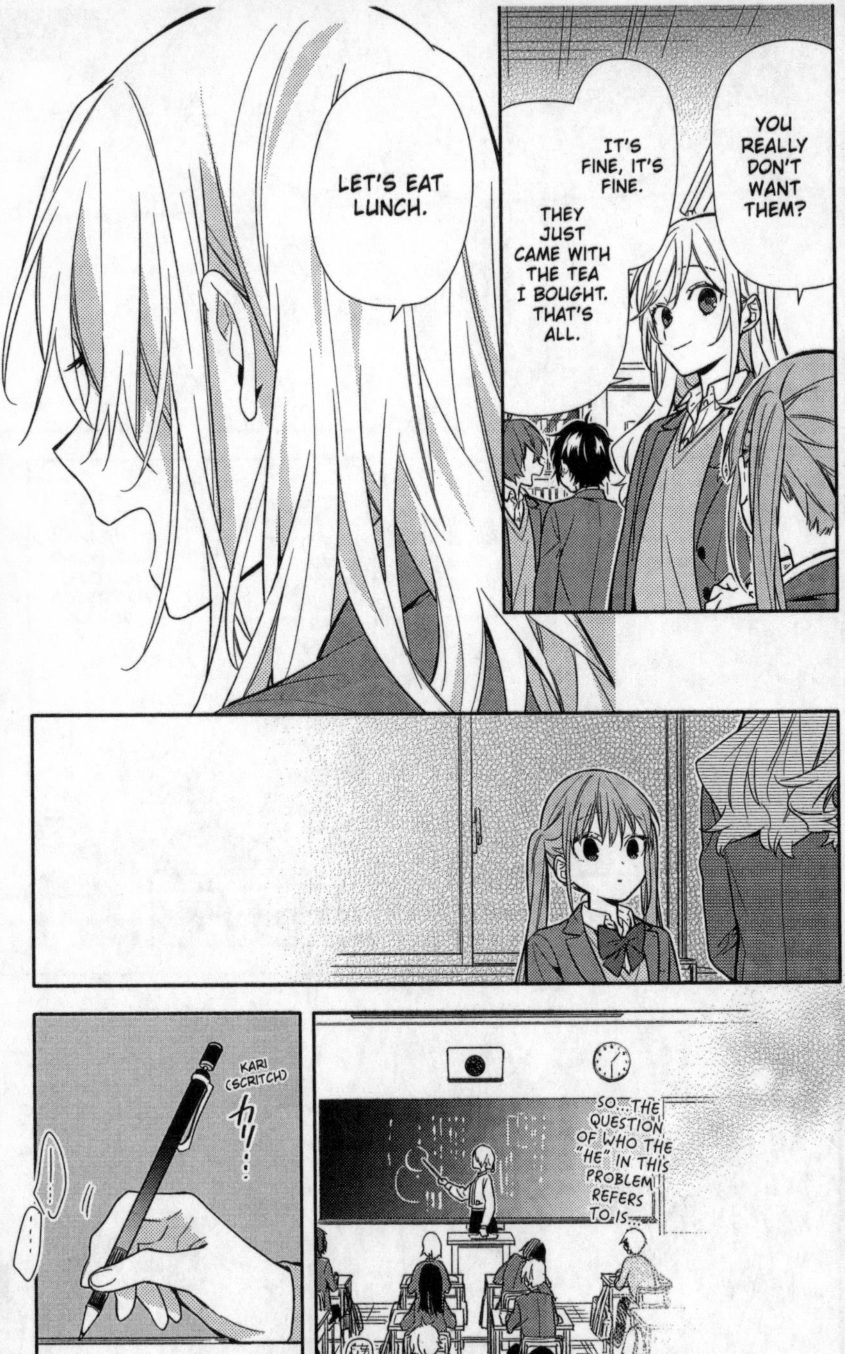
YOU REALLY DON'T WANT THEM?
IT'S FINE, IT'S FINE.
THEY JUST CAME WITH THE TEA I BOUGHT. THAT'S ALL.
LET'S EAT LUNCH.
SO...THE QUESTION OF WHO THE "HE" IN THIS PROBLEM REFERS TO IS...
KARI (SCRITCH)
カリ…
...!

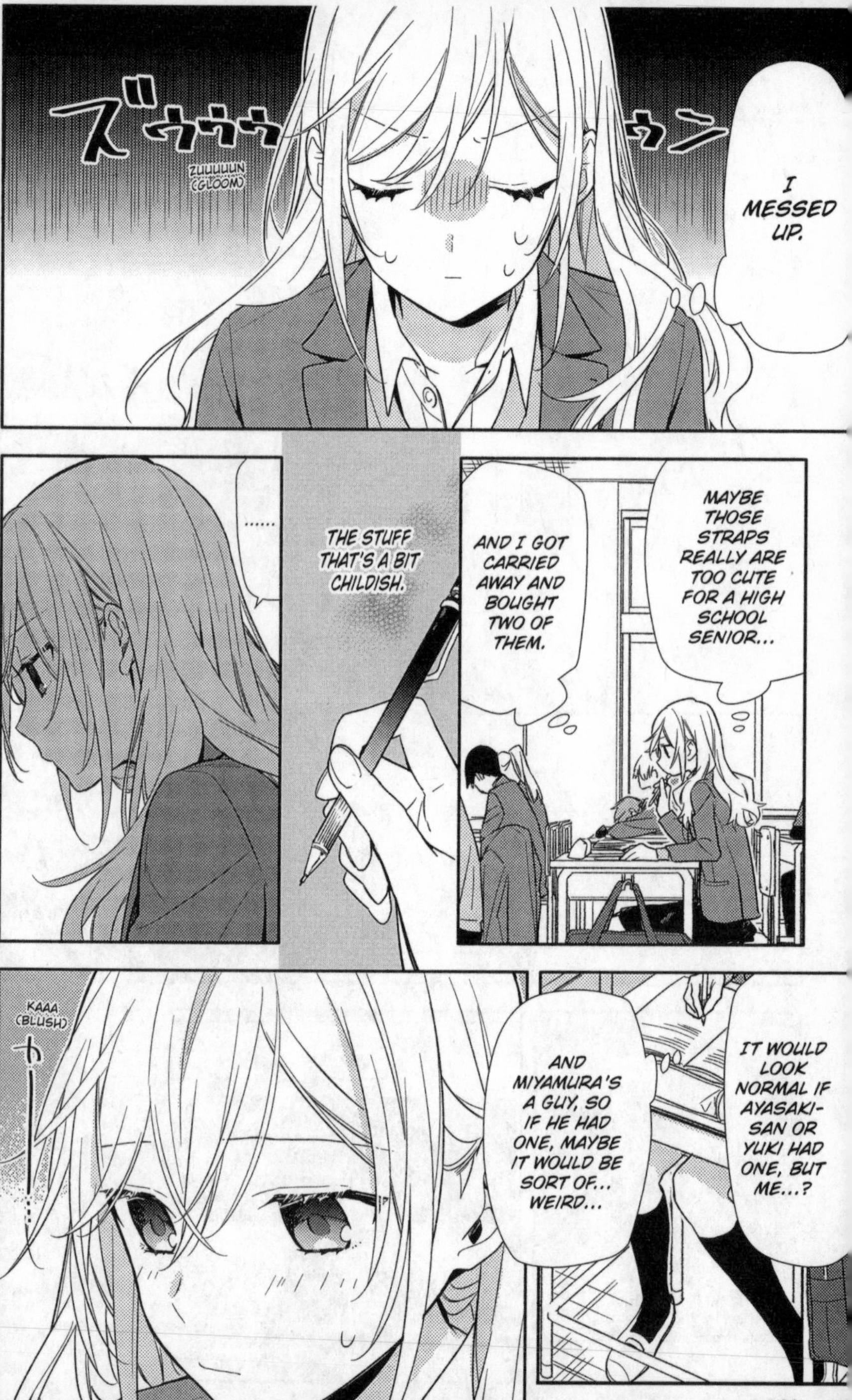
ズウウウ
ZUUUUUN (GLOOM)
ウン
I MESSED UP.
MAYBE THOSE STRAPS REALLY ARE TOO CUTE FOR A HIGH SCHOOL SENIOR...
AND I GOT CARRIED AWAY AND BOUGHT TWO OF THEM.
THE STUFF THAT'S A BIT CHILDISH.
......
IT WOULD LOOK NORMAL IF AYASAKI-SAN OR YUKI HAD ONE, BUT ME...?
AND MIYAMURA'S A GUY, SO IF HE HAD ONE, MAYBE IT WOULD BE SORT OF... WEIRD...
KAAA (BLUSH)

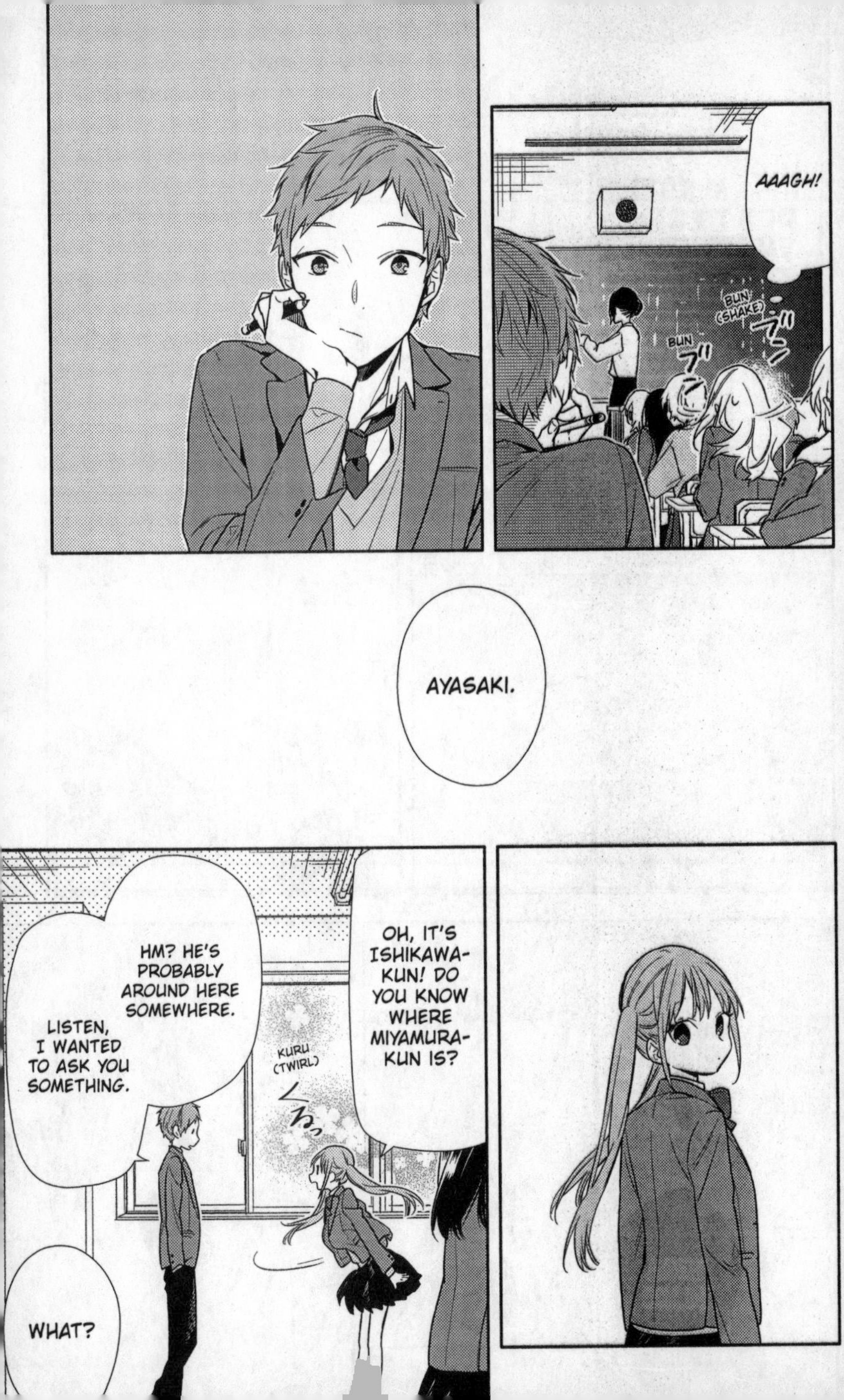
AAAGH!
BUN (SHAKE)
BUN
AYASAKI.
OH, IT'S ISHIKAWA-KUN! DO YOU KNOW WHERE MIYAMURA-KUN IS?
KURU (TWIRL)
HM? HE'S PROBABLY AROUND HERE SOMEWHERE.
LISTEN, I WANTED TO ASK YOU SOMETHING.
WHAT?

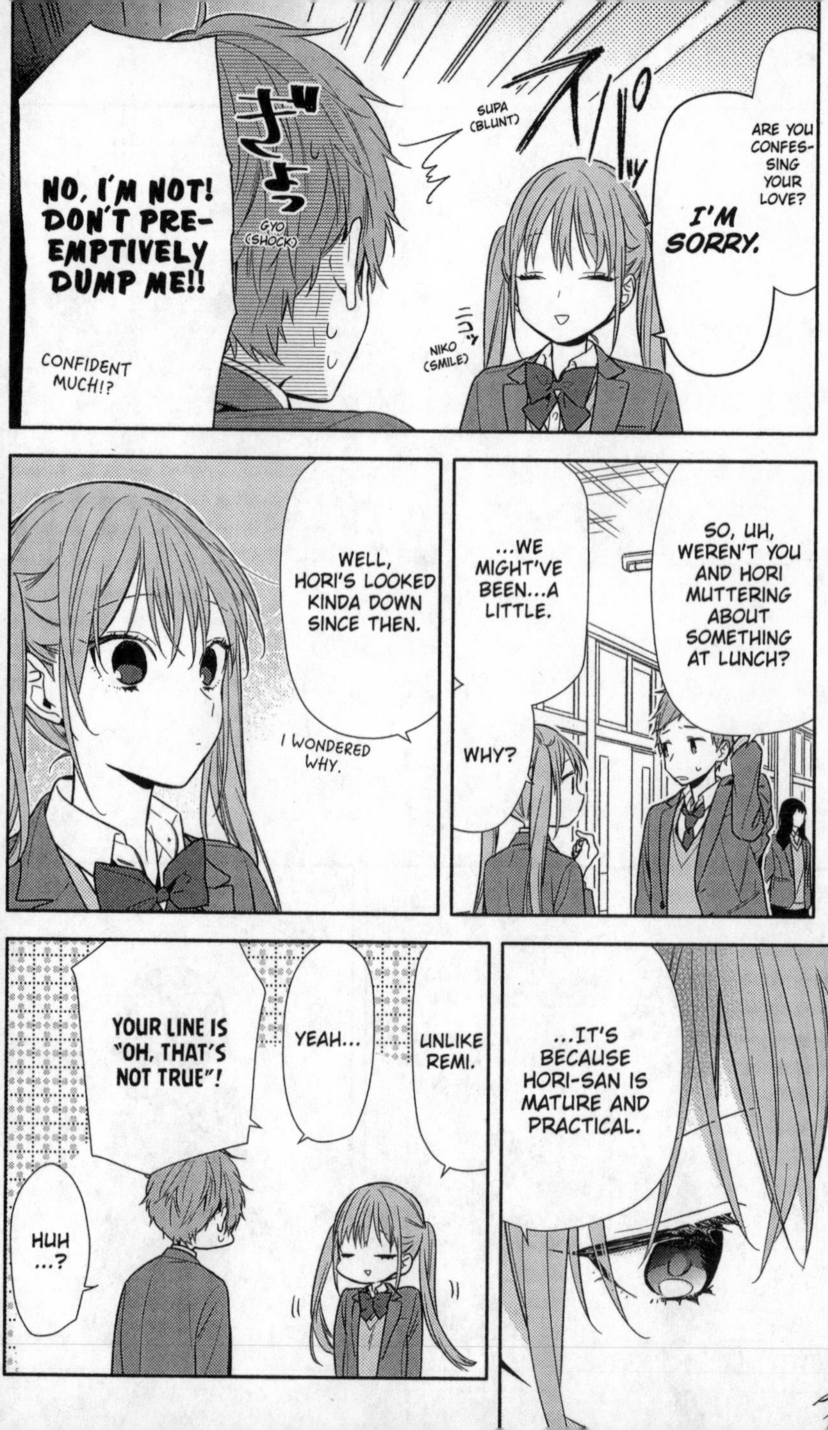
ARE YOU CONFESSING YOUR LOVE?
I'M SORRY.
スパッ
SUPA (BLUNT)
ニコッ
NIKO (SMILE)
ぎょっ
GYO (SHOCK)
NO, I'M NOT! DON'T PRE-EMPTIVELY DUMP ME!!
CONFIDENT MUCH!?
SO, UH, WEREN'T YOU AND HORI MUTTERING ABOUT SOMETHING AT LUNCH?
...WE MIGHT'VE BEEN...A LITTLE.
WHY?
WELL, HORI'S LOOKED KINDA DOWN SINCE THEN.
I WONDERED WHY.
...IT'S BECAUSE HORI-SAN IS MATURE AND PRACTICAL.
UNLIKE REMI.
YEAH...
YOUR LINE IS "OH, THAT'S NOT TRUE"!
HUH...?

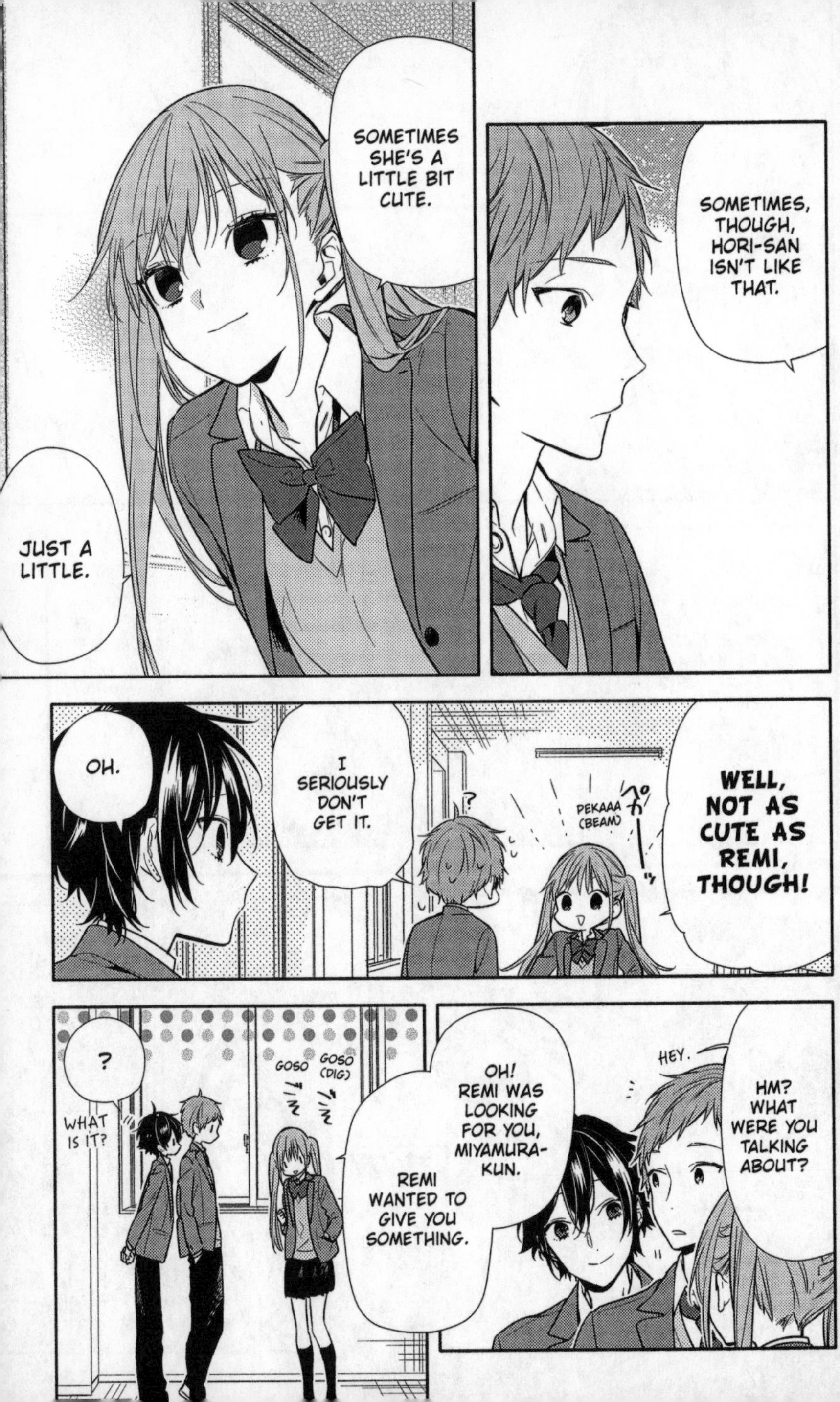
SOMETIMES, THOUGH, HORI-SAN ISN'T LIKE THAT.
SOMETIMES SHE'S A LITTLE BIT CUTE.
JUST A LITTLE.
WELL, NOT AS CUTE AS REMI, THOUGH!
PEKAAA (BEAM)
?
I SERIOUSLY DON'T GET IT.
OH.
HM? WHAT WERE YOU TALKING ABOUT?
HEY.
OH! REMI WAS LOOKING FOR YOU, MIYAMURA-KUN.
REMI WANTED TO GIVE YOU SOMETHING.
GOSO GOSO (DIG)
?
WHAT IS IT?

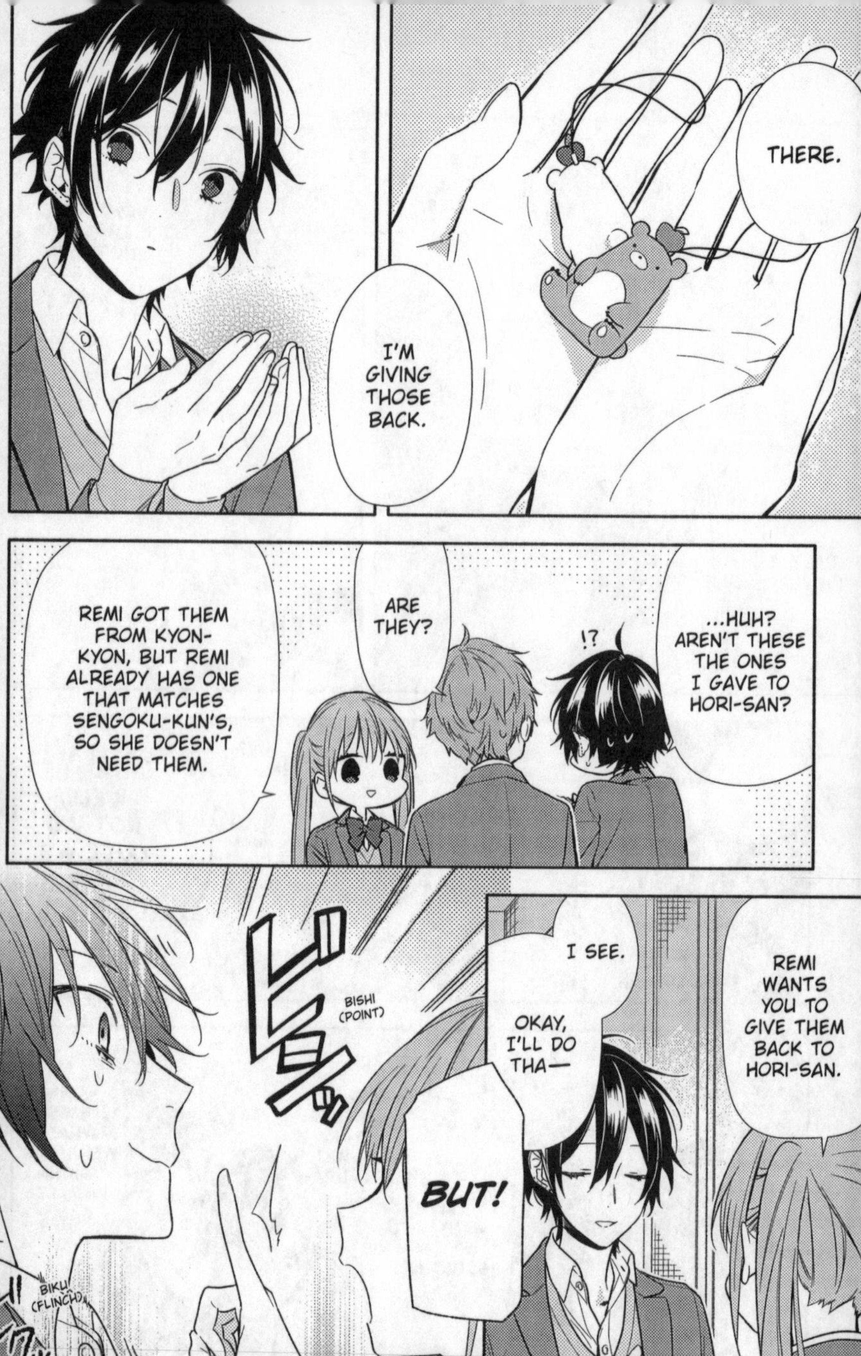
THERE.
I'M GIVING THOSE BACK.
...HUH? AREN'T THESE THE ONES I GAVE TO HORI-SAN?
!?
ARE THEY?
REMI GOT THEM FROM KYON-KYON, BUT REMI ALREADY HAS ONE THAT MATCHES SENGOKU-KUN'S, SO SHE DOESN'T NEED THEM.
REMI WANTS YOU TO GIVE THEM BACK TO HORI-SAN.
I SEE.
OKAY, I'LL DO THA—
BISHI (POINT)
BUT!
BIKU (FLINCH)

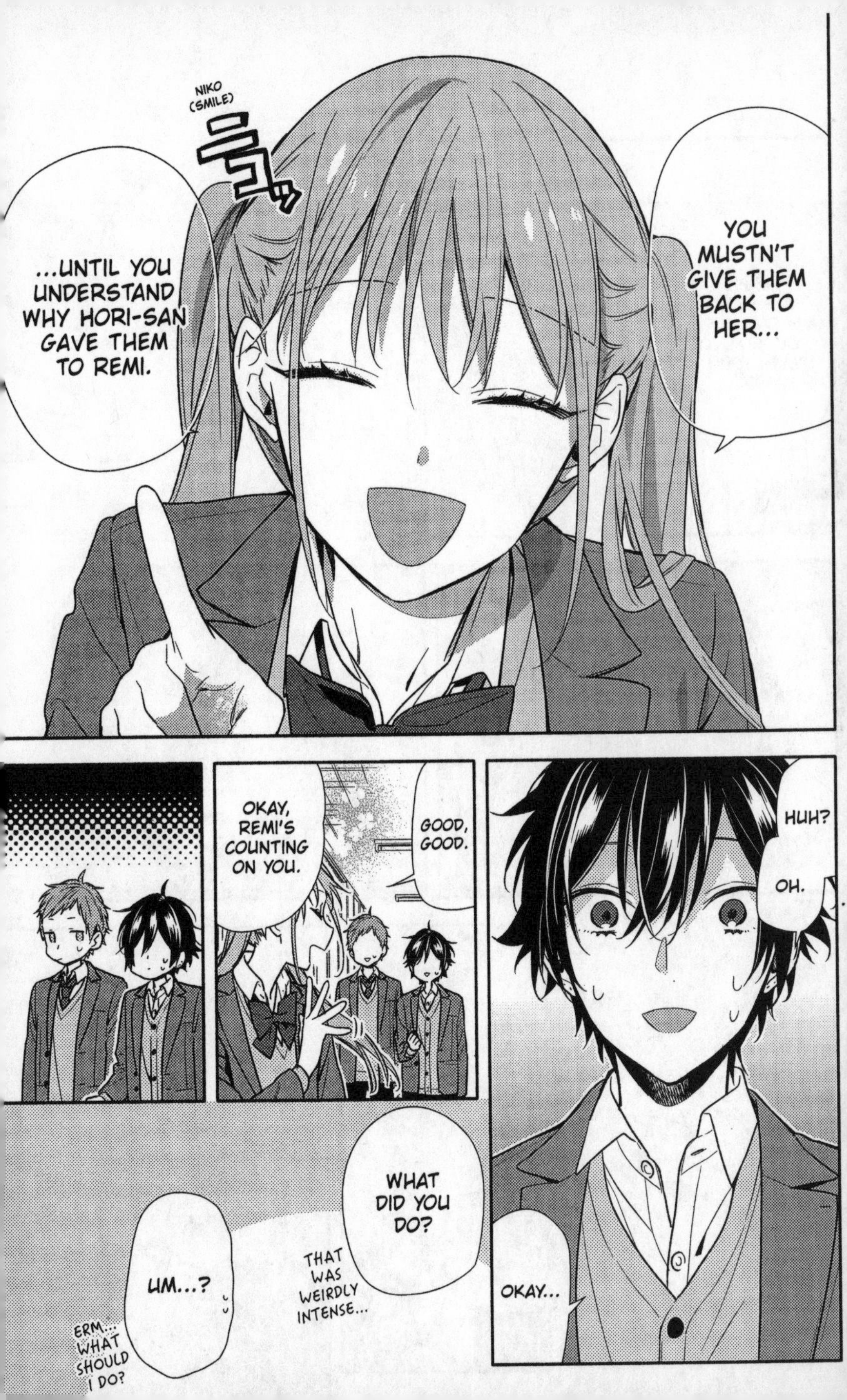
YOU MUSTN'T GIVE THEM BACK TO HER...
NIKO (SMILE)
...UNTIL YOU UNDERSTAND WHY HORI-SAN GAVE THEM TO REMI.
HUH?
OH.
OKAY...
GOOD, GOOD.
OKAY, REMI'S COUNTING ON YOU.
WHAT DID YOU DO?
THAT WAS WEIRDLY INTENSE...
UM...?
ERM... WHAT SHOULD I DO?

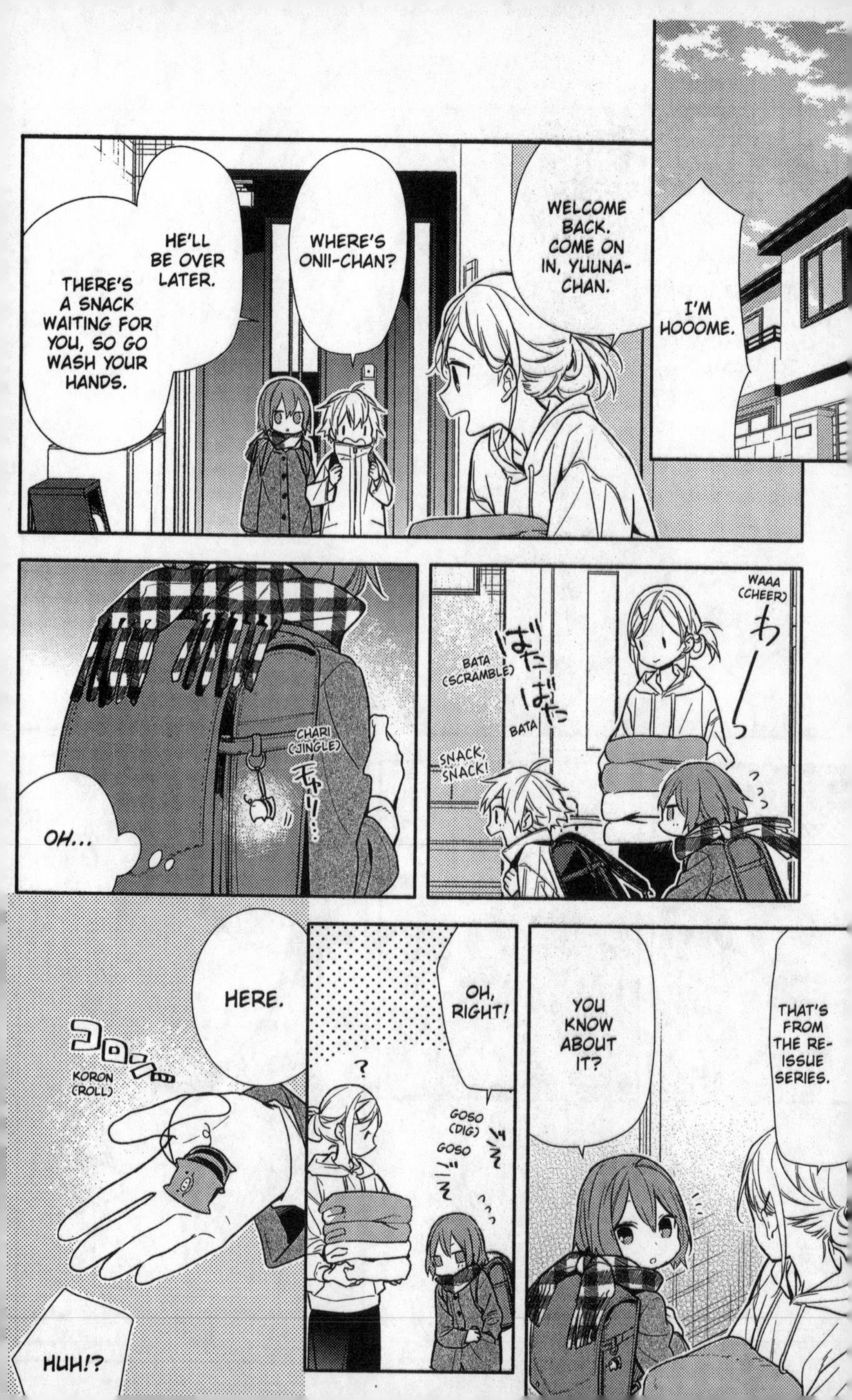
I'M HOOOME.
WELCOME BACK. COME ON IN, YUUNA-CHAN.
WHERE'S ONII-CHAN?
HE'LL BE OVER LATER.
THERE'S A SNACK WAITING FOR YOU, SO GO WASH YOUR HANDS.
わー
WAAA (CHEER)
ばた
BATA (SCRAMBLE)
ばた
BATA
SNACK, SNACK!
チャリ…
CHARI (JINGLE)
OH...
THAT'S FROM THE RE-ISSUE SERIES.
YOU KNOW ABOUT IT?
OH, RIGHT!
?
ごそ
GOSO (DIG)
ごそ
GOSO
HERE.
コロン…
KORON (ROLL)
HUH!?

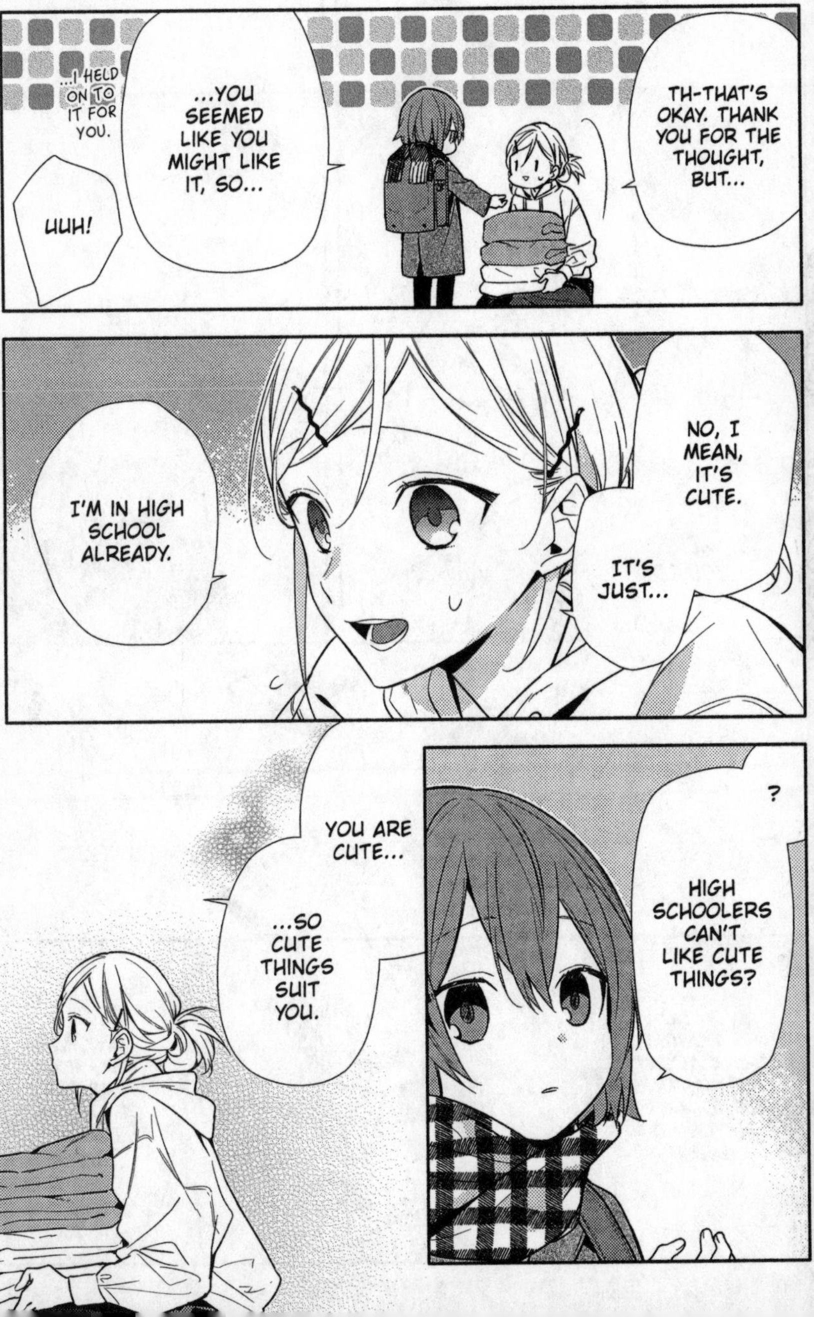
TH-THAT'S OKAY. THANK YOU FOR THE THOUGHT, BUT...
...YOU SEEMED LIKE YOU MIGHT LIKE IT, SO...
...I HELD ON TO IT FOR YOU.
UUH!
NO, I MEAN, IT'S CUTE.
IT'S JUST...
I'M IN HIGH SCHOOL ALREADY.
?
HIGH SCHOOLERS CAN'T LIKE CUTE THINGS?
YOU ARE CUTE...
...SO CUTE THINGS SUIT YOU.

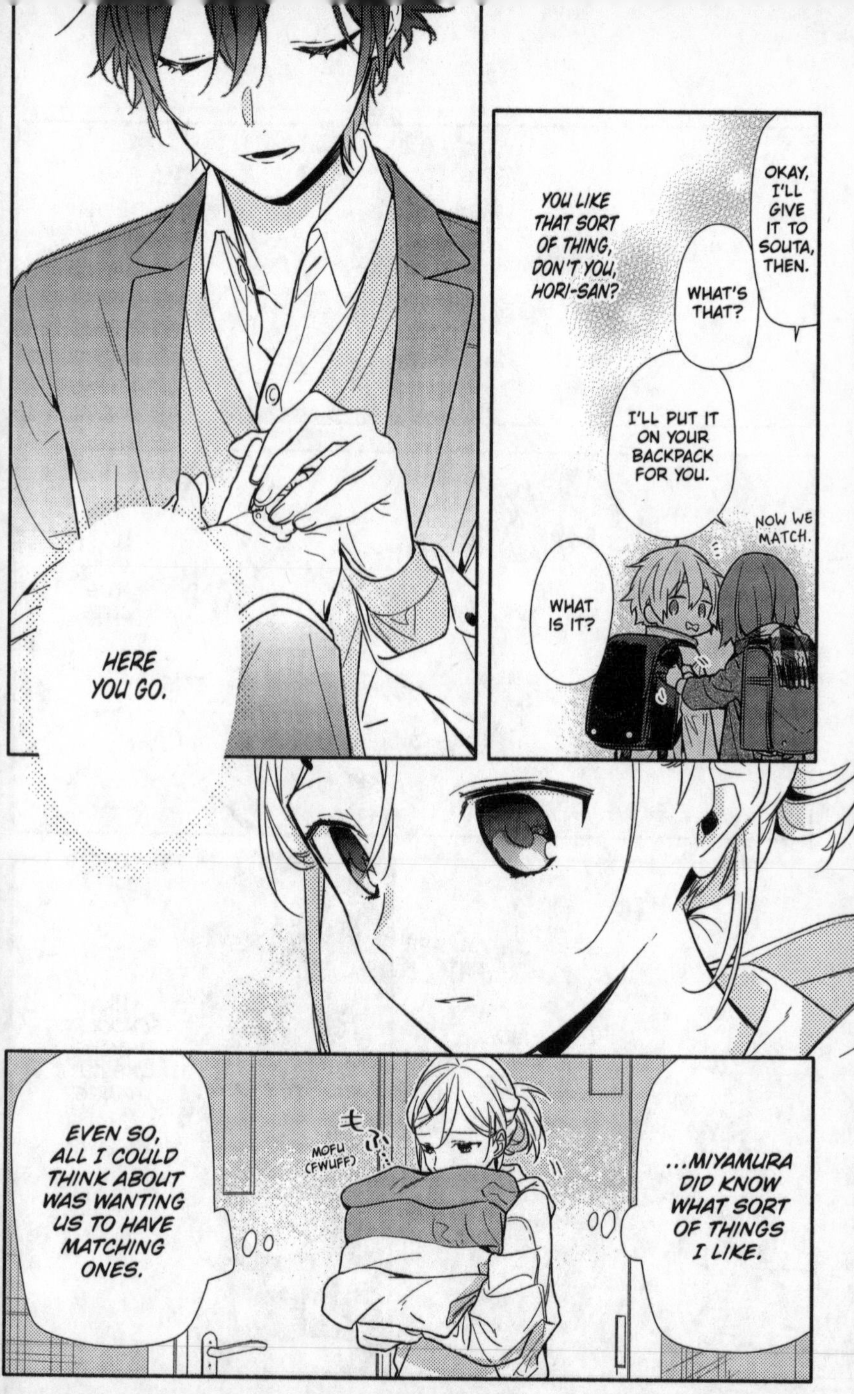
OKAY, I'LL GIVE IT TO SOUTA, THEN.
YOU LIKE THAT SORT OF THING, DON'T YOU, HORI-SAN?
WHAT'S THAT?
I'LL PUT IT ON YOUR BACKPACK FOR YOU.
NOW WE MATCH.
WHAT IS IT?
HERE YOU GO.
...MIYAMURA DID KNOW WHAT SORT OF THINGS I LIKE.
MOFU (FWUFF)
EVEN SO, ALL I COULD THINK ABOUT WAS WANTING US TO HAVE MATCHING ONES.

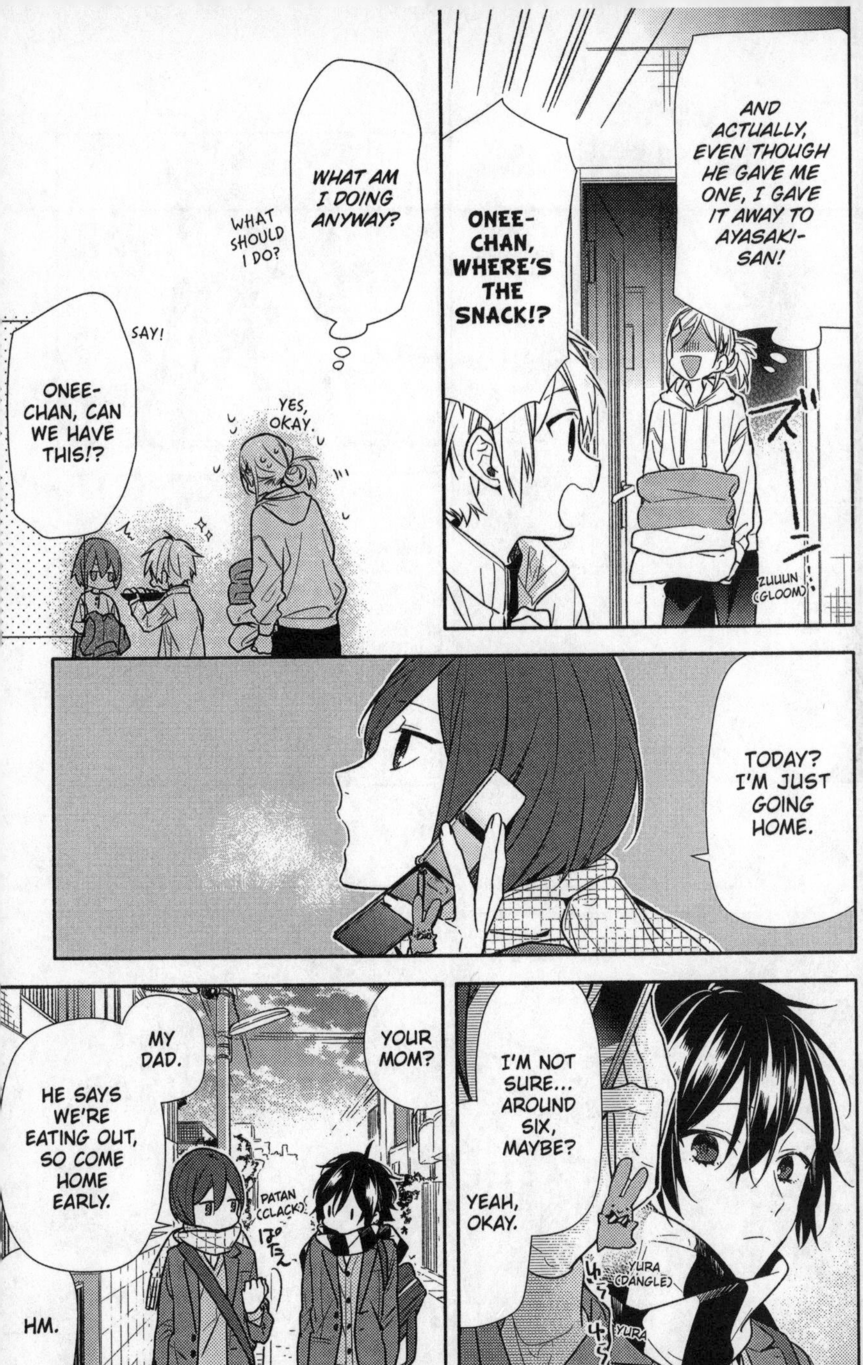
AND ACTUALLY, EVEN THOUGH HE GAVE ME ONE, I GAVE IT AWAY TO AYASAKI-SAN!
ONEE-CHAN, WHERE'S THE SNACK!?
ZUUUN (GLOOM)
WHAT AM I DOING ANYWAY?
WHAT SHOULD I DO?
YES, OKAY.
SAY!
ONEE-CHAN, CAN WE HAVE THIS!?
TODAY? I'M JUST GOING HOME.
I'M NOT SURE... AROUND SIX, MAYBE?
YEAH, OKAY.
YURA (DANGLE)
YURA
YOUR MOM?
PATAN (CLACK)
MY DAD.
HE SAYS WE'RE EATING OUT, SO COME HOME EARLY.
HM.

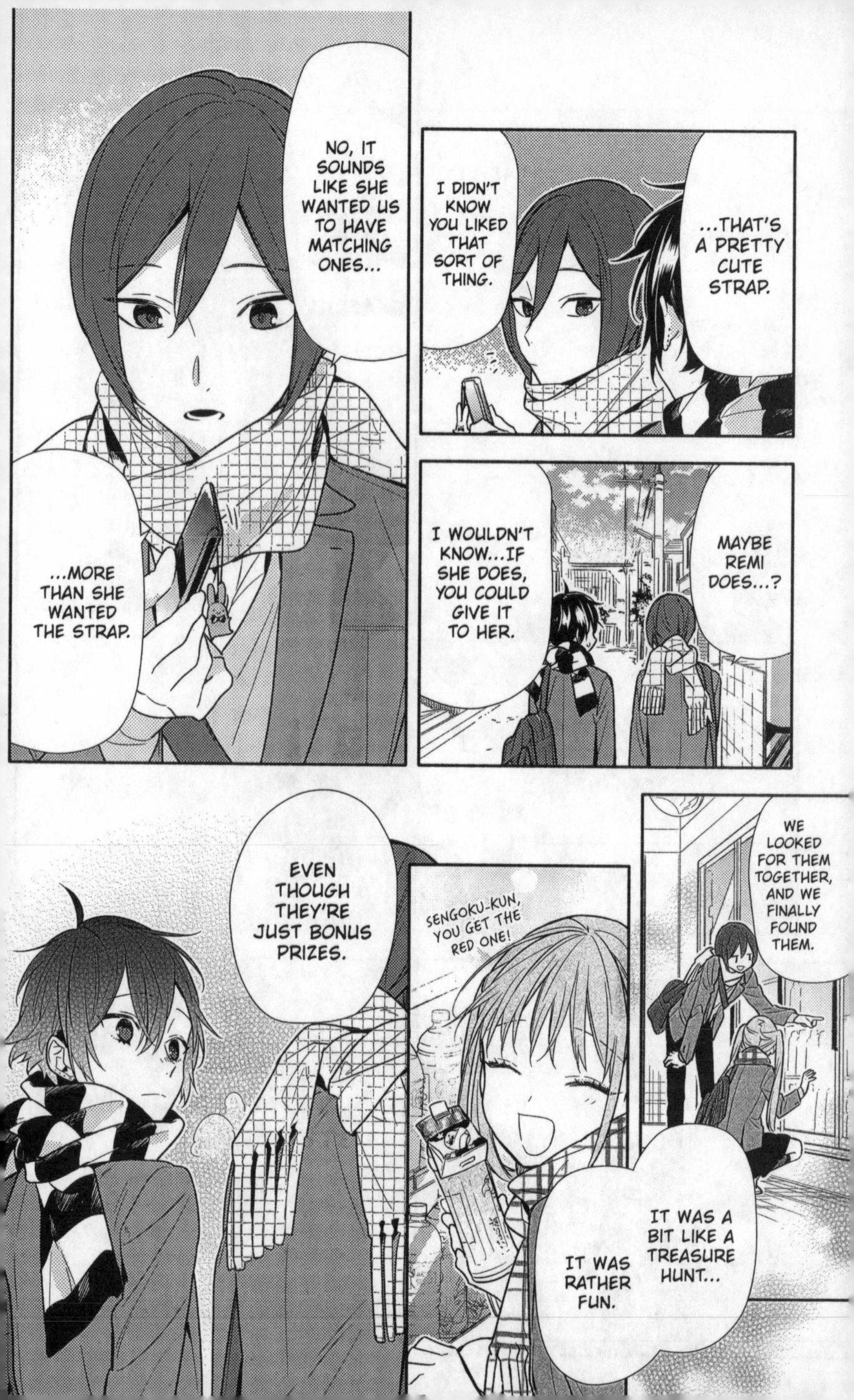
...THAT'S A PRETTY CUTE STRAP.
I DIDN'T KNOW YOU LIKED THAT SORT OF THING.
MAYBE REMI DOES...?
I WOULDN'T KNOW...IF SHE DOES, YOU COULD GIVE IT TO HER.
NO, IT SOUNDS LIKE SHE WANTED US TO HAVE MATCHING ONES...
...MORE THAN SHE WANTED THE STRAP.
WE LOOKED FOR THEM TOGETHER, AND WE FINALLY FOUND THEM.
SENGOKU-KUN, YOU GET THE RED ONE!
IT WAS A BIT LIKE A TREASURE HUNT...
IT WAS RATHER FUN.
EVEN THOUGH THEY'RE JUST BONUS PRIZES.

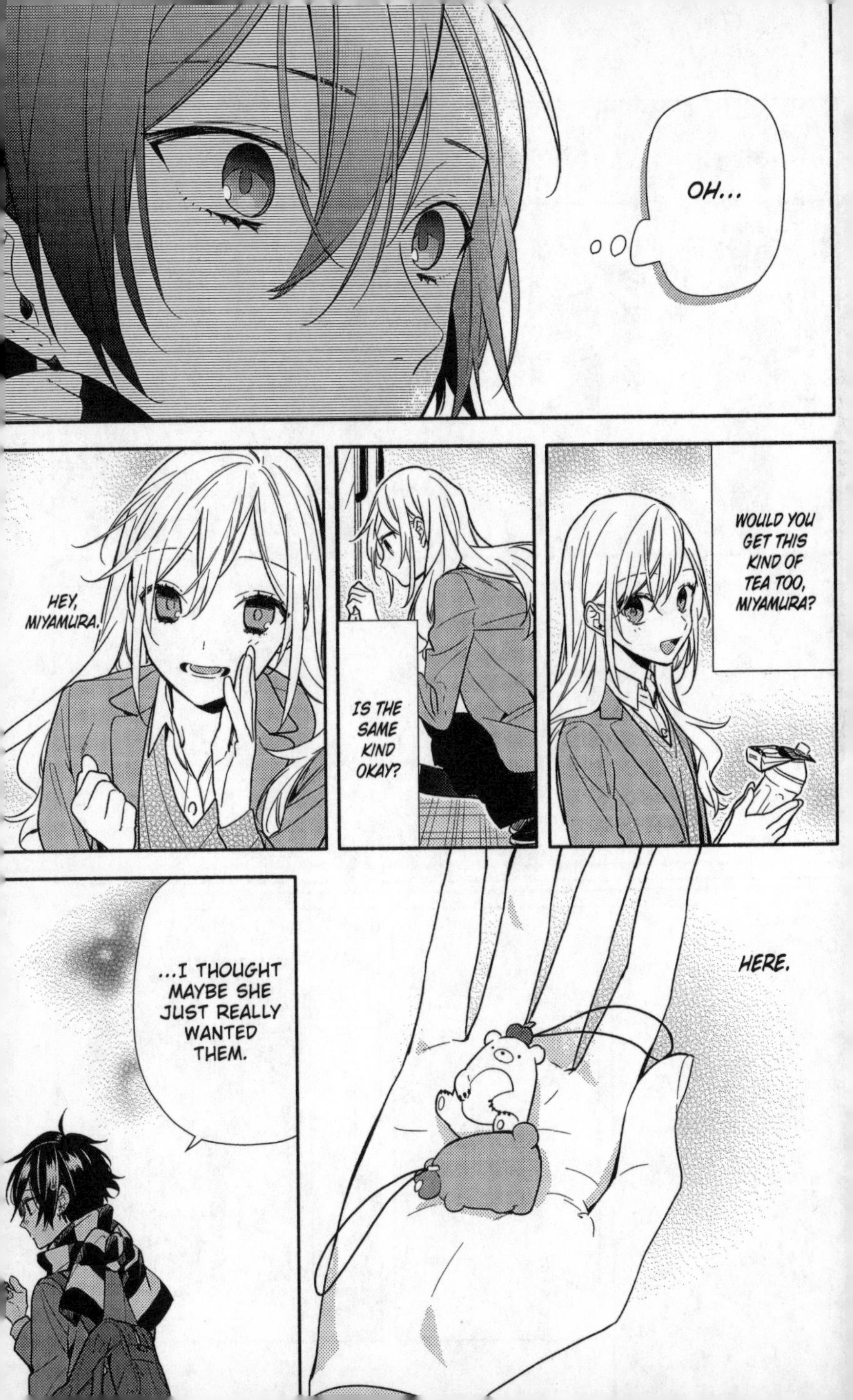
OH...
WOULD YOU GET THIS KIND OF TEA TOO, MIYAMURA?
IS THE SAME KIND OKAY?
HEY, MIYAMURA.
HERE.
...I THOUGHT MAYBE SHE JUST REALLY WANTED THEM.

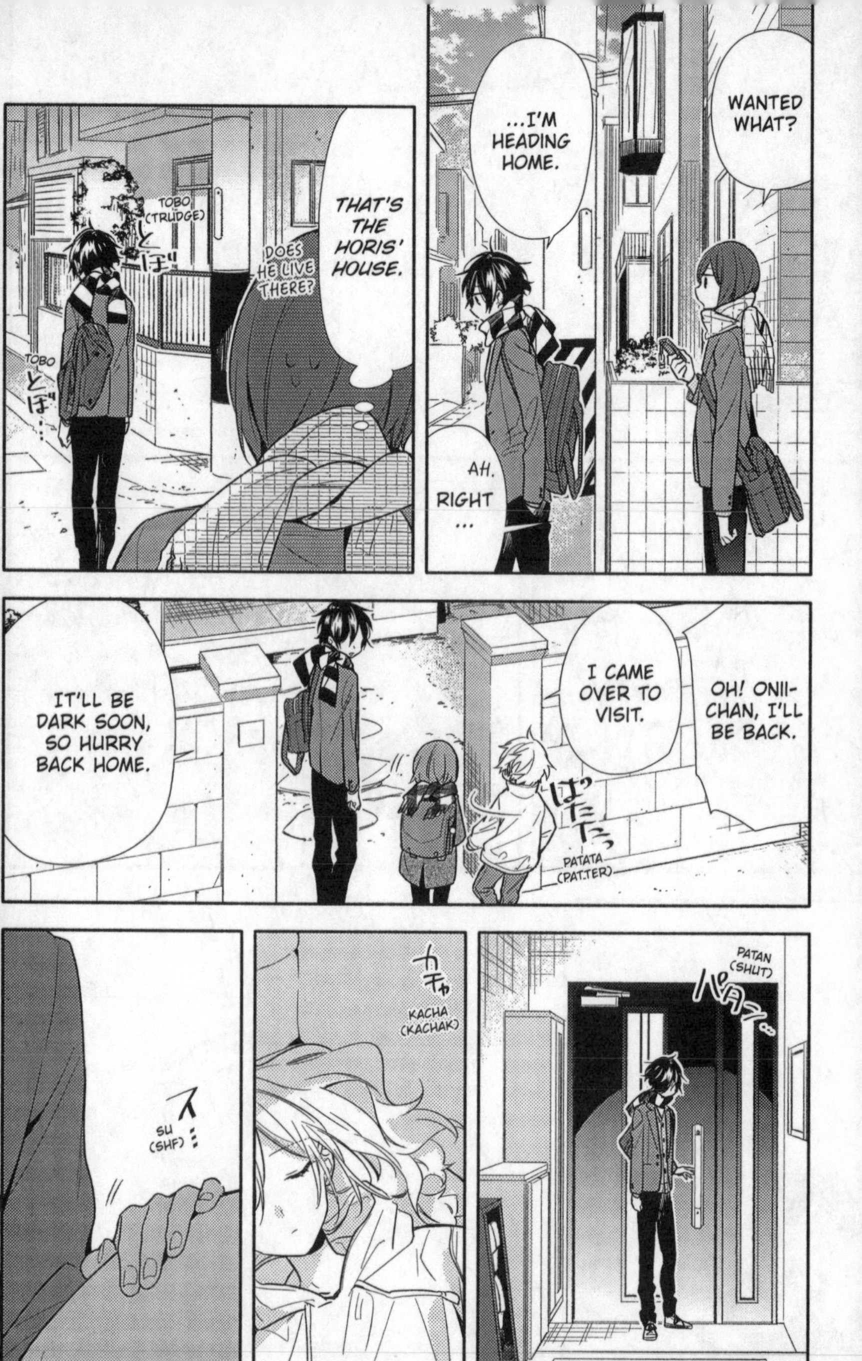
WANTED WHAT?
...I'M HEADING HOME.
AH. RIGHT ...
THAT'S THE HORIS' HOUSE.
DOES HE LIVE THERE?
TOBO (TRUDGE)
TOBO
OH! ONII-CHAN, I'LL BE BACK.
I CAME OVER TO VISIT.
PATATA (PATTER)
IT'LL BE DARK SOON, SO HURRY BACK HOME.
PATAN (SHUT)
KACHA (KACHAK)
SU (SHF)

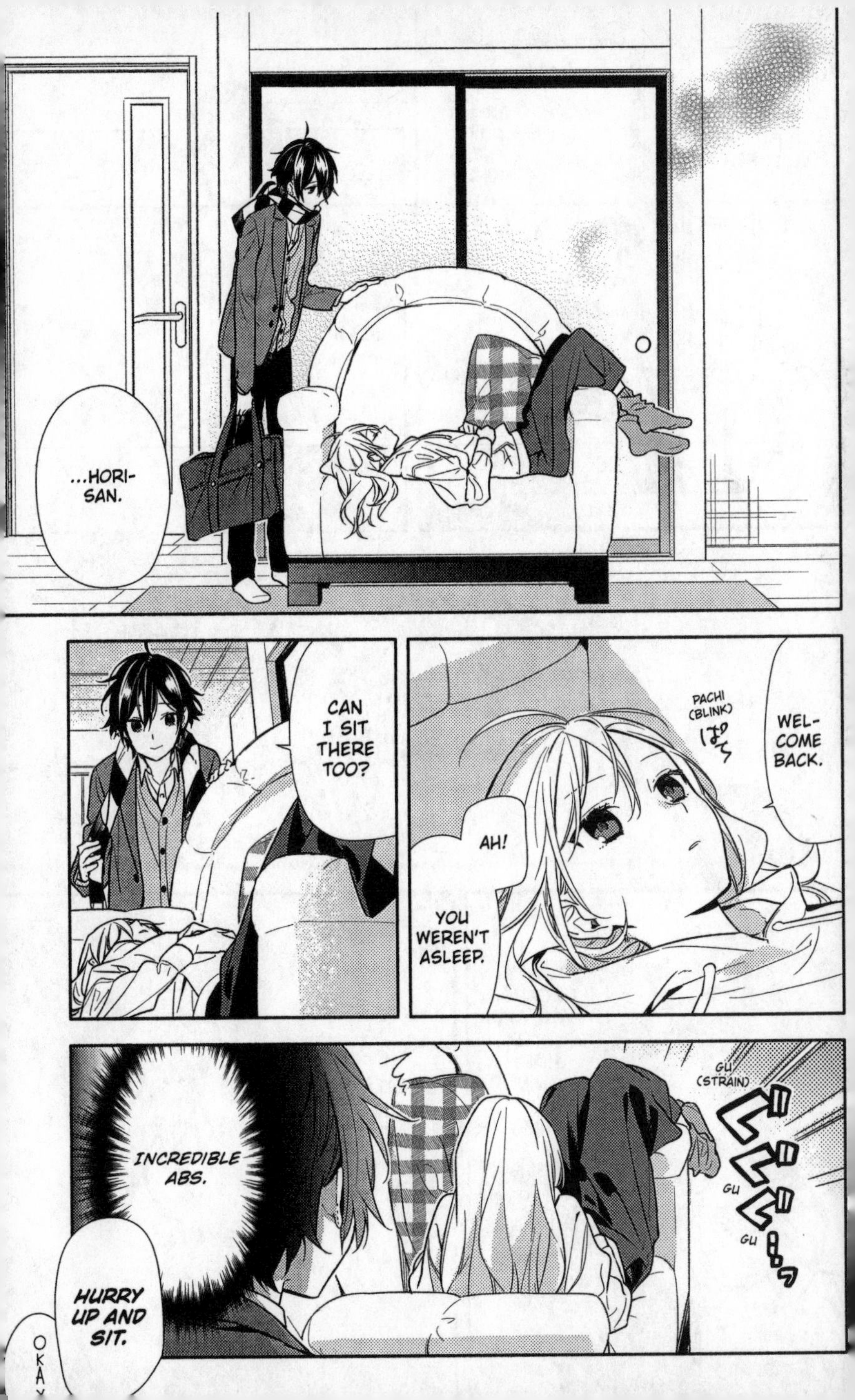
...HORI-SAN.
WEL-COME BACK.
PACHI (BLINK)
AH!
YOU WEREN'T ASLEEP.
CAN I SIT THERE TOO?
GU (STRAIN)
GU
GU
INCREDIBLE ABS.
HURRY UP AND SIT.
OKA

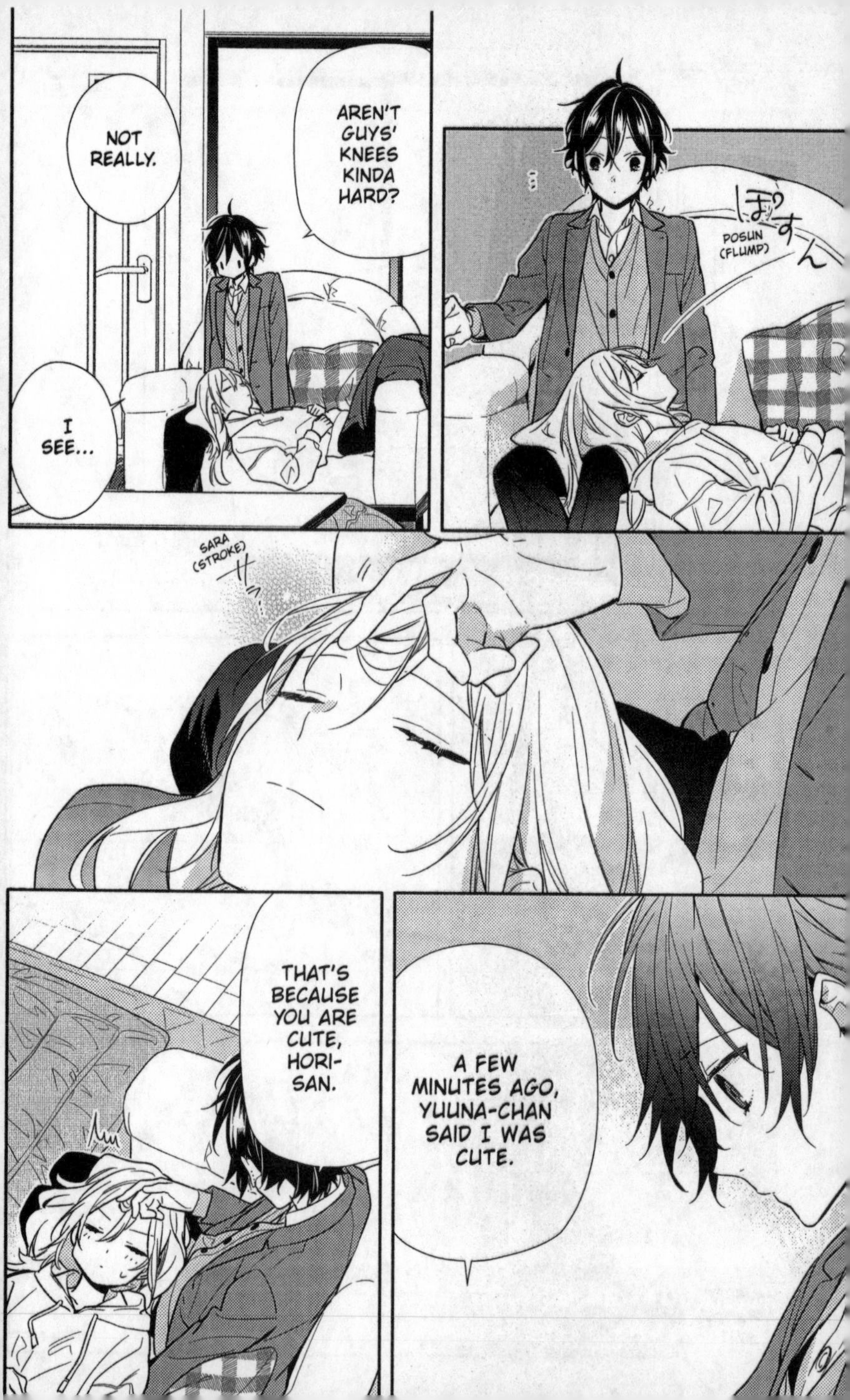
ぽすん
POSUN (FLUMP)
AREN'T GUYS' KNEES KINDA HARD?
NOT REALLY.
I SEE...
SARA (STROKE)
A FEW MINUTES AGO, YUUNA-CHAN SAID I WAS CUTE.
THAT'S BECAUSE YOU ARE CUTE, HORI-SAN.

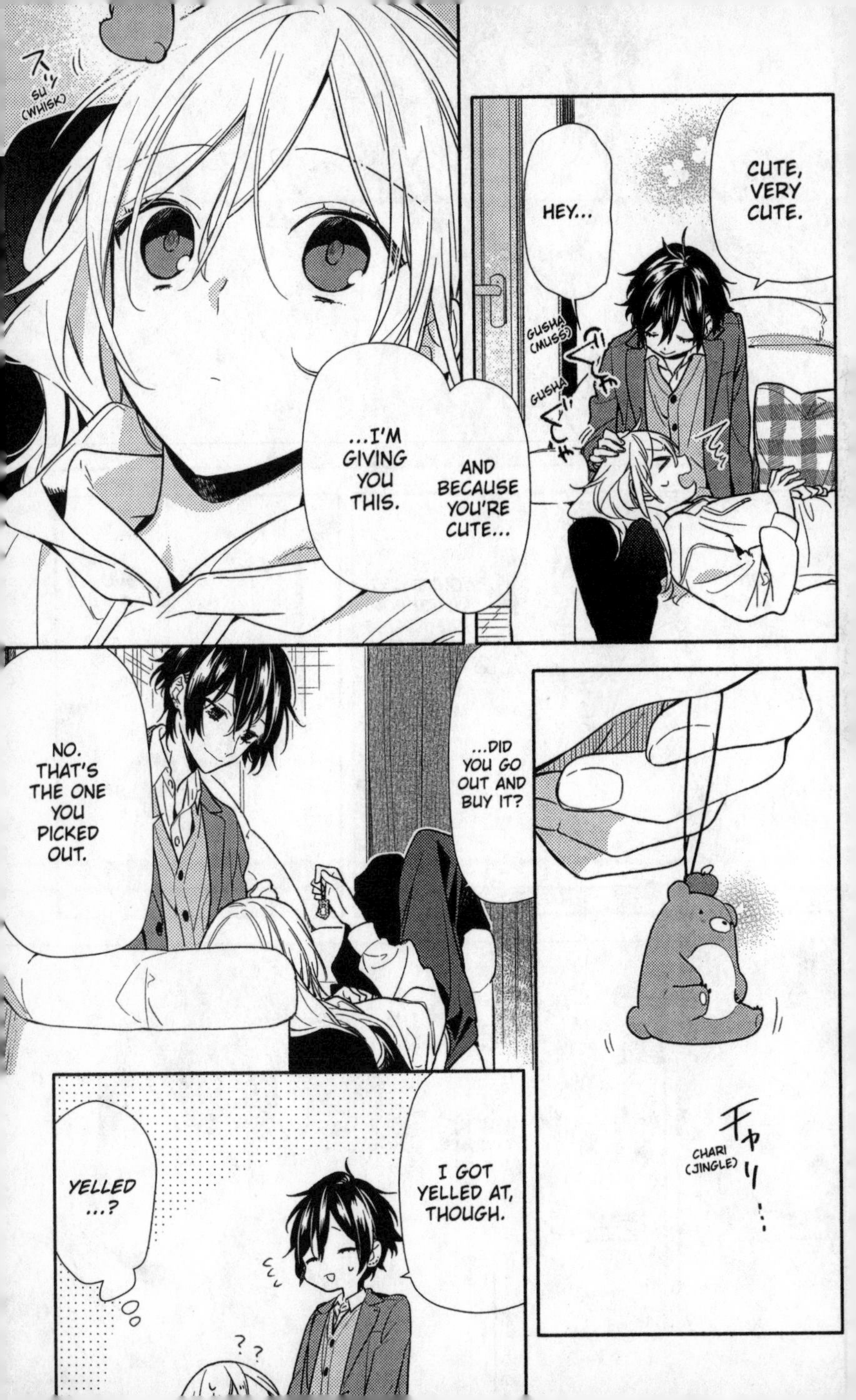
CUTE, VERY CUTE.
HEY...
GUSHA (MUSS)
GUSHA
SU (WHISK)
AND BECAUSE YOU'RE CUTE...
...I'M GIVING YOU THIS.
CHARI (JINGLE)
...DID YOU GO OUT AND BUY IT?
NO. THAT'S THE ONE YOU PICKED OUT.
I GOT YELLED AT, THOUGH.
YELLED ...?

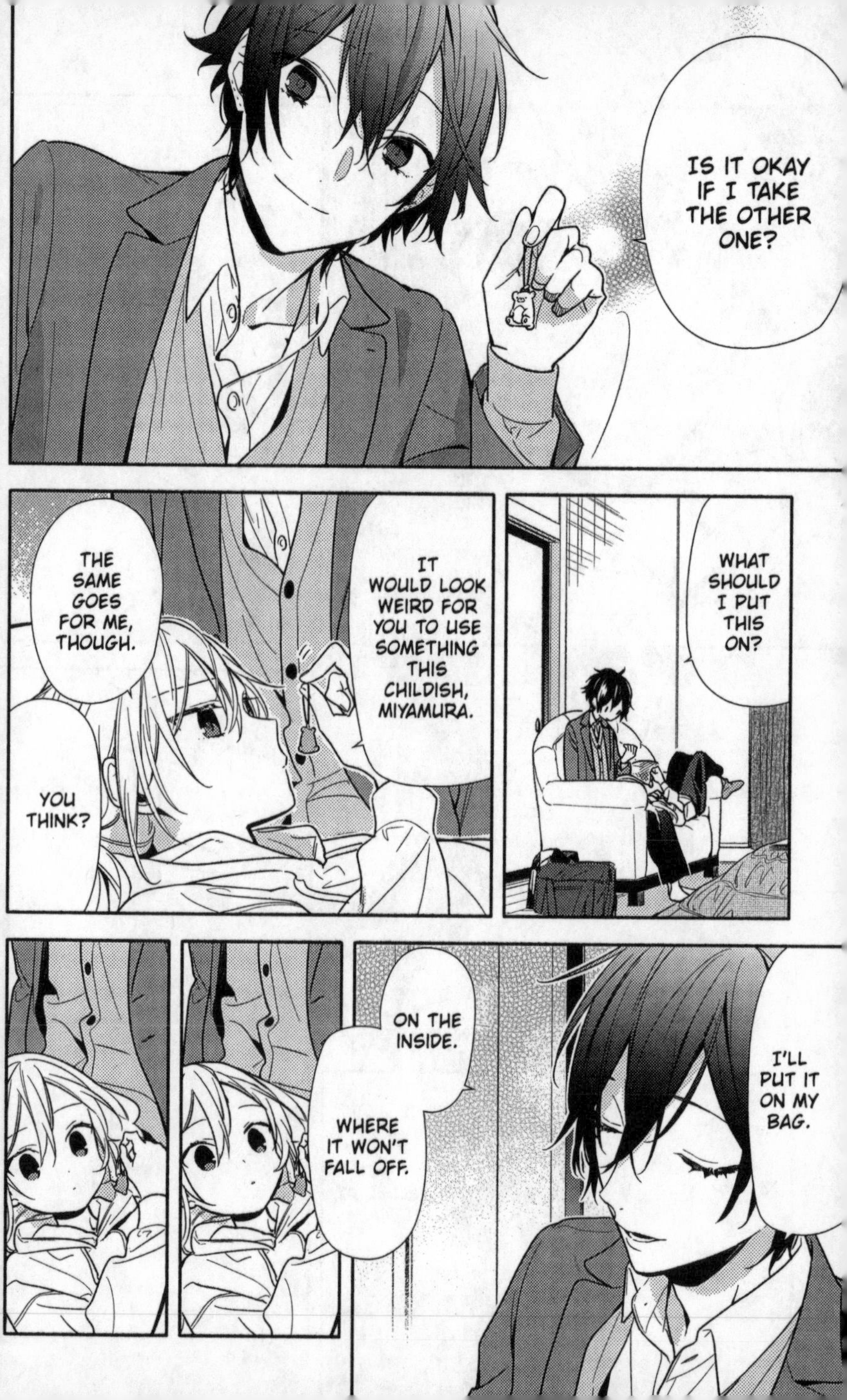
IS IT OKAY IF I TAKE THE OTHER ONE?
WHAT SHOULD I PUT THIS ON?
IT WOULD LOOK WEIRD FOR YOU TO USE SOMETHING THIS CHILDISH, MIYAMURA.
THE SAME GOES FOR ME, THOUGH.
YOU THINK?
I'LL PUT IT ON MY BAG.
ON THE INSIDE.
WHERE IT WON'T FALL OFF.

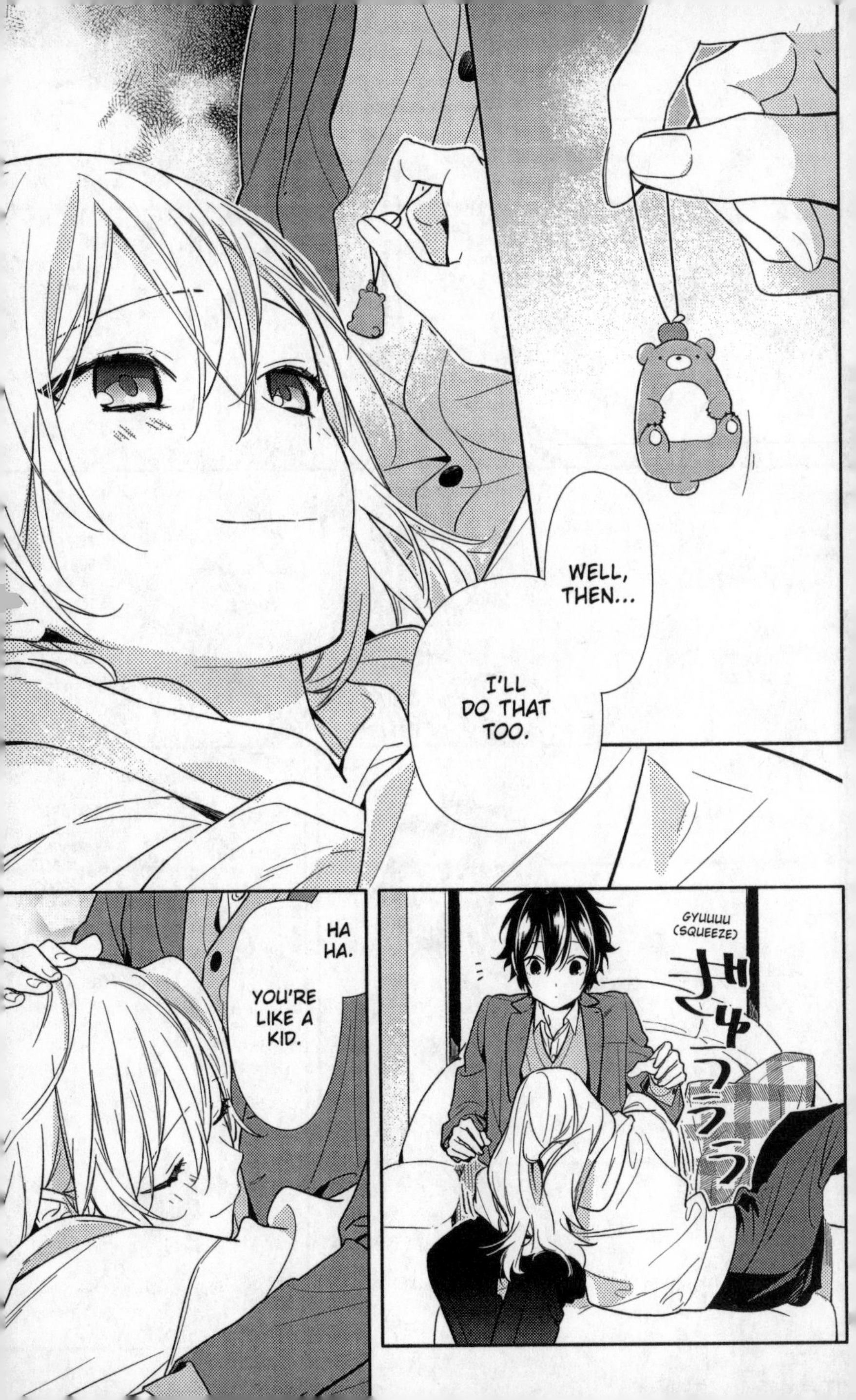
WELL, THEN...
I'LL DO THAT TOO.
GYUUUU (SQUEEZE)
ぎゅううう
HA HA.
YOU'RE LIKE A KID.

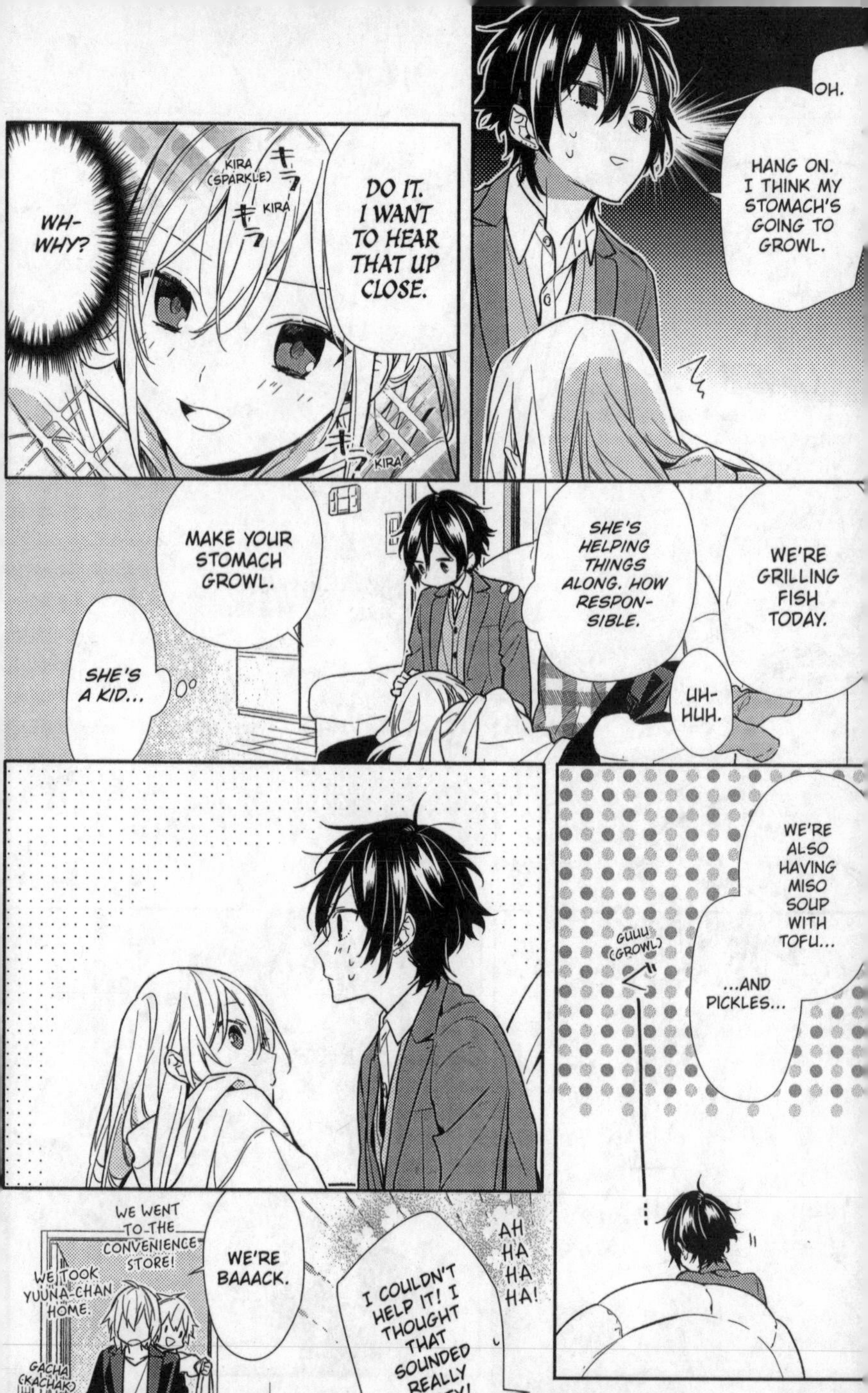
OH.
HANG ON. I THINK MY STOMACH'S GOING TO GROWL.
KIRA (SPARKLE)
KIRA
DO IT. I WANT TO HEAR THAT UP CLOSE.
WH- WHY?
KIRA
WE'RE GRILLING FISH TODAY.
UH-HUH.
SHE'S HELPING THINGS ALONG. HOW RESPONSIBLE.
MAKE YOUR STOMACH GROWL.
SHE'S A KID...
WE'RE ALSO HAVING MISO SOUP WITH TOFU...
...AND PICKLES...
GUUU (GROWL)
AH HA HA HA!
I COULDN'T HELP IT! I THOUGHT THAT SOUNDED REALLY TASTY!
WE'RE BAAACK.
WE WENT TO THE CONVENIENCE STORE!
WE TOOK YUUNA-CHAN HOME.
GACHA (KACHAK)

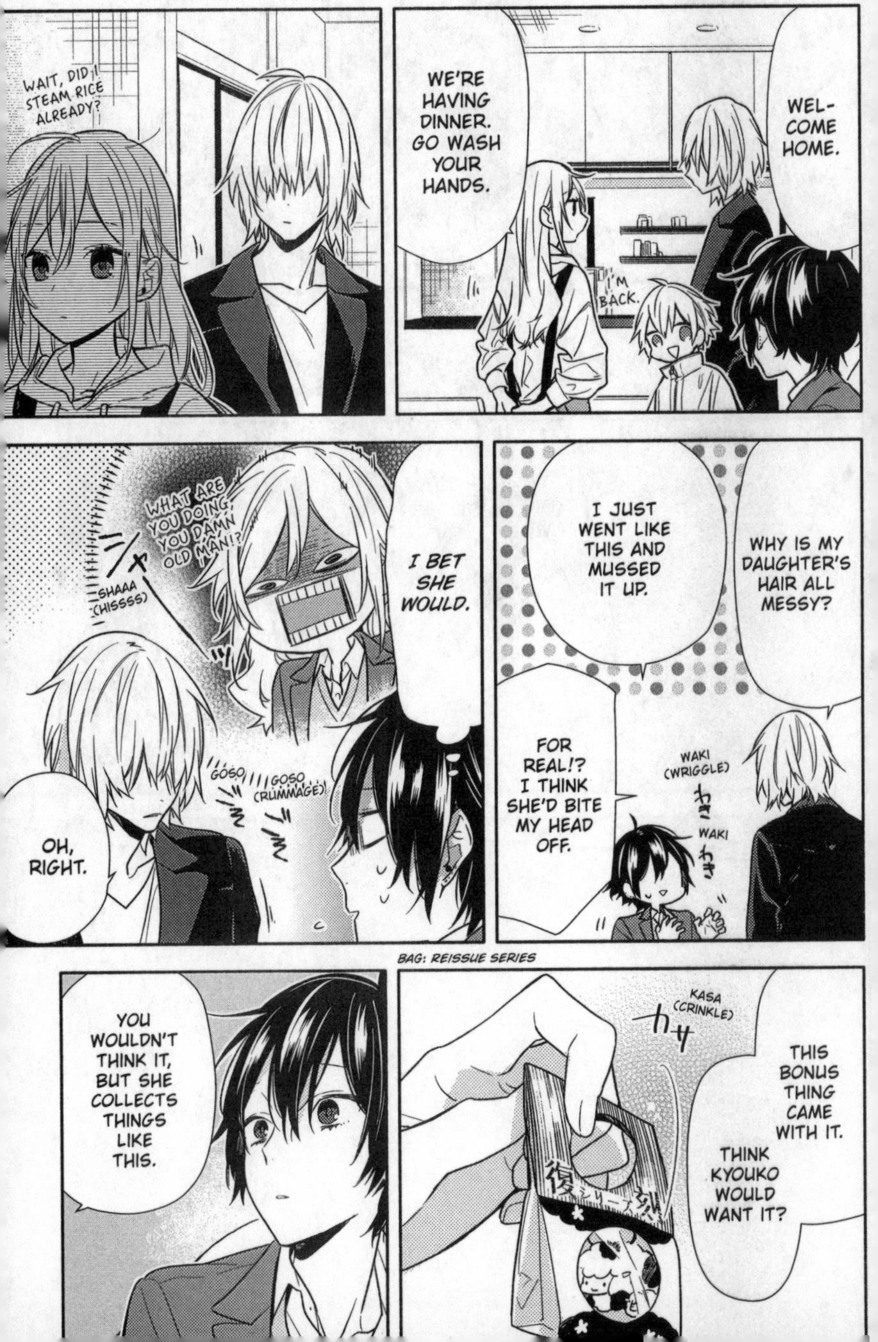
WEL-COME HOME.
I'M BACK.
WE'RE HAVING DINNER. GO WASH YOUR HANDS.
WAIT, DID I STEAM RICE ALREADY?
WHY IS MY DAUGHTER'S HAIR ALL MESSY?
I JUST WENT LIKE THIS AND MUSSED IT UP.
FOR REAL!? I THINK SHE'D BITE MY HEAD OFF.
WAKI (WRIGGLE)
WAKI
I BET SHE WOULD.
WHAT ARE YOU DOING, YOU DAMN OLD MAN!?
SHAAA (HISSSS)
GOSO GOSO (RUMMAGE)
OH, RIGHT.
BAG: REISSUE SERIES
KASA (CRINKLE)
THIS BONUS THING CAME WITH IT.
THINK KYOUKO WOULD WANT IT?
YOU WOULDN'T THINK IT, BUT SHE COLLECTS THINGS LIKE THIS.

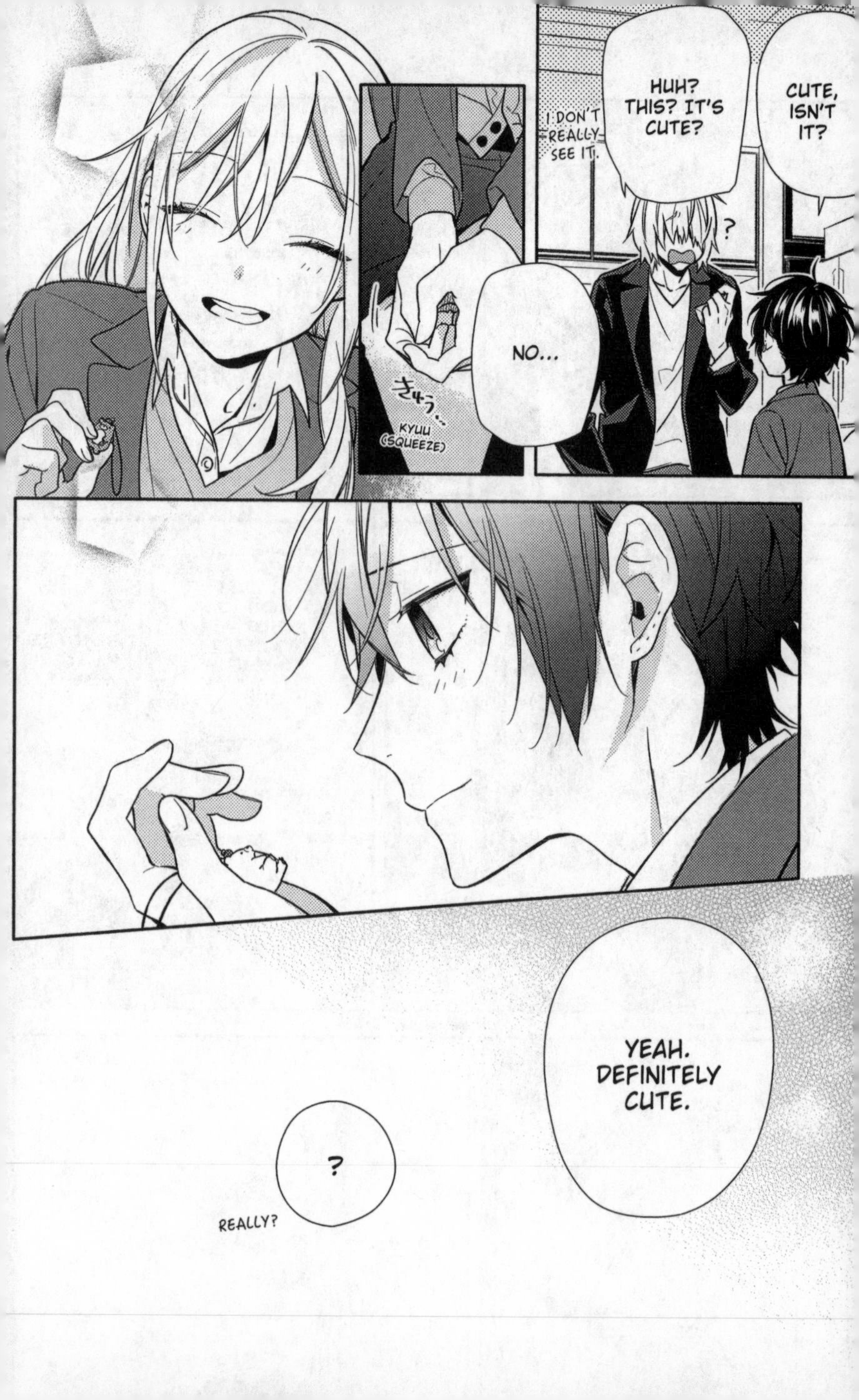
CUTE, ISN'T IT?
HUH? THIS? IT'S CUTE?
I DON'T REALLY SEE IT.
?
NO...
きゅう...
KYUU (SQUEEZE)
YEAH. DEFINITELY CUTE.
?
REALLY?

HORIMIYA

HORIMIYA

Page·100

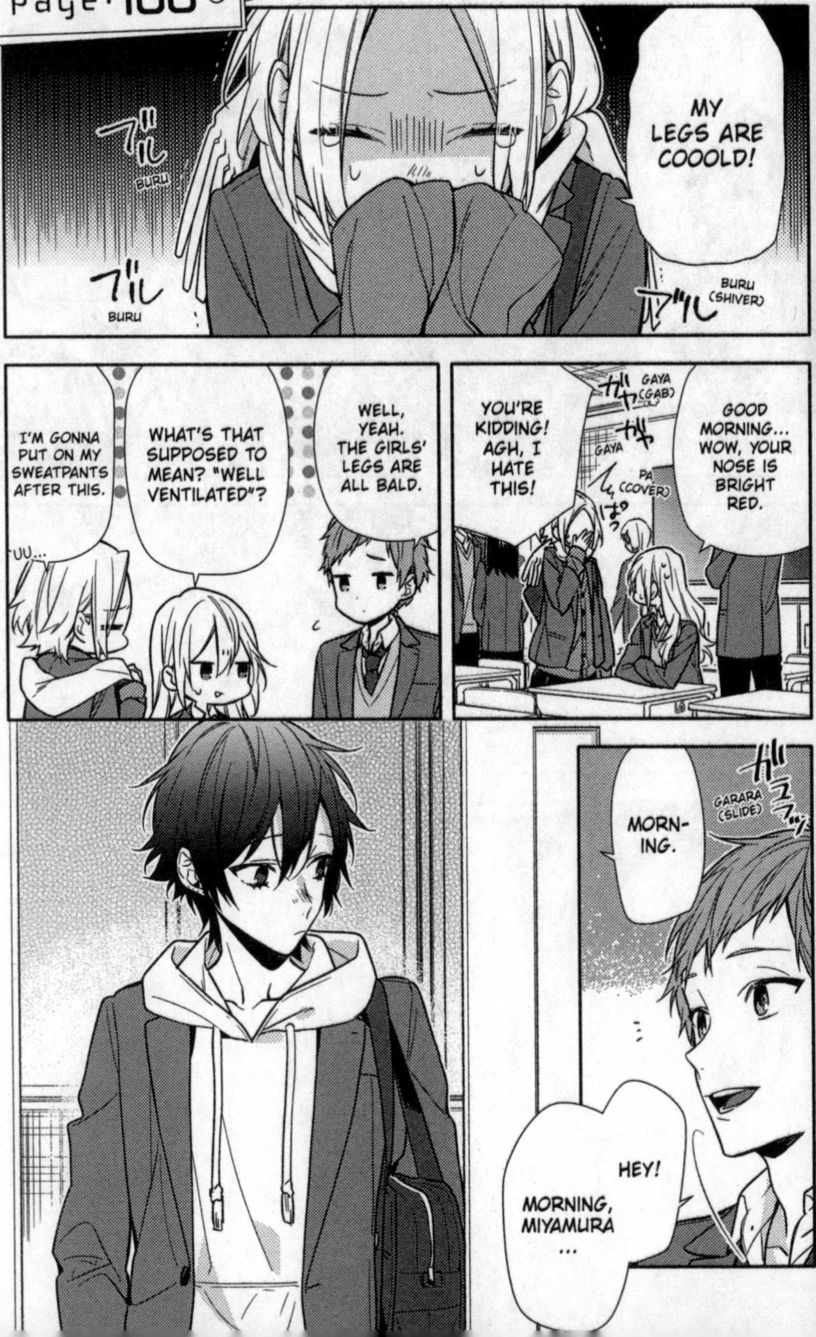
MY LEGS ARE COOOLD!
BURU (SHIVER)
BURU
BURU
GOOD MORNING... WOW, YOUR NOSE IS BRIGHT RED.
GAYA (GAB)
GAYA
PA (COVER)
YOU'RE KIDDING! AGH, I HATE THIS!
WELL, YEAH. THE GIRLS' LEGS ARE ALL BALD.
WHAT'S THAT SUPPOSED TO MEAN? "WELL VENTILATED"?
I'M GONNA PUT ON MY SWEATPANTS AFTER THIS.
UU...
GARARA (SLIDE)
MORN-ING.
HEY!
MORNING, MIYAMURA ...

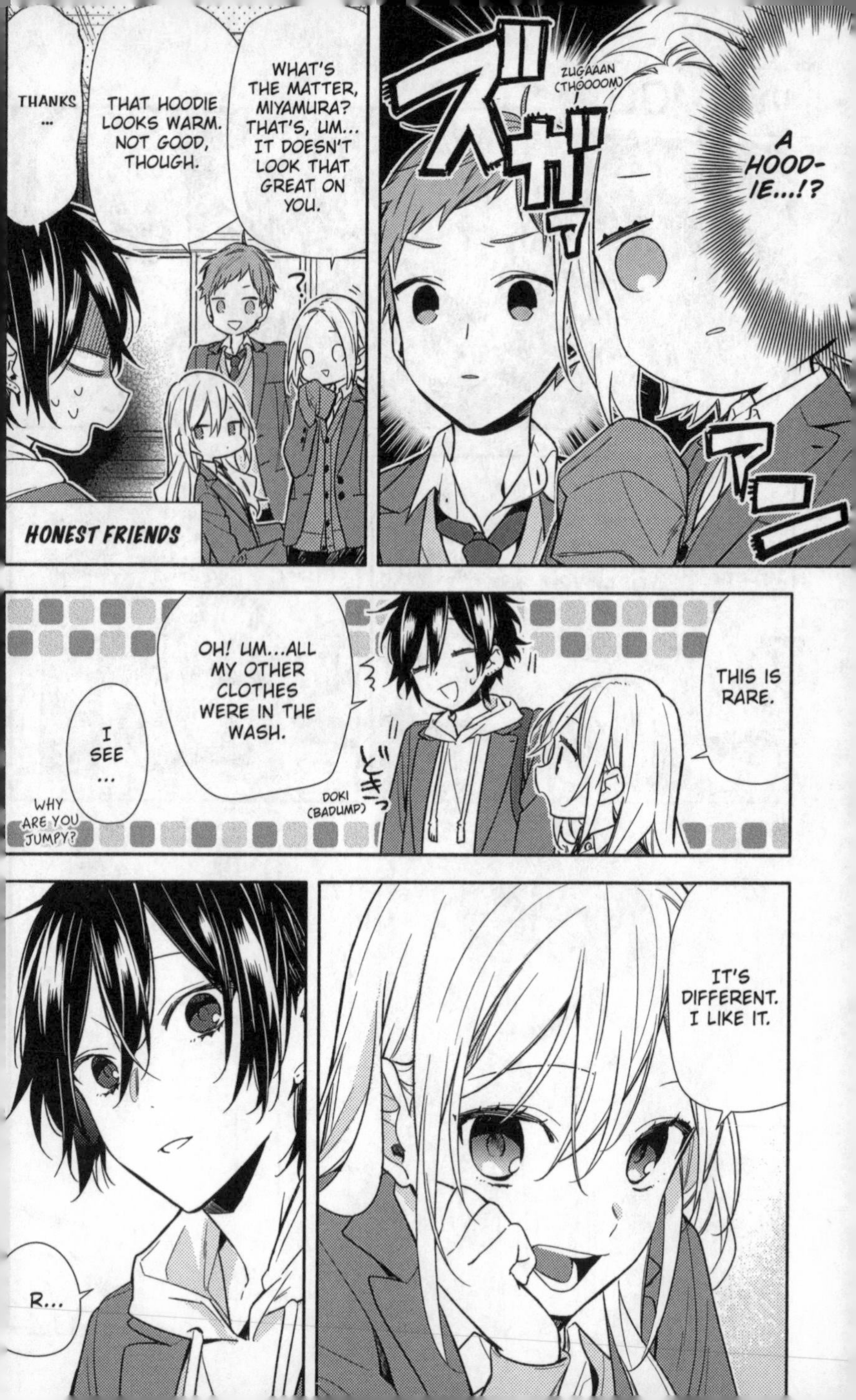
ZUGAAAN (THOOOOM)
A HOODIE...!?
WHAT'S THE MATTER, MIYAMURA? THAT'S, UM... IT DOESN'T LOOK THAT GREAT ON YOU.
THAT HOODIE LOOKS WARM. NOT GOOD, THOUGH.
THANKS...
HONEST FRIENDS
THIS IS RARE.
OH! UM...ALL MY OTHER CLOTHES WERE IN THE WASH.
DOKI (BADUMP)
I SEE...
WHY ARE YOU JUMPY?
IT'S DIFFERENT. I LIKE IT.
R...

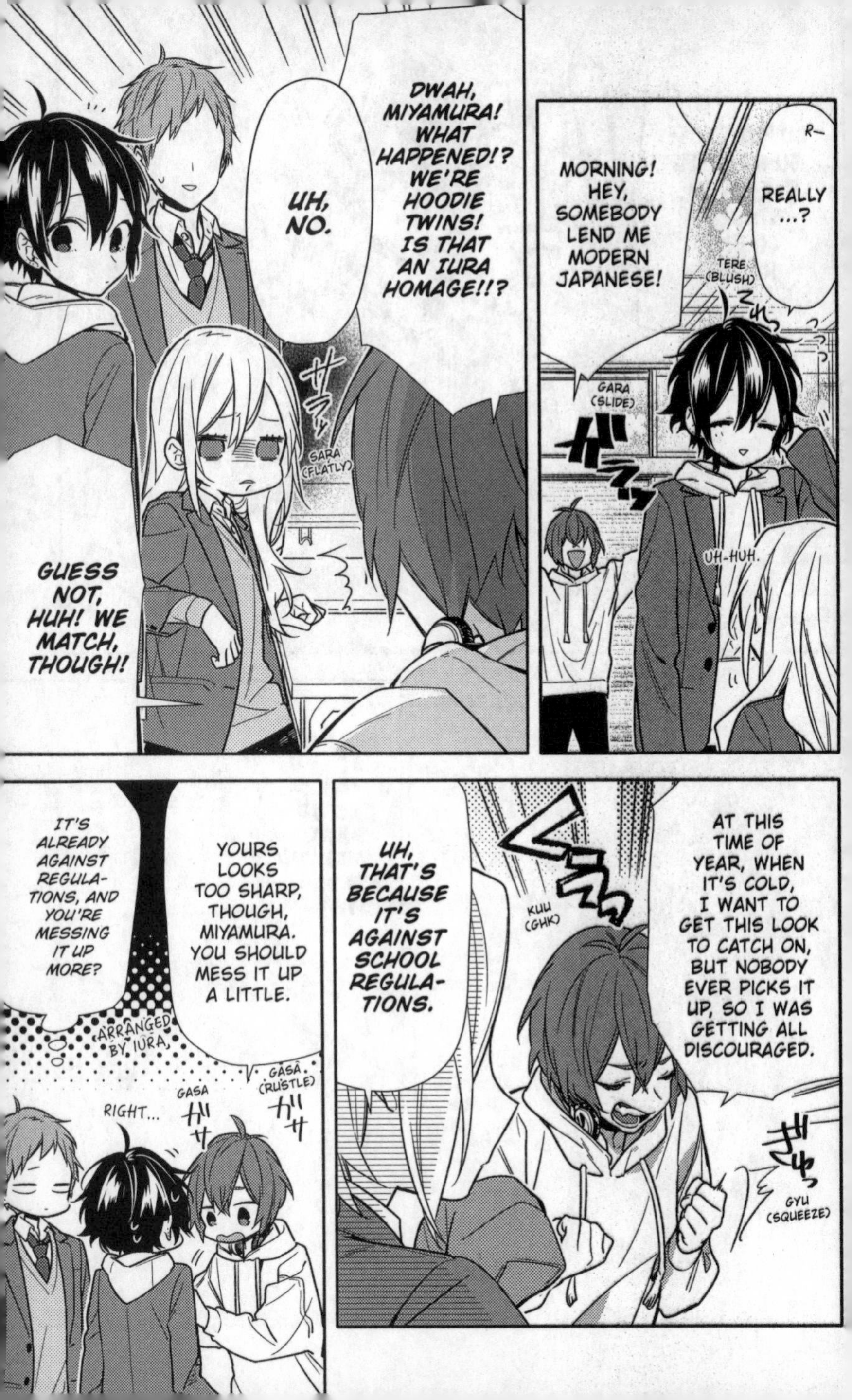
R—
REALLY ...?
MORNING! HEY, SOMEBODY LEND ME MODERN JAPANESE!
TERE (BLUSH)
GARA (SLIDE)
UH-HUH.
DWAH, MIYAMURA! WHAT HAPPENED!? WE'RE HOODIE TWINS! IS THAT AN IURA HOMAGE!!?
UH, NO.
SARA (FLATLY)
GUESS NOT, HUH! WE MATCH, THOUGH!
AT THIS TIME OF YEAR, WHEN IT'S COLD, I WANT TO GET THIS LOOK TO CATCH ON, BUT NOBODY EVER PICKS IT UP, SO I WAS GETTING ALL DISCOURAGED.
KUU (GHK)
UH, THAT'S BECAUSE IT'S AGAINST SCHOOL REGULATIONS.
GYU (SQUEEZE)
YOURS LOOKS TOO SHARP, THOUGH, MIYAMURA. YOU SHOULD MESS IT UP A LITTLE.
IT'S ALREADY AGAINST REGULATIONS, AND YOU'RE MESSING IT UP MORE?
ARRANGED BY IURA
GASA (RUSTLE)
GASA
RIGHT...

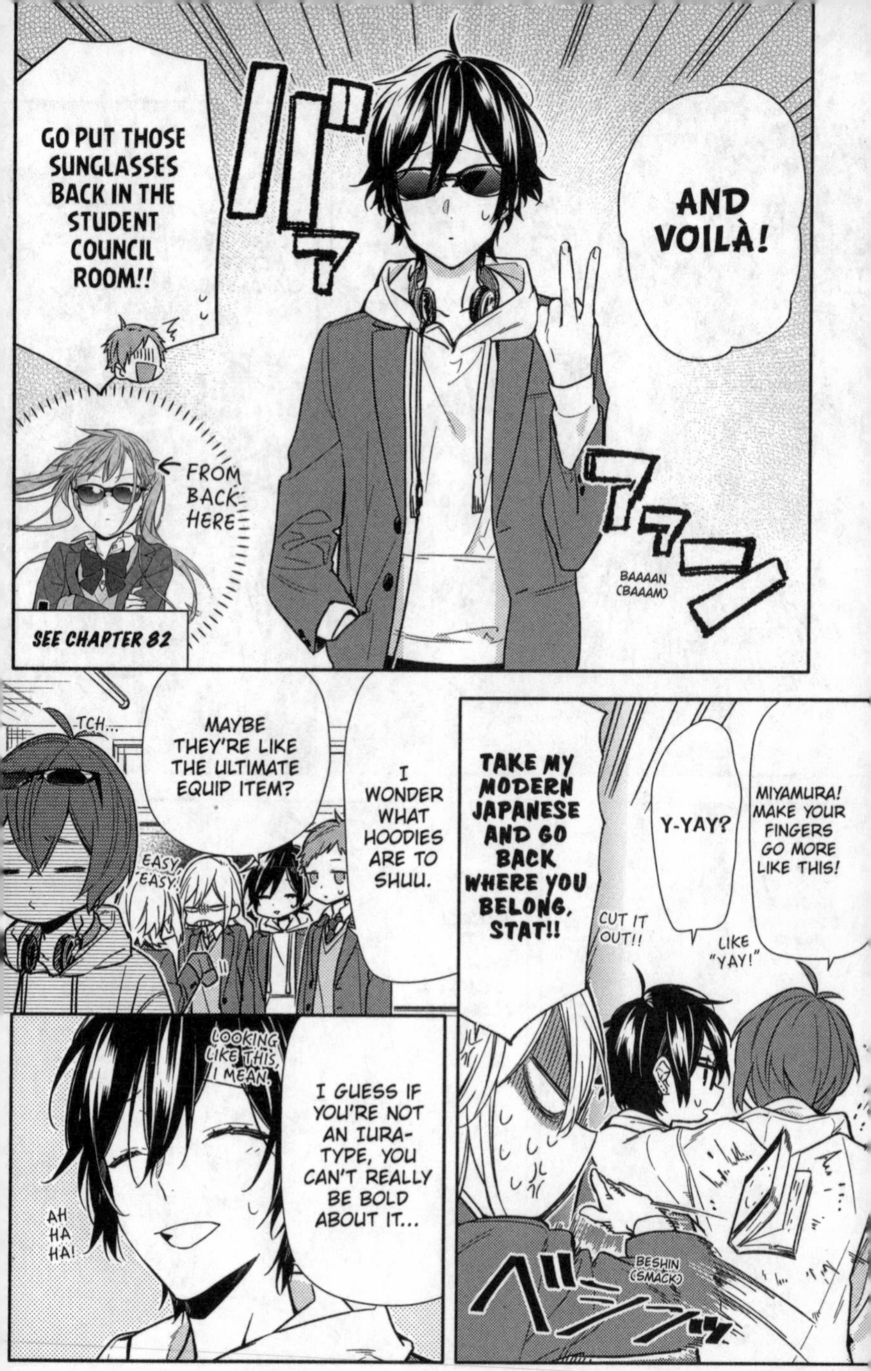
AND VOILÀ!
BAAAAN (BAAAM)
GO PUT THOSE SUNGLASSES BACK IN THE STUDENT COUNCIL ROOM!!
FROM BACK HERE
SEE CHAPTER 82
MIYAMURA! MAKE YOUR FINGERS GO MORE LIKE THIS!
LIKE "YAY!"
Y-YAY?
CUT IT OUT!!
TAKE MY MODERN JAPANESE AND GO BACK WHERE YOU BELONG, STAT!!
BESHIN (SMACK)
I WONDER WHAT HOODIES ARE TO SHUU.
MAYBE THEY'RE LIKE THE ULTIMATE EQUIP ITEM?
TCH...
EASY, EASY.
LOOKING LIKE THIS, I MEAN.
I GUESS IF YOU'RE NOT AN IURA-TYPE, YOU CAN'T REALLY BE BOLD ABOUT IT...
AH HA HA!

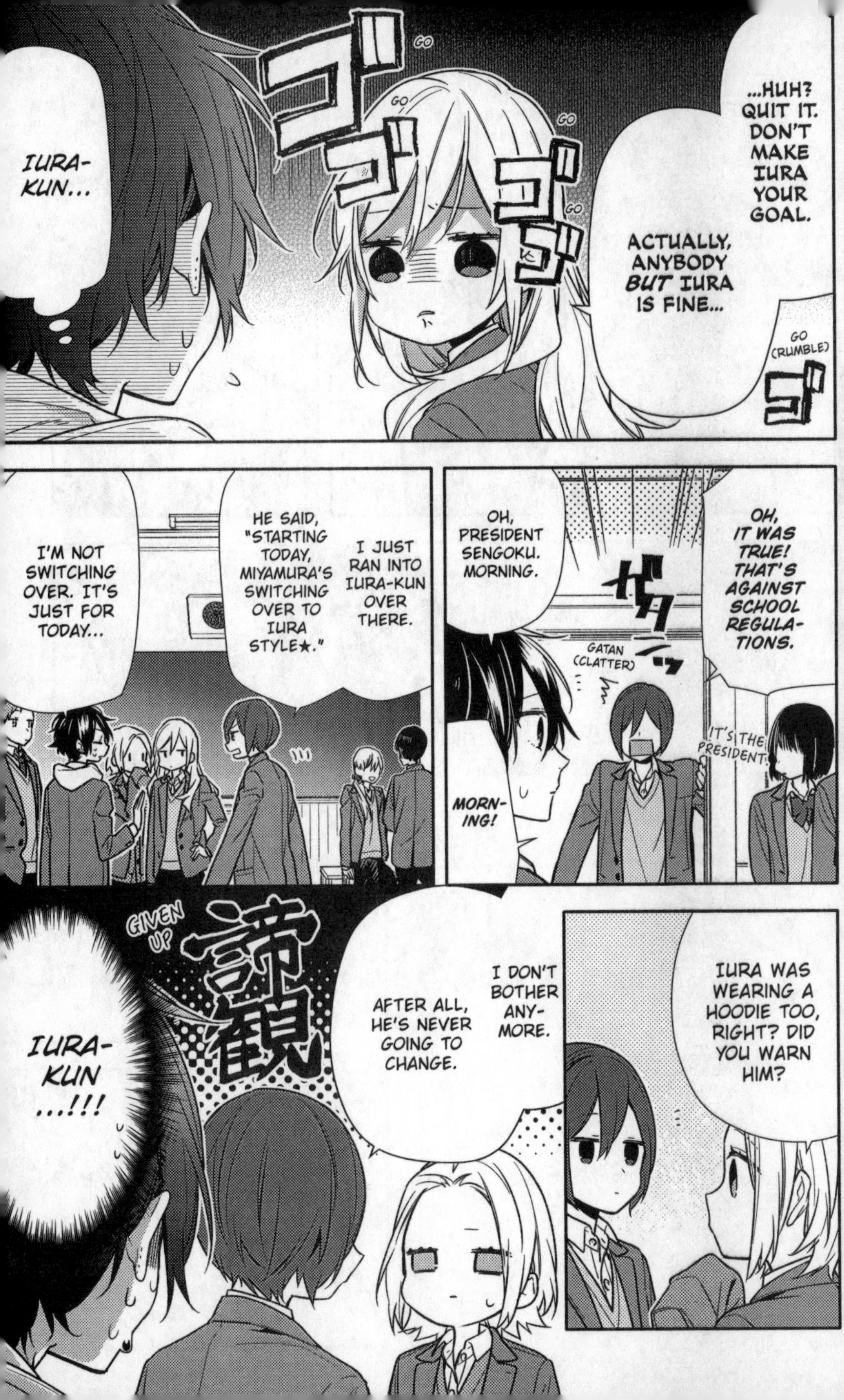

...HUH? QUIT IT. DON'T MAKE IURA YOUR GOAL.
ACTUALLY, ANYBODY *BUT* IURA IS FINE...
GO (RUMBLE)
GO
GO
GO
GO
IURA-KUN...
OH, *IT WAS TRUE! THAT'S AGAINST SCHOOL REGULATIONS.*
GATAN (CLATTER)
IT'S THE PRESIDENT.
OH, PRESIDENT SENGOKU. MORNING.
MORNING!
I JUST RAN INTO IURA-KUN OVER THERE.
HE SAID, "STARTING TODAY, MIYAMURA'S SWITCHING OVER TO IURA STYLE★."
I'M NOT SWITCHING OVER. IT'S JUST FOR TODAY...
IURA WAS WEARING A HOODIE TOO, RIGHT? DID YOU WARN HIM?
I DON'T BOTHER ANYMORE.
AFTER ALL, HE'S NEVER GOING TO CHANGE.
GIVEN UP
IURA-KUN ...!!!

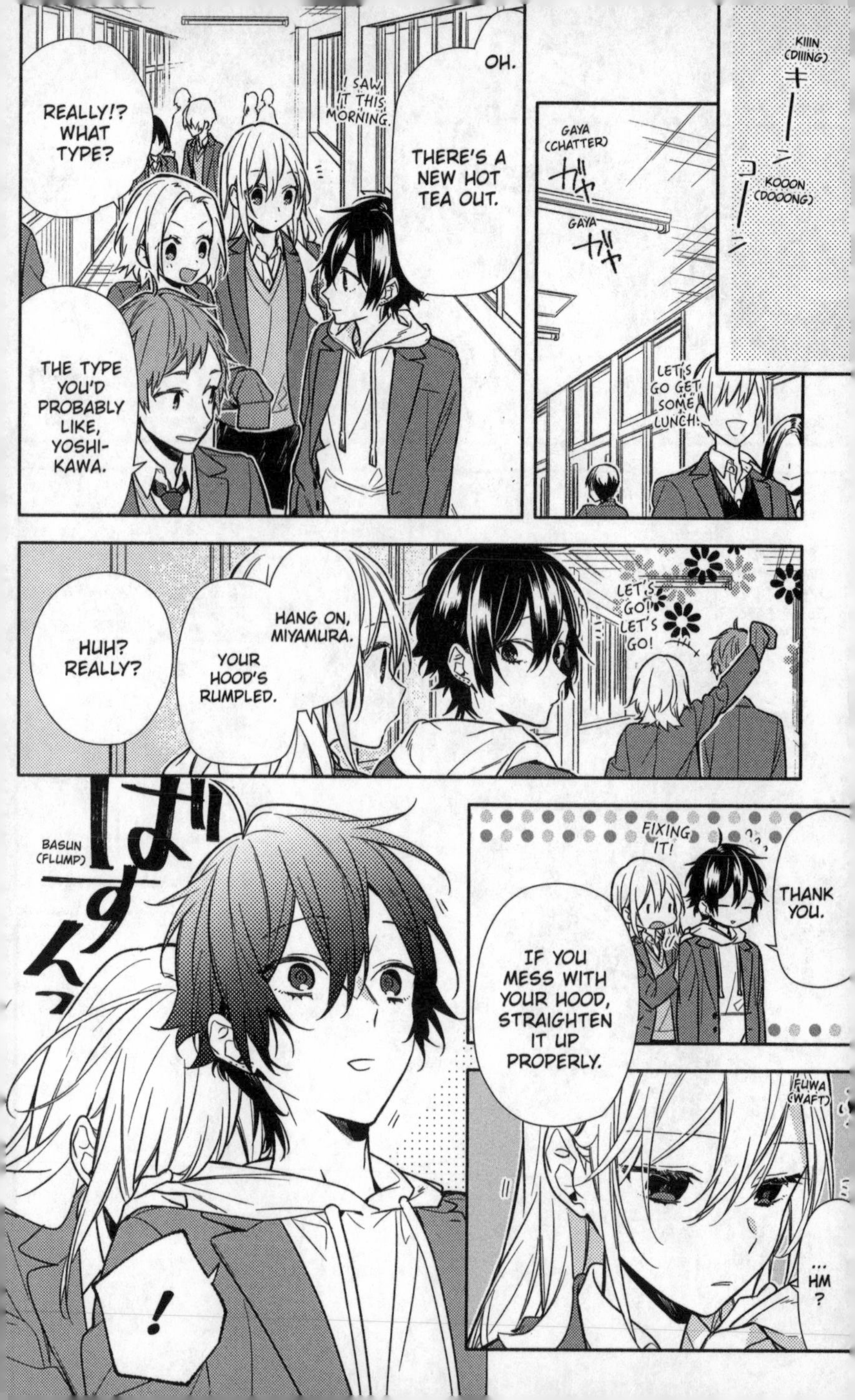
KIIIN (DIIING)
KOOON (DOOONG)
GAYA (CHATTER)
GAYA
LET'S GO GET SOME LUNCH!
OH.
I SAW IT THIS MORNING.
THERE'S A NEW HOT TEA OUT.
REALLY!? WHAT TYPE?
THE TYPE YOU'D PROBABLY LIKE, YOSHIKAWA.
LET'S GO! LET'S GO!
HANG ON, MIYAMURA.
YOUR HOOD'S RUMPLED.
HUH? REALLY?
FIXING IT!
THANK YOU.
IF YOU MESS WITH YOUR HOOD, STRAIGHTEN IT UP PROPERLY.
FUWA (WAFT)
...HM?
BASUN (FLUMP)
!

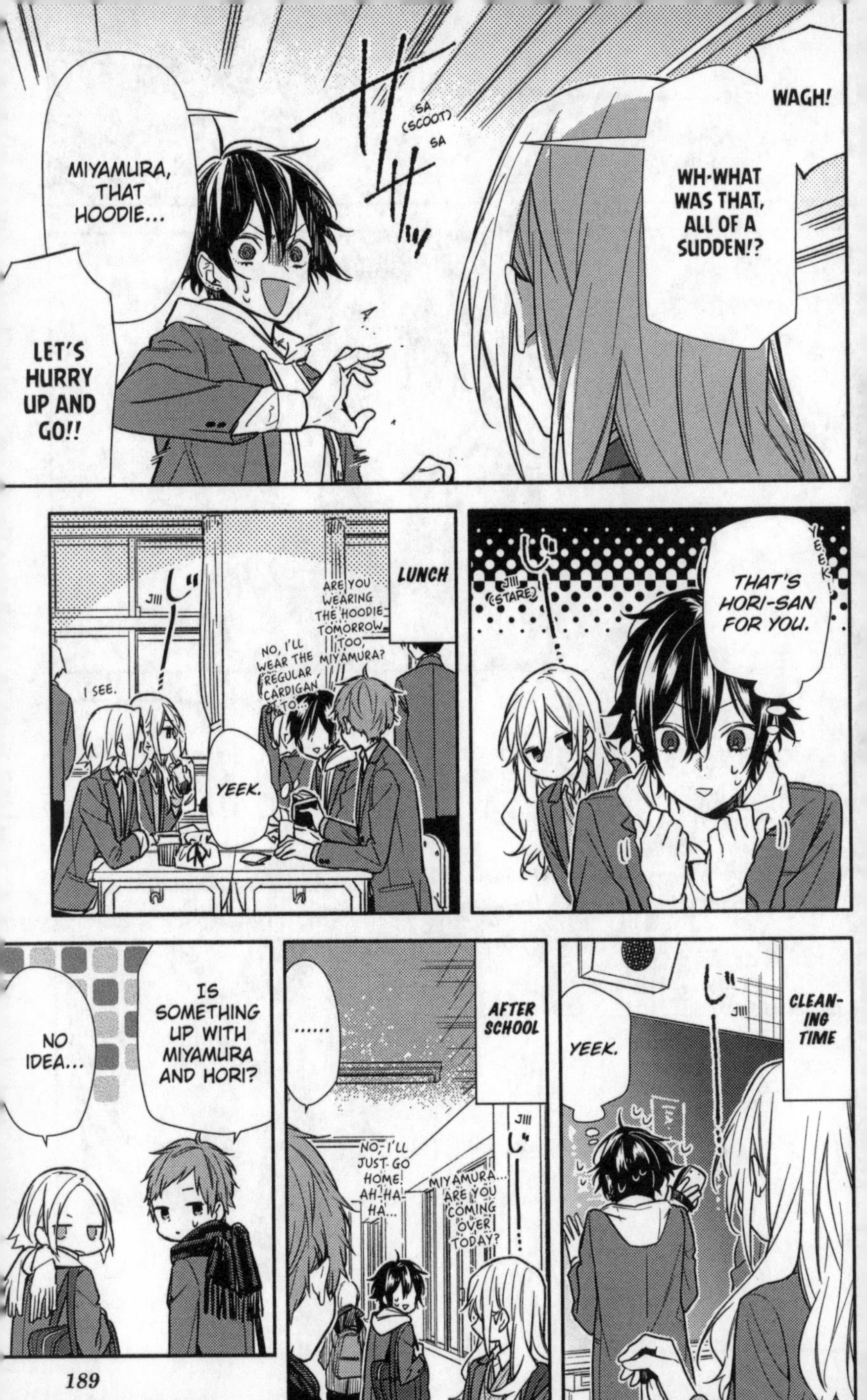

WAGH!
WH-WHAT WAS THAT, ALL OF A SUDDEN!?
SA (SCOOT)
SA
MIYAMURA, THAT HOODIE...
LET'S HURRY UP AND GO!!
YEEK...
JIII (STARE)
THAT'S HORI-SAN FOR YOU.
LUNCH
ARE YOU WEARING THE HOODIE TOMORROW TOO, MIYAMURA?
NO, I'LL WEAR THE REGULAR CARDIGAN TO...
JIII
I SEE.
YEEK.
CLEAN-ING TIME
JIII
YEEK.
AFTER SCHOOL
......
JIII
MIYAMURA... ARE YOU COMING OVER TODAY?
NO, I'LL JUST GO HOME! AH-HA HA...
IS SOMETHING UP WITH MIYAMURA AND HORI?
NO IDEA...

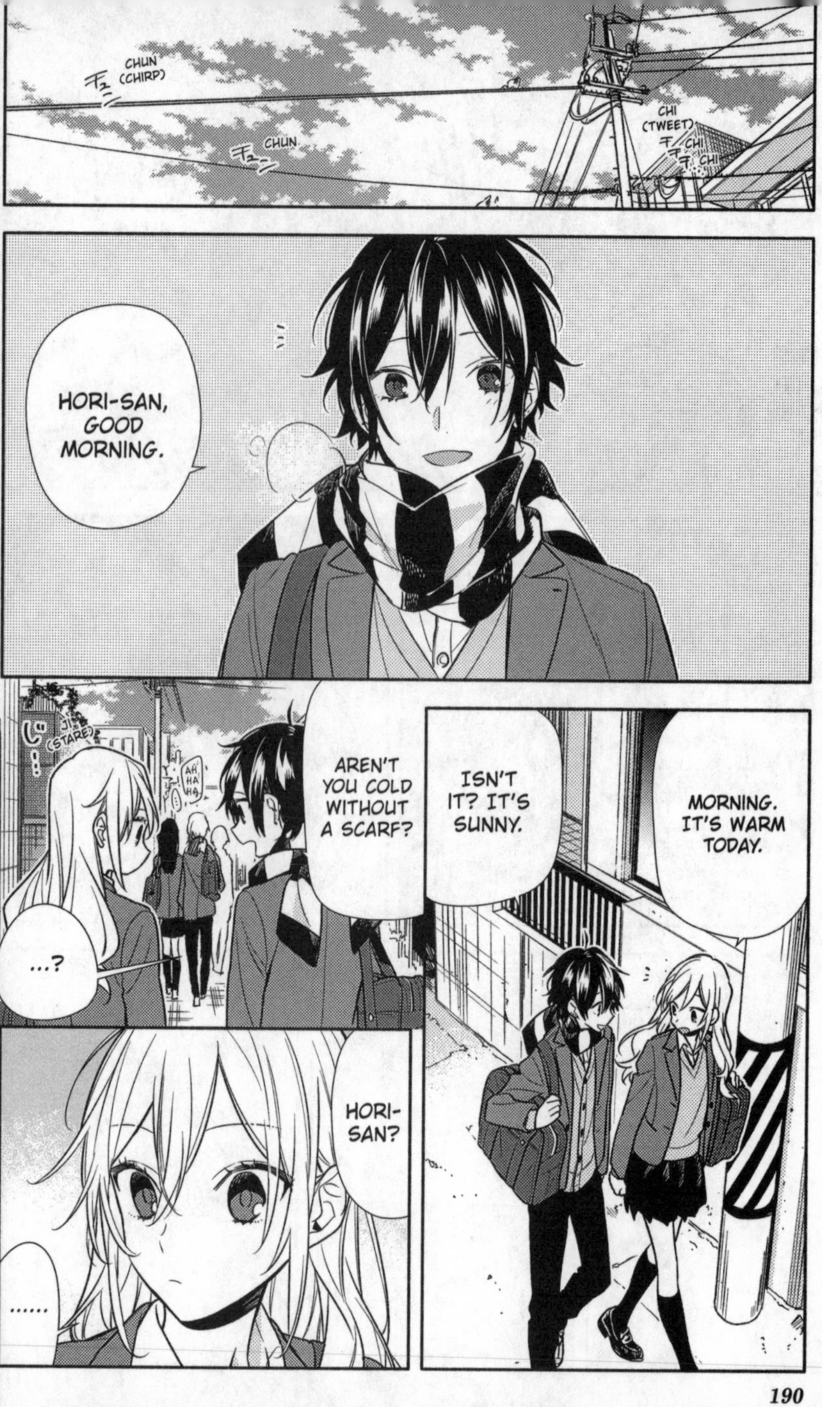

CHI (TWEET)
CHI
CHI
CHUN (CHIRP)
CHUN
HORI-SAN, GOOD MORNING.
MORNING. IT'S WARM TODAY.
ISN'T IT? IT'S SUNNY.
AREN'T YOU COLD WITHOUT A SCARF?
JI (STARE)
AH HA HA
...?
HORI-SAN?
......

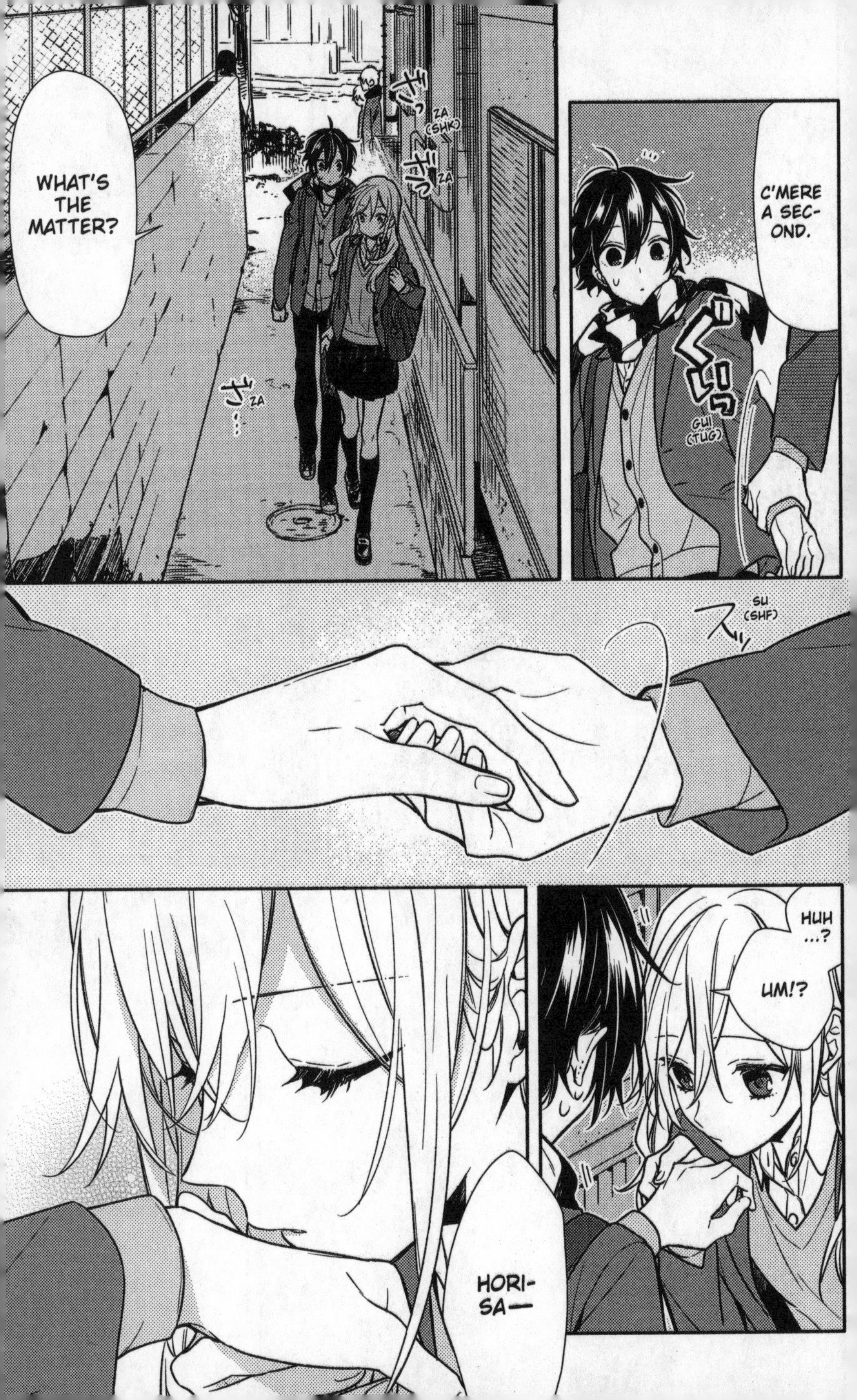
C'MERE A SEC-OND.
GUI (TUG)
ZA (SHK)
ZA
WHAT'S THE MATTER?
ZA
SU (SHF)
HUH ...?
UM!?
HORI-SA—

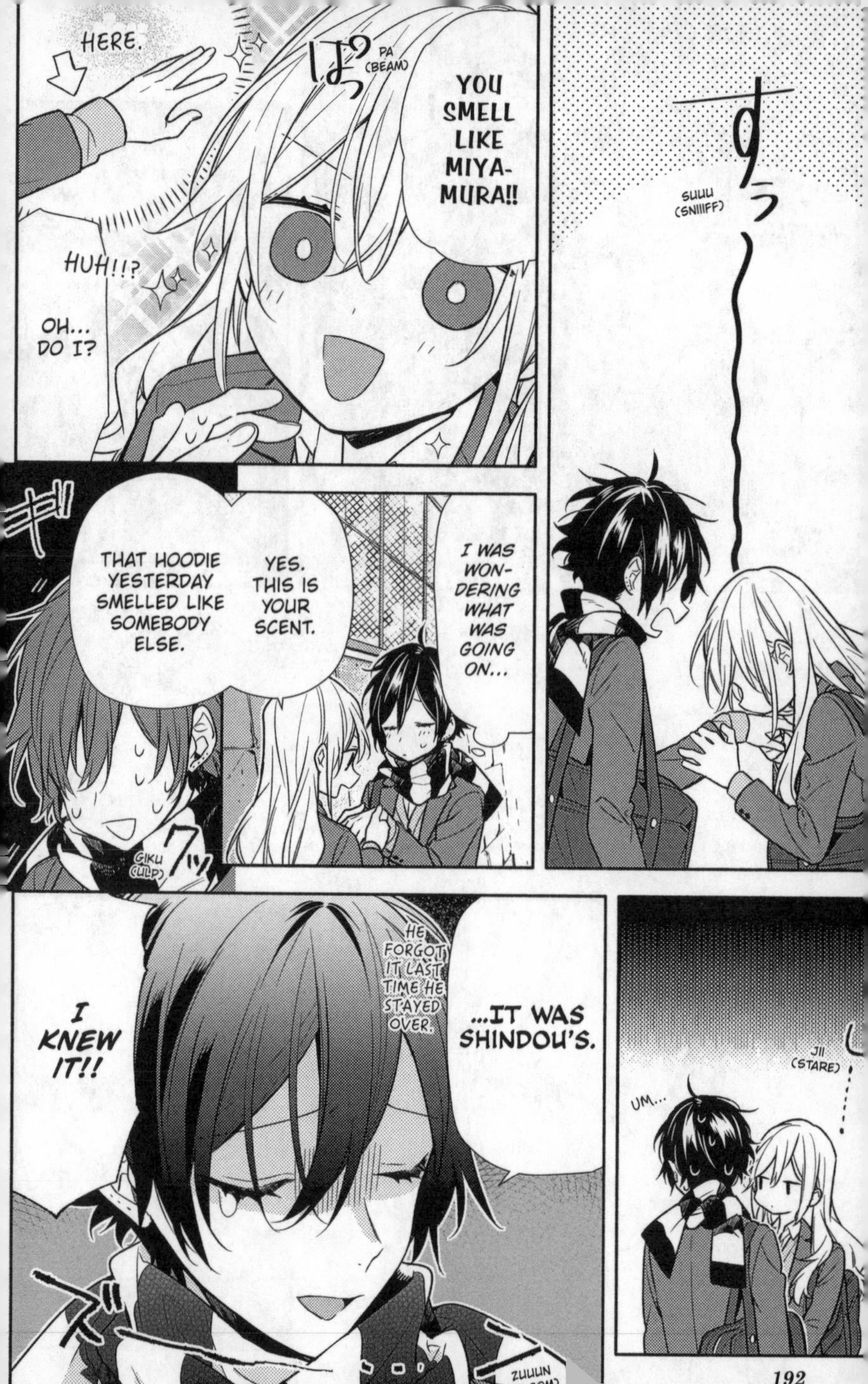
SUUU (SNIIIFF)
YOU SMELL LIKE MIYAMURA!!
PA (BEAM)
HERE.
HUH!!?
OH... DO I?
I WAS WONDERING WHAT WAS GOING ON...
YES. THIS IS YOUR SCENT.
THAT HOODIE YESTERDAY SMELLED LIKE SOMEBODY ELSE.
GIKU (GULP)
JII (STARE)
UM...
...IT WAS SHINDOU'S.
HE FORGOT IT LAST TIME HE STAYED OVER.
I KNEW IT!!
ZUUUN (GLOOM)

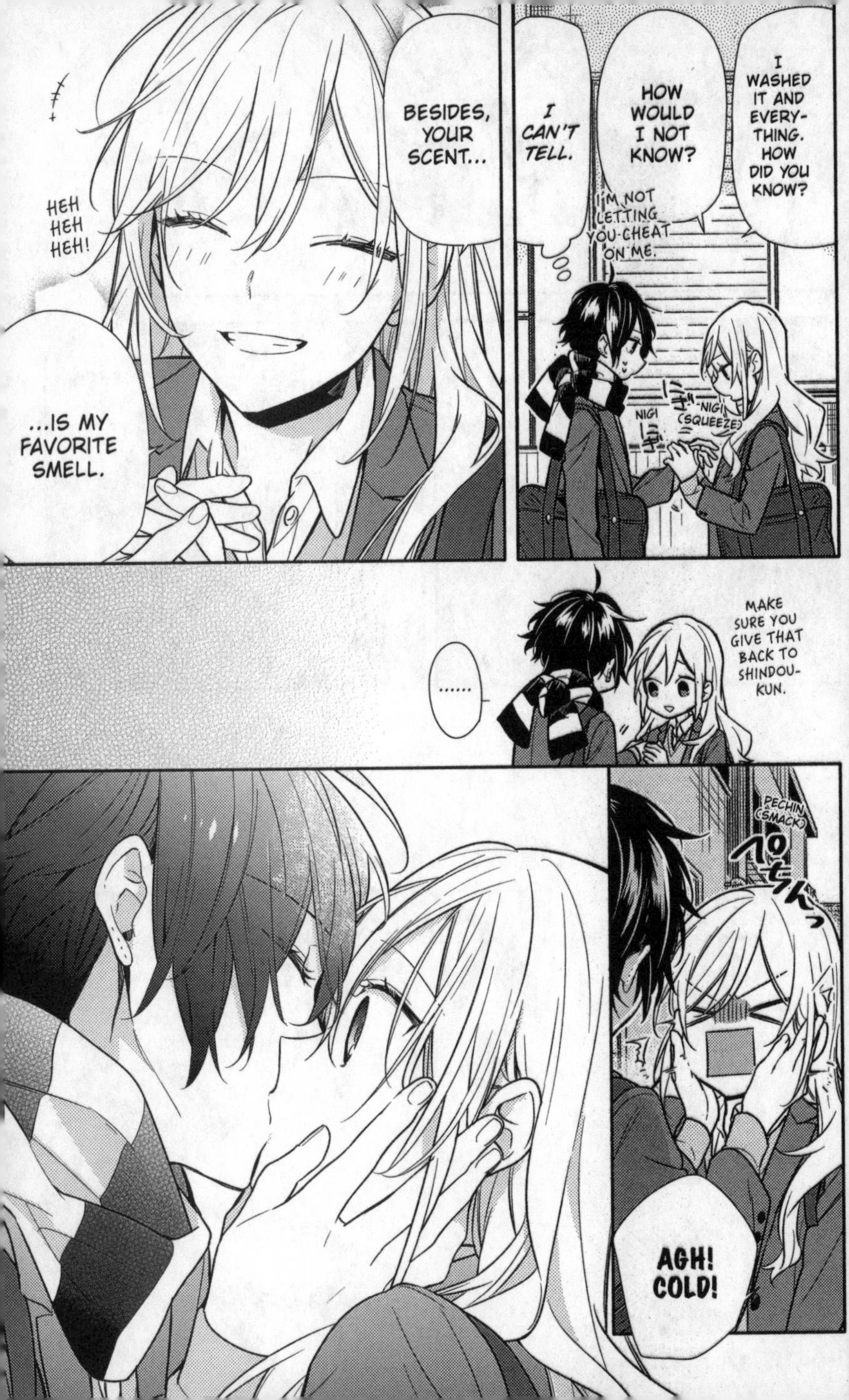

I WASHED IT AND EVERYTHING. HOW DID YOU KNOW?
HOW WOULD I NOT KNOW?
I'M NOT LETTING YOU CHEAT ON ME.
I CAN'T TELL.
NIGI NIGI (SQUEEZE)
BESIDES, YOUR SCENT...
...IS MY FAVORITE SMELL.
HEH HEH HEH!
MAKE SURE YOU GIVE THAT BACK TO SHINDOU-KUN.
......
PECHIN (SMACK)
AGH! COLD!

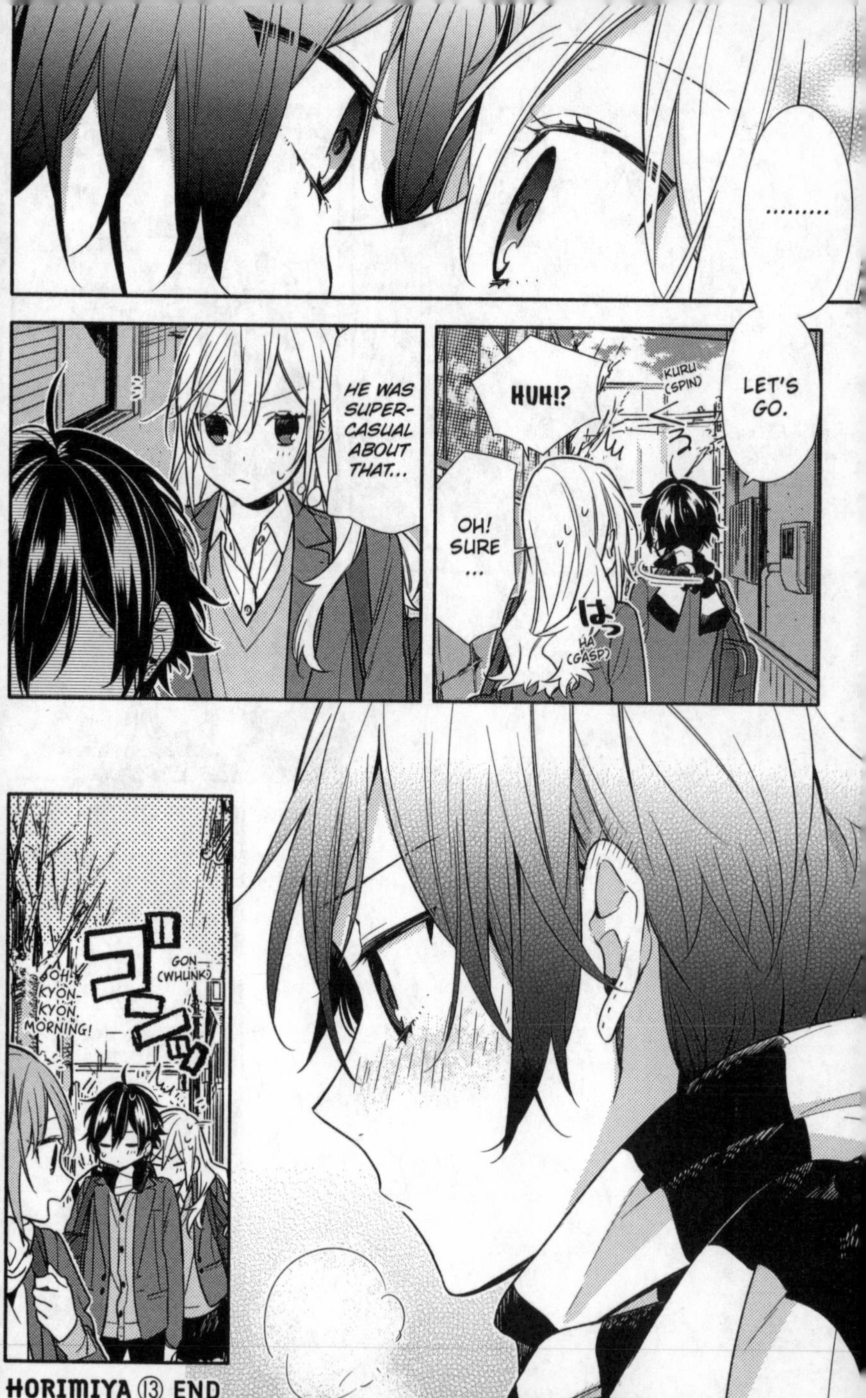
....
LET'S GO.
KURU (SPIN)
HUH!?
OH! SURE ...
はっ
HA (GASP)
HE WAS SUPER-CASUAL ABOUT THAT...
GON (WHUNK)
OH! KYON-KYON. MORNING!

HORIMIYA ⑬ END

Translation Notes

Page 29 – -*senpai*, -*san*
These are honorifics appended to the end of a person's name to indicate their status in relation to the speaker. -*senpai* is used when addressing an upperclassman or colleague of higher rank, and -*san* is used in all situations, only being left out when speaking informally—usually with friends.

Page 80 – *Onii-san*
A polite term used when referring to someone's older brother or a man you're meeting for the first time.

Page 126 – Test of courage
In Japan, a "test of courage" is a visit to a scary location, typically at night, as part of a dare. The spookiest time of year in Japan is summer, which is when such impromptu tests are usually held.

Page 138 – Mobster
The word Souta uses here is *mononoke*, or "apparition." He was looking for the word *kedamono*, or "beast."

Page 139 – Brother compound
In Japanese, the term "brother complex" is shortened to *burakon*. In this case, Kyousuke somehow comes up with the term *puraban*, which are plastic sheets that shrink in the oven, typically used for arts and crafts. You may know them as Shrinky Dinks.

To Be Continued...

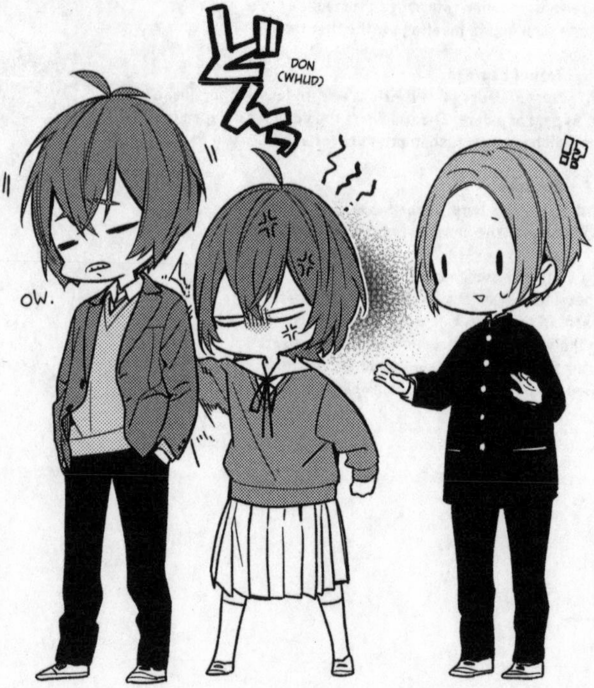
!?
DON
(WHUD)
OW.

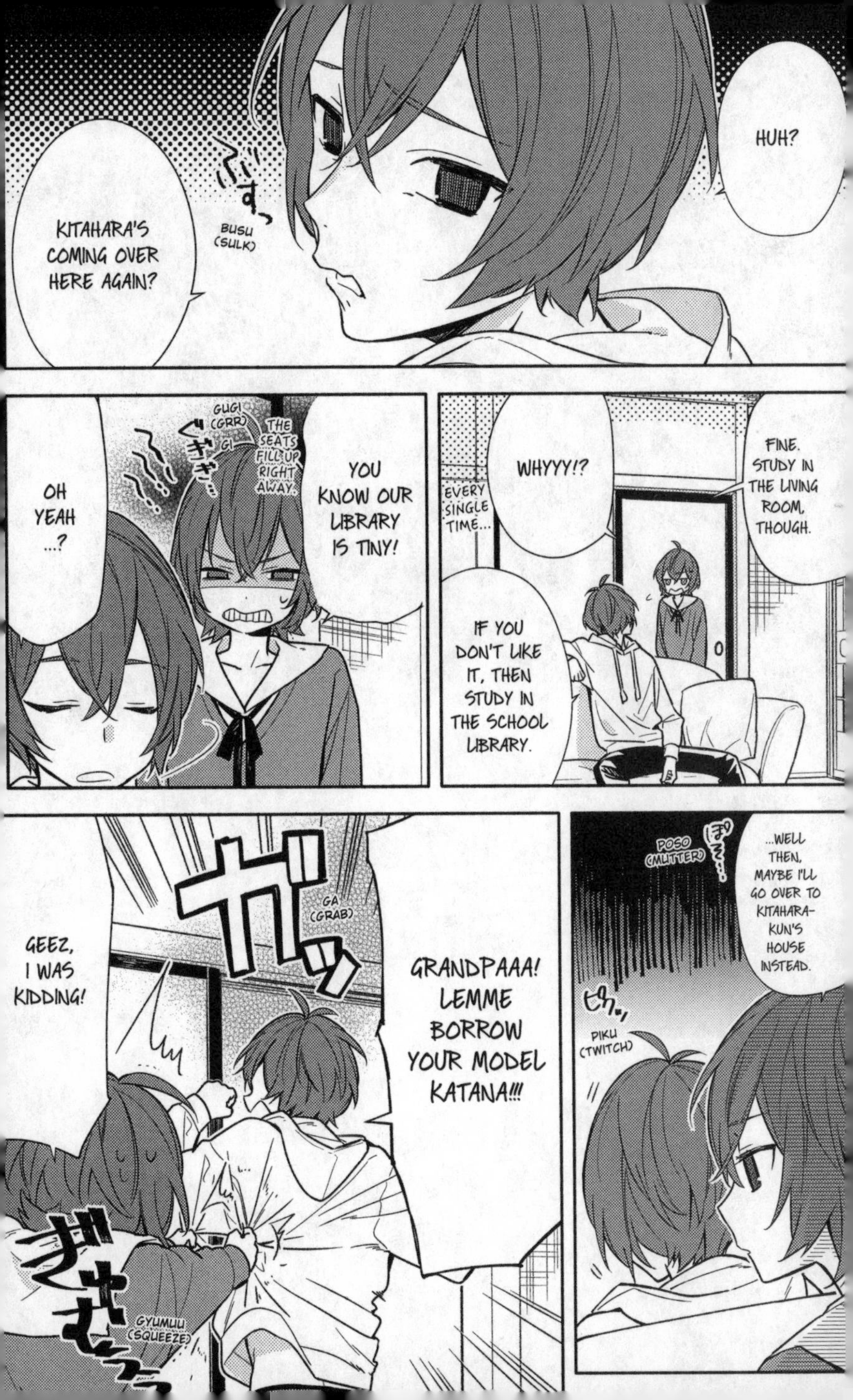
HUH?
ぶすっ
BUSU (SULK)
KITAHARA'S COMING OVER HERE AGAIN?
FINE. STUDY IN THE LIVING ROOM, THOUGH.
WHYYY!?
EVERY SINGLE TIME...
IF YOU DON'T LIKE IT, THEN STUDY IN THE SCHOOL LIBRARY.
YOU KNOW OUR LIBRARY IS TINY!
THE SEATS FILL UP RIGHT AWAY.
GUGI (GRR) GI
OH YEAH ...?
...WELL THEN, MAYBE I'LL GO OVER TO KITAHARA-KUN'S HOUSE INSTEAD.
POSO (MUTTER)
PIKU (TWITCH)
GRANDPAAA! LEMME BORROW YOUR MODEL KATANA!!!
ガッ
GA (GRAB)
GEEZ, I WAS KIDDING!
GYUMUU (SQUEEZE)

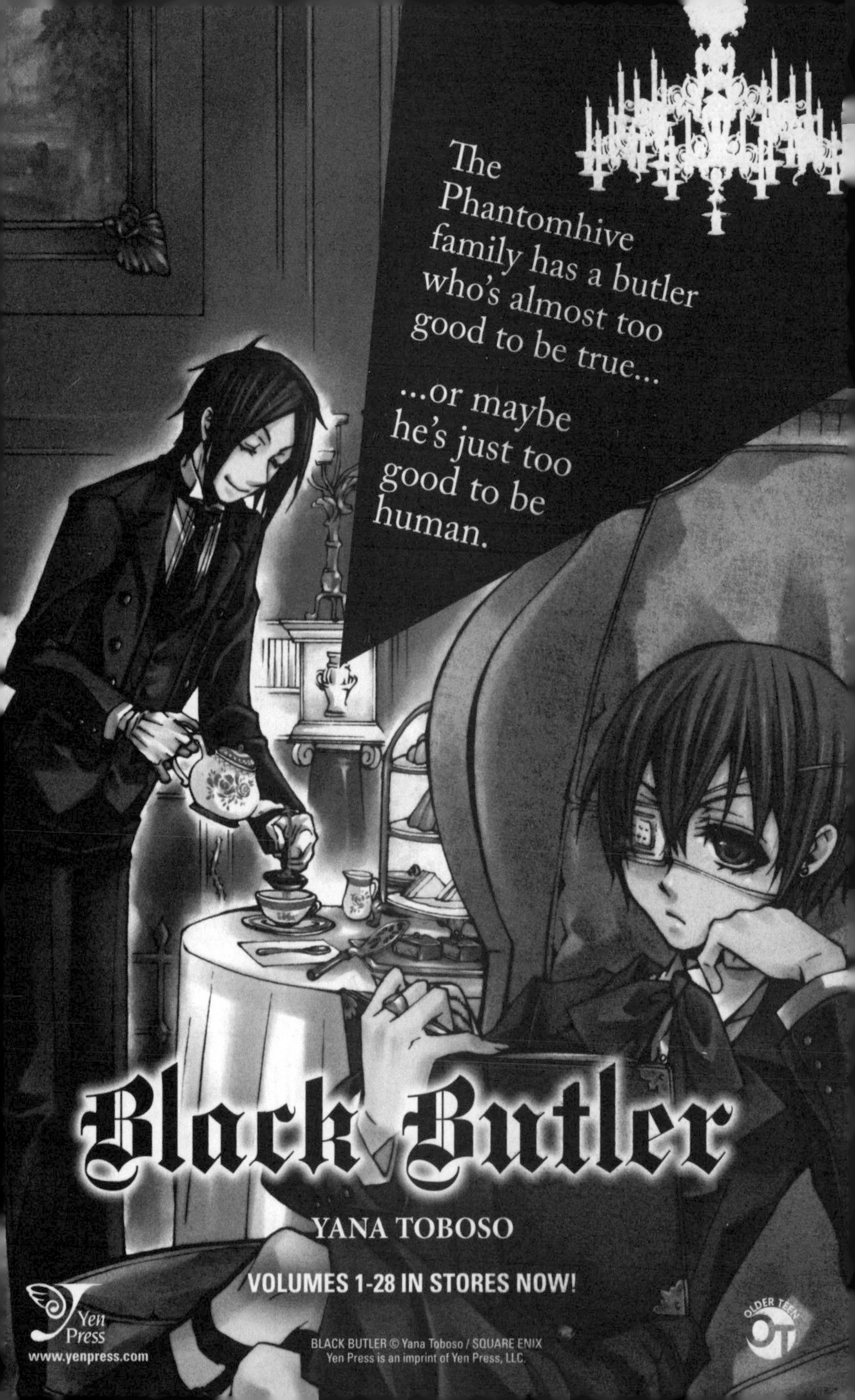
The Phantomhive family has a butler who's almost too good to be true...
...or maybe he's just too good to be human.
Black Butler
YANA TOBOSO
VOLUMES 1-28 IN STORES NOW!
Yen Press
www.yenpress.com
BLACK BUTLER © Yana Toboso / SQUARE ENIX
Yen Press is an imprint of Yen Press, LLC.
OLDER TEEN
OT

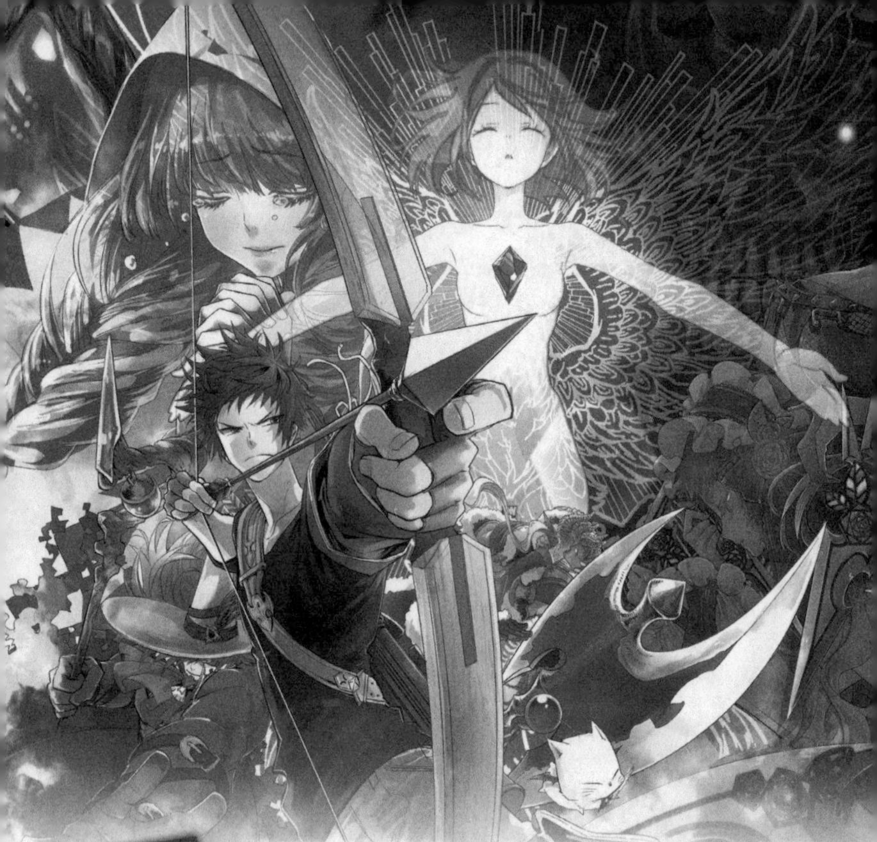

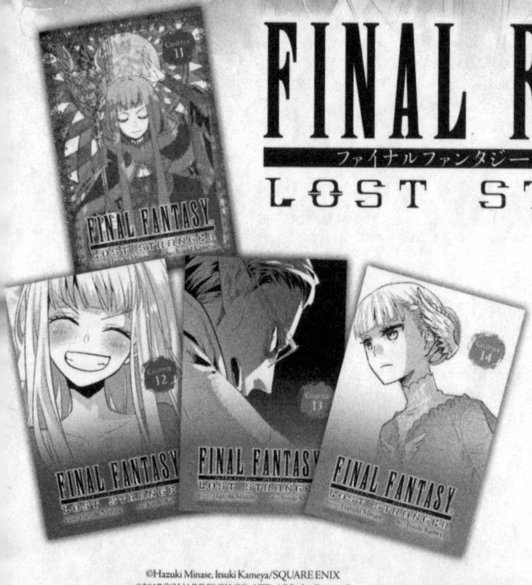

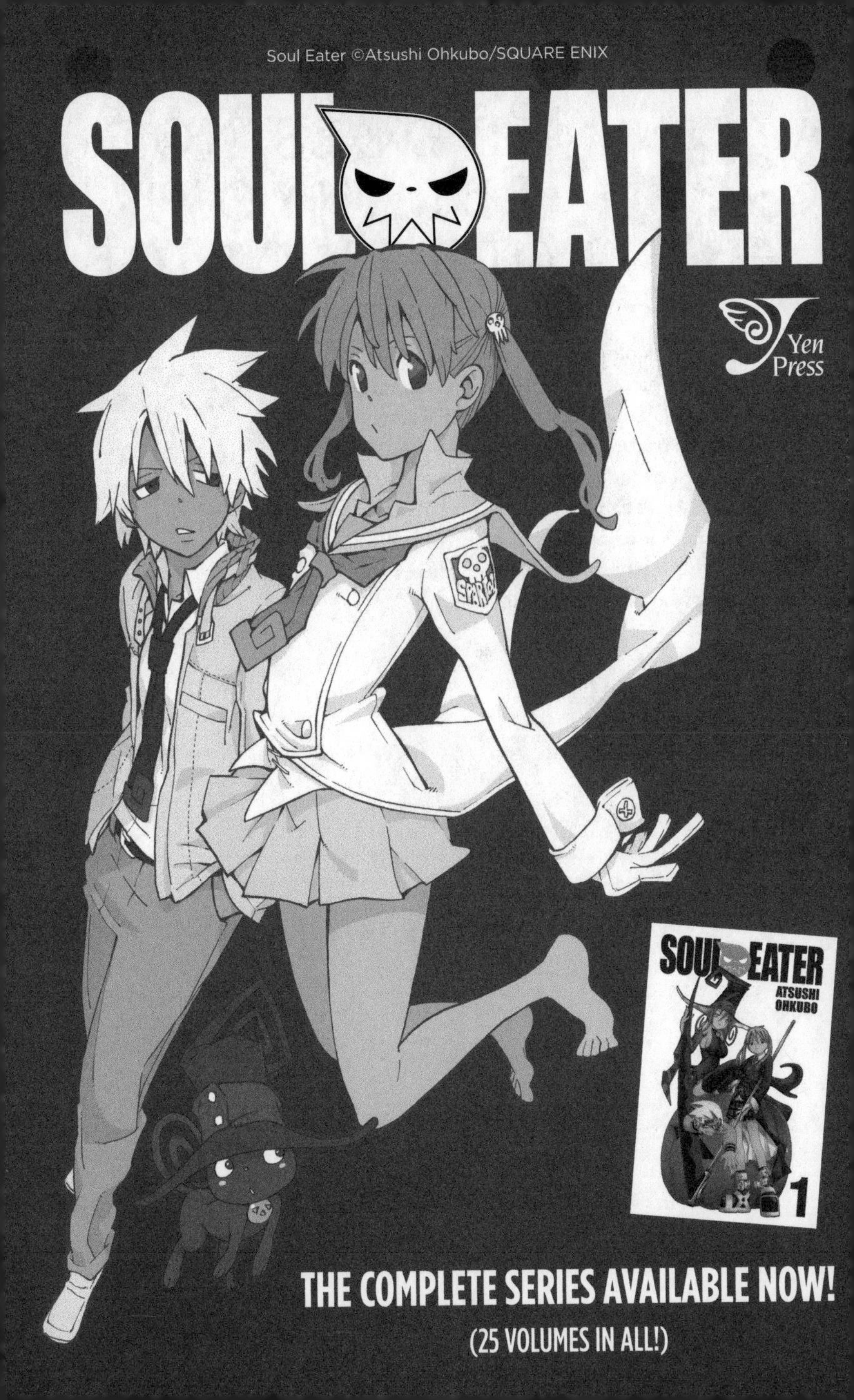
Soul Eater ©Atsushi Ohkubo/SQUARE ENIX
SOUL EATER
Yen Press
SOUL EATER
ATSUSHI OHKUBO
1
THE COMPLETE SERIES AVAILABLE NOW!
(25 VOLUMES IN ALL!)

Karino Takatsu, creator of
SERVANT x SERVICE, presents:

My Monster Girl's Too Cool For You

**Burning adoration melts
her heart...literally!**

In a world where *youkai* and
humans attend school together,
a boy named Atsushi Fukuzumi
falls for snow *youkai* Muku Shiroishi. Fukuzumi's passionate feelings
melt Muku's heart...and the rest of her?! The first volume of an
interspecies romantic comedy you're sure to fall head over heels for
is now available!!

YenPress.com

**Read new installments of this series every
month at the same time as Japan!**

CHAPTERS AVAILABLE NOW AT E-TAILERS EVERYWHERE!

© Karino Takatsu/SQUARE ENIX CO., LTD.

THE POWER
TO RULE THE
HIDDEN WORLD
OF SHINOBI...

THE POWER
COVETED BY
EVERY NINJA
CLAN...

...LIES WITHIN
THE MOST
APATHETIC,
DISINTERESTED
VESSEL
IMAGINABLE.

Nabari No Ou

Yuhki Kamatani

COMPLETE SERIES NOW AVAILABLE

FINAL FANTASY TYPE-0™

Art: TAKATOSHI SHIOZAWA
Character Design: TETSUYA NOMURA
Scenario: HIROKI CHIBA

The cadets of Akademeia's Class Zero are legends, with strength and magic unrivaled, and crimson capes symbolizing the great Vermilion Bird of the Dominion. But will their elite training be enough to keep them alive when a war breaks out and the Class Zero cadets find themselves at the front and center of a bloody political battlefield?!

HERO × Daisuke Hagiwara

Translation: Taylor Engel
Lettering: Alexis Eckerman

HORIMIYA vol. 13
© HERO · OOZ
© 2019 Daisuke Hagiwara / SQUARE ENIX CO., LTD. First published in Japan in 2019 by SQUARE ENIX CO., LTD. English translation rights arranged with SQUARE ENIX CO., LTD. and Yen Press, LLC through Tuttle-Mori Agency, Inc.

English translation © 2020 by SQUARE ENIX CO., LTD.

Yen Press
150 West 30th Street
New York, NY 10001

Visit us at yenpress.com · facebook.com/yenpress · twitter.com/yenpress · yenpress.tumblr.com · instagram.com/yenpress

First Yen Press Edition: January 2020

Yen Press is an imprint of Yen Press, LLC. The Yen Press name and logo are trademarks of Yen Press, LLC.

The publisher is not responsible for websites (or their content) that are not owned by the publisher.

Library of Congress Control Number: 2015960115

ISBNs: 978-1-9753-5964-5 (paperback)
978-1-9753-5965-2 (ebook)

10 9 8 7 6 5 4 3 2

BVG

Printed in the United States of America